FREEDOM, TECHNOLOGY, AND THE FIRST AMENDMENT

By
Jonathan W. Emord

PACIFIC RESEARCH INSTITUTE FOR PUBLIC POLICY
San Francisco, California

This book is a product of the Center for Applied Jurisprudence of
the Pacific Research Institute for Public Policy.

Copyright © 1991 by Pacific Research Institute for Public Policy. All
rights reserved. No part of this publication may be reproduced,
stored in a retrieval system, or transmitted in any form or by any
means, electronic, mechanical, photocopy, recording, or otherwise,
without the prior written consent of the publisher.

ISBN 0-936688-37-9 (hard); 0-936488-38-7 (pbk.)

Printed in the United States of America.

Pacific Research Institute for Public Policy
177 Post Street
San Francisco, CA 94108
(415) 989-0833

Library of Congress Cataloging-in-Publication Data

Emord, Jonathan, 1961–
    Freedom, technology, and the First Amendment / by Jonathan
Emord.
        p.   cm.
    Includes bibliographical references and index.
    ISBN 0-936688-37-9 (hard) : $29.95. — ISBN 0-936488-38-7 (pbk.) : $12.95
    1. Freedom of the press—United States.   2. Telecommunication—Law and legislation—United States.
    3. Mass media—Law and legislation—United States.   I. Pacific Research Institute for Public
Policy.   II. Title
    KF4774.E46   1991
    342.73 '0853—dc20
    [347.302853]   90-20205
                                                                            CIP

For Ern, Jen, Michelle,
and all who cherish freedom

CONTENTS

ACKNOWLEDGMENTS

The creation of this volume has been an obsession of mine for the past three years. During those years, I have benefited greatly from the counsel, insights, and research assistance of a group of individuals whose credentials and talents are well known and well respected. I share with them a deep conviction to those fundamental freedoms protected by the First Amendment, an amendment I have long regarded as the cornerstone of American liberty.

I owe a debt of gratitude to two gentlemen in particular for their painstaking review of each manuscript copy, for their critical comment on each theory, and for their faithful adherence to principle: William H. Mellor, President of the Pacific Research Institute, sponsor of this project, and Director of the Center for Applied Jurisprudence; and Fred S. McChesney, Robert W. Thompson Chair of Law and Public Policy at Emory University School of Law and Chairman of the First Amendment Task Force of the Center for Applied Jurisprudence. In addition, the members of the First Amendment Task Force of the Center for Applied Jurisprudence have graciously taken time from their busy schedules to read the manuscripts, to critically comment on them, and to provide invaluable recommendations that have been liberally adopted in this work. I am extremely grateful to Randy E. Barnett, Associate Professor of Law at the Illinois Institute of Technology, Chicago-Kent College of Law; Lillian R. BeVier, Henry L. and Grace Doherty Charitable Foundation Professor of Law at the University of Virginia School of Law; Clint D. Bolick, Director of the Landmark Center for Civil Rights; Thomas Hazlett, Assistant Professor of Agricultural Economics at the University of California at Davis; Sam Kazman, General Counsel for the Competitive Enterprise Institute; Thomas B. Kelley of Cooper and Kelley; Douglas W. Kmiec, Professor of Law and Director, Thomas J. White Center of Law and Government at the University of Notre Dame; William E. Lee, Professor at the Henry W. Grady College of Journalism and Mass Communication at the University of Georgia; Michael W. McConnell, Professor of Law at the University of Chicago Law School; Matthew L. Spitzer, William T. Dalessi Professor of Law at the University of Southern California Law Center; and Gerrit Wormhoudt of Fleeson, Gooing, Coulson & Kitch.

I am indebted to Leonard P. Liggio, Distinguished Senior Scholar at the Institute for Humane Studies for his historical insights; to Henry Geller, Esq., for his expert critical analysis; to Benjamin J. Lambiotte for challenging me to consider certain perspectives on the law previously unknown to me; to John C. Hollar, Esq., and William E. Kennard, Esq., two of the communications bar's finest practitioners and scholars, for their critical insights; to Douglas Webbink for sharing with me his views on property rights theories as applied to broadcasting; to Robert Louis du Treil, Ronald Rackley, Garrison C. Cavell, Karl D. Lahm, and William P. Suffa, five of the nation's finest broadcast consulting engineers, for their learned edits on the sections relating to technical matters; to Mark S. Weinstein, Esq., for his friendship, guidance, and incontrovertible commitment to free principles; to Richard J. Bodorff, Esq., for his meticulous editing and critical analysis and for his honesty, intellect, and compassionate heart; to Congressman Jon Kyl and his staff for affording me access to rare volumes from the Library of Congress; to Karen Corr, Ricky A. Pursley, Beth Smith, Judy Little, Janet Reid, and Georgia Sullivan for their research assistance; and to the library staffs of the Library of Congress, the University of Virginia School of Law Library, George Mason University School of Law Library, and the Broadcast Pioneers Library.

In June 1989, The Liberty Fund, Inc., sponsored a conference on "Free and Responsible Individuals versus Prior Restraint," which I had the privilege of attending and from which I benefited. I am grateful for the contributions made by the conference participants and, in particular, by Dr. Richard L. Stroup of the Department of Economics at Montana State University and Director of the Political Economy Research Center; Dr. William C. Dennis, Program Fund Officer of The Liberty Fund, Inc.;

Michael Krauss, Professor of Law at George Mason University School of Law; Fred L. Smith, Jr., of the Competitive Enterprise Institute; and Dr. Bruce Yandle of the Department of Economics at Clemson University.

The Pacific Research Institute has provided the funding for this project from its inception. The delightful staff of the Institute has made each First Amendment Task Force meeting enjoyable and scintillating and the production of this volume a pleasurable experience. I thank them for their exceptional efforts.

The readability of this volume has been greatly improved by the stylistic editing of Sheldon L. Richman, Senior Editor at the Institute for Humane Studies, by the copyediting of Barbara B. Hart and Linda C. Rosen, and by the proofreading of Karen Stough. They have ably transformed the sometimes stilted prose of a lawyer into a work that is accessible to all.

My secretaries, Lori Ramsey and Yvette Ormsby, have labored tirelessly to compose the typewritten manuscripts and the final prepublication text. I owe them much.

I cannot close without mentioning how very fortunate I have been to have a wife as kind, loving, and intelligent as Michelle. She has assisted me with my research, challenged my draftsmanship, and revealed precious bits of knowledge all along the way. If only I could begin to repay her for the happiness she has given me.

PREFACE

The federal and state regulatory labyrinth that controls and structures the nation's electronic mass media violates the First Amendment. This volume explores the fundamental purpose and meaning of the First Amendment and demonstrates that only a property-rights model, such as that present in the print media context, can ensure adequate protection for the freedom of speech and press as we enter the twenty-first century.

Technology is now carrying us into the greatest age of mass communication the world has ever known. The principal threat to the development of the new media is not something unknown and mysterious. It is the same enemy of freedom that has always prevented civilized man from enjoying an unencumbered right to exchange information: the government. This book concerns government regulation of the press and the threat that government poses to the core values embodied by the First Amendment's free speech and press clause.

If our freedom of speech and press is to retain its meaning and protected status in the new media age, the current regulatory regime must give way to a free, self-governing media marketplace, one where the constitutional standards of the print media apply to all modes of communication.

In the twenty-first century, technology will afford the American public a profusion of new means to send and receive ideas and information. From the home, each person will command access to more information, opinion, and entertainment than ever before. For the first time, each person will be able to publish to hundreds or thousands of others in the United States and abroad at comparatively low costs. As with the advent of the first international broadcasts, so too in this new age, the world once again will seem to grow smaller as the common store of knowledge grows larger.

The advent of a nationwide series of interactive switched broadband voice, audio, video, and data fiber optic digital networks will come to pass by the early twenty-first century. These fiber optic networks will be the communication transit systems for the great bulk of new-age information and opinion. They will make possible a great increase in the gross national product, in the rapidity with which economic transactions may be consummated, in the development of a global economic and information marketplace, and in the sophistication of the average consumer.

Today, the average American home includes a telephone (and, often, a computer modem) for interactive voice and data communication. It also includes several reception services, for example, multichannel cable, over-the-air television, video cassette recorders, compact disc players, stereo systems, and radios. In the average American home of tomorrow, the once-separate television, telephone, compact disc player, video cassette recorder, and home computer and printer will be replaced by a great multi-operational unit that will have integrated voice, audio, video, and data transmission, retrieval, and reception capabilities. The technology of tomorrow will bring the office and consumer market to the home through a computer keyboard, a video screen, and a printer. As a result, the workplace will become a part of life at home and mass marketing will become further honed, enabling producers to satisfy the individualized needs of each consumer.

It will be possible to conduct elaborate video and data searches to compare prices and characteristics of advertised goods and services with those not advertised but available in other markets. It will be possible within the span of but a few minutes to sample different kinds of information through computer searches of databases across the country. Legal, medical, and financial consulting will be obtainable at home on demand. For the first time each person will have the power to publish information directly from the home to mass audiences. Each person will be able to send live or recorded voice, audio, video, and data messages across the fiber-optic lines to targeted recipients in the United States and abroad. As never before, the vast majority of Americans will be able to participate directly in the commercial, academic, political, social, and entertainment marketplaces around the globe.

Those who wish to market their products will be able to precisely target interested audiences in a less-expensive and more efficient manner than through the current mass media. Producers will be able to reach those consumers most interested in a product with ease and will be able to elicit far more information from them about a product's desirable and undesirable features.

Tomorrow's world marketplace of commercial goods and services, academic information and opinion, and news and entertainment will be extraordinarily diverse and will permit dramatic increases in the pace of innovation and in public awareness about all facets of life. The new communications marketplace will belong to consumers. They will be able to select precise categories of information, opinion, or entertainment from among innumerable offerings and will be able to exclude unwanted items with ease. Americans will be able to participate in regional and national surveys of their opinions on political, social, or economic questions and will be able to receive the tabulated results moments later. In these and sundry other ways, the exchange of information and opinion in the America of tomorrow will occur in high volume, at light speed, and to much greater effect than is now possible.

This is the realistic promise of new-age technologies now under development. These advancements must come to pass if the great benefits of freedom of speech and press are to be realized in the next century. The critical issues concern how soon we may reap the benefits of these new technologies and whether those empowered to regulate will resist the urge to do so or will erect new obstacles to technological progress and freedom under the guise of some new "public interest" standard. If history repeats itself, regulations will be imposed. However, if those in power can learn from past mistakes and can embrace the full protective compass of the First Amendment as their guide, we will witness the rapid development of the most beneficial communications age the world has ever known.

Unleashing this progress and protecting freedom will require the elimination of those government barriers that now abridge the speech and press freedom and that prevent or retard innovation and new competition in the media marketplace. New legal barriers must be erected *against* government controls. These barriers will prevent the government from encroaching on the private sphere of communication and will enable free will rather than censorship to characterize communication in the next century. To help ensure that individual free choice does reign over matters of speech and press, this book calls for a rededication to the old First Amendment and an application of *that* amendment to the new press.

Jonathan W. Emord
Washington, D.C.

PART I

DEFINING THE CORE VALUES OF THE FIRST AMENDMENT

In pursuance of the wishes thus expressed, the first Congress that assembled under the Constitution proposed certain amendments, which have since, by the necessary ratifications, been made a part of it; among which amendments is the article containing, among other prohibitions on the Congress, an express declaration that they should make no law abridging the freedom of the press.

*Without tracing farther the evidence on this subject, it would seem scarcely possible to doubt that no power whatever over the press was supposed to be delegated by the Constitution, as it originally stood, and that the amendment was intended as a positive and absolute reservation of it.**

---

*James Madison, "Report on the Virginia Resolutions," 1799–1800, IV, *The Debates in the Several State Conventions on the Adoption of the Federal Constitution* . . . 572 (J. Elliot ed. 1836).

1

BASIC ASSUMPTIONS AND OBJECTIVES

The First Amendment has served as a severe restriction on government power over speech[1] and the press.[2] Almost all conflicts redressable by the amendment have concerned governmental attempts to suppress ideas[3] or information[4] deemed offensive or harmful by those in power. Many of these conflicts have called into question the fundamental meaning of freedom in our republic, for they have often forced us to assess whether the unorthodox message of a single spokesman may be constitutionally silenced by those with political power to do so.[5] The government has chosen to suppress speech for a variety of reasons: to defend majoritarian values,[6] to ensure opportunities for expression by politically favored groups,[7] to prevent the use of speech forums for purposes disfavored by our representatives,[8] or to protect the political base of support relied upon by the elected to retain power.[9]

The government's periodic suppression of speech may be an ineluctable by-product of democratic processes, particularly during periods of popular passion. (It is, of course, a *modus operandi* for regimes with unlimited powers.) In our democracy, elected officials have often found suppression of unpopular speech a facile and irresistible means to curry favor with constituents.[10] This political reaction comes as no surprise to public choice theorists who have understood that self-interest motivates almost all of us to one degree or another, including (or perhaps, most especially) politicians.[11] The politicians' proclivity to suppress unpopular speech is an old one. It precedes the First Amendment,[12] continues to this day in spite of the amendment, and will no doubt continue long into the future.[13]

Even without resort to constitutional analysis, we know, viscerally, that political suppression of speech sacrifices our personal liberty and autonomy. It separates from us a *freedom* that is an inherent product of the human mind, the freedom to choose which subjects to debate.

Moreover, the process of political suppression vests a particularly malevolent power in government. It leaves us at the mercy of censors empowered to determine *who* may be privileged to speak or write and *what*, from the lexicon of known or "approved" ideas and information, others may be *allowed* to hear or see. In this way, our individual freedom can be supplanted by the power of government. Freedom to discern for ourselves the merit and utility of a message is replaced by the judgment of a censor who discerns for us, without our consent, which messages we may safely consider. As a result, we are denied both intellectual self-fulfillment and the ability to freely impart our ideas to others. The consequence is a transformation of the " 'marketplace of ideas' from an 'uninhibited, robust and wide open' one into an inhibited, insipid and delimited one."[14]

Moreover, it is emphatically *political* suppression of speech, rather than *private* limitations on opportunities for speech, that poses the greatest threat to liberty.[15] Seven distinct aspects of political suppression can be contrasted with their private analogues to establish the point.

1. Political suppression is pervasive. It prohibits disapproved speech by *all* owners of regulated speech forums,[16] or it prohibits entire categories of speech from being uttered or published.[17] Private limitations merely foreclose single opportunities for speech. They leave the speaker the option of relying on competing means to disseminate his or her message.

2. Political suppression is, of course, in service to a *political* agenda—the policy favored by a party constituency that has the power to impose its preferences on others through law. Private limitations do not involve public policy determinations and do not typically have a political character. Private limitations are usually the result of *economic* choices by the forum owner, who seeks not pervasive legal control over others but rather simple profit maximization, the most efficient application of his or her own resources. The profit motive knows no single political creed and does not mandate the establishment of a particular vision of truth, liberty, justice, and fairness. The profit motive does not depend on the application of coercive force to attain objectives; it relies on consumer choice.

3. Political suppression is usually unalterable by efforts at self-help, because resorting to private action to circumvent suppression is often unlawful. Private limitations are necessarily confined to a property owner's speech forum and so may be circumvented by a competing use of another speech forum.
4. Just as political suppression is capable of precluding certain disapproved speakers from having access to the press, it is also capable of ensuring that certain favored speakers are guaranteed access to the press. This enforced access denies forum owners a speech or press right in favor of others preferred by the state. Private limitations can never extinguish the liberty of speakers to utter views in their own forums.
5. Political suppression is enforceable by the government's executive departments, which, because they possess a lawful monopoly on the use of police power, may, at their discretion, incarcerate, try, and punish transgressors. Private limitations cannot lawfully be enforced through private incarceration or punishment of transgressors; rather, private parties wishing to protect their property rights must, in almost every instance, bring their grievances to the police and to the courts.
6. Political suppression may be accomplished by using the government's virtually inexhaustible purse, which can outbid any private party in securing ownership over the means of communication, or by using its takings and eminent domain powers. The private sector simply cannot compete against these methods of acquiring control over the means of communication.
7. Last, by operational definition government is an absolute monopoly. Except for what is left of the systems of federalism and separation of powers, government, by legal fiat, has no competition. Therefore, political suppression is pervasive, self-sustaining, and sometimes damning. Private limitations are made in an environment rife with competition, where forum owners have an economic incentive to disseminate useful information that other forum owners choose not to disseminate. One voice is spoken in the midst of a plethora of competitors. Therefore, private limitations are limited to a specific area defined by ownership, are counteracted by others who have an economic incentive to do so, are changeable, and depend on popular demand.

It is for these reasons that people have far more to fear from, for example, a ban on speech by the Beijing government following the massacre in Tiananmen Square than they do from, say, the decision by certain book vendors not to sell Salman Rushdie's *The Satanic Verses*. The silencing of dissenting voices in communist China was pervasive and brutally absolute. The decision of some not to sell Rushdie's book did not prevent the book from becoming a best seller. Accordingly, because it is the government that poses the greatest, most pervasive threat to preserving liberty of speech and the press, this volume is dedicated to analyzing that menace.

ENDNOTES

1. *See, e.g., Abrams v. United States,* 250 U.S. 616, 630 (1919) (Holmes, J., dissenting); *Whitney v. California,* 274 U.S. 357, 375 (1927) (Brandeis, J., concurring); *United States v. Schwimmer,* 279 U.S. 644, 654–655 (1929) (Holmes, J., dissenting); *West Virginia State Bd. of Education v. Barnette,* 319 U.S. 624, 642 (1943); *Cohen v. California,* 403 U.S. 15, 21 (1971); *Texas v. Johnson,* 109 S. Ct. 2533 (1989); *United States v. Eichman,* 58 L.W. 4744 (1990).

2. *See, e.g., Near v. Minnesota ex rel. Olson,* 283 U.S. 697, 716 (1931); *New York Times Co. v. Sullivan,* 376 U.S. 254, 270 (1964); *New York Times Co. v. United States,* 403 U.S. 713 (1971); *Board of Education, Island Trees Union Free School v. Pico,* 457 U.S. 853, 857 (1982).

3. *See, e.g., Police Department of Chicago v. Mosley,* 408 U.S. 92, 95 (1972) ("[T]he First Amendment means that government has no power to restrict expression because of its message, its ideas, its subject matter, or its content").

4. *See, e.g., Virginia State Bd. of Pharmacy v. Virginia Citizens Consumer Council, Inc.,* 425 U.S. 748, 765 (1976) ("So long as we preserve a predominantly free enterprise economy, the allocation of our resources in large measure will be made through numerous private economic decisions. It is a matter of public interest that those decisions, in the aggregate, be intelligent and well informed. To this end the free flow of information is indispensable").

5. *See, e.g., West Virginia State Bd. of Education v. Barnette,* 319 U.S. 624 (1943) (Jehovah's witnesses on religious grounds refused to salute the flag in violation of state law); *Tinker v. Des Moines School District,* 393 U.S. 503 (1969) (junior high students who wore black arm bands in protest of the Vietnam war were suspended from school for violating school policy against such protest); *Cohen v. California,* 403 U.S. 15 (1971) (individual opposed to the draft stood in a county courthouse wearing a jacket upon which were inscribed the words "Fuck the Draft" in violation of a state breach of the peace law); *Wooley v. Maynard,* 430 U.S. 705 (1977) (Jehovah's witness on religious grounds masked the New Hampshire state motto "Live Free or Die" on his license plate in violation of the state's law); *Texas v. Johnson,* 109 S. Ct. 2533 (1989); and *United States v. Eichman,* 58 L. W. 4744 (1990) (individuals opposed to the Constitution, policies, or statutes of the United States government burned American flags in protest contrary to state and federal law).

6. *See, e.g., Cohen v. California,* 403 U.S. 15 (1971).

7. *See, e.g., Pacific Gas and Electric Company v. Public Utilities Commission of California,* 475 U.S. 1 (1986).

8. *See, e.g, Red Lion Broadcasting Co. v. FCC,* 395 U.S. 367.

9. *See, e.g., Buckley v. Valeo,* 424 U.S. 1 (1976); *see also* Epstein, *Modern Republicanism—Or the Flight from Substance,* 97 YALE L. J. 1633, 1644 (1988) ("campaign restrictions work to the systematic advantage of incumbency of both parties").

10. *See, e.g., Times Film Corp. v. Chicago,* 365 U.S. 43, 69 (1969) (Warren, C. J., dissenting).

11. *See generally* J. BUCHANAN & G. TULLOCK, THE CALCULUS OF CONSENT (1962).

12. *See generally* L. LEVY, EMERGENCE OF A FREE PRESS (1985).

13. *See, e.g., Times Film Corp. v. Chicago,* 365 U.S. 43, 69 (1969) (Warren, C. J., dissenting).

14. *See* Emord, *The First Amendment Invalidity of FCC Ownership Regulations,* 38 CATH. U. L. REV. 401, 464 (1989).

15. For the contrary proposition, *see, e.g.,* Barron, *Access to the Press—A New First Amendment Right,* 80 HARV. L. REV. 1641 (1967); Fiss, *Free Speech and Social Structure,* 71 IOWA L. REV. 1405 (1986).

16. *See, e.g., Syracuse Peace Council,* 2 FCC Rcd. 5043 (1987), *reconsideration denied,* 3 FCC Rcd. 2035 (1988), *aff'd,* 867 F.2d 654 (D.C. Cir. 1989), *cert. denied,* 110 S. Ct. 717 (1990).

17. *See, e.g., Chaplinsky v. New Hampshire,* 315 U.S. 568 (1942); *FCC v. Pacifica Foundation,* 438 U.S. 726 (1978).

2

THE IMPORTANCE OF HISTORY AND SECURE MEANING

Most contemporary legal scholars argue that constitutional history is not relevant to interpretation of the Constitution. They seek to infuse the Constitution with modern meanings reflective of their own social, political, or economic values. The view that fundamental changes in the Constitution should be reserved to the people through the amendment process set forth in Article V has given way to the view that the power to alter the Constitution's fundamental meaning is rightfully inherent in the Supreme Court's authority to decide cases.

In subsequent chapters we will examine the currently popular academic theories of First Amendment construction. At this juncture, let us briefly consider the essential arguments against historically based construction of the Constitution and the reasons why, contrary to these arguments, we must understand the intellectual history underlying the document before we may presume to say what it means.

According to the reigning academic view, the Constitution is not a permanent framework for a limited federal republic, but a *tabula rasa;* constitutional law is not a prescription for the maintenance of power, but a form of politics.[1] "[C]onstitutional interpretation should be in some sense 'open,' or what I call 'possibilistic,' " writes Robin West, a contemporary scholar. The document is to be "open to multiple interpretations, which [should] *at least* include interpretations capable of facilitating progressive causes and policies," she writes.[2] Another scholar, Erwin Chemerinsky, believes "[t]he judicial role is to articulate the meaning of basic values

11

in the contemporary context and to protect these values from unjustified infringement."[3] He finds it "desirable for society to have an institution, such as the judiciary, that is accorded great discretion in imparting specific, modern content to constitutional provisions."[4]

Through the elimination of traditional barriers to the broad exercise of judicial discretion, the currently popular academic view invites jurists to transform the Constitution from a document that embodies limitations on the exercise of government power into a document that promotes and even requires the application of power in service to a *political* agenda—an agenda devised not by the Congress but by the courts. In this way, plans for the redistribution of income, speech power, voting power, and economic opportunity from a set of *disfavored* people (the political majority and the economically successful) to a set of *favored* people (the political minority or the economically unsuccessful) have been translated into *constitutional* requirements. As Frank Michelman sees it, under a *proper* system of constitutional construction, the "equal protection" clause of the Fourteenth Amendment must be read to mandate government provision of a minimum level of social welfare for each person, complete with a constitutional entitlement to food, shelter, clothing, health care, and "effective participation" in the political system.[5]

This kind of constitutional construction is the approach favored by most legal academicians for attaining, through judicial fiat, political objectives that they believe may not be attainable through democratic processes, namely, various redistributionist schemes. The arguments for what may be termed "Relativist" construction create a basis in constitutional law for circumventing the policy making function of the legislature with an oligarchic expedient: the judicial authority of the courts.

At least five principal arguments have been advanced to justify the various forms of Relativist construction. Different permutations of each argument have been presented in the legal scholarship:

1. Our ancestors' time is not our time; their answers cannot be ours. Alexander Bickel first hinted at this sentiment in *The Least Dangerous Branch:*

    > [A]s time passes, fewer and fewer relevantly decisive choices are to be divined out of the tradition of our founding. Our problems have grown radically different from those known to the Framers, and we have had to make value choices that are effectively new, while maintaining continuity with tradition.[6]

2. We cannot know our tradition; our view of the past is inevitably colored by our perceptions of the present. Paul Brest has written:

> [W]e can never understand the past in its own terms, free from our prejudices or preconceptions. We are hopelessly imprisoned in our own world views; we can shed some preconceptions only to adopt others, with no reason to believe that they are the conceptions of the different society that we are trying to understand.[7]

3. Tradition should not be a source for discerning constitutional values because such construction causes the rules laid down by past majorities to bind nonconsenting present majorities. In *Democracy and Distrust,* John Hart Ely wrote:

> There are . . . serious theoretical problems with tradition as a source of constitutional values. Its overtly backward-looking character highlights its undemocratic nature: it is hard to square with the theory of our government the proposition that yesterday's majority, assuming it was a majority, should control today's. . . . Reliance on tradition therefore seems consistent with neither the basic theory of popular control nor the spirit of the majority-checking provisions to which we are seeking to give content.[8]

4. Historiography is value laden, not value neutral. There is an historical basis to buttress almost every conceivable interpretation of the Constitution. Therefore, historically based construction is in fact no different from modern value construction in its interpretive flexibility. Erwin Chemerinsky has written:

> Historiographers persuasively argued that the process of historical examination is inevitably interpretive and influenced by the values of the historian. Reading constitutional history for original intent cannot be value neutral because of the subjective process of deciding whose intent counts (the drafters? the ratifiers? which ones?), of ascertaining which of their views matter, and of determining the intent of large numbers of people who often had different objectives. . . . [I]nterpretation based on tradition faces exactly the same dilemma as originalism. As with originalism, supporters [of historical construction] . . . must identify why tradition should control interpretation. . . . Given American history's diversity, a tradition can be found to support or condemn almost any practice.[9]

5. The Framers of the Constitution did not intend to create a permanent constitutional understanding. According to Jefferson Powell, the Framers of the Constitution did not understand their "personal intentions"

to be "a definitive or even particularly valuable guide to constitutional construction." [10]

Viewed within the prism of history, the Constitution is by design a framework for the establishment of a limited federal republic. The framework is not a catalogue of specific rules, but an embodiment of broad principles that define the scope and purpose of federal power in the first three articles and that provide limitations on the exercise of that power in the Bill of Rights. The movement to abandon constitutional history is based on an assumption that there are no constitutional values worth preserving in these provisions; that there is no danger in substituting new, untried principles of jurisprudence for old, proven ones; and that there is no threat to liberty in shifting the power to alter the fundamental meaning of the Constitution from the people, through the formal amendment process set forth in Article V, to the courts, through the exercise of judicial discretion.

The movement to abandon constitutional history is also based on the assumption that stable protection for rights against the novel exercise of government power has negligible or no value when compared with the need to accommodate social, economic, or political changes through an ever-changing constitutional order.

In the scholarship advocating the abandonment of history, there is a remarkable absence of discussion about the dangers posed by official abuse in a government that assumes new, plenary powers to change the nation's basic charter and to exercise jurisdiction over areas previously beyond the reach of government. There is no discussion of the dangers of abuse inherent in the judiciary's assumption of new authority to redefine rights long understood and exercised by the American people. Each American exercises rights secure in the knowledge that the Constitution provides these rights stable protection. Without this security, our freedoms will, in a very real sense, be compromised or lost.

The dangers of abuse that exist in the Relativists' constitutional order are numerous and bode ill for maintaining freedom and limited government. Furthermore, the arguments for abandoning history have established neither the necessity nor the desirability of rejecting long-standing principles of constitutional law developed during the popular rebellion that ultimately produced the Constitution and its amendments. The Relativists' arguments have not proven that a principled understanding tested by the pragmatic experiences of the people is inferior to novel principles derived from the minds of judges and tested nowhere except in those minds.

Consider the following specific refutations of the arguments against historically based construction enumerated above.

1. Unquestionably, Alexander Bickel is correct when he points out that we are confronted with many problems that are radically different from those that confronted the Constitution's Framers. However, the mere fact that we are confronted with new problems does not in itself establish that the fundamental principles underlying any particular constitutional provision have no applicability in our time or have such limited applicability as to be irrelevant today. Additionally, social change does not itself justify judicial usurpation of the power to alter the Constitution, a power vested in the people by Article V. Furthermore, the need to apply the Constitution to new factual circumstances does not require interpreting the Constitution in a manner that disserves or violates its fundamental principles.

2. Paul Brest is undoubtedly correct when he asserts that in judging the facts of a case, individual prejudices creep into the analysis, causing the reasoning and, less frequently, the results to differ from jurist to jurist. However, this universal condition does not make reliance on history a suspect approach. It does not establish that it is too difficult to discern from the historical record the paramount principles that have justified a particular constitutional provision. It also does not establish that it is too difficult to tailor decisions so that they will support rather than contravene these principles. By probing into the historical record, we *can* identify the popular philosophical bases that underlie any particular provision of the Constitution. That there may be more than one philosophical basis and more than one possible interpretation of the philosophical bases does not make the historical method illegitimate, nor does it necessarily obscure meaning. Rather, it adds to the possible meanings of the constitutional provision. That there may be conflicting bases for interpretation does not prevent the jurist from selecting the one that best comports with the overall design and purpose of the Constitution.

3. John Hart Ely's argument that historically based construction causes past majorities to prevail over nonconsenting present ones misconstrues the purpose of an historical focus. The purpose is not to ensure that past majorities govern today's majority, but to ensure that the trust placed in the Constitution by the American people (who have come to rely on stable constitutional meaning) is not compromised by the exercise of judicial discretion. In short, in its proper sphere, Congress makes sure

that popular majoritarian values are embodied in the law. It is, however, the duty of the courts to make sure that the fundamental principles underlying constitutional rights are not transgressed as a result of the usurpation of power by *any* branch of the government.

4. Erwin Chemerinsky's argument is correct in its recognition that all judicial interpretation is value laden. However, he fails to take into account the fact that some forms of interpretation are more value laden than others and therefore less stable. Judicial interpretation exercised to preserve the fundamental principles underlying the Constitution is less value laden, is more methodological and pragmatic, and is more protective of rights long enjoyed by the American people than an interpretation that is open-ended or based entirely on the ideological preferences of the interpreter. Open-ended, or Relativist, interpretation is, of course, boundless and so provides no predictable meaning. It has no certain methodology; it does not require a search through the historical record to discover meaning. It is inherently ideological and, therefore, entirely subjective. It differs markedly based on who the judge is. The judge privileged to decide a constitutional question is free to define rights according to his or her own sense of justice in a manner that may or may not protect rights actually understood and enjoyed by the American people. Indeed, left to their own devices, judges who adopt the open-ended or Relativist approach are free to enhance the rights of some to the detriment of others. In contrast, forms of interpretation that are bound by a need to make decisions conform to the principles underlying the Constitution will ensure far greater stability in the protection of rights, far greater uniformity in decisions, and far greater assurance to the American people that existing liberties will not be sacrificed to attain short-term, partisan objectives.

Furthermore, Erwin Chemerinsky states the obvious when he explains that, with enough searching, one can find an historical basis to support just about any practice. However, it is not self-evident—indeed it is contrary to fact—that there are endless numbers of principles that actually underlie the Constitution's provisions. In the underlying principles, judges may discern grounds for developing a constitutional jurisprudence—one that protects rights on the basis of core constitutional values and that provides stability in the protection of rights, leaving the ultimate power to make basic changes to the people in accordance with Article V.

5. Jefferson Powell's argument that the Framers did not intend their constitutional preferences to be permanent rests on a weak foundation. In a well-documented article entitled "The Constitution's Accommodation of Social Change," Philip A. Hamburger has submitted evidence that the Framers and ratifiers of the Constitution generally understood that "constitutional law was permanent."[11] While there were differences among the Framers and ratifiers over the meaning of the Constitution, there was a consensus that the Constitution's meaning was to be permanent. Even had the Framers and ratifiers intended their Constitution to be only a temporary framework, the value of relying on historical analysis would not thereby be repudiated. For those who seek to interpret the Constitution in accordance with the principles underlying it, the fact that some Framers may not have intended their original understandings to govern the document is irrelevant. The focus is on the principles protected by the provision in issue, not on the specific intentions of any one Framer or group of Framers or ratifiers.

In the case of the freedom of speech and press, there is a rich, principled intellectual history preceding the adoption of the First Amendment. This history is the by-product of an actual struggle to secure protection for freedoms long denied. As opposed to a system of open-ended or Relativist construction, a system of historically based construction will better ensure that the amendment's meaning, as actually understood and experienced by the American people, will not be lost or sacrificed. Thus this latter system preserves that trust which the people place in the Constitution, a trust that is necessary if our republic is to survive.

It should not come as a surprise that the past legal and philosophical struggles to imbue the law with protections for the freedom of speech and press are in fact a great source of meaning for the freedom. Indeed, all scholars in the Western world, whether they admit it or not, draw from this legacy in formulating values they deem worthy of protection under the First Amendment. They may find certain by-products of the freedom more valuable than others, but they cannot help but borrow from the essential principles wrought through the struggle of men to be free. No matter how much some people would like to disclaim the importance of constitutional history to an understanding of the meaning of the Constitution, that history is in fact a great, if not the greatest, source of meaning.

Tangible enjoyments of free speech and press have whetted the public appetite for freedom and have given assurance through repetition, void of legal punishment, that such experiences reside securely in a private province, protected from the state. In a limited federal republic, which our government designedly is, people expect that speech and press freedom will not suddenly become illegal or subject to regulation. We *could* redefine the freedom of speech and press in accordance with our own predilections, no matter how far afield we strayed from the original constitutional plan. However, that redefinition would result in a grave injustice to the American people, for it is the freedom that Americans actually enjoy and have historically enjoyed that we must, at a minimum, protect.

Article V recognizes that in our polity, despite the paramount necessity of protecting minority rights, a constitutional change of any fundamental nature must be agreed to by almost all of us. If a supermajority of Americans believe the Constitution does not serve them, they retain the right to revise it. This power has long been recognized as a great savior of republics such as ours, because it avoids the need for revolution to effect basic changes in the legal order that sometimes become necessary. It also prevents the majority from suffering a sudden loss in constitutional protection at the hands of a judicial minority.

Comprehending the philosophical grounds that led our ancestors to risk incarceration and to sacrifice their lives in the fight to secure the freedom of speech and press is the essential first step in understanding the meaning of that freedom. To avoid the mistakes of past regimes whose transgressions of fundamental liberties fomented strife and revolution, we must understand our history. We must always bear in mind that the freedom we define is not ours individually to change. The freedom of speech and press is rightly regarded by the American people as theirs; we each share in this sovereign right, and not a single one of us possesses a legitimate power to fundamentally redefine it.

Fundamental changes in the protection of the freedom affect every American. We therefore need to approach the First Amendment with humility. We must respect those core values that it protects and that form the fundamental reason why the amendment was made a part of our Constitution. Once we understand *why* our Constitution includes a protection for freedom of speech and press, we will know *what* we must protect if the freedom is to retain its status as a truly sovereign right of the people.

THE PURPOSE OF THIS HISTORICAL STUDY

The following historical study is not intended to resolve the debate over what consensus, if any, existed between 1789 and 1791 regarding the proper meaning of the terms "speech" and "press" within the First Amendment.[12] Various writers, such as Leonard Levy and Jeffrey Smith, have focused on different aspects of the historical tradition and have come to different conclusions.[13]

This study's purpose is to document that government has historically posed the greatest threat to speech and press liberty and to establish that the central purpose of the First Amendment is to disarm the government of any power to trench on that liberty. Comprehension of any precise eighteenth-century definition of the terms "speech" and "press" is not necessary to appreciate the philosophical underpinnings for and purpose of this great restraint on government power. Consequently, the disagreement about the eighteenth-century understanding of these terms is merely noted here in passing.

Levy has argued that no popular consensus existed between 1789 and 1791 concerning the meaning of the terms "speech" and "press." Indeed, the Blackstonian conception of a free press predominated in the law.[14] Levy has asserted that the First Amendment did not eliminate the law of seditious libel but went only so far as to protect the Blackstonian common law view: that is, a mere freedom from prior restraint but not a freedom from punishment for matters once published.[15]

Although before 1985 Levy had largely ignored a great body of evidence that demonstrated that the *actual press practice* in the late eighteenth century (despite infrequent prosecutions for seditious libel) had been in accord with an expansive definition of speech and press,[16] in his latest work Levy now recognizes that the press abounded with antigovernment scurrility. Nevertheless, Levy continues to believe that the *law* of seditious libel was largely unaffected by these practices.[17]

Others, like Smith, have found preservation of the *actual freedom* of the press to be the principal focus of First Amendment protection in the late eighteenth century.[18] Smith believes that the freedom designedly protected by the amendment far exceeded the Blackstonian definition and had, by 1789, rendered that view of the law anachronistic.[19]

The conundrums presented by these conflicting views are fascinating, but they need not be resolved to comprehend the essential focus of and the core values protected by the First Amendment. The historical consensus and the plain meaning of the evidence support the view that above all else the First Amendment stands as a denial of government control over speech and the press, whatever those terms may mean. Moreover, this same evidence establishes that the First Amendment was designed to protect a private sphere in which ideas and information would be freely exchanged.

By studying the historic speech and press conflicts between man and the state, we may observe how the core values of the First Amendment became part of the American tradition of liberty and how those values have defined our Western conception of individual freedom. We may also observe how colonial governments used their primitive regulatory tools to invade the sphere of private speech and press. This observation will help us understand that contemporary governments' suppression of speech and press is but part of an historical pattern.

The history presented in the next several chapters focuses on the development of the Radical Whig philosophy of speech and press. The philosophy arose in England in the late seventeenth century and gained great popularity in America during the eighteenth century. It has been underemphasized in constitutional scholarship but is of vital significance for comprehending the origins of press freedom in America.

ENDNOTES

1. *See, e.g.,* Michelman, *Bringing the Law to Life: A Plea for Disenchantment,* 74 CORNELL L. REV. 256–69 (1989).
2. West, *Progressive and Conservative Constitutionalism,* 88 MICH. L. REV. 641, 648 (1990).
3. E. CHEMERINSKY, INTERPRETING THE CONSTITUTION 129 (1987).
4. *Id.*
5. Michelman, *Welfare Rights in a Constitutional Democracy,* 1979 WASH. U. L. Q. 659, 677.
6. A. BICKEL, THE LEAST DANGEROUS BRANCH 39 (1962).
7. Brest, *The Misconceived Quest for the Original Understanding,* 60 B. U. L. REV. 204, 221–22 (1980).
8. J. ELY, DEMOCRACY AND DISTRUST 62–63 (1980).
9. Chemerinsky, *Foreword: The Vanishing Constitution,* 103 HARV. L. REV. 43, 92, 94 (1989).
10. *See* Powell, *The Original Understanding of Original Intent,* 98 HARV. L. REV. 885, 944 (1985).
11. *See* Hamburger, *The Constitution's Accommodation of Social Change,* 88 MICH. L. REV. 239, 327 (1989).

12. Some First Amendment scholars adhere to the view that the Framers' *"only purpose"* in adopting the amendment was to "sustain the process of representative self-government." BeVier, *Justice Powell and the First Amendment's "Societal Function": A Preliminary Analysis,* 68 VA. L. REV. 177 (1982). *See also* BeVier, *The First Amendment and Political Speech: An Inquiry into the Substance and Limits of Principle,* 30 STAN. L. REV. 299 (1978); R. Bork, *Neutral Principles and Some First Amendment Problems,* 47 IND. L. J. 1 (1971) [*but see* R. Bork, THE TEMPTING OF AMERICA 333 (1990) where Bork reiterates that he now finds the views he articulated in his *Indiana Law Journal* article to posit "an unworkable rule." *See also Ollman v. Evans,* 750 F. 2d 970, 1002 (1984) (Bork, C. J., concurring)]. Other scholars believe the amendment to have been designed to prohibit prior restraints on speech and press but to permit prosecutions post-publication for seditious libel. *See, e.g.,* Note, *The Founding Fathers and Political Speech: The First Amendment, the Press and the Sedition Act of 1798,* ST. LOUIS U. PUB. L. REV. 395 (1987); L. LEVY, EMERGENCE OF A FREE PRESS (1985); W. BERNS, THE FIRST AMENDMENT AND THE FUTURE OF AMERICAN DEMOCRACY (1976); W. BERNS, FREEDOM, VIRTUE AND THE FIRST AMENDMENT (1957). Still others contend that the historical scholarship underlying the Framers' intent supports an expansive conception of the speech and press liberty. *See* J. SMITH, PRINTERS AND PRESS FREEDOM (1988); Smith, *Prior Restraint: Original Intentions and Modern Interpretations,* 28 WM. & MARY L. REV. 439 (1987); Mayton, *Seditious Libel and the Lost Guarantee of Freedom of Expression,* 84 COLUM. L. REV. 91 (1984); Anderson, *The Origins of the Press Clause,* 30 UCLA L. REV. 455 (1983); Bogen, *The Origins of Freedom of Speech and Press,* 42 MD. L. REV. 429 (1983); D. Teeter, *A Legacy of Expression: Philadelphia Newspapers and Congress During the War for Independence* (1966) (unpublished dissertation, University of Wisconsin, Madison, Ph.D., School of Journalism); M. Yodelis, *Boston's Second Major Paper War: Economics, Politics, and the Theory and Practice of Political Expression in the Press, 1763–1775* (1971) (unpublished dissertation, University of Wisconsin, Madison, Ph.D., School of Journalism).

13. *Compare* L. LEVY, EMERGENCE OF A FREE PRESS (1985) *with* J. SMITH, PRINTERS AND PRESS FREEDOM (1988).

14. L. LEVY, EMERGENCE OF A FREE PRESS 269 (1985).

15. Explains Levy:

> What is clear is that no evidence suggests an understanding that a constitutional guarantee of free speech or press meant the impossibility of future prosecutions of seditious utterances. . . . Freedom of speech and press, as the evidence demonstrates, was not understood to include a right to broadcast sedition by words. The security of the state against libelous

advocacy or attack outweighed any social interest in open expression, at least through the period of adoption of the First Amendment. The thought and experience of a life-time, indeed the taught traditions of law and politics extending back many generations, supplied an *a priori* belief that freedom of political discourse, however broadly conceived, stopped short of seditious libel.

L. LEVY, EMERGENCE OF A FREE PRESS 269 (1985).

16.   *Compare* L. LEVY, LEGACY OF SUPPRESSION: FREEDOM OF SPEECH AND PRESS IN EARLY AMERICAN HISTORY (1963) *with* L. LEVY, EMERGENCE OF A FREE PRESS (1985).

17.   Writes Levy:

The amendment protected the *freedom* of the press, not the press. The freedom of the press and of political discourse generally had so widened in scope that seditious libel had become a narrow category of verbal offenses against government, government officials, and government policies. To be sure, the legal definition of seditious libel remained what it had been from the time of Hawkins to Mansfield: malicious, scandalous falsehoods of a political nature that tended to breach of the peace, instill revulsion or contempt in the people, or lower their esteem for their rulers. But prosecutions were infrequent, the press habitually scurrilous. Government forebore, realizing that prosecutions might fail or backfire because critics represented strong factions, and, often, influential men. Moreover, public opinion, except in times of crisis like Shay's [sic] Rebellion, tended to distrust an administration that sought to imprison its critics. The press could not have endured as aspersive and animadvertive as it was without public support. For the most part people understood that scummy journalism unavoidably accompanied the benefits to be gained from a free press. People seem to have understood that critics vented unfavorable opinions in order to excite a justifiable contempt for the government; to prosecute those critics seemed to immunize from criticism public officials who probably deserved to be disliked or distrusted. That was the teaching of *Cato's Letters* and of the Zenger case.

L. LEVY, EMERGENCE OF A FREE PRESS 271 (1985).

18.   *See* J. SMITH, PRINTERS AND PRESS FREEDOM (1988); Baldasty, *Toward an Understanding of the First Amendment, Boston Papers, 1782–1791,* 3 JOURNALISM HISTORY 25–30, 32 (1976); Yodelis-Smith and Baldasty, *Criticism of Public Officials and Government in the New Nation,* 4 J. COMM. INQUIRY 53–74 (1979); Anderson, *The Origins of the Press Clause,* 30 UCLA L. REV. 455–541 (1983).

19.   Following his history of antigovernment press practices in the eighteenth century, Smith concludes:

> Although early Americans believed that false aspersions could be a form of personal injury, they understood that a self-governing people required information and that any authority for government suppression was a greater threat to freedom than even the most irresponsible journalism. Courts have often ignored this willingness to trust the marketplace of ideas, and some historians have asserted that such tolerance hardly existed, but the revolutionary generation knew from its experience that the press could serve as an effective check on the abuse of power. Realizing that freedom of expression would always be endangered, those who demanded and ratified the First Amendment used the strongest possible terms in attempting to preserve a fundamental right for themselves and for future generations.

J. SMITH, PRINTERS AND PRESS FREEDOM 167 (1988).

3

THE BIRTH OF THE MECHANICAL PRESS AND THE STRUGGLE TO MAKE IT FREE

[T]he art of Printing will so spread knowledge that the common people, knowing their own rights and liberties, will not be governed by way of oppression.[1]

The history of the press in England and America reveals a disturbing pattern of government and press entanglement that has obstructed free communication. From King Henry VIII's time to our own, the government has always sought control over the means of disseminating ideas and information. To gain that control, government has often entered into a *quid pro quo* arrangement with the press. In exchange for printers ceding to the government content control, they have been granted legal protection from competition, affording them rates of return on sales that have exceeded the market rate (what economists term "monopoly rents"). The licensing of the printing press and, later, of the broadcast and cable press has been part of this broader pattern of press/state symbiosis.

The unholy marriage between press and state dates back 500 years and recommences each time technological innovation provides mankind with a new mode of mass communication. The first press-state union in Western history took place at the end of the fifteenth century just as the printing press made its debut in England.

William Caxton (1424?–1491) first introduced printing to England with a press that he established at Westminster in 1476.[2] He likely did so not at the behest of Henry VI but in coordination with a number of men of letters who might well have been his patrons.[3] Caxton was soon followed by other printers who began press work in London and Westminster.[4] By 1523, England had about thirty-three printers and booksellers that were publishing and disseminating literature.[5]

Throughout the sixteenth century, the Crown, principally through the Privy Council and the Courts of Star Chamber, kept the slowly proliferating press in check. The Council and the Courts of Star Chamber, quick to condemn religious heresies and statements disrespectful of the King and his counselors, prosecuted individuals and printers for sedition of various kinds.[6] As the press published more controversial material of a religious or political nature, the control exerted by the King and the Privy Council increased precipitously.[7]

In an early effort to co-opt the press, Henry VIII in 1528 decreed that no book bound outside England could be sold in England, thereby affording native printers protection from external competition. The Crown also entered the printing business by establishing the King's Stationer, whose powers were expanded into control over the general printing trade throughout the sixteenth century. The office was highly prized and received a monopoly over the distribution of foreign books. Well-behaved printers favored by the Crown could be appointed as royal printers and paid handsomely for their work so long as they did not offend the Crown.[8] The position of royal printer came with a heavy dose of censorship imposed by the Crown's overseers.[9] The King further increased his control over the content of the press by issuing patents of monopoly to his favorite printers. Patent holders were awarded an exclusive right to publish a particular kind of work, such as the Bible, in accordance with the King's prerogative.[10] In exchange for these privileges, the royal printers and the officers of the King's Stationer Company assisted the Crown in suppressing printing disfavored by His Majesty.[11]

As early as 1529, Henry VIII took a further step toward suppressing free speech and press (a step that would often be repeated) when he banned a number of Protestant works deemed heretical. He issued a proclamation that explained the act as necessary to protect his subjects from corruption:

> [C]ertain heretical and blasphemous books lately made, [have been] privily sent into this realm by the disciples, fautors, and adherents of said Martin Luther, and other heretics . . . [T]he king's subjects are likely to be corrupted, unless his highness (as Defender of the Faith) do put to his most gracious help and royal authority . . . wherefore his highness chargeth and straitly commandeth all and every [one of] his lords spiritual and temporal, judges, justices of [the] peace, sheriffs, mayors, bailiffs, constables, etc. . . . [to see that] no person or persons do from henceforth presume to bring into this realm, or do sell,

receive, take, or detain any book or work, printed or written, which is made, or hereafter shall be made against the faith catholic, or against the holy decrees, laws, and ordinances of holy church, or in reproach, rebuke, or slander of the king, his honorable council, or his lords spiritual or temporal.[12]

Although executions were relied on to discourage violations of the proclamation, printers and booksellers persisted in distributing noxious works, provoking the King to establish a licensing system in 1530.[13] He did so with the sternest admonition:

[N]o manner of person or persons take upon hym or them to printe any boke or bokes in englische tong, concernynge holy scripture, not before this tyme printed within this realme, ontyll such tyme as the same boke or bokes be examyned and approued by the ordinary of the diocese, where the said bokes shalbe printed: And that the prynter thereof, upon euery of the sayde bokes so examyned, do sette the name of the examynour or examynours, with also his owne name upon the sayd bokes, as he wyll answere to the kinges highnes, at his uttermoste peryll.[14]

The system of licensing afforded the Crown the greatest success in controlling printed matter. It gave the King considerable power to promote the circulation of works favorable to his religious and political policies. Despite occasional popular revolts against censorship and the persistent efforts of factions, such as the Puritans "who moved a secret press around England to produce the Martin Marprelate tracts in 1588 and 1589,"[15] the system of licensing with its monopoly rents kept the press in England under the control of the Crown until at least the middle to late seventeenth century.

With the increasing distribution of pamphlets and the development of the art of printing during the seventeenth century, greater numbers of people entered the ranks of the literati. Inspired by the Puritan Reformation, groups such as the Independents and the Levellers joined John Milton in advocating greater freedom of inquiry. In the 1640 Leveller movement, John Lilburne, Richard Overton, and William Walwyn, among others, generated tracts critical of government censorship and licensing. They appealed for the government to "hear all voices and judgments" and countenance "all mens understandings" so those seeking knowledge could "be more conveniently informed."[16]

In their fight for religious toleration, the Independents, the Levellers, and men such as John Milton advocated an end to the Licensing Act of 1643 on grounds that the prior restraint discouraged learning and the discovery of truth.[17] John Locke similarly advocated a tolerance for opposing points of view short of seditious expressions.[18] However, these voices of dissent, the most remarkable of the period from the 1640s until the 1720s, did little to effect immediate changes in government controls.

Between 1640 and 1643, the royal power over the press was systematically removed from the Crown by Parliament. The first major movement occurred with the abolition of the popularly dreaded Courts of Star Chamber in 1641.[19] From 1641 until 1694 and the expiration of the Printing Act, Parliament remained the principal organ of government responsible for censorship.

It was not until George III's reign (1760–1820) that the press in England exerted an independent influence so great that government efforts at censorship inspired significant opposition. Rising literacy caused the newspaper (which first appeared in the 1640s) to become an accepted and vital medium. By 1694, pressure from the growing number of independent printers began to mount against the censorial acts of Parliament. In a petition to the House of Lords, independent printers protested that the Licensing Act of 1692 "subjects all Learning and true Information to the arbitrary Will and Pleasure of a mercenary, and perhaps ignorant Licenser; destroys the Properties of Authors in their Copies; and sets up many Monopolies."[20] Arrayed against the independents stood the armies of co-opted printers who had long enjoyed their artificial monopoly protection and thus vehemently opposed an end to licensing, despite the transgressions of their liberties.[21] Against mounting public pressure, Parliament refused to reenact the Licensing Act, and it expired.

By the time of George III's accession to the throne in 1760, some ninety newspapers thrived in London. An attempt to reimpose prior restraints on the press through licensing restrictions or to enforce a vigorous general prosecution against the press would have met with stiff opposition from a growing class of politically conscious Britishers.[22] The class consisted of readers and debaters from all stations in life. They shared a passion for polemics and a thirst for knowledge, and they congregated in London coffee houses, which became centers of political communication.[23]

From 1700 forward, the British government's only remaining usable vehicles for suppressing speech and the press consisted of the doctrines of seditious libel[24] and breach of legislative privilege.[25] Since Sir Edward Coke's 1606 Star Chamber decision, *De Libellis Famosis,* a criminal libel could be found to have been perpetrated against a private person under the theory that a private libel "provokes revenge and therefore tends, however remotely, to a breach of the peace."[26] A criminal libel could also be found to have been perpetrated against the government ("an even greater offense") under the theory that such a libel not only produces a breach of the peace "but also the scandal of government."[27]

By the mid-eighteenth century, the accepted legal view was that articulated by Sir William Blackstone in his *Commentaries:*

> The liberty of the press . . . consists in laying no previous restraints upon publications, and not in freedom from censure for criminal matter when published. Every freeman has an undoubted right to lay what sentiments he pleases before the public: to forbid this is to destroy the freedom of the press; but if he publishes what is improper, mischievous, or illegal, he must take the consequences of his own temerity.[28]

Under this Blackstonian model, the "truth" of a libel, rather than being a defense to a libel charge, was deemed in aggravation of it, "because it was more provocative [and] thereby [increased] . . . the tendency to breach of the peace or [exacerbated] . . . the scandal against the government."[29]

THE RISE OF A PHILOSOPHY OF FREEDOM

Freedom of Speech is the great Bulwark of Liberty; they prosper and die together; And it is the Terror of Traytors and Oppressors, and a Barrier against them. It produces excellent Writers, and encourages Men of fine Genius.[30]

Simultaneous with the waning of government control of the British press in the late seventeenth century, there arose a philosophy of freedom so powerful in its popular appeal that it influenced opinion not only in England but also in the colonies. This philosophy was brought to the fore by the eighteenth-century Radical Whigs; their views became a popular polemical passion in the colonies that swept the revolutionary generation and eventually led to the inclusion of a free speech and press clause in the First Amendment to the U.S. Constitution.

The law of England had undergone a significant change throughout the eighteenth century (from prohibiting unlicensed printing to permitting it with the threat of prosecution post-publication). However, an avant-garde group, the "coffee house radicals," remained dissatisfied. They took their political cues from the radical social and political thought of the English Civil War and of the Commonwealth period. They united these sentiments with the philosophical legacy of the opposition politicos and religious dissenters of the seventeenth century to produce "the extreme 'left' under George III," the Radical Whigs.[31]

Among the coffee house radicals, two of the most beloved and prolific polemicists of the time were John Trenchard and Thomas Gordon. Trenchard (1662–1723) was "a west-country squire of ample means and radical ideas, . . . [a] 57-year-old veteran of the pamphlet wars that surrounded the Glorious Revolution."[32] Gordon (?–1750) was "a clever young Scott . . . fresh from Aberdeen University" who moved to London "to make his fortune, equipped with little but a sharp tongue and a ready wit."[33] The two met in 1719.[34]

Trenchard and Gordon were most notable in the American colonies for their collection of 138 piercing essays concerning civil and religious liberty that were republished in book form and entitled *Cato's Letters*. The essays were first published serially in *The London Journal* from 1720 to 1723[35] and were thereafter collected in four volumes that, due to their renown, "went through six editions between 1723 and 1755."[36]

Clinton Rossiter has found *Cato's Letters* the single most important political influence on the colonial mind: "Locke, Bolingbroke, Sidney, Addison, and Gordon and Trenchard were, so far as the colonists were concerned, the great men of [the Whig] . . . tradition, and the greatest of these were Gordon and Trenchard."[37] Rossiter finds that "[n]o one can spend any time in the newspapers, library inventories, and pamphlets of colonial America without realizing that *Cato's Letters* rather than Locke's *Civil Government* was the most popular, quotable, esteemed source of political ideas in the colonial period."[38] Among their letters on liberty, Trenchard and Gordon dedicated four to the freedoms of speech and press.[39]

Trenchard and Gordon believed liberty "the unalienable Right of Mankind."[40] They argued that men in government must, when exercising "discretionary Power," "answer for that Discretion to those that trust them," the people.[41] This Whig view was precisely the reverse of that held by the Tories. The Tory view provided a philosophical basis for state control: that the King was answerable to God but his subjects were answerable to him.[42]

Of all *Cato's Letters*, the two most famous in the colonies were Letters No. 15, "Of Freedom of Speech; That the Same is inseparable from Publick Liberty," and No. 32, "Reflections upon Libelling." Letter No. 15 was an extraordinarily enlightened article for its time, quite popular in England among Whigs and in America among the vast majority of colonists.[43] In that essay, Trenchard and Gordon defined "Freedom of Speech" as the right not just of the governors but "of every Man, as far as by it he does not hurt and control the Right of another," and this limitation "is the only Check which it ought to suffer, the only Bounds which it ought to know."[44]

Trenchard and Gordon believed this degree of free speech "essential to free Government."[45] They perceived a property in one's speech and also understood the rights of property and speech to "always go together."[46]

The writings of Trenchard and Gordon on speech and press set forth three essential values that have been recognized repeatedly in modern times as the fundamental elements of the freedom. These three values are expressed as: (1) a right of the individual to expose corruption and to criticize those in power to ensure that they remain responsive to the people, (2) a right of the individual to propagate knowledge and to engage in discourse and debate in the search for truth, and (3) a right of the individual to control his thoughts and his expression for intellectual self-development and self-fulfillment.

THE ORIGINS OF THE SELF-GOVERNMENT/ CHECKING-VALUE MODEL

Out of the opposition political movement, of which Trenchard and Gordon were a part, arose the view that Lockean natural rights could best be secured through a watchful press. Criticism of government was viewed as an essential means to bring into public scrutiny acts of wrong-doing or misguided policies that in turn could inspire public revulsion and political reaction.

Trenchard and Gordon could not accept the notion that one "ought to speak well" of even wicked leaders to preserve the public peace and abide by His Majesty's legal prerogative.[47] "[T]o do publick Mischief, without hearing of it, is only the Prerogative and Felicity of Tyranny," they wrote; "[a] free People will be showing they are so, by their Freedom of Speech."[48] Because government is nothing but the "part and Business of the People," Trenchard and Gordon counseled that it "ought to be the Ambition, of all honest Magistrates, to have their Deeds openly examined, and publickly scanned."[49] They sought a broad canvass of public men and measures, so that when public men "are honest, they [may] be publickly known, that they may be publickly commended," and so that when "they be knavish or pernicious, they [may] be publickly exposed, in order [that they may] . . . be publickly detested."[50]

Having surveyed the Roman and English histories of speech and press freedom, they concluded that "[a]ll Ministers . . . who were Oppressors, or intended to be Oppressors, have been loud in their Complaints against Freedom of Speech, and the License of the Press; and always restrained, or endeavored to restrain, both."[51] The consequence of this has been that

"Writers" have been "brow-beaten" and "punished . . . violently" and their works have been "burnt."[52] The understanding Trenchard and Gordon derived from this history of suppression was that "[b]y [their suppression of speech] . . . [Ministers] shewed how much Truth alarmed them, and how much they were at Enmity with Truth."[53]

Trenchard and Gordon's second letter on the freedoms of speech and press concerns the subject of libel. Entitled "Reflections upon Libelling," Letter No. 32 defined their understanding of the permissible scope of libel prosecutions. They defined "libelling" as "a sort of writing that hurts particular Persons, without doing Good to the Publick."[54] As for exposing the "Wickedness" of public men and measures, Trenchard and Gordon believed such exposure the "duty which every Man owes to Truth and his Country" and which "can never be a Libel in the Nature of Things."[55] For Trenchard and Gordon, great constraints on government power were deemed of major import. It was better to err on the side of permitting many hurtful libels than on the side of a zealous effort to suppress them.[56] To avoid a too-aggressive prosecution of libels, Trenchard and Gordon also called for tolerance of even false and bilious harangues, finding them unbelievable in nature and thus harmless. Repeatedly, they implored readers to tolerate as much as possible *all* libels to avoid the danger of a general prosecution that could destroy the "End of Writing":

> Of all Sorts of Libels, scurrilous ones are certainly the most harmless and contemptible: Even Truth suffers by Ill-Manners; and Ill-Manners prevent the Effect of Lies. The Letter in the *Saturday's Post* of the 27th past does, I think, exceed all the Scurrilities which I have either heard, or seen, from the Press or the Pulpit. The Author of it must surely be mad: He talks as if Distraction were in his Head, and a Firebrand in his Hand; and nothing can be more false. . . . The Paper is a Heap of Falsehood and Treason, delivered in the Style and Spirit of *Billingsgate*. . . .
>
> However, as bad as that Letter is, (and, I think, there cannot be a worse) Occasion will never be taken from scurrilous and traitorous Writing, to destroy the End of Writing. . . .
>
> I must own, that I would rather many Libels should escape, than the Liberty of the Press be infringed; yet no man in *England* thinks worse of Libels than I do.[57]

The next letter in Trenchard and Gordon's series on speech and press is Letter No. 100, "Discourse upon Libels."[58] In this one, the two Whigs again addressed alleged libels on governmental men and measures. Here they noted the hypocrisy presented by those partisans who, when "in

Power[,] . . . were unwilling to have their Actions scanned and censured" but who, when out of power, "thought it very hard not to be allowed the Liberty to utter their Groans."[59] They reiterated the theme of Letter No. 32 that toleration of libels is prudent to "preserve the Advantages of Liberty of Speech, and Liberty of Writing (which secures all other Liberties)."[60] They explained that it is of "less consequence . . . that an innocent Man should be now and then aspersed, than that all Men should be enslaved."[61]

From *Cato's Letters* No. 15, 32, and 100, a fundamental value of speech and press is identified: government must tolerate public criticism of its men and measures so that truth about government can surface and so that the people can remain sovereign. Modern scholars have incorporated these values of speech and press freedom into theories that have great influence in academic circles. Vincent Blasi has written extensively concerning the "checking value" of free speech and press,[62] and Alexander Meiklejohn is renowned for his treatment of the "self-government" rationale for free speech and press.[63]

THE ORIGINS OF THE MARKETPLACE OF IDEAS/ SEARCH FOR TRUTH MODEL

Echoing the theme from Milton's *Areopagitica,*[64] Trenchard and Gordon condemned the practice whereby parties in power seek to promote their own political views and to suppress opposing ones. They did not extol the benefits of liberal discussion merely in religion and politics but also in philosophy and science. They understood that the search for truth would necessarily produce errors in judgment. However, they believed that if knowledge of errors were suppressed, unknowing others might err. They also believed that if errors were not exposed in public debate, then public ignorance would be perpetuated.

If men are permitted to "preach or reason publickly and freely upon certain Subjects, as for Instance, upon Philosophy, Religion, or Government," they may do so "wrongly, irreligiously, or seditiously . . . ," the two gentlemen reasoned. They may "pervert and mislead an ignorant and unwary Person." However, if men are prohibited from preaching or reasoning thusly, "the World must soon be over-run with Barbarism, Superstition, Injustice, Tyranny, and the most Stupid Ignorance."[65] In sum, by denying the public a misleading, irreligious, or seditious message, the government would succeed only in causing the public to be deprived of essential knowledge.

Returning to the notion that truth has inherent superiority in a competition of ideas, Trenchard and Gordon deemed it "senseless to think that any Truth can suffer by being thoroughly searched, or examined into; or that the Discovery of it can prejudice true Religion, equal Government, or the Happiness of Society, in any respect."[66] Rather, "Truth has so many Advantages above Error, that she wants only to be shewn, to gain Admiration and Esteem."[67]

In these passages from Letter No. 100, the two Whigs set forth the fundamental bases for what has become known as the "Marketplace of Ideas/Search for Truth" rationale—that through a free and open encounter of ideas, truth will come to the fore and will tend to triumph over falsehood. In our time, Justices Holmes and Brandeis have been given greatest credit for popularizing the "Marketplace of Ideas" and "Search for Truth" free speech and press rationales.[68] Indeed, Justice Holmes originated the "marketplace of ideas" metaphor.[69]

THE ORIGINS OF THE PERSONAL AUTONOMY/ SELF-FULFILLMENT MODEL

Trenchard and Gordon wrote that "[w]ithout Freedom of Thought, there can be no such Thing as Wisdom." They recognized that the freedom of speech and press was valuable because it promoted intellectual development as well as the exchange of information and opinion. The two Whigs believed it a "blessed Time, when you might think what you would, and speak what you thought!"[70] They also believed that each person had a property right in his speech and submitted that "in those wretched Countries where a Man cannot call his Tongue his own, he can scarce call any Thing else his own."[71]

They valued a freedom for people to "search Nature, . . . investigate her Works . . . and discover [her] hidden and darling Secrets" and to explore religion, believing the quest for knowledge in itself a process that must be free from governmental constraints if it is to advance the cause of mankind.[72]

In these passages from Letters No. 15 and 100, Trenchard and Gordon identified the rudimentary elements of what has become known as the "Autonomy" and "Self-Fulfillment" rationales: the quest for knowledge and the need to share information and ideas with others are fundamental aspects of the freedom of speech and press, deserving of protection from government. In recent years, Martin Redish and C. Edwin Baker have been principal advocates of the Autonomy and Self-Fulfillment rationales for speech and press liberty.[73]

THE INDOMITABLE JOHN WILKES: A CLASSIC "CATONIST"

[A] fellow who stood near His Majesty had the audacity to hallow out, "Wilkes and Liberty for ever!"[74]

The elements in *Cato's Letters* that form the Radical Whig free speech and press theory became the credo of one of the eighteenth century's most controversial political figures, John Wilkes. Wilkes's travails became a toast of the times in England and revolutionary America. Through a decade-long attack on the government of George III, and particularly the Tory administration of Lord Bute, Wilkes established himself as a hero in both countries.[75] His ribald opposition became emblematic of the kind of liberality for which Radical Whigs yearned. What Parliament regarded as Wilkes's "excesses" were understood by the Radical Whigs to be an Englishman's birthright. In short, the broad canvass of government men and measures contained in Wilkes's written works became in practice what Cato stood for in theory. Virtually all Radical Whigs of the time, particularly those in colonial America, celebrated this flouting of free press restrictions.

Explains Robert A. Rutland: "John Wilkes' problems after the 1763 publication of *North Briton* No. 45 were well known in America, where great sympathy was created by the arrest of Wilkes and 48 others under general warrants signed by the secretaries of state, Lords Halifax and Egremont."[76] Leonard Levy found Wilkes to be, like Cato, a continental hero in America "extolled for [his] . . . defense of virtually unfettered political discussion."[77] Bernard Bailyn has commented that "John Wilkes' career was crucial to the colonists' understanding" of themselves; "his fate, the colonists came to believe, was intimately involved with their own."[78] Bailyn finds that Wilkes's most famous publication, *North Briton* No. 45, "was as celebrated in the colonies as it was in England, and more generally approved of."[79]

Beginning in 1755, a British weekly Whig publication, the *Monitor*, and its editor, Arthur Beardmore, began to take umbrage at the measures of the Tory administration.[80] In 1762, the administration sought to counteract the influence of the *Monitor* with its favored press organ, the *Briton*, which was edited by T. G. Smollet.[81] To confound the Tory effort, the Whig opposition produced yet another newspaper, the *North Briton*, edited and authored by John Wilkes and Charles Churchill.[82] Shortly after the *North Briton*'s appearance, the government's supporters produced yet another paper for their side, the *Auditor,* edited by Arthur Murphy.[83] "The newspaper battle was on and continued throughout the summer of 1762; the *Briton* and the *Auditor* versus the *North Briton* and the *Monitor*"[84] (some titles of which must have been wistfully chosen).[85]

Between June 1762 and April 1763, the *North Briton* heaped sometimes caustic and scandalous abuse on the administration of George III and, in particular, on Lord Bute.[86] Its principal editor, John Wilkes, was a member of Parliament. In *North Briton* No. 45, which at the time was thought to be his last edition, Wilkes commented on the King's speech at the opening session of Parliament. Although critical of certain men and measures, Wilkes's commentary was mild by modern standards.[87] However, it provoked the ire of the administration whose minister, George Grenville, and secretaries of state, Lords Egremont and Halifax, succeeded in having Wilkes arrested and imprisoned[88] and, upon a general warrant, in having his private study ransacked and certain of his papers confiscated.[89]

Shortly after his imprisonment, Wilkes was released to Westminster Hall on a writ of *habeas corpus.* A throng of well-wishers accompanied him.[90] Following a presentation by his counsel of reasons why Wilkes ought to be released, the presiding judge adjourned the court for three days.[91] Back in court, before a gallery full of supporters, Wilkes pled:

> My lords . . . the Liberty of all peers and gentlemen, and, what touches me more sensibly, that of all the meddling and inferior set of people, who stand most in need of protection, is in my case this day to be finally decided upon a question of such importance as to determine at once whether English Liberty shall be a reality or a shadow.[92]

Chief Justice Pratt responded: "The person of a Member ought to be sacred . . . unless it is absolutely necessary to confine him to prevent further mischief. We are therefore all of [the] opinion that Mr. Wilkes is entitled to the privileges of Parliament, and therefore he must be discharged."[93] Thereby, Pratt, without passing on the legal issue of a libel, determined that Wilkes, because of his legislative privilege, could not be detained.

With his freedom restored, Wilkes resumed his crusade against the government of George III. He paid a foreman, Michael Cury, to operate his printing press.[94] He scheduled for printing an obscene parody entitled "Essay on Women," written under the pseudonym of Dr. Warburton, Bishop of Gloucester.[95] He also ordered his printer to republish 2,000 copies of the infamous *North Briton* No. 45.[96] These works set in motion, Wilkes fled to Paris.[97]

Upon receipt of copies of Wilkes's "Essay on Women" and notice of the republication of *North Briton* No. 45, the House of Commons acted. The House denounced the essay as a "most scandalous, obscene, and impious libel" and resolved that *North Briton* No. 45 was a "false, scandalous, and seditious libel."[98] It ordered that all copies of *North Briton* No. 45 be burned.[99]

Upon his return from Paris, Wilkes was summoned to Parliament to account for his libels.[100] He protested that he was not well enough to appear.[101] He then eluded the authorities by a Christmas Eve escape from Britain, across the English Channel, and back to Paris.

Wilkes was thereafter convicted in absentia for seditious and obscene libel and pronounced an "outlaw."[102] Despite the conviction, Wilkes did not let his pen rest. He continued to write letters and tracts to his countrymen, engendering a good deal of sympathy for his cause.[103] He returned from France in 1768 as an international celebrity. In spite of his fame, he had to serve a twenty-two month prison term for his libels.[104] He was also obliged to pay a 1,000 pound fine.[105] Wilkes's hardship, however, was not as bleak as it might at first appear. As an international *cause célèbre* for the Whig opposition, he received gifts and food from compatriots in England and the colonies during his incarceration.[106] Moreover, he was thrice elected to Parliament while in prison,[107] although denied his seat each time.

John Wilkes's irreverent and indefatigable opposition to the administration of George III epitomized the kind of spirited canvassing of men and measures that was called for in *Cato's Letters*. His strident exercise of the liberty of speech and press stretched the bounds of that freedom.

Wilkes's cause was associated in colonial "minds with great opposition to the government that passed the Stamp Act and the Townshend Duties, that was flooding the colonies with parasite placemen, and that appeared to be making inroads into the constitution."[108] The colonists viewed Wilkes as one of their own, struggling for their ideals. In 1769, William Palfrey wrote to Wilkes: "the fate of Wilkes and America must stand or fall together."[109] The deprivation of Wilkes's hallowed rights cut deeply against the American grain.

The ideals espoused by Cato and the actions taken by Wilkes were the respective script and theatrics of a British free speech and free press drama that, when staged in the American colonies, met with near universal applause. The American mind, in a state of rebellion, decried any deprivation of natural rights. Americans were duly impressed by the principles of Cato and by Wilkes's bold opposition, and they became enthralled with the Radical Whig expansive conception of the speech and press freedom.

ENDNOTES

1. Samuel Hartlib, friend of John Milton, London, Oct. 25, 1641, *quoted in* F. SIEBERT, FREEDOM OF THE PRESS IN ENGLAND 1476–1776 192 (1952).
2. F. SIEBERT, FREEDOM OF THE PRESS IN ENGLAND 1476–1776 22 (1952).
3. *Id.* at 24.
4. *Id.* at 24–25.
5. *Id.* at 25.
6. From the end of the fifteenth century until 1695, the press in England labored under the omnipresent threat of judicial or legislative punishment for one or more of the following: treason, Scandalum Magnatum (i.e., false news), heresy, licensing act violations, breach of legislative privilege, and seditious libel. The control of the presses was considered a royal prerogative. During most of the period, unlicensed presses were illegal. *See* Hamburger, *The Development of the Law of Seditious Libel and the Control of the Press,* 37 STAN. L. REV. 661 (1985); L. LEVY, TREASON AGAINST GOD (1981); W. HAWKINS, A TREATISE OF THE PLEAS OF THE CROWN (1716).
7. F. SIEBERT, FREEDOM OF THE PRESS IN ENGLAND 1476–1776 30 (1952).
8. *Id.* at 32–33.
9. *Id.* at 37.
10. *Id.* at 38–39.
11. *Id.* at 167.
12. *Quoted in Id.*
13. *Id.* at 46.
14. *Quoted in Id.* at 46.
15. J. SMITH, PRINTERS AND PRESS FREEDOM 20 (1988).
16. L. LEVY, EMERGENCE OF A FREE PRESS 90 (1985).
17. In *Areopagitica,* Milton wrote "that [the Licensing Act] will be primely to the discouragement of all learning and the stop of truth, not only by disexercising and blunting our abilities in what we know already, but by hindering and cropping the discovery that might be yet further made both in religious and civil wisdom." *Quoted in* M. HUGHES, JOHN MILTON COMPLETE POEMS AND MAJOR PROSE 720 (1957). However, Milton did not go so far as to repudiate the law of libel: "I deny not but that it is of greatest concernment in the church and commonwealth to have a vigilant eye how books demean themselves as well as men; and thereafter to confine, imprison, and do sharpest justice on them as malefactors." *Id.*

18. *See* John Locke, *A Letter Concerning Toleration, in* 6 THE WORKS OF JOHN LOCKE 4 (1811); *see also* L. LEVY, EMERGENCE OF A FREE PRESS 98–100 (1985) (wherein Levy contends that Locke's toleration, like that of Milton, did not extend to Catholics, atheists, or Jews).

19. F. SIEBERT, FREEDOM OF THE PRESS IN ENGLAND 1476–1776 260 (1952).

20. *Quoted in Id.* at 260.

21. *Id.*

22. "For more than a century, newspapers and pamphlets had been strewn across the tables of clubs, inns, taverns and coffeehouses and had fueled animated exchanges which filled the air along with tobacco smoke. London had nearly ninety newspapers in 1760. . . ." J. SMITH, PRINTERS AND PRESS FREEDOM 22 (1988).

23. J. BREWER, PARTY IDEOLOGY AND POPULAR POLITICS AT THE ACCESSION OF GEORGE III 149 (1976).

24. *See* Hamburger, *The Development of the Law of Seditious Libel and Control of the Press,* 37 STAN. L. REV. 661, 663 (1985).

25. For example, on June 4, 1721, the House of Commons debated "how to deal with two men who had arrested the servant of a member [of Parliament], and were accused, also, of uttering uncomplimentary words against the House itself. It was finally decided that they should ride one horse, bareback, seated back to back, from Westminster to the Exchange, each wearing on his breast a paper on which was [placed] the following inscription: 'For arresting a servant to a member of the House of Commons of Parliament.' This sentence was pronounced by the speaker." M. CLARKE, PARLIAMENTARY PRIVILEGE IN THE AMERICAN COLONIES 105–6 (1943).

26. 3 Coke's *Reports* 254 (1606).

27. L. LEVY, EMERGENCE OF A FREE PRESS 7 (1985).

28. 4 W. BLACKSTONE, COMMENTARIES ON THE LAWS OF ENGLAND 151–52 (1765–1769); L. LEVY, EMERGENCE OF A FREE PRESS 12–13 (1985).

29. L. LEVY, EMERGENCE OF A FREE PRESS 12 (1985).

30. 1 J. TRENCHARD & T. GORDON, CATO'S LETTERS (L. Levy, gen. ed.) 100 (Letter No. 15, *Of Freedom of Speech: That the Same is inseparable from Publick Liberty, Feb. 4, 1720*) (1971 reprint).

31. *See* B. BAILYN, 1 PAMPHLETS OF THE AMERICAN REVOLUTION 1750–1776 28–29 (1965).

32. *Id.* at 29.

33. *Id.* at 30.

34. *See* C. ROSSITER, SEEDTIME OF THE REPUBLIC 140 (1953).

35. *See* B. BAILYN, 1 PAMPHLETS OF THE AMERICAN REVOLUTION 1750–1776 30 (1965).

36. L. LEVY, EMERGENCE OF A FREE PRESS 109 (1985). Writing in the Dedication to the sixth edition of *Cato's Letters,* Thomas Gordon (John Trenchard

had since passed away) wrote in 1755: "Let me add, that these Letters are still so well received by the Public, that the last Edition has been long since sold off, and for above three years past it was scarcely possible to find a set of them, unless in public auctions. I mention this, that the present Edition may not seem owing to the frequent Quotations made from them in our late Party-hostilities. I flatter myself, that, as these Papers contain Truths and Reasons eternally interesting to human Society, they will at all Times be found seasonable and useful. They have already survived all the Clamor and Obloquy of Party, and indeed are no longer considered as Party-Writings, but as impartial Lessons of Liberty and Virtue." 1 J. TRENCHARD & T. GORDON, CATO'S LETTERS (L. Levy, gen. ed.) xviii–xix (1971 reprint).

37.   C. ROSSITER, SEEDTIME OF THE REPUBLIC 141 (1953).

38.   *Id. See also* E. COOK, LITERARY INFLUENCES IN COLONIAL NEWSPAPERS 1704–1750, 81–83, 125–126, 129, 137, 139, 159, 257, 265 (1912); F. TOLLES, MEETING HOUSE AND COUNTING HOUSE 178–79 (1948); F. McDONALD, NORVUS ORDO SECLORUM 47, 59, 70, 76 (1985); H. TREVOR COLBOURN, THE LAMP OF EXPERIENCE: WHIG HISTORY AND THE INTELLECTUAL ORIGINS OF THE AMERICAN REVOLUTION 26–27 (1793); C. ROBBINS, THE EIGHTEENTH-CENTURY COMMONWEALTH MAN, STUDIES IN THE TRANSACTION, DEVELOPMENT, AND CIRCUMSTANCE OF ENGLISH LIBERAL THOUGHT FROM THE RESTORATION OF CHARLES II UNTIL THE WAR WITH THE THIRTEEN COLONIES 115–25 (1959); D. JACOBSON, THE ENGLISH LIBERTARIAN HERITAGE, FROM THE WRITINGS OF JOHN TRENCHARD AND THOMAS GORDON IN THE INDEPENDENT WHIG AND CATO'S LETTERS xvii–lx (1965).

Bernard Bailyn has also found that *Cato's Letters* were adored in the colonies. States Bailyn:

> Republished entire or in part again and again in the colonies, "quoted in every colonial newspaper from Boston to Savannah," and referred to repeatedly in the pamphlet literature, the writings of Trenchard and Gordon ranked in the minds of the Americans with the treatises of Locke as the most authoritative statement of the nature of political liberty and above Locke as an exposition of the social sources of the threats it faced.

B. BAILYN, 1 PAMPHLETS OF THE AMERICAN REVOLUTION 1750–1776 30 (1965).

Forrest McDonald notes that *Cato's Letters* were "widely read by American patriots." F. McDONALD, NORVUS ORDO SECLORUM 47 (1985). Jeffrey Smith finds that editions of *Cato's Letters* "were immensely popular in America, where journalists and political theorists praised and imitated the authors." J. SMITH, PRINTERS AND PRESS FREEDOM 25 (1988).

Because of their wide circulation and revered status in America, *Cato's Letters* appear to have held a uniquely central place in colonial political thought. Consequently, through a careful study of *Cato's Letters* we may better understand the colonists' view of liberty.

39. 1 J. TRENCHARD & T. GORDON, CATO'S LETTERS (L. Levy, gen. ed.) 96 (Letter No. 15, *Of Freedom of Speech; That the Same is inseparable from Publick Liberty,* Feb. 4, 1720) (1971 reprint); 1 J. TRENCHARD & T. GORDON, CATO'S LETTERS (L. Levy, gen. ed.) 246 (Letter No. 32, *Reflections upon Libelling,* June 10, 1721); 2 J. TRENCHARD & T. GORDON, CATO'S LETTERS (L. Levy, gen. ed.) 292 (Letter No. 100, *Discourse upon Libels,* Oct. 27, 1722) (1971 reprint); 2 J. TRENCHARD & T. GORDON, CATO'S LETTERS (L. Levy, gen. ed.) 300 (Letter No. 101, *Second Discourse upon Libels,* Nov. 3, 1722) (1971 reprint).

40. 2 J. TRENCHARD & T. GORDON, CATO'S LETTERS (L. Levy, gen. ed.) 214 (Letter No. 59, *Liberty Proved to be the Unalienable Right of All Mankind,* Dec. 30, 1721) (1971 reprint).

41. 2 J. TRENCHARD & T. GORDON, CATO'S LETTERS (L. Levy, gen. ed.) 215 (Letter No. 59, *Liberty Proved to be the Unalienable Right of All Mankind,* Dec. 30, 1721) (1971 reprint).

42. For expositions in defense of the Divine Right of Kings, *see, e.g.,* R. FILMER, OBSERVATIONS CONCERNING THE ORIGINAL AND VARIOUS FORMS OF GOVERNMENT (1666); R. FILMER, PATRIARCHA, OR THE NATURAL POWER OF KINGS (1680); R. FILMER, OBSERVATIONS CONCERNING THE ORIGINAL OF GOVERNMENT UPON MR. HOBS LEVIATHAN, MR. MILTON AGAINST SALMASIUS, H. GROTIUS DE JURE BELLI (1652); R. FILMER, THE NECESSITY OF THE ABSOLUTE POWER OF ALL KINGS (1648). For an attack upon the Divine Right of Kings and an exposition on the origins of natural rights, see 1 J. LOCKE, TWO TREATISES ON GOVERNMENT (P. Laslett ed. 1960).

43. L. LEVY, FREEDOM OF THE PRESS FROM ZENGER TO JEFFERSON: EARLY AMERICAN LIBERTARIAN THEORIES xxiii (1966). "Trenchard and Gordon helped popularize a radical Whig theme which gained wide acceptance during the eighteenth century. Newspaper and pamphlet writers preached the necessity of popular vigilance and journalistic surveillance." J. SMITH, PRINTERS AND PRESS FREEDOM 63 (1988).

44. 1 J. TRENCHARD & T. GORDON, CATO'S LETTERS (L. Levy, gen. ed.) 96 (Letter No. 15 *Of Freedom of Speech, That the Same Is inseparable from Publick Liberty,* Feb. 4, 1720) (1971 reprint).

45. *Id.*

46. *Id.*

47. *Id.* at 97.

48. *Id.*

49. *Id.*
50. *Id.* at 100.
51. *Id.* at 101.
52. *Id.* at 101–2.
53. *Id.* at 102.
54. J. TRENCHARD & T. GORDON, CATO'S LETTERS (L. Levy, gen. ed.) 246 (Letter No. 32, *Reflections upon Libelling,* June 10, 1721) (1971 reprint).
55. *Id.* at 247.
56. *Id.* at 252.
57. *Id.* at 252–53.
58. 2 J. TRENCHARD & T. GORDON, CATO'S LETTERS (L. Levy, gen. ed.) 292 (Letter No. 100, *Discourse upon Libels,* Oct. 27, 1722) (1971 reprint).
59. *Id.* at 293.
60. *Id.* at 294.
61. *Id.*
62. *See* Blasi, *The Checking Value in First Amendment Theory,* 1977 AM. B. FOUND, RES. J. 521; *see also* H. KALVEN, A WORTHY TRADITION: FREEDOM OF SPEECH IN AMERICA 69–70 (1988); Kalven, *The New York Times Case: A Note on "The Central Meaning of the First Amendment,"* 1964 SUP. CT. REV. 191, 205.
63. *See, e.g.,* A. MEIKLEJOHN, FREE SPEECH AND ITS RELATION TO SELF-GOVERNMENT 16–17 (1948); BeVier, *The First Amendment and Political Speech: An Inquiry into the Substance and Limits of Principle,* 30 STAN. L. REV. 299, 304–22 (1978); Meiklejohn, *The First Amendment Is an Absolute,* 1961 SUP. CT. REV. 245, 255–57.
64. In an address to Parliament, *Areopagitica* (1644), John Milton advocated an end to the Licensing Act of 1643, alleging that prior restraint on the press discouraged learning and the discovery of truth:

    > And though all the winds of doctrine were let loose to play upon the earth, so Truth be in the field, we do injuriously by licensing and prohibition to misdoubt her strength. Let her and Falsehood grapple; who ever knew Truth put to the worse, in a free and open encounter.

    Quoted in M. HUGHES, JOHN MILTON COMPLETE POEMS AND MAJOR PROSE 746 (1957).
65. 2 J. TRENCHARD & T. GORDON, CATO'S LETTERS (L. Levy, gen. ed.) 296–97 (Letter No. 100, *Discourse upon Libels,* Oct. 27, 1722) (1971 reprint).
66. *Id.*
67. *Id.* at 298–300.
68. *See, e.g., Abrams v. United States,* 250 U.S. 616, 630 (1919) (Holmes, J., dissenting); *Whitney v. California,* 274 U.S. 357, 375 (1927) (Brandeis, J.,

concurring); *see also* Duval, *Free Communication of Ideas and the Quest for Truth: Towards a Teleological Approach to First Amendment Adjudication*, 41 GEO. WASH. L. REV. 161, 188–94 (1972).

69.   See *Abrams v. United States*, 250 U.S. 616, 630 (1919).

70.   1 J. TRENCHARD & T. GORDON, CATO'S LETTERS (L. Levy, gen. ed.) 96, 99 (Letter No. 15, *Of Freedom of Speech; That the Same is inseparable from Publick Liberty*, Feb. 4, 1720) (1971 reprint).

71.   *Id.* at 96.

72.   2 J. TRENCHARD & T. GORDON, CATO'S LETTERS (L. Levy, gen. ed.) 297 (Letter No. 100, *Discourse upon Libels*, Oct. 27, 1722) (1971 reprint).

73.   *See, e.g.*, M. REDISH, FREEDOM OF EXPRESSION: A CRITICAL ANALYSIS 47–48 (1984); Redish, *The Value of Free Speech*, 130 U. PA. L. REV. 591 (1982); Baker, *Realizing Self-Realization: Corporate Political Expenditures and Redish's The Value of Free Speech*, 130 U. PA. L. REV. 646 (1982). Although Professor Scanlon may be credited with the first modern development of the Autonomy theory of free speech [*see* Scanlon, *A Theory of Freedom of Expression*, 1 Phil. & Pub. Aff. 216 (1972)], he has since recanted his earlier view [*see Freedom of Expression and Categories of Expression*, 40 U. PITT. L. REV. 519 (1979)].

74.   From *Gent's Magazine*, 1769, at 268, *quoted in* GEORGE RUDÉ, WILKES AND LIBERTY 71 (1962).

75.   1 B. BAILYN, PAMPHLETS OF THE AMERICAN REVOLUTION 1750–1776 70–71 (1965).

76.   1 THE PAPERS OF GEORGE MASON 1725–1792 290n (R. Rutland ed. 1970).

77.   L. LEVY, EMERGENCE OF A FREE PRESS 62 (1985).

78.   1 B. BAILYN, PAMPHLETS OF THE AMERICAN REVOLUTION 1750–1776 70 (1965). "Wilkes was celebrated in toasts and popular demonstrations throughout [Britain]. When Wilkes won reelection to Parliament in 1768, Benjamin Franklin witnessed mobs illuminating London for two nights and 'requiring gentlemen and ladies of all ranks as they passed in their carriages to shout for Wilkes and liberty, marking the same words on all their coaches with chalk, and No. 45 on every door.' Franklin considered it 'really an extraordinary event' to find such support for 'an outlaw and exile, of bad personal character, not worth a farthing.' " J. SMITH, PRINTERS AND PRESS FREEDOM 23 (1988).

79.   1 B. BAILYN, PAMPHLETS OF THE AMERICAN REVOLUTION 1750–1766 70 (1965).

80.   F. SIEBERT, FREEDOM OF THE PRESS IN ENGLAND 1476–1776 376 (1952).

81.   *Id.*

82.   *Id.*

83.   *Id. See also* G. RUDÉ, WILKES AND LIBERTY 20 (1962).

84.   F. SIEBERT, FREEDOM OF THE PRESS IN ENGLAND 1476–1776 376 (1952).

85. "[T]he *North Briton,* as its name suggests, was both a direct riposte to [the *Briton*] . . . and a satirical commentary on the widely-held belief that the new administration was over-heavily staffed with Scots and over-tender to Scottish interests." G. RUDÉ, WILKES AND LIBERTY 21 (1962).

86. Lord Bute's "alleged intimacy with the King's mother, the Princess Dowager, was a subject of constant comment." G. RUDÉ, WILKES AND LIBERTY 21 (1962). In the first issue of the *North Briton,* Wilkes waxed eloquent on the value of a free press to check governmental excesses:

> The liberty of the press is the birthright of a Briton, and is justly esteemed the firmest bulwark of the liberties of this country. It has been the terror of all bad ministers; for their dark and dangerous designs, or their weakness, inability, and duplicity, have thus been detected and shown to the public, generally in too strong and just colors for them to bear up against the odium of mankind. . . . A wicked and corrupt administration must naturally dread this appeal to the world; and will be for keeping all the means of information from the prince, parliament, and people.

John Wilkes, *North Briton* No. 1, Sat., June 5, 1762, at 1–2 (London: W. Bingley, 1769).

87. G. RUDÉ, WILKES AND LIBERTY 22 (1962).

88. *Id.* at 23.

89. L. LEVY, EMERGENCE OF A FREE PRESS 145 (1985).

90. G. RUDÉ, WILKES AND LIBERTY 26 (1962).

91. *Id.* "As Wilkes left the court room, he was greeted with thunderous shouts of 'Liberty! Liberty! Wilkes forever!' " *Id.*

92. *Id.* at 26–27.

93. *Id.* at 27.

94. *Id.* at 31.

95. *Id.*

96. *Id.*

97. *Id.*

98. *Id.* at 33.

99. L. LEVY, EMERGENCE OF A FREE PRESS 145 (1985).

100. G. RUDÉ, WILKES AND LIBERTY 34 (1962).

101. *Id.*

102. L. LEVY, EMERGENCE OF A FREE PRESS 145 (1985).

103. *Id.* at 145–46.

104. *Id.* at 146.

105. *Id.*

106.   "Wilkes was housed in comfortable seclusion in a first floor of the prison with windows overlooking St. George's Fields. Gifts, food-parcels, delicacies, money, commemorative medallions and other tokens of respect and affection poured in from every part of England and even from the Sons of Liberty at Boston and the House of Assembly of South Carolina." G. RUDÉ, WILKES AND LIBERTY 57 (1962). "[Wilkes's] return from exile in 1768 and subsequent election to Parliament were major events to Americans. Toasts were offered to him throughout the colonies, and substantial contributions to his cause as well as adulatory letters were sent by Sons of Liberty in Virginia, Maryland, and South Carolina." 1 B. BAILYN, PAMPHLETS OF THE AMERICAN REVOLUTION 1750–1776 70 (1965).

107.   L. LEVY, EMERGENCE OF A FREE PRESS 146 (1985).

108.   1 B. BAILYN, PAMPHLETS OF THE AMERICAN REVOLUTION 1750–1776 70 (1965); *see also* Maier, *John Wilkes and American Disillusionment with Britain,* 20 WM. & MARY Q. 375–95 (1963).

109.   1 B. BAILYN, PAMPHLETS OF THE AMERICAN REVOLUTION 1750–1776 71 (1965).

4

THE ATLANTIC CROSSING OF RADICAL WHIG THEORY

Before the revolution . . . we were all good Whigs, cordial in [our] . . . free principles, and in [our] . . . jealousies of the executive Magistrate.[1]

Radical Whig thought was celebrated in the American colonies from the 1730s to the 1780s.[2] Indeed, the colonists "devoured" Whig theory.[3] To say simply that this tradition of opposition thought was quickly transmitted to America and widely appreciated there is to understate the fact. Opposition thought, in the form it took at the turn of the seventeenth century and in the early eighteenth century, thoroughly saturated the colonial mind. There seems never to have been a time after the Hanoverian succession when these writings were not central to American political expression or were absent from popular politics.

British and American "merchants, politicians, publishers, [and] intellectuals . . ." residing in trading towns exchanged large amounts of opposition literature and news.[4] Americans temporarily living "in the nation's chief trading towns all deliberately and self-consciously sought to keep the communities on both sides of the Atlantic informed of . . . every political development."[5] A great deal of information was passed by merchants who traded from one or the other side of the Atlantic, or by those who had business or familial ties across the ocean. Opposition party sources in England supplied the colonies with a "flood of newspapers, pamphlets, and letters."[6]

This exchange of information would only seem natural given the close sociopolitical connections between the two English-speaking peoples. The British were fascinated by their American counterparts, and vice versa. Moreover, the political hostilities between the Whig colonists and the Tory administration of George III necessarily focused each on the other's popular politics.

Americans were avid readers of Whig opposition literature and saw to it that the coffee house radicals' handiwork was published, republished, and widely circulated.[7] Regarding free speech and press, the writings of Trenchard and Gordon had perhaps the greatest currency. In 1775, for example, fifty-three copies of Trenchard and Gordon's weekly *Independent Whig*, bound in book form, were available in Philadelphia.[8] Several copies of *Cato's Letters* also circulated in that city.[9] "[A]stonishing quantities" of *Cato's Letters* were imported into the colonies generally.[10]

Moreover, almost every significant event touching on speech evoked from colonists the hallowed principles of Cato. In 1735, the *New York Weekly Journal* reprinted excerpts from *Cato's Letters* on the freedom of speech and press before the famous trial of John Peter Zenger for seditious libel.[11] In 1767, John Dickinson appears to have drawn from *Cato's Letters* in drafting his "Letters from a Farmer in Pennsylvania to the Inhabitants of the English Colonies."[12] The works of Trenchard and Gordon appear to have influenced the Continental Congress when in 1774 its members adopted an "Address to the Inhabitants of Quebec."[13]

Cato's most popular essay, Letter No. 15, "Of Freedom of Speech; That the Same is inseparable from Publick Liberty," was quoted repeatedly throughout the colonies.[14] Bernard Bailyn has found the *New York Weekly Journal*, in particular, a "veritable anthology of the writings of Trenchard and Gordon."[15] Clinton Rossiter has found excerpts from *Cato's Letters* in several newspapers published during the colonial period, including the following: the Boston-based *New-England Courant* editions of September 11 to October 30, 1721, and July 9, 1722; the New York-based *American Weekly Mercury* editions of February 20, March 29, April 19, June 7, and June 21, 1722; February 11 to March 3, 1724; March 13, 1729; and April 9 to June 4, 1730; the *New-York Weekly Journal* editions of November 12, 1733, to November 11, 1734; July 7 to 21 and August 25 to September 22, 1735; the Philadelphia-based *Pennsylvania Gazette* editions of April 1 to May 13 and June 10, 1736; the *Boston Gazette* editions of May 12 to 19, 1735; and the Charleston-based *South-Carolina Gazette* editions of July 29 and August 8, 1748.[16]

Because of the high degree of literacy among the colonists and the wide distribution of newspapers in the colonies,[17] the repeated publication of these selected writings is quite significant.[18] Outright expressions of reverence for Cato also exist. For example, in 1774, Josiah Quincy, Jr., included in a bequest to his son the works he thought would place "the spirit of liberty" upon him: "Algernon Sidney's works,—John Locke's works,—Lord Bacon's works,—Gordon's Tacitus,—and *Cato's Letters*."[19]

Moreover, Leonard Levy has found *Cato's Letters* accessible to or in the library inventories of those who were among the American revolutionary and constitutional elite. Explains Levy:

> John Dickinson, John Adams, and Thomas Jefferson quoted Cato; Jefferson had a copy of *Cato's Letters* in his personal library. Many private libraries, college libraries, and bookstores had copies of *Cato's Letters*. Benjamin Franklin recommended that students read *Cato's Letters* . . . Chief Justice William Cushing of Massachusetts in 1789 inquired of John Adams whether Cato was right in advocating that truth could not be a libel in matters involving government, religion, and society. David Ramsey in his near contemporary history of the Revolution, commenting on the popularity of "fashionable authors, who have defended the cause of liberty," wrote: "*Cato's Letters*, the Independent Whig, and such productions were common." Old John Adams, reminiscing about the coming of the American Revolution, began his list of "fashionable reading" among Americans of the late colonial period with *Cato's Letters*. In the history of political liberty as well as of freedom of speech and press, no eighteenth century work exerted more influence than *Cato's Letters*.[20]

The evidence of wide acceptance of the Radical Whig ideology espoused by Cato is compelling. Again and again, the colonial printers and colonists wrapped themselves in the mantle of Cato when seeking to make a point about inalienable rights or to defend themselves against governmental deprivations of those rights. This history establishes that the colonists were in near universal agreement: the free speech and press philosophy of Cato was their own. The broad conceptions of free speech and press that are espoused in *Cato's Letters* were transformed into bedrock in America. The American colonial and revolutionary experience with these conceptions appears to have expanded their scope and enhanced their importance. Although the decidedly Anglophilic colonial courts clung tenaciously to the Blackstonian conception of the speech and press liberty, increasingly the people—as expressed in the tracts, newspapers, and jury verdicts of the time—adopted Cato's view.

ENDNOTES

1. Thomas Jefferson *quoted in* C. ROSSITER, SEEDTIME OF THE REPUBLIC 143 (1953).

2. D. Bogen, *The Origins of Freedom of Speech and Press*, 42 MD. L. REV. 429, 445 (1983).

3. B. BAILYN, THE IDEOLOGICAL ORIGINS OF THE AMERICAN REVOLUTION 43–44 (1967).

4. J. BREWER, PARTY IDEOLOGY AND POPULAR POLITICS AT THE ACCESSION OF GEORGE III 202–3, 205 (1976).

5. *Id.* at 205.

6. B. BAILYN, THE IDEOLOGICAL ORIGINS OF THE AMERICAN REVOLUTION 132 (1967); *see also* W. FULLER, THE AMERICAN MAIL 112, 117 (1972) (discussing the common practice among newspaper editors of exchanging newspapers to obtain news intelligence).

7. B. BAILYN, THE IDEOLOGICAL ORIGINS OF THE AMERICAN REVOLUTION 133 (1967).

8. D. L. Teeter, *A Legacy of Expression: Philadelphia Newspapers and Congress During the War for Independence, 1775–1783* 23 (1966) (unpublished dissertation, University of Wisconsin, Madison, Ph.D., School of Journalism).

9. *Id.*

10. C. ROSSITER, SEEDTIME OF THE REPUBLIC 492n (1953).

11. *See* R. Buel, *Freedom of the Press in Revolutionary America: The Evolution of Libertarianism 1760–1820, in* THE PRESS AND THE AMERICAN REVOLUTION 69 (B. Bailyn & J. Hench eds. 1980); *see also* A BRIEF NARRATIVE OF THE NEW YORK WEEKLY JOURNAL 9–12 (S. Katz ed. 1972).

12. *See* R. Buel, *Freedom of the Press in Revolutionary America: The Evolution of Libertarianism 1760–1820, in* THE PRESS AND THE AMERICAN REVOLUTION 69 (B. Bailyn & J. Hench eds. 1980).

13. *Id.*

14. *See* Rabban, *The Ahistorical Historian: Leonard Levy on Freedom of Expression in Early American History,* 37 STAN. L. REV. 795, 806 (1985).

15. B. BAILYN, THE IDEOLOGICAL ORIGINS OF THE AMERICAN REVOLUTION 43 (1967).

16. C. ROSSITER, SEEDTIME OF THE REPUBLIC 492n (1953).

17. *See* Leder, *The Role of Newspapers in Early America "In Defense of Their Own Liberty"* 1 THE HUNTINGTON LIBRARY QUARTERLY 1 (1966). "Philadelphia printers—and indeed all American printers of the late eighteenth century—were publishers for a continent. Their newspapers or broadsides or printed sermons travelled by post-rider's saddlebag, by stage, and by sailing ships to all of the thirteen colonies and beyond." D. L. Teeter, *A Legacy of Expression: Philadelphia Newspapers and Congress During*

the War for Independence, 1775–1783 54 (1966) (unpublished dissertation, University of Wisconsin, Madison, Ph.D., School of Journalism).

18. The abundance of these writings indicates that a pervasive and extreme market demand for Whig principles compelled printers to abandon their typical preference for balance in debate in order to become partisans. For a discussion of the pecuniary emphasis of the colonial printing trade, *see* Botein, *Printers and the American Revolution, in* THE PRESS AND THE AMERICAN REVOLUTION 15 (B. Bailyn & J. Hench eds. 1980). By a margin of perhaps as much as two to one, colonial printers came to openly favor the Whig view in their publications. *Id.* at 32.

19. B. BAILYN, THE IDEOLOGICAL ORIGINS OF THE AMERICAN REVOLUTION 45 (1967).

20. L. LEVY, EMERGENCE OF A FREE PRESS 114 (1985).

5

THE AMERICAN COLONISTS'
REJECTION OF BLACKSTONE
IN FAVOR OF CATO

*I have for a long Time observed, that Men who bawl out loudest for
shutting up the Press, or having it open only for their own Party, are of
tyrannical Principles, and Enemies to Liberty both in Church and State,
and would be glad to keep the People in the most abject Slavery.*[1]

The press practice in early America reveals the great influence that Radical
Whig principles had over the colonial mind. From the 1730s until Independence, colonial printers persisted in publishing articles assailing men in power
and their policies. This history bespeaks an extraordinary commitment to
press liberty. It also reveals an essential antigovernment focus.

Far from affording sheepish allegiance to the Crown's power brokers,
colonial printers often risked their reputations, fortunes, and liberties to
condemn governors whose actions they believed to be corrupt or tyrannical. The colonial struggle for a free press was but a further extension
of the Radical Whig movement which, although conceived in England, grew
to full maturity in America.

Early in the colonial experience, an ideological divide grew between
the colonists and the colonial power brokers (the governors and legislators).
The colonists increasingly adhered to John Locke's conceptions of natural
rights.[2] The ruling authorities, who received their grant of power from the
King of England, maintained Tory sentiments favoring the traditional Divine
Right of Kings. The speech and press conflicts in the colonies, like those

in England, were at root a consequence of the collision of these two views of the source of sovereignty. One view led independently minded members of the Whig opposition to disagree with their rulers in speech and print. The other view led haughty governors of Tory sentiments to take offense and seek to silence the opposition. Invariably, governors first sought to encourage the legislators to drag offending printers before the Bar of the Assembly for reprimand or punishment. If this method failed, governors resorted to court action via the doctrine of seditious libel. Before 1735, only a half dozen trials for seditious libel are believed to have occurred in the colonies.[3] The principal means to suppress the press was legislative punishment for breach of privilege.[4]

In the colonies, as in England, the exchange of monopoly rents for control over content was relied on to ensure the dissemination of information and opinion to the liking of colonial authorities. By the time of the American Revolution, each colony had its own official newspaper whose printer was paid handsomely for printing what the legislature and the governor wanted. The printer was also given the exclusive right to print the proceedings of the legislature. In addition, the very lucrative position of Postmaster could be bestowed on a printer who adhered to the official orthodoxy.

Under what would now be viewed as a grossly expanded theory of legislative privilege, colonial legislatures were able to send the House's sergeant-at-arms off to apprehend anyone who, by speech or action, allegedly breached the peace of the House.[5] Typically, the offender would be forced to prostrate himself before the assembly and beg forgiveness for the transgressions.[6]

If not believed or if unrepentant, the accused would be placed in the custody of the sergeant-at-arms (and usually detained in the officer's own home) for trial before the House.[7] In the "trial," members would agree either (1) simply to interrogate the culprit and dismiss him following satisfactory answers (if the transgression were deemed trifling) or (2) to produce witnesses against him, cross-examine him, and subject him to a penalty ("a reprimand at the bar of the house," fines, imprisonment, or physical punishment, if the transgression were deemed grave).[8]

Mary Patterson Clarke has documented a few examples believed to typify legislative suppression of speech and press during the colonial period. In 1696 in Maryland, a man accused of "abusing the assembly" was fined 1,000 pounds of tobacco, ordered to pay fees, and required to give bail for an appearance at a provincial court.[9] Another man, an English merchant, alleged to have "[heaped] vile abuse" on the House and governor, was sentenced by the assembly to receive "thirty-nine lashes on the bare back," pay the sheriff's fees for performing the flogging, and beseech the House's forgiveness for upsetting their "quiet and rest."[10] In 1767, the Virginia House of Burgesses, in response to the service of a writ on one of the burgesses, summoned a Mr. James Pride. He pled illness as an excuse for not showing. The House then sent two physicians to examine him. The man was then arrested by the sergeant-at-arms. Unrepentant, he printed in the *Virginia Gazette* a justification for his actions. For this, he was reprimanded before the House; sent to jail (expressly deprived of a pen, ink, and paper); and fed only bread with "no strong drink whatsoever."[11]

Before the mid-1720s and before *Cato's Letters* reached the colonies, the documented instances of Whig opposition to suppression of free speech and press were few. However, after the mid-1720s, the rift between an increasingly boisterous colonial press and a thin-skinned ruling class widened. Despite the rift, there were only about six known cases of seditious libel trials in the entire period, and all but one occurred before 1735.

In the 1760s and 1770s, an emboldened press emerged in the colonies as the number of colonial printers and newspapers multiplied. Between 1763 and 1775 "the number of master printers at work in colonial America increased from forty-seven to eighty-two," and "the number of newspapers that they published doubled from twenty-one in 1763 to forty-two in 1775."[12] Although in the 1720s the nation had only thirty newspapers, "[b]y 1790 the nation had almost a hundred newspapers, most of them weeklies, but a few semi-weeklies and eight dailies."[13] The power gained by numbers (both of printers and of devoted readers) made any general prosecution of the press virtually impossible. It made even selected prosecutions of printers, as in the case of Alexander McDougall in 1771, an almost guaranteed political faux pas because of the great difficulty of obtaining a guilty verdict from a jury.

THE CASE OF JOHN PETER ZENGER

Although not the first case of a trial for seditious libel in the colonies, the prosecution of John Peter Zenger in August 1735 was undoubtedly the most renowned.[14] The case arose out of a conflict between a profligate governor of New York, William Cosby, who "was interested only in those aspects of the governorship that brought in money . . ." and one of the nation's first party paper publishers, John Peter Zenger, who had a passion for *Cato's Letters*.[15]

From the start of the *New York Weekly Journal* in 1733 to his prosecution in 1735, Zenger filled his paper with fillips in essay form that castigated Governor Cosby's administration.[16] Many essays were from *Cato's Letters*.[17] Zenger identified Governor Cosby only by innuendo. The *New York Weekly Journal* also featured advertisements, including sham ads written by Zenger himself. In one such ad, Zenger lambasted the government newspaper, the *New York Gazette,* and called for the capture of a "large Spaniel," by which he no doubt meant the Governor.[18] The ad read as follows:

A large Spaniel, of about Five Foot Five Inches High, has lately stray'd from his Kennel, with his mouth full of fulsome Panegyrics, and in his Ramble dropped them in the *New York Gazette*; . . . Whatsoever will strip the said Panegyrics of all their Fulsomeness, and send the Beast back to his Kennel, shall have the Thanks of all honest men, and all reasonable charges.[19]

In an extensive newspaper debate, William Bradford, editor of the state-supported *New York Gazette,* defended the "virtues" of libel law. Zenger took issue with the proposition that the government's judges could ever be impartial in their construction of the meaning of words alleged to be libelous.[20] Zenger preferred for the government to allow readers to be their own judges.[21]

These and other Zenger writings provoked the wrath of Governor Cosby. However, the Governor appears to have refrained from seeking the prosecution of Zenger on grounds of seditious libel until Zenger published "two scandalous songs" following the victory of the anti-Cosby, pro-Whig "Morrisite" faction in the New York City municipal elections.[22]

On January 28, 1735, New York's Attorney General filed an "information" against Zenger, charging him with seditious libel. Zenger was arrested.[23] While Zenger was in prison, James Alexander continued to publish the *Journal* and retained for Zenger the renowned attorney Andrew Hamilton, "reputedly the best lawyer in America."[24] The trial began on August 4, 1735.[25] Zenger pled not guilty.[26] In defense, Hamilton admitted that Zenger had published the allegedly libelous tracts (a matter that, in libel trials of the time, was the principal factual contention).[27] Given the regnant Blackstonian conception of the law, the Attorney General appears to have expected that an end would soon come to the matter:

[A]s Mr. Hamilton has confessed printing and publishing these libels, I think the jury must find a verdict for the King; for supposing they were true, the law says that they are not the less libelous for that; nay indeed the law says their being true is an aggravation of the crime.[28]

Addressing himself more to the jury than to the court (particularly since at least six of the jurors were of the pro-Zenger Morrisite faction),[29] Hamilton argued that proof of the printing of the alleged libel was not enough, but that the Attorney General would also have to prove the libel's *falsity*. Moreover, Hamilton argued that the prevailing state of the law (that is, that truth was a factor in *aggravation* of a libel) was a relic from the dreaded days of the Star Chamber Court. He implied that the Attorney General and the court were seeking to reimpose that hated regime.[30]

Extending his point further, Hamilton played on the jury's sense of local loyalty and prejudice and on the Morrisite faction's sympathies. He submitted that it would be a "strange doctrine" to "press everything for law here which is so in England."[31] Rather, he explained that "[i]n England so great a regard and reverence is had [for] the judges, that if any man strikes another in Westminster Hall while the judges are sitting he shall lose his right hand and forfeit his land and goods for so doing." But such, said Hamilton, is not the law "within the Province of New York."[32]

The Attorney General reiterated the state of the law of libel, explaining, "we have nothing to prove; you have confessed the printing and publishing,"[33] noting that falsity need not be proved. Chief Justice James DeLancey acted on the point. "You cannot be admitted, Mr. Hamilton, to give the truth of a libel in evidence," he said. "A libel is not to be justified; for it is nevertheless a libel that it is *true*."[34] Following further attempts by Hamilton at undercutting the Justice's ruling, DeLancey warned:

> [T]he . . . Court is of opinion, you ought not to be permitted to prove the facts in the papers: These are the words of the book, "It is far from being a justification of a libel, that the contents thereof are true, or that the person upon whom it is made had a bad reputation, since the greater appearance there is of truth in any malicious invective, so much the more provoking it is."[35]

Hamilton persisted nevertheless, forcing the Chief Justice to implore sternly that Hamilton stop his wayward course: "After the Court [has] declared [its] opinion, it is not good manners to insist upon a point in which you are overruled."[36]

But Hamilton continued and appealed to the jurors' Whiggish hearts with lines reminiscent of Cato:

> I will go so far into Mr. Attorney's doctrine as to agree that if the faults, mistakes, nay even the vices of such a person be private and personal, and don't affect the peace of the public, or the liberty or property of our neighbor, it is unmanly and unmannerly to expose them either by word or by writing. But when a ruler

of a people brings his personal failings, but much more his vices, into his administration, and the people find themselves affected by them . . . that will alter the case mightily, and all the high things that are said in favor of rulers, and of dignities, and upon the side of power, will not be able to stop people's mouths when they feel themselves oppressed.[37]

This statement caused the Attorney General to warn: "Pray Mr. Hamilton, have a care what you say, don't go too far . . . , I don't like those liberties."[38] Hamilton pressed on nonetheless. He inveighed against maladministration and asked the jury to recognize a natural right to criticize government men and measures, stating, "it is natural . . . it is a right which all free men claim" that they "are entitled to complain when they are hurt."[39] Hamilton called on the jury not merely to determine the facts in the case but also to construe the law.[40]

In his closing instruction to the jury, Justice DeLancey tried to set the case aright, explaining that Hamilton had taken "great pains . . . to show how little regard juries are to pay to the opinion of judges." The Justice informed the jurors that it was their duty to determine whether the words of Zenger quoted in the Attorney General's information "make a libel" under the law.[41] After "only a few minutes," the jury returned with its verdict: not guilty.[42]

The case gained considerable notoriety in the colonies and in England. It was "widely read and frequently reprinted."[43] "Pamphlets and newspapers everywhere printed accounts of the trial, and colonists who had been hitherto indifferent to controversies over liberty and authority discussed it with interest."[44] Benjamin Franklin sold copies of James Alexander's 1736 *Narrative* of the case and published his own essay in defense of Hamilton's argument.[45] Franklin's essay, which appeared in four parts, "used the marketplace of ideas concept, identified freedom of expression as a natural right and pillar of free government, and chronicled the suppressive tactics of despots who 'constantly encouraged prosecutions of words.' "[46]

The *Zenger* case did not affect the way in which the royal judges interpreted the law of libel, but it did establish precedent for colonists to thwart seditious libel prosecutions by returning jury verdicts for the hapless libel defendants. It also propounded the view that seditious libel was wrought from the wicked Star Chamber Courts, was a mortal threat to a natural right, and was a vehicle for a profligate ministry to conceal its transgressions from the public.[47]

THE CASE OF BENJAMIN EDES AND JOHN GILL

The rift between the governors and the governed continued to widen as the intensity of the revolutionary conflict increased. In 1768 in the Province of Massachusetts Bay, another colonial jury blocked a governor's attempt to convict two printers of seditious libel. The printers, Benjamin Edes and John Gill ("spokesmen for Sam Adams and the radical party"),[48] took issue with a charge to the grand jury given by the Chief Justice of the Massachusetts Supreme Court, Thomas Hutchinson, in the August term, 1767.[49] The Chief Justice lamented that "[p]retty high Notions of the Liberty of the Press" had "prevailed of late among us."[50] He warned that this liberty consisted only in a right to publish "without License."[51] It did not consist in "a Liberty of reviling and calumniating all Ranks and Degrees of Men with Impunity, all Authority with Ignominy."[52]

Edes and Gill did not abide by the Chief Justice's definition and made their sentiments known by publishing a reply that quoted liberally from *Cato's Letters* No. 15, "Of Freedom of Speech; That the Same is inseparable from Publick Liberty."[53] Throughout the year, Edes and Gill maintained their defense of a freedom to canvass government men and measures.

In a 1768 charge to the grand jury, Chief Justice Hutchinson warned that "[n]o Government . . . would have tolerated those libellous pieces which we have seen in the publick prints." These articles, he said, reminded him of "one [John] Wilkes, of whom you all have heard—and whom, I am sorry to say it, some among us show too great a Desire to imitate."[54] But Edes and Gill would not be stopped by such official criticism.

In early February 1768, they published an article that severely denounced Massachusetts Governor Francis Bernard. "[W]hen a diabolical Thirst for Mischief is the alone Motive of your Conduct," they wrote, "you must not wonder if you are treated with open Dislike; for it is impossible, how much we endeavor it, to *feel* any Esteem for a Man like you."[55] In particular, the piece criticized Governor Bernard for inducing "a worthy Minister of State [in England]" to "form a most unfavorable Opinion of the Province . . . and some of [its] most respectable Inhabitants."[56] The critique concluded with this searing passage:

[I]t is certain that Men totally abandoned to Wickedness, can never merit our Regard, be their Stations ever so high.

> If such Men are by God
> appointed
> The Devil may be the Lord's
> anointed.

It was signed "A TRUE PATRIOT."[57]

On March 3, 1768, the Governor's Council, with characteristic disdain, described the article as a "false, scandalous and impudent Libel."[58] The Council found the work "not only an Insult on the General Court; not only an Insult on the King's Authority, and the Dignity of his Government, but as it concludes with the most unwarrantable Profaneness, an Insult upon the King of Kings."[59]

Once the Council's address had been published, Governor Bernard ordered it to be sent to the Massachusetts House of Representatives.[60] The House, dominated by Radical Whigs whose sympathy lay with Edes and Gill, not only refused to endorse the submission of the matter to a grand jury,[61] but, paraphrasing Cato, defended the printers' right to present their views:

> The Liberty of the Press is a great Bulwark of the Liberty of the People: It is therefore the incumbent Duty of those who are constituted the Guardians of the People's Right to defend and maintain it.[62]

Undaunted, Governor Bernard turned to Chief Justice Hutchinson for a grand jury indictment. In his charge to the grand jury, Hutchinson again defined the liberty of the press to consist of no prior restraints.[63] He instructed the jury that robbing a person of his "Reputation" is worse than taking away his "Property."[64] He counseled that "a bad Ruler" is properly answerable to Great Britain for "any Misdemeanor.[65] The province has "a good King" in George III, he explained, and that king "can *easily* have [Governor Bernard] . . . removed." Hutchinson was quick to remark: "I am sure, I do not believe our present Governor is deserving of such Treatment: I am myself fully convinced of his Uprightness and Integrity."[66] In his final instruction to the jury, Hutchinson appears to have understood how violent the public rancor would be if the jury were to issue a Bill for Libelling:

> In doing your Duty and in the Observance of your Oath, you may cause a Clamor against you; Reproach may be thrown on you; you may be vilified and slandered;—but remember your own Consciences.[67]

The jurors consulted their consciences, then refused to issue a Bill for Libelling.[68]

In apparent exasperation at how taken the public had become with the notion that seditious libel prosecution was a vehicle for suppression, in a 1769 charge to the grand jury, Hutchinson explained: "I do not mention the Matter of Libels to you, Gentlemen—I am discouraged!—My repeated charges to Grand Juries, on this Head, both in this and other counties, being so entirely neglected."[69]

The *Boston Gazette* carried a strident defense, written by Sam Adams, of the grand jury's decision. The article explained that "[t]here is nothing so *fretting* and *vexatious,* nothing so justly TERRIBLE to tyrants, and their tools and abettors, as a FREE PRESS."[70] Adams thought the "reason" for this "obvious": A free press is "the bulwark of the People's Liberties" (quoting Cato) and "is ever watched by those who are forming plans for the destruction of the People's Liberties, with an *envious* and *malignant* eye."[71]

THE CASE OF ALEXANDER MCDOUGALL

More than thirty years after the *Zenger* case established jury suasion as a means to obstruct seditious libel prosecution, juries, openly flouting the Blackstonian law, continued to block prosecutions.[72] Of the half-dozen or so trials for seditious libel, the only one after *Zenger* in 1735 was the highly celebrated trial of Alexander McDougall in 1771.[73] McDougall, one of the Sons of Liberty, allegedly libelled the Assembly of New York[74] by writing an anonymous broadside, an "Address to the Betrayed Inhabitants of New York," criticizing the New York Assembly for "voting moneys to support the King's troops." The broadside was to be published in the *New York Gazette.*[75]

McDougall was prosecuted in the court of Chief Justice Daniel Horsmanden and said not a word in his own defense except to demand a jury trial.[76] He was thereafter imprisoned for two and a half months. During his imprisonment, news of the case was broadcast throughout the colonies.[77] McDougall was heralded as "America's Wilkes" and the seemingly magical number "45" from that infamous edition of the *North Briton* was revived as a rallying cry for McDougall's liberty.[78] Leonard Levy explains:

> McDougall himself consciously posed as the American Wilkes and turned his imprisonment into a theatrical triumph, while his supporters used the free press issue as an anti-administration weapon. Forty-five, the number of the *North Briton* that had earned Wilkes his conviction for seditious libel, became the talismanic symbol of libertarianism and of the American cause against England. On the forty-fifth day of the year, for example, forty-five Liberty Boys dined

in honor of McDougall on forty-five pounds of beef from a forty-five-month-old bull, drank forty-five toasts to liberty of the press and its defenders, and after dinner marched to the city jail to salute McDougall with forty-five cheers.[79]

The state's principal witness, the *Gazette*'s publisher, James Parker, died before McDougall could be tried.[80] However, the Assembly, using the breach-of-legislative-privilege doctrine, ordered McDougall to appear and beg its pardon.[81] He refused despite threats of being forced to undergo the infamous *peine forte et dure,* that is, to lay spread-eagle "on the ground and have heavy metal weights placed upon his body."[82] He was imprisoned and, although a court issued a writ of habeas corpus in order that he might appear before a magistrate, he was detained, illegally, until the end of the legislative session.[83]

The colonial experience with freedom of speech and press from the 1730s until Independence reveals a solid commitment by the colonists to the Radical Whig philosophy of Cato. Colonial printers were quick to infuse the press with criticism of government men and measures. Colonial governors adhered to the old Anglophilic view defined in Blackstone's *Commentaries.* However, public approbation for Cato's view of freedom of speech and press caused the citizenry to abandon the Blackstonian conception. As a consequence, after the 1735 *Zenger* trial, prosecutions for seditious libel ceased to be a serious threat[84] because juries refused to return guilty verdicts. By the mid-1770s, with pressures mounting for a split with Great Britain, the principal underlying theoretical basis for seditious libel (the Divine Right of Kings) had been thoroughly discredited:

> But where, say some, is the King of America? I'll tell you, friend, he reigns above, and doth not make havoc on mankind like the royal brute of Great Britain. Yet that we may not appear to be defective even in earthly honors, let a day be solemnly set apart proclaiming the charter; let it be brought forth placed on the divine law, the Word of God; let a crown be placed thereon, by which the world may know, that so far as we approve of monarchy, that in America the law is King. For as in absolute governments the King is law, so in free countries the law ought to be King; and there ought to be no other.[85]

ENDNOTES

1.   Thomas Fleet, editor, the *Boston Evening-Post*, Mar. 30, 1741, *quoted in* M. Yodelis, *Boston's Second Major Paper War: Economics, Politics, and the Theory and Practice of Political Expression in the Press, 1763–1775* 18

(1971) (unpublished dissertation, University of Wisconsin, Madison, Ph.D., School of Communications).

2. *See, e.g.,* T. Emerson, *Colonial Intentions and Current Realities of the First Amendment,* 125 U. Pa. L. Rev. 737 (1977).

3. *See* L. Levy, Emergence of a Free Press 17 (1985).

4. *See* Leder, *The Role of Newspapers in Early America "In Defense of Their Own Liberty,"* 1 The Huntington Library Quarterly 2, at note 3. Jeffrey A. Smith estimates that during the entire colonial period there were "at least twenty instances" where "legislatures summoned and interrogated journalists who published writings critical of the provincial government." J. Smith, Printers and Press Freedom 8 (1988).

5. *See, e.g.,* M. Clarke, Parliamentary Privilege in the American Colonies 103 (1943).

6. *Id.* at 103-4.

7. *Id.* at 104.

8. *Id.*

9. *Id.* at 104-5.

10. *Id.* at 105.

11. *Id.* at 105-6.

12. Botein, *Printers and the American Revolution, in* The Press and the American Revolution 41 (B. Bailyn & J. Hench eds. 1980).

13. J. Burns, The Vineyard of Liberty 90 (1982).

14. A Brief Narrative of the Case and Tryal of John Peter Zenger Printer of the New York Weekly Journal 26 (S. Katz ed. 1972).

15. *Id.* at 2, 9, 11.

16. *Id.* at 9.

17. *Id.* at 9-10.

18. *Id.* at 9; E. Cook, Literary Influences in Colonial Newspapers 1704-1750 125-27 (1912).

19. E. Cook, Literary Influences in Colonial Newspapers 1704-1750 125 (1912).

20. A Brief Narrative of the Case and Tryal of John Peter Zenger Printer of the New York Weekly Journal 13 (S. Katz ed. 1972).

21. *Id.*

22. *Id.* at 17. The songs and numerous other excerpts from *The New York Weekly Journal* are contained in appendices to A Brief Narrative of the Case and Tryal of John Peter Zenger Printer of the New York Weekly Journal (S. Katz ed. 1972).

23. *Id.* at 18.

24. *Id.* at 22.

25. *Id.* at 23.

26. *Id.* at 61.

27. *Id.* at 62.
28. *Id.*
29. *Id.* at 21–22.
30. *Id.* at 66.
31. *Id.* at 67.
32. *Id.*
33. *Id.* at 69.
34. *Id.*
35. *Id.* at 74.
36. *Id.* at 75.
37. *Id.* at 79.
38. *Id.*
39. *Id.* at 81.
40. *Id.* at 24.
41. *Id.* at 100.
42. *Id.* at 23.
43. L. LEVY, EMERGENCE OF A FREE PRESS 37, 44 (1985).
44. C. ROSSITER, SEEDTIME OF THE REPUBLIC 30 (1953).
45. J. SMITH, PRINTERS AND PRESS FREEDOM 121 (1988).
46. *Id.*
47. *See, e.g.,* L. LEVY, EMERGENCE OF A FREE PRESS 37 (1985).
48. *Id.* at 65.
49. *See* REPORTS OF CASES ARGUED AND ADJUDGED IN THE SUPERIOR COURT OF JUDICATURE OF THE PROVINCE OF MASSACHUSETTS BAY, BETWEEN 1761 AND 1772 236–37 (J. Quincy, Jr., ed. 1865).
50. *Id.* at 244.
51. *Id.*
52. *Id.*
53. A. SCHLESINGER, PRELUDE TO INDEPENDENCE: THE NEWSPAPER WAR ON BRITAIN 1764–1776 96 (1958).
54. *See* REPORTS OF CASES ARGUED AND ADJUDGED IN THE SUPERIOR COURT OF JUDICATURE OF THE PROVINCE OF MASSACHUSETTS BAY, BETWEEN 1761 AND 1772 263 (1865). The Chief Justice related a Wilkes anecdote that Wilkes "was once asked, while he was writing, how far a Man in an English Government might go, in his Publications, and not come within the Laws of High Treason. To which he answered, he was just then trying to see how far he could go." *Id.*
55. *Id.* at 271.
56. *Id.*
57. *Id.* at 271–72.
58. *Id.* at 273.
59. *Id.*

60. *Id.* at 274.
61. L. Levy, Emergence of a Free Press 66 (1985).
62. *See* Reports of Cases Argued and Adjudged in the Superior Court of Judicature of the Province of Massachusetts Bay, Between 1761 and 1772 275 (J. Quincy, Jr., ed. 1865).
63. *Id.* at 266.
64. *Id.* at 267.
65. *Id.*
66. *Id.* at 267–68.
67. *Id.* at 269.
68. *Id.* at 270.
69. *Id.* at 309.
70. *Id.* at 278.
71. *Id.*
72. During the consideration of the libel matter by the Province, Edes and Gill made a mockery of the landmark British seditious libel case, *De Libellis Famosis,* when they printed the parody, "*Libel* on a *Lobster,*" which read:

A *libel* on a *Lobster.*

I hope none will be offended; but I really prefer a
Crab to a *Lobster.**

Libellus Famosus.

* See 5 Report 125.

A libel on Crabs

I Care not a Farthing who is offended;
I would not give one Lobster for
Ten Crabs.*

Famosus Libellus.

* See Westminster Journal.

Id. at 276–77.
73. *See* L. Levy, Emergence of a Free Press 17, 77 (1985).
74. *Id.* at 45.
75. *See* Nelson, *Seditious Libel in Colonial America,* 3 Am. J. L. Hist. 169 (1959); S. Botein, *Printers and the American Revolution in* The Press and the American Revolution 29 (B. Bailyn & J. Hench eds. 1980).
76. *See* L. Levy, Emergence of a Free Press 77 (1985).
77. *Id.*
78. *Id.* at 79.

79. *Id.*
80. *Id.*
81. *Id.* at 80.
82. *Id.*
83. *Id.* at 81.
84. M. Yodelis, *Boston's Second Major Paper War: Economics, Politics, and the Theory and Practice of Political Expression in the Press, 1763–1780* 8 (1971) (unpublished dissertation, University of Wisconsin, Madison, Ph.D., School of Communications).
85. Thomas Paine, "Common Sense," *reprinted in* P. FONER, THE LIFE AND MAJOR WRITINGS OF THOMAS PAINE 29 (1974). "*Common Sense* was published by Robert Bell in January, 1776, and became an immediate sensation. . . . The demand for the pamphlet was immense, with the printers receiving notes from their correspondents such as that to Thomas Bradford from William Whitcroft in Annapolis: 'Please to send down by the Post three or four dozen pamphlets of Common Sense with the Conditions the money shall be remitted to you as soon as I know the price of them.' " D. L. Teeter, *A Legacy of Expression: Philadelphia Newspapers and Congress During the War for Independence, 1775–1783* (1966) (unpublished dissertation, University of Wisconsin, Madison, Ph.D., School of Journalism).

6

THE REVOLUTIONARY COMMITMENT TO A FREE PRESS

The colonial experience placed America in the vanguard of a budding movement for freedom of speech and press. This experience led the colonists' first representative assembly to recognize the freedom of speech not in the traditional Anglophilic terms of Blackstone but in holistic, natural rights terms. On October 26, 1774, the First Continental Congress approved an "Address to the Inhabitants of Quebec," which contained in it an "exposition on the fundamental rights of the colonists."[1] The Continental Congress defined the press freedom in very broad terms:

> The last right we shall mention, regards the freedom of the press. The importance of this consists, besides the advancement of truth, science, morality, and arts in general, in its diffusion of liberal sentiments on the administration of Government, its ready communication of thoughts between subjects, and its consequential promotion of union among them, whereby oppressive officers are shamed or intimidated, into more honorable and just modes of conducting affairs.[2]

In further developing this liberty in the text of the Address, the Continental Congress, quoting Montesquieu, explained that free speech, perhaps more so than any other right, is the root liberty: "The enjoyment of liberty, and even its support and preservation, consists in every man's being allowed to speak his thoughts, and lay open his sentiments."[3] The Continental Congress had formally recognized the Radical Whig theory of a free press. Thus, the colonial press's activities and the colonists' struggle against Anglophilic suppression of the press had borne fruit.

In May 1776, the Continental Congress advised each colony to create its own government, separate from Britain.[4] Except for Rhode Island and Connecticut, each obliged by establishing its own state constitution.[5] Of these eleven states, nine had provisions in their constitutions to protect freedom of speech or the press.

David Anderson has grouped these into four archetypal categories. His first archetype is the one drafted by George Mason in Virginia's Declaration of Rights of 1776.[6] Virginia was the first state to act on the advice of the Continental Congress. The language chosen for the amendment is from *Cato's Letters* No. 15 and reads: "Freedom of Speech is the great Bulwark of Liberty."[7] The connection to Cato is unmistakable. As Frederick Schauer explains:

> We know . . . that [Mason] . . . was personally familiar with the writings of John Trenchard and Thomas Gordon, published anonymously in England in the first half of the eighteenth century under the pseudonym "Cato," and reprinted in almost every colonial newspaper. Indeed, the specific "bulwark of liberty" language, contained not only in the Virginia Declaration of Rights, but also in a Resolution of the Massachusetts House eight years earlier, comes directly from *Cato's Letters*.[8]

The Virginia Declaration reads: "That the freedom of the Press is one of the greatest bulwarks of liberty, and can never be restrained but by despotic Governments."[9]

North Carolina's Declaration of Rights of 1776 is patterned after the Virginia Declaration. It reads: "That the freedom of the press is one of the greatest bulwarks of liberty, and therefore ought never to be restrained."[10]

The second archetype is that of Maryland's Declaration of Rights of 1776, which provides: "That the liberty of the press ought to be inviolably preserved."[11] It was copied verbatim by Delaware for its Declaration of Rights and was also copied with slight modifications by Georgia and South Carolina for their constitutions.[12] The Georgia article reads: "Freedom of the press and trial by jury to remain inviolate forever."[13] The South Carolina article reads: "That the liberty of the press be inviolably preserved."[14]

The third archetype is that of the Massachusetts Declaration of Rights of 1780, which provides: "The liberty of the press is essential to the security of freedom in a state: it ought not, therefore, to be restrained in this Commonwealth."[15] New Hampshire's Bill of Rights of 1783 was patterned after Massachusetts' model. In part, it reads: "The Liberty of the Press is essential to the security of freedom in a state; it ought, therefore, to be inviolably preserved."[16]

Uniquely, Pennsylvania, the fourth archetype, included "speech," explicitly, as well as "press" in its Declaration of Rights of 1776: "That the people have a right to freedom of speech, and of writing, and publishing their sentiments; therefore the freedom of the press ought not to be restrained."[17] In addition, within Pennsylvania's constitution proper, it had a second press clause: "The printing presses shall be free to every person who undertakes to examine the proceedings of the legislature, or any part of government."[18]

These constitutional protections were the by-products of popular revolutions to secure in *written* form the *natural* rights to speech and press that had been the Radical Whig rallying cry. The focus of the colonists' philosophy of natural rights was an individualistic one.

George Mason, a Virginia planter with little formal legal training, was responsible for drafting the vast majority of Virginia's Declaration of Rights of 1776,[19] which by 1789 became a *cause célèbre* throughout Europe.[20] James Madison sat with Mason on the committee charged with drafting the declaration. Madison, himself not a lawyer,[21] nevertheless possessed a wealth of knowledge of English common law; that knowledge would have enabled him to tailor the declaration to express English common law meanings and to prevent the sweeping breadth suggested by the phraseology of the press clause. He chose not to do so. No evidence exists of any written statement by Madison that would support a limitation on the scope of the press clause. Rather, Madison's consent to the declaration is indicative of his preference for the lay radical language and, in particular, the protection offered by the natural rights conception of the liberty, over what must have then seemed an outmoded doctrine (the British common law conception of seditious libel). Indeed, the very first section of the declaration gives the meaning intended, and that meaning was a natural rights, not a common law, understanding:

> That all men are by nature equally free and independent, and have certain rights, of which, when they enter into a state of society, they cannot, by any compact, deprive or divest their posterity; namely, the enjoyment of life and liberty, with the means of acquiring and possessing property, and pursuing and obtaining happiness and safety.[22]

Robert A. Rutland found a commitment to natural rights throughout the nine colonies that sought written constitutional protection for rights. The drafters preferred the natural rights conception.[23] Pennsylvania's Declaration of Rights of 1776 also contained a natural rights preface before its catalogue of civil liberties: "Whereas all government ought to be instituted and supported for the security and protection of the community as such, and to enable the individuals who compose it to enjoy their natural rights . . . and whenever these great ends of government are not obtained, the people have [a] right, by common consent to change it."[24] Vermont's Declaration of Rights of 1777 repeats the Pennsylvania language verbatim.[25]

Delaware's Declaration of Rights of 1776 is steeped in "compact theory" and other doctrinal language of natural rights. Section 1 of the declaration reads: "That all government of right originates from the people, is founded in compact only, and [is] instituted solely for the good of the whole."[26] Maryland's Declaration of Rights of 1776 repeats the Delaware declaration verbatim.[27]

Georgia's Constitution of 1777, in a manner analogous to the Declaration of Independence, begins with a discussion of the abuses of "the legislature of Great Britain," deeming such conduct "repugnant to the common rights of mankind" and as obliging all Americans "to assert the rights and privileges they are entitled to by the laws of nature and reason."[28]

Massachusetts' Declaration of 1780 begins with a "Preamble" that defines the rights it will protect to be "natural rights." It reads:

> The end of the institution, maintenance and administration of government, is to secure the existence of the body-politic; to protect it; and to furnish the individuals who compose it, with the power of enjoying, in safety and tranquility, their natural rights, and the blessings of life.[29]

New Hampshire's Bill of Rights of 1783, too, is an embodiment of natural rights philosophy. Section II reads: "All men have certain natural, essential, and inherent rights: among which are—the enjoying and defending [of] life and liberty—acquiring, possessing and protecting property—and, in a word, of seeking and obtaining happiness."[30]

The American conception of civil liberties became a part of these first revolutionary documents. That conception had grown apart from the common law of England and had been infused with the Radical Whig conceptions of liberty that the colonists prized. One of the critical questions to face the newly liberated states was whether a national government formed by their union should also contain written constitutional strictures against the exercise of power to violate civil rights.

ENDNOTES

1. "Address to the Inhabitants of Quebec, 1774," *reprinted in* 1 THE ROOTS OF THE Bill of RIGHTS 221 (B. Schwartz ed. 1980).
2. 1 JOURNALS OF THE CONTINENTAL CONGRESS, 1774–1789 108 (1968).
3. *Id.* at 110.
4. "Connecticut Declaration of Rights, 1776," *reprinted in* 2 THE ROOTS OF THE BILL OF RIGHTS 289 (B. Schwartz ed. 1980).
5. *Id.*
6. "Virginia Declaration of Rights, 1776," *reprinted in* 2 THE ROOTS OF THE BILL OF RIGHTS 234 (B. Schwartz ed. 1980). Technically, Thomas Ludwell Lee most likely wrote the language on the parchment. However, whether this was at Mason's explicit instruction or just with his acquiescence is unknown. *See* 1 THE PAPERS OF GEORGE MASON 1725–1792 281n (R. Rutland ed. 1970).
7. George Mason was well aware of *Cato's Letters*; on May 18, 1776, before the Committee discussion of a Declaration of Rights, the *Virginia Gazette* carried the text of Letter No. 15 on freedom of speech. *See* 1 THE PAPERS OF GEORGE MASON 1725–1792 281n (R. Rutland ed. 1970).
8. Schauer, *Free Speech and Its Philosophical Roots in* THE FIRST AMENDMENT, THE LEGACY OF GEORGE MASON 133 (T. Shumate ed. 1985).
9. Anderson, *The Origins of the Press Clause,* 30 UCLA L. REV. 464 (1983).
10. *Id.* at 464n.
11. *Id.* at 464–65.
12. *Id.* at 465.
13. *Id.* at 538.
14. *Id.* at 538–39.
15. *Id.* at 465.
16. *Id.*
17. *Id.*
18. *Id.*
19. "Virginia Declaration of Rights, 1776," *reprinted in* 2 THE ROOTS OF THE BILL OF RIGHTS 234 (B. Schwartz ed. 1980).
20. Rutland, *George Mason and the Origins of the First Amendment,* N.Y. ST. B. J. 8, 12 (November 1987).
21. *See* R. RUTLAND, JAMES MADISION, THE FOUNDING FATHER 6 (1987). *See also* Bogen, *The Origins of Freedom of Speech and Press,* 42 MD. L. REV. 429, 440, n.52 (1983) ("From Mason to Madison, the development of charter language protecting freedom of speech and of the press was in the hands of politicians who studied government rather than [in the hands of] lawyers").
22. "Virginia Declaration of Rights, 1776," *reprinted in* 2 THE ROOTS OF THE BILL OF RIGHTS 234 (B. Schwartz ed. 1980).

23. R. RUTLAND, THE BIRTH OF THE BILL OF RIGHTS, 1776–1791 42 (1983). "Without bothering to examine the niceties of law, the Revolutionary legislators swept aside doubt by giving full expression to guarantees of civil liberty. Indeed, the whole catalog of human rights which colonists reviewed during the years preceding Lexington-Concord had been regarded not as common law rights, but as natural rights." *Id. See also* C. ROSSITER, SEEDTIME OF THE REPUBLIC, 383 (1953); R. KETCHAM, JAMES MADISON: A BIOGRAPHY 290–91 (1971).

24. "Pennsylvania Declaration of Rights, 1776," *reprinted in* 2 THE ROOTS OF THE BILL OF RIGHTS 263 (B. Schwartz ed. 1980).

25. "Vermont Declaration of Rights, 1777," *reprinted in* 2 THE ROOTS OF THE BILL OF RIGHTS 319 (B. Schwartz ed. 1980).

26. "Delaware Declaration of Rights, 1776," *reprinted in* 2 THE ROOTS OF THE BILL OF RIGHTS 276 (B. Schwartz ed. 1980).

27. "Maryland Declaration of Rights, 1776," *reprinted in* 2 THE ROOTS OF THE BILL OF RIGHTS 280 (B. Schwartz ed. 1980).

28. "Georgia Constitution, 1777," *reprinted in* 2 THE ROOTS OF THE BILL OF RIGHTS 291 (B. Schwartz ed. 1980).

29. "Massachusetts Declaration of Rights, 1780," *reprinted in* 2 THE ROOTS OF THE BILL OF RIGHTS 339 (B. Schwartz ed. 1980).

30. "New Hampshire Bill of Rights, 1783," *reprinted in* 2 THE ROOTS OF THE BILL OF RIGHTS 375 (B. Schwartz ed. 1980).

7

A CONSTITUTION WITHOUT POWER OVER THE PRESS

The liberty of the press was the tyrant's scourge—it was the true friend and firmest supporter of civil liberty; therefore why pass it by in silence?[1]

The Constitutional Convention and the Federalist/Antifederalist ratification struggle reveal that the unamended Constitution afforded the new central government no power to regulate the press. Federalists argued that no power had been granted to the new central state over speech and the press. The Antifederalists' complaint was not that some power had been given but that a positive denial of central government power over speech and the press was lacking in the new Constitution and that this omission was a fatal defect, for it left the precious liberties of the American people unguarded.

At the Philadelphia Constitutional Convention of 1787, little mention was made of the need for a bill of rights. On August 20, 1787, Charles Pinckney of South Carolina submitted to the Convention a free press proposal for inclusion in the Constitution after consideration by the Committee of Detail. It would have provided that "[t]he liberty of the Press shall be inviolably observed [*sic:* probably preserved]."[2] Pinckney again brought up the point on September 14, 1787, joined this time by Elbridge Gerry of Massachusetts. On this occasion, Roger Sherman of Connecticut argued against the proposal: "It is unnecessary," he said. "The power of Congress does not extend to the Press."[3]

The question was voted down at Sherman's suggestion, seven states to four (the four being Massachusetts, Maryland, Virginia, and South

Carolina).[4] Notably, James Madison voted in favor of the proposal. This appears to be the full extent of Convention consideration of the addition of a press protection. However mild the dispute at the Convention, the lack of such a provision in the Constitution of 1787 proved to be a principal bone of contention in the ratification debates.

Within weeks after the Convention ended, Antifederalist efforts to block ratification of the Constitution had begun. In a letter from James Madison to Thomas Jefferson dated October 24, 1787, the rumblings began to be felt by that father of the Constitution and prospective Federalist:

> Col. [George] Mason left Phila[delphia] in an exceedingly ill humor indeed. A number of little circumstances arising in part from the impatience which prevailed towards the close of the business, conspired to whet his acrimony. He returned to Virginia with a fixed disposition to prevent the adoption of the plan if possible. He considers the want of a Bill of Rights as a fatal objection.[5]

George Mason, "the first to sound the alarm,"[6] did not wait long to list his "Objections." He voiced them outside the state house in Philadelphia,[7] and he sent a copy to General George Washington along with a letter dated October 7, 1787.[8] Foremost among his objections was that "[t]here is no declaration of rights; and the laws of the general government being paramount to the laws and constitutions of the several states, the declaration of rights, in the separate states, are no security."[9] Colonel Mason noted particularly that the document contained "no declaration of any kind for preserving the liberty of the press."[10]

James Wilson of Pennsylvania was one of the first Federalists to articulate that faction's principal opposition to a bill of rights. In a 1787 "Address to a Meeting of the Citizens of Philadelphia," Wilson explained that the new Constitution did not grant to the government powers beyond those expressly provided in the instrument.[11] On the subject of the "liberty of the press," Wilson asked: "[W]hat control can proceed from the government, to shackle or destroy that sacred palladium of national freedom?"[12] He then answered: "[T]he proposed system possesses no influence whatever upon the press; and it would have been merely nugatory, to have introduced a formal declaration upon the subject."[13] Indeed, Wilson argued that the provision of a declaration could be construed as an implication that "some degree of power was given," when that was not the case.[14] This Federalist argument was perceived as a weak one, and the Antifederalists endeavored to exploit the weakness.

In Massachusetts, Elbridge Gerry argued to the state legislature that the new Constitution did not secure "the liberties of America" and that he was duty bound to oppose it.[15] He said that "without the security of a bill of rights," the new government could not protect the rights of the people.[16] In his "Observations on the New Constitution and the Federal and State Conventions," Gerry explained in a more developed fashion his fear of the Constitution's failure to erect a barrier against the exertion of government power over speech and the press. Wrote Gerry:

> There is no security in the proffered system, either for the rights of conscience or the liberty of the Press: Despotism[,] usually while it is gaining ground, will suffer men to think, say, or write what they please; but when once established . . . the most unjust restrictions may take place in the first instance, and an imprimatur on the Press in the next, may silence the complaints, and forbid the most decent remonstrations of an injured and oppressed people.[17]

Roger Sherman of Connecticut, who had professed at the Convention that no power had been given to the new central state concerning speech or the press, reiterated his view that the clamor for a bill of rights was altogether nonsensical, for the security of freedom rested in the "nature" of the government, not in "parchment barriers."

> Of a very different nature . . . is all that sublimity of nonsense and alarm, that has been thundered against [the proposed Constitution] in every shape of metaphoric terror, on the subject of a bill of rights, the liberty of the press, rights of conscience, rights of taxation and election, trials in the vicinity, freedom of speech, trial by jury, and a standing army. These last are undoubtedly important points, much too important to depend on mere paper protection. . . . The only real security that you can have for all your important rights must be in the nature of your government.[18]

Richard Henry Lee argued for a bill of rights in Pennsylvania before the document was sent to the states for ratification.[19] In the Continental Congress, Lee argued that amendments to the Constitution were necessary including, among other essential rights to be protected, the freedom of the press. He was unable to convince the majority to follow his lead.[20] He nevertheless persisted in arguing eloquently for amendments. In his fourth letter from "The Federal Farmer," dated October 15, 1787, Lee continued to appeal for amendments to the Constitution; he explained how even in the absence of a direct delegation of power to Congress over the press, that body could still violate the press's liberty.

I confess I do not see in what cases the Congress can, with any pretence of right, make a law to suppress the freedom of the press; though I am not clear, that Congress is restrained from laying any duties whatever on certain pieces printed, and perhaps Congress may require large bonds for the payment of these duties. Should the printer say, the freedom of the press was secured by the constitution of the state in which he lived, Congress might, and perhaps, with great propriety, answer, that the federal constitution is the only compact existing between them and the people; in this compact the people have named no others, and therefore Congress, in exercising the powers assigned them, and in making laws to carry them into execution are restrained by nothing beside the federal constitution.[21]

In a letter from Sam Adams to Lee, that old Massachusetts patriot warned that in the new Constitution "the Seeds of Aristocracy . . . spring even before the Conclusion of our struggle for natural Rights of Men, Seeds which like a Canker Worm lie at the Root of free Governments."[22] Approximately a dozen newspapers "from the Maine woods to tidewater North Carolina"[23] began to publish Antifederalist essays in opposition to the Constitution. Foremost among the printers to take issue with the proposed constitution was Eleazer Oswald of Philadelphia, printer of the *Independent Gazetteer.*[24]

The Antifederalists held sway over significant segments of the populace in Massachusetts, Rhode Island, Virginia, New York, and North Carolina.[25] Those constitutional convention delegates who had left the Convention early, such as Robert Yates, John Lansing, and Luther Martin, formed powerful alliances with Elbridge Gerry and George Mason in their effort to block ratification.[26] Jefferson, although in Paris at the time, did receive much correspondence from friends and foes of the Constitution. In a December 8, 1788, letter to Jefferson, James Madison described the opposition to the Constitution as "formidable."[27]

From October 27, 1787, until August 16, 1788, James Madison, Alexander Hamilton, and John Jay wrote eighty-five letters that supported the Constitution and that were published in the newspapers of New York City.[28] In Federalist No. 84, Hamilton argued (as had James Wilson) that a bill of rights was "not only unnecessary" but "would even be dangerous."[29] Asked Hamilton: "[W]hy declare that things shall not be done which there is no power to do?"[30] In particular reference to the liberty of the press, Hamilton queried: "Why . . . should it be said that the liberty of the press shall not be restrained, when no power is given by which restrictions may be imposed?"[31]

The Antifederalists were, of course, unsuccessful in blocking ratification of the Constitution, although they were successful in getting several states, including Pennsylvania, Massachusetts, Maryland, South Carolina, North Carolina, New Hampshire, Virginia, and New York to adopt recommendations that the Constitution be amended.[32] The Antifederalists did block ratification in Rhode Island and North Carolina.[33] Although the Antifederalists were largely unsuccessful in their immediate quest to block ratification of the Constitution, their remonstrations brought to the fore the fact that the new government was to possess no power over the press. Moreover, their struggle for express protections for the fundamental rights of the people was to beget lasting justifications for freedom against governmental encroachments.

ENDNOTES

1. James Lincoln in a speech during the South Carolina Ratifying Convention, Wednesday, Jan. 16, 1788, *quoted in* 4 THE ROOTS OF THE BILL OF RIGHTS 744 (B. Schwartz ed. 1980).

2. NOTES OF DEBATES IN THE FEDERAL CONVENTION OF 1787 REPORTED BY JAMES MADISON 485–86, 640 (A. Koch ed. 1966).

3. *Id.* at 640.

4. *Id.* at 640n.

5. 1 THE PAPERS OF GEORGE MASON 1725–1792 1007 (R. Rutland ed. 1970). In explaining the lack of a Bill of Rights, George Washington wrote to the Marquis de Lafayette on April 28, 1788:

    [T]here was not a member of the convention, I believe, who had the least objection to what is contended for by the advocates for a Bill of Rights. . . . The first, where the people evidently retained every thing, which they did not in the express terms give up, was considered nugatory as you will find to have been more fully explained by Mr. Wilson and others; and, as to the second, it was only the difficulty of establishing a mode, which should not interfere with the fixed modes of any of the States, that induced the convention to leave it as a matter of future adjustment.

    1 THE WASHINGTON PAPERS (S. Padover ed. 1955) 247.

6. R. RUTLAND, THE ORDEAL OF THE CONSTITUTION 32 (1966).

7. *Id.* Mason drafted his objections on the "blank pages of his copy of the 'Committee on Stile and Arrangement' report." R. RUTLAND, THE BIRTH OF THE BILL OF RIGHTS 1776–1791 120 (1971). Copies of the objections were quickly circulated to Mason's friends and, subsequently, were printed and distributed "throughout the Republic." *Id.*

8. C. KENYON, THE ANTIFEDERALISTS 191 (1985).

9. *Id.* at 192.

10. G. Mason, *Objections to the Proposed Federal Constitution, 1787, reprinted in* 2 THE ROOTS OF THE BILL OF RIGHTS 446 (B. Schwartz ed. 1980).

11. J. Wilson, *An Address to a Meeting of the Citizens of Philadelphia, 1787, reprinted in* 3 THE ROOTS OF THE BILL OF RIGHTS 528 (B. Schwartz ed. 1980).

12. *Id.* at 529.

13. *Id.*

14. *Id.*

15. R. RUTLAND, THE BIRTH OF THE BILL OF RIGHTS 1776–1791 123 (1971).

16. *Id.*

17. E. Gerry, *Observations on the New Constitution and the Federal and State Conventions, 1788, reprinted in* 3 THE ROOTS OF THE BILL OF RIGHTS 486 (B. Schwartz ed. 1980).

18. R. Sherman, *Letters of a Countryman, 1787, reprinted in* 3 THE ROOTS OF THE BILL OF RIGHTS 539 (B. Schwartz ed. 1980).

19. *Id.* at 139.

20. *Id.* at 120–21.

21. R. Lee, *Letter IV, October 15, 1787, reprinted in* 3 THE ROOTS OF THE BILL OF RIGHTS 474 (B. Schwartz ed. 1980).

22. R. RUTLAND, THE BIRTH OF THE BILL OF RIGHTS 1776–1791 145 (1971).

23. R. RUTLAND, THE ORDEAL OF THE CONSTITUTION 38 (1966).

24. *Id.*

25. *Id.* at 313.

26. R. RUTLAND, THE BIRTH OF THE BILL OF RIGHTS 1776–1791 119 (1971).

27. *Madison to Jefferson, 1788, reprinted in* 5 THE ROOTS OF THE BILL OF RIGHTS 992 (B. Schwartz ed. 1980).

28. THE FEDERALIST viii (C. Rossiter ed. 1961).

29. *Id.* at 513.

30. *Id.*

31. *Id.*

32. R. RUTLAND, THE BIRTH OF THE BILL OF RIGHTS 1776–1791 141–54 (1971); 5 THE ROOTS OF THE BILL OF RIGHTS 983–84, 1167 (B. Schwartz ed. 1980).

33. R. RUTLAND, THE BIRTH OF THE BILL OF RIGHTS 1776–1791 174 (1971).

8

THE QUEST FOR A POSITIVE DENIAL OF GOVERNMENT POWER OVER THE PRESS

The crucial turn of events for securing a bill of rights took place in the mind of James Madison. Madison appears to have been influenced, at least in part, by the advice of his good friend Thomas Jefferson, who, during the ratification struggle, was living in Paris while serving as America's Minister to France.[1] Having informed Jefferson in a letter dated October 24, 1787, of Colonel Mason's objections to the Constitution, Madison next encountered Jefferson's views on the subject. In a letter sent from Paris on December 20, 1787, Jefferson informed Madison of "what I do not like" about the Constitution of 1787, listing "[f]irst the omission of a bill of rights providing clearly and without the aid of sophisms for freedom of religion, freedom of the press, protection against standing armies, restriction against monopolies, the eternal and unremitting force of the habeas corpus laws, and trials by jury in all matters of fact triable by the laws of the land and not by the law of Nations."[2] Jefferson believed "a bill of rights . . . [to be] what the people are entitled to against every government on earth, general or particular, and what no just government should refuse, or rest on inference."[3] Jefferson expounded on these same sentiments in a letter to William Stephens Smith sent from Paris February 2, 1788. In that letter, he expressed astonishment at the absence of language in the Constitution guarding against the government's exercise of power over fundamental rights, including freedom of the press. But he hoped that in time all would "come about."[4]

In a letter dated October 17, 1788, Madison let Jefferson know that, for his part, he might soon "come about"; Madison wrote that although he never thought the omission of a bill of rights "a material defect," he now favored such a bill, for "it might be of use" and "could not be of disservice."[5] In the same letter, Madison addressed dangers inherent in majoritarian control over government power, which he feared could, if left unchecked by some counterbalancing force, invade the private sphere, and produce oppression.[6] He also articulated his view "that absolute restrictions in cases that are doubtful, or where emergencies may overrule them, ought to be avoided." He explained that no bill of rights could avoid being overridden "in extraordinary cases." He posited one such case: "Should a Rebellion or insurrection alarm the people as well as the Government, and a suspension of the Hab[eas] Corp[us] be dictated by the alarm, no written prohibitions on earth would prevent the measure."[7]

In a letter dated March 15, 1789, Jefferson answered Madison's points. Jefferson explained that, in the hands of the judiciary, a bill of rights could prove an effective safeguard. "In the arguments in favor of a declaration of rights, you omit one which has great weight with me," wrote Jefferson, "the legal check which it puts in the hands of the judiciary."[8] Jefferson also explained that just as the new Constitution grants specific powers, so too should it "guard us against . . . abuses of power within the field submitted."[9]

On reflection, Madison decided to support a bill of rights. He did so, at least in part, for political reasons: to quell the Antifederalist clamor for a second Constitutional Convention[10] and perhaps to secure his election to Congress.[11] James Madison informed his political supporters that he would favor a bill of rights "[n]ot because they are necessary, but because they can produce no possible danger, and may gratify some gentlemen's wishes."[12] In a January 2, 1789, letter to George Eve, a campaign worker in his congressional district, Madison emphasized that it was his "sincere opinion" that a bill of rights protecting the "rights of conscience in the fullest latitude" and "the freedom of the press" should be enacted in the first Congress.[13]

Madison lost a bid for the U.S. Senate in large part because of his perceived opposition to a bill of rights and Patrick Henry's machinations to promote that view among the state assemblymen and the people.[14] Madison's concerns about the reaction of a rights-sensitive public that believed him an enemy of liberty surfaced in a January 14, 1789, letter he wrote to George Washington:

> I fear, from the vague accounts which circulate, that the federal candidates are likely to stand in the way of one another. This is not the case however

in my district. The field is left entirely to Monroe & myself. The event of our competition will probably depend on the part to be taken by two or three descriptions of people, whose decision is not known, if not yet to be ultimately formed. I have pursued my pretensions much further than I had premeditated; having not only made great use of epistolary means, but actually visited two Counties, Culpeper & Louisa, and publicly contradicted the erroneous reports against me. It has been very industriously inculcated that I am dogmatically attached to the Constitution in every clause, syllable & letter, and therefore not a single amendment will be promoted by my vote, either from conviction or a spirit of accommodation. This is the report most likely to affect the election, and most difficult to be combated with success within the limited period.[15]

Madison defeated James Monroe in his race for the U.S. House in good measure because of his switch in position on the need for a bill of rights.[16] Once elected, Madison turned quickly to the business of fulfilling his promise to amend the Constitution. He looked to his home state for guidance.

A Virginia amendment committee composed of such ardent Antifederalists as Patrick Henry and George Mason had been formed to draft amendments for submission to Congress.[17] Forty were specified, including a "20-article bill of rights" and "20 other articles listing perceived defects in the Constitution."[18] The Bill of Rights "was essentially Mason's Virginia Declaration of Rights, one major modification being the addition of [a] . . . provision for freedom of speech in addition to that on freedom of the press."[19] In considering these and other state recommended amendments, Madison "drew heavily" on the Virginia Declaration of Rights that he helped adopt.[20] Indeed "[m]uch of the wording [chosen by Madison for his bill of rights] is Mason's [own] from the Virginia Declaration of Rights as recast in the recommendations of 24 and 27 June 1788."[21] This choice should have come as no surprise, for Madison "had a personal role in framing" the Virginia Declaration of Rights.[22]

The nexus between Mason and Madison in Virginia's Declaration of Rights of 1776 is crucial. Mason, familiar with the writings of Cato,[23] had supported making Cato's "Bulwark of Liberty" language a part of that declaration and had chosen to rest the declaration on a natural rights foundation. By choosing to follow this tradition, in particular, and to promote the Antifederalist amendments, in general, Madison held out the promise that he would invest the Constitution of the United States with a catalogue of natural rights protections.

JAMES MADISON KEEPS HIS PROMISE

On May 4, 1789, Madison attempted to acquire the indulgence of the House (then debating import and tonnage duties) to hear his proposed amendments to the Constitution on May 25. Not until June 8, 1789, however, was he able to steal away the attention of the House from the business of structuring the new government long enough to consider his amendments.[24]

The House was reluctant to concern itself with the matter. For example, James Jackson asked that the members be tolerant of the new constitution, give it "a fair trial," and let it be examined "by experience."[25] He believed it "certainly imprudent" to amend the document without having "test[ed] what its errors are."[26]

Madison persisted, explaining that the amendments he proposed came "from a very respectable number of our constituents" and, in light of the "anxiety which prevails in the public mind," were necessary to "quiet" that discontentment.[27] He stressed that "a great number of our constituents . . . are dissatisfied" with the Constitution but would likely join in support of it if the House were to "expressly declare the great rights of mankind secured under this constitution."[28]

Madison emphasized that his amendments would provide security to "the great mass of the people who" opposed the Constitution for its failure to provide "effectual provisions against encroachments on particular rights."[29] He then introduced the amendments. Among them was one on the freedoms of speech, writing, publishing, and the press:

> The people shall not be deprived or abridged of their right to speak, to write, or to publish their sentiments; and the freedom of the press, as one of the great bulwarks of liberty, shall be inviolable.[30]

The "bulwark of liberty" language had been transplanted from *Cato's Letters* No. 15 to the Virginia Declaration of Rights of 1776 and, finally, to the floor of the House. Madison also proposed a free press amendment specifically directed at the states:

> No State shall violate the equal rights of conscience, or the freedom of the press, or the trial by jury in criminal cases.[31]

After delivering the full list of rights he sought to secure in the Constitution, Madison expounded on their significance. As to freedom of the press, Madison explained that in Great Britain the legislature had rendered the value of rights "altogether indefinite."[32] He noted that although "able advocates" had resisted violations of "freedom of the press" by Parliament, no written source of protection, not even the Magna Charta, contained provisions to protect "the great rights, the trial by jury, freedom of the press, or liberty of conscience."[33] Indeed, Madison concluded that under the current laws of Great Britain (in the case of speech, the Blackstonian Common Law) "[t]he freedom of the press and rights of conscience, those choicest privileges of the people, are unguarded."[34] Madison viewed his proposed speech and press protection to be, on the federal level, a companion to the similarly worded state protections that collectively would establish fixed barriers against the exercise of government power over speech and the press. Explained Madison:

> The people of many States have thought it necessary to raise barriers against power in all forms and departments of Government, and I am inclined to believe, if once bills of rights are established in all the States as well as the federal constitution, we shall find that . . . upon the whole, they will have a salutary tendency.[35]

Madison succinctly defined the overall purpose of his bill of rights:

> [W]hatever may be the form which the several States have adopted in making declarations in favor of particular rights, the great object in view is to limit and qualify the powers of Government, by excepting out of the grant of power those cases in which the Government ought not to act, or to act only in a particular mode. They point these exceptions sometimes against the abuse of the executive power, sometimes against the legislative, and, in some cases, against the community itself; or, in other words, against the majority in favor of the minority.[36]

In advocating the extension of the conscience, press, and jury trial protections to the state governments, Madison stated that he wished "to extend this interdiction . . . because it is proper that every Government should be disarmed of powers to trench upon those particular rights."[37]

Adopting the counsel of Jefferson that a bill of rights in the hands of the judiciary would be more than a parchment barrier to accretions of power by government, Madison argued to his congressional colleagues that effective barriers could be erected through judicial means:

> It is true, there are a few particular States in which some of the most valuable articles have not, at one time or other, been violated; but it does not follow but they may have, to a certain degree, a salutary effect against the abuse of power. If they are incorporated into the constitution, independent tribunals of justice will consider themselves in a peculiar manner the guardians of those rights; they will be an impenetrable bulwark against every assumption of power

in the legislative or executive; they will be naturally led to resist encroachment upon rights expressly stipulated for in the constitution by the declaration of rights.[38]

There was little hardy discussion over Madison's amendments. On the free press provision, however, there is one revealing statement from James Jackson. His statement is indicative of how much the practice of tolerating liberal criticism of government men and measures had come to be accepted by the First Congress. Jackson argued that a bill of rights was unnecessary. As an example, he noted that despite the fact that a member of the House had been "attacked in the public newspapers," the House had not harkened back to the law of colonial times by summoning the writer to appear before the House "for a breach of [legislative] privilege."[39] Instead, the writer stood unmolested, a tribute to the new regime's tolerance.

On July 21, 1789, Congress sent the proposed amendments to a select committee, the Committee of Eleven, of which Madison himself was a member.[40] In committee, Madison's original language was revised,[41] albeit because of the absence of a select committee record, it is impossible to tell whether all of the changes to the speech and press provision were merely stylistic.[42] The committee version read:

The freedom of speech, and of the press, and the right of the people peaceably to assemble, and consult for their common good, and to apply to the Government for the redress of grievances, shall not be infringed.[43]

On August 15, 1789, the House agreed to the select committee's version of the amendment on speech, press, and assembly.[44] Reflecting on this achievement, Madison declared that same day: "[W]e have asserted the right sufficiently in what we have done; if we mean nothing more than this, that the people have a right to express and communicate their sentiments and wishes, we have provided for it already. The right of freedom of speech is secured; the liberty of the press is expressly declared to be beyond the reach of this government."[45] On August 24, 1789, the House formally proposed the amendments that it desired be appended to the Constitution.[46]

The Senate became the next battleground. Madison's speech and press amendment directed at the states was a quick casualty, eliminated by vote of the Senate.[47] The Senate's journal reveals that on September 3, 1789, the free speech, press, and assembly amendment was considered.[48] Because the Senate proceedings were not open to the public,[49] it is impossible to know with reasonable certainty what views prevailed there in consideration of the amendment. On September 4, 1789, the Senate agreed to its own version of the amendment:

That Congress shall make no law, abridging the freedom of speech, or of the press, or the right of the people peaceably to assemble and consult for their common good, and to petition the government for a redress of grievances.[50]

On September 9, 1789, the Senate combined the speech and press amendment with the religion clauses. It also eliminated the "and consult for their common good" segment of the earlier revision.[51] This last Senate version was then adopted and submitted to the House. A conference committee[52] reformed the establishment clause language slightly to create the current version of the First Amendment:

Congress shall make no law respecting an establishment of religion, or prohibiting the free exercise thereof; or abridging the freedom of speech, or of the press; or the right of the people peaceably to assemble, and to petition the Government for a redress of grievances.[53]

The final ratification of the First Amendment on December 15, 1791, signaled a triumph for those who desired to declare explicitly that the new constitution afforded the federal government no power over speech and press. The amendment was to be a barrier that, through proper judicial interpretation, would prevent the government from encroaching on the private sphere of speech and press activity in America.

PARCHMENT BARRIERS

Although the first American Congress, uniquely among governments of the world, had disclaimed any power over speech and press, the central question, then as now, was whether mere words etched in parchment could prevent the recurrence of a centuries-old government pattern of encroachment on the press.

Even were this American moment just an historical anomaly, the First Amendment was clearly a triumph for Cato and the Radical Whigs. Their seventy-year quest to render protection against the censorial power of the state a part of the supreme law had finally borne fruit. As Madison would later state in proud reflection on the achievement: "If we advert to the nature of Republican Government, we shall find that the censorial power is in the people over the Government, and not in the Government over the people."[54]

The amendment served as an express assurance that the freedom of speech and press was beyond the reach of the new central state. The core values of speech and press freedom were to be self-sustaining and self-governing in a private sphere where independent judgments of individuals would predominate.

It was not long, however, before the intoxication of power led men to regard the First Amendment as a mere "parchment barrier" that could be easily rent in the headlong rush of politicians to attain partisan objectives. The Sedition Act of 1798[55] resurrected the law of seditious libel in service to the incumbent Federalist Party. The Act was allegedly necessary to guard American neutrality against French influences[56] but in fact was used as a vehicle to silence the Republicans.[57] The Act forced James Madison to articulate more fully his understanding of the antigovernment focus of the amendment.

Madison enumerated his objections in his "Report on the Virginia Resolutions" in the Virginia House of Delegates: (1) the Sedition Act presumes the existence of "a power not delegated by the Constitution," (2) the power "is expressly and positively forbidden" by the First Amendment, and (3) the power "is levelled against the right of freely examining public characters and measures, and of free communication thereon, which has ever been justly deemed the only effectual guardian of every other right."[58]

Madison understood the First Amendment to be "a denial to Congress of all power over the press."[59] He explained that the British common law view that freedom of the press consists merely in "an exemption from all previous restraint" was not "the American idea of it; since a law inflicting penalties on printed publications would have a similar effect with a law authorizing a previous restraint on them."[60] Madison found the "security of the freedom" to lie not only in exemption from prior restraints but also in exemption "from the subsequent penalty of laws."[61] Madison stated that the English common law view of the press "cannot . . . be the standard of [the] freedom in the United States."[62] Rather, in the United States, the First Amendment constituted "a positive denial of any power whatever on the subject."[63] Wrote Madison:

> In every state, probably, in the Union, the press has exerted a freedom in canvassing the merits and measures of public men, of every description, which has not been confined to the strict limits of the common law. On this footing the freedom of the press has stood; on this foundation it yet stands.[64]

Confronted with public indignation against the Sedition Act and the Federalists' loss at the polls to the Jeffersonian Republicans, Congress refused to renew the Act in 1801.[65] President Thomas Jefferson pardoned all of those convicted and put an end to almost all prosecutions under the

Act, "including those instituted against Federalist editors."[66] Despite the change in administrations, the public disapprobation for the Sedition Act, and a profusion of essays in the press decrying censorship, the post–Sedition Act period did not usher in a change in jurisprudential outlook. As before the Revolution, the courts by and large adhered to the Blackstonian conception of press liberty. In fact, the Blackstonian view continued to dominate American jurisprudence on issues of speech and press well into the first part of the twentieth century.

THE LEGACY OF SIR WILLIAM BLACKSTONE

From 1798 until 1931, the federal courts and most state courts steadfastly adhered to the law of Blackstone: that prior restraint was prohibited, but punishment for matter once published was permissible. The longevity of Blackstone in the courts is attributable not merely to the reverence that nineteenth-century judges had for common law precedents. It is also due to the courts' failure to form any developed theory of speech and press liberty and to the fact that not until the second decade of the twentieth century did the Supreme Court apply the First Amendment to the states.[67] In 1925, the Court incorporated the First Amendment into the "liberty" term of the Fourteenth Amendment and thereby made it applicable to the states.[68]

From the time of the Pennsylvania Supreme Court decision in *Republica v. Oswald*[69] in 1788 until Justice Harlan's dissent in *Patterson v. Colorado*,[70] there appears to have been no significant development of a First Amendment theory that could be relied on to undermine the Blackstonian construct. In *Ex Parte Jackson,* the Court *in dicta* wrote of the "[l]iberty of circulating" publications as being "essential to" freedom of the press.[71] However, in context, this language was used as a basis to justify excluding lottery materials from the U.S. mail under the rationale that although Congress has no power to prevent the private circulation of publications, it had an inherent authority to exclude material from the government's mail system on the basis of its content.[72] Furthermore, this liberty of circulating was not applied to protect private parties in subsequent precedent from 1878 to 1897.

In 1897, the Supreme Court reiterated that the Bill of Rights did not apply to the states and made it clear that in "the fundamental law" "inherited from our English ancestors" the "freedom of speech and of the press . . . does not permit the publication of libels, blasphemous or indecent articles, or other publications injurious to public morals or private reputation."[73]

In fact, the "fundamental law" would not permit an unlicensed speech in a public commons. In the 1798 case of *Davis v. Massachusetts,* the Supreme Court refused to recognize a liberty to speak unobtrusively in a public commons under the theory that "absolutely or conditionally to forbid public speaking in a highway or public place is no more an infringement of the rights of a member of the public than for the owner of a private house to forbid it in his house."[74] This remained the law for forty years.

From 1800 until the 1860s few events replicated the kind of large-scale challenge to the freedom of speech and press posed by the Sedition Act of 1798. There were instances of censorship by government during this period; however, the government imposed no general system of licensure and engaged in no national campaign of prosecution against seditious libel, and so the press was able to develop in a comparatively free environment. Michael Gibson has noted that the Postmaster General acquiesced in Southern censorship of abolitionist mail in 1859.[75] Of course, during the Civil War many civil rights were violated: at least one newspaper was closed down by the government in New York City, editors of "Copperhead" persuasion were imprisoned, and field correspondents' reports were sometimes censored.[76] Nevertheless, these actions came amid distinguishable circumstances that limited their impact as precedents and did not prevent the proliferation of "a lively press, flourishing publishing houses, and abundant speech making" throughout the nation.[77]

In the mid-1860s and throughout the 1870s, the free speech and press environment changed drastically as Congress enacted laws that directly regulated speech through obscenity proscriptions, additional restrictions on the use of the mails, and limitations on the speech rights of immigrants with unpopular beliefs.[78] During this period, the law of Blackstone remained largely intact.

In his 1907 decision in *Patterson v. Colorado,* Justice Holmes wrote for the Court concerning a state contempt conviction handed down after someone published views critical of how state court judges handled a pending case.[79] Holmes had little difficulty in discerning the law. The First Amendment did not apply to the states (although for purposes of argument Holmes assumed that it did) and, despite the fact that prior restraints on publications were outlawed, "subsequent punishment[s]" were permissible whether the publication propagated truth or falsity.[80]

In a number of cases involving the speech of political extremists or political or religious dissenters, the Court adhered to the Blackstonian precedent. For example, *Turner v. Williams* upheld the government's decision to deport a British alien who admitted in a public speech, which concerned a predicted global workers' strike, that he was an anarchist.[81] It was not deemed unlawful for the government to punish what the state perceived to be "bad tendencies" in pursuit of the public welfare, provided no prior restraints were imposed.

During and shortly after World War I, the law schools began to define many of the First Amendment theories that still predominate in the law. These theories were based on several of the rationales in favor of free speech and press that had led to the First Amendment's inclusion in the Constitution. The theories appear to have greatly influenced the Supreme Court. In particular, Justices Oliver Wendell Holmes and Louis D. Brandeis abandoned their earlier adherence to Blackstone and began to take an expansive view of the First Amendment. Theodore Schroder, Roscoe Pound, Thomas Cooley, Ernst Freund, Henry Schofield, and, most particularly, Zechariah Chafee, Jr., were among the academics who contributed a body of scholarship that helped convince Holmes and Brandeis that the Blackstonian view disserved the core values of the First Amendment. In reliance on this scholarship, Holmes and Brandeis ensconced the law with the elements of modern free speech and press theory.[82]

In 1917, during World War I, Congress enacted the Espionage Act that, among other things, prohibited the willful promotion of "insubordination, disloyalty, muting, or refusal of duty, in the military or naval forces" or the obstruction of recruitment efforts. Holmes wrote three decisions in 1919 in which convictions under the Act were sustained: *Schenck v. United States*,[83] *Frohwerk v. United States*,[84] and *Debs v. United States*.[85] In these cases, Holmes sustained a conviction for the publication and dissemination of a circular opposing the draft, a conviction for the publication of views sympathetic to Germany during the war, and a conviction for the utterance of views glorifying socialism.[86] In no case was there any evidence of imminent danger or violence. Nevertheless, in each case Holmes, consistent with his Blackstonian views, found the mere "tendency" to promote criminal acts sufficient to warrant government suppression.[87]

Just eight months after *Schenck* was decided, Holmes underwent a change of heart, writing his most eloquent dissent in favor of free speech. In *Abrams v. United States*,[88] he called for "free trade in ideas." Brandeis joined Holmes in articulating new theoretical grounds for an expansive conception of free speech and press. In his dissent in *Schaefer v. United States*[89] and in his concurrence in *Whitney v. California*,[90] Brandeis emphasized the value of protecting minority views and the value of ideological contest to the discovery and spread of political truth. The Holmes and Brandeis dissents and concurrences presaged the writing of majority opinions embodying their theories.

In 1930, Charles Evans Hughes, returning to the Court as Chief Justice following an unsuccessful bid for the presidency, sided with Holmes and Brandeis. Owen Roberts also arrived and made it apparent that he too sided with Holmes, Brandeis, and Hughes on speech and press issues. The majority coalition of Hughes, Holmes, Brandeis, Stone, and Roberts soon transformed the Court's First Amendment jurisprudence into one far more sympathetic to the core values underlying the amendment. The transformation took place in *Stromberg v. California*.[91] The modern era of First Amendment construction is in large measure built atop the underpinnings constructed by Justices Holmes and Brandeis.

From 1930 forward, the essential question has not been whether the First Amendment may be applied to deprivations of speech and press freedoms but rather whether the state's interests in regulation of the press should supersede the individual's interest in the free dissemination of ideas and information. The system of constitutional interpretation chosen by the interpreter is the all-important factor in resolving these cases.

ENDNOTES

1. 3 THE ROOTS OF THE BILL OF RIGHTS 592 (B. Schwartz ed. 1980).
2. *Jefferson to Madison, 1787, reprinted in* 3 THE ROOTS OF THE BILL OF RIGHTS 606 (B. Schwartz ed. 1980).
3. *Id.* at 607.
4. Wrote Thomas Jefferson to William Stephens Smith:

    I own it astonishes me to find such a change wrought in the opinions of our countrymen since I left them, as that three fourths of them should be contented to live under a system which leaves to their governors the power of taking from them the trial by jury in civil cases, freedom of religion, freedom of the press, freedom of commerce, the habeas corpus laws, and of yoking them with a standing army. This is a degeneracy in the principles of liberty. . . . But I hope it will all come about.

    Jefferson to William Stephens Smith, 1788, reprinted in 3 THE ROOTS OF THE BILL OF RIGHTS 609 (B. Schwartz ed. 1980).
5. Wrote James Madison to Thomas Jefferson:

    My own opinion has always been in favor of a bill of rights; provided it be so framed as not to imply powers not meant to be included in the enumeration. At the same time I have never thought the omission a material defect, nor been anxious to supply it even by subsequent amendment, for any other reason than that it is anxiously desired by others. I have favored it because I supposed it might be of use, and if properly executed could not be of disservice. I have not viewed it in an important light—1. because I conceive that in a certain degree, though not in the extent argued by Mr. Wilson, the rights in question are reserved by the manner in which the federal powers are granted [and] 2. because there is great reason to fear that a positive declaration of some of the most essential rights could not be obtained in the requisite latitude.

Madison to Jefferson, 1788, reprinted in 3 THE ROOTS OF THE BILL OF RIGHTS 615 (B. Schwartz ed. 1980).

6.   Wrote James Madison to Thomas Jefferson:

Wherever the real power in a Government lies, there is the danger of oppression. In our Governments the real power lies in the majority of the Community, and the invasion of private rights is chiefly to be apprehended, not from acts of Government contrary to the sense of its constituents, but from acts in which the Government is the mere instrument of the major number of the Constituents.

Madison to Jefferson, 1788, reprinted in 3 THE ROOTS OF THE BILL OF RIGHTS 616 (B. Schwartz ed. 1980).

See also Thomas Jefferson's letter to David Humphreys, dated March 18, 1789, in which he presents his view of the threat from government as it specifically pertains to the speech and press liberties, explaining:

I am one of those who think it a defect that the important rights, not placed in security by the frame of the constitution itself, were not explicitly secured by a supplementary declaration. There are rights, which it is useless to surrender to the government, and which yet, governments have always been fond to invade. These are the rights of thinking, and publishing our thoughts by speaking or writing: the right of free commerce: the right of personal freedom.

Jefferson to David Humphreys, 1789, reprinted in 5 THE ROOTS OF THE BILL OF RIGHTS 1000 (B. Schwartz ed. 1980).

7.   *Madison to Jefferson, 1788, reprinted in* 3 THE ROOTS OF THE BILL OF RIGHTS 617 (B. Schwartz ed. 1980).

8.   *Jefferson to Madison, 1789, reprinted in* 3 THE ROOTS OF THE BILL OF RIGHTS 620 (B. Schwartz ed. 1980).

9.   *Id.* at 621.

10.   5 THE ROOTS OF THE BILL OF RIGHTS 1006 (B. Schwartz ed. 1980).

11. In a July 31, 1789, letter to his son John, George Mason argued that Madison favored a bill of rights at the last minute out of a desire to quash the principal opposition to his election to the House. Wrote Mason: "[T]he *Fact* was, Mr. Madison [knew that he coul]'d not be elected, without making some such Promises." 1 THE PAPERS OF GEORGE MASON 1725–1792 1164 (R. Rutland ed. 1970).

12. R. RUTLAND, THE BIRTH OF THE BILL OF RIGHTS 1776–1791 173 (1971).

13. Wrote James Madison to George Eve:

> [I]t is my sincere opinion that the Constitution ought to be revised, and that the first Congress meeting under it, ought to prepare and recommend to the States for ratification, the most satisfactory provisions for all essential rights, particularly the rights of Conscience in the fullest latitude, the freedom of the press, trials by jury, security against general warrants & c.

R. RUTLAND, THE BIRTH OF THE BILL OF RIGHTS 1776–1791 195–96 (1971).

14. *Id.* at 190–91.

15. *Madison to Washington, 1789, reprinted in* 5 THE ROOTS OF THE BILL OF RIGHTS 998 (B. Schwartz ed. 1980).

16. R. RUTLAND, THE BIRTH OF THE BILL OF RIGHTS 1776–1791 192–96 (1971).

17. *Id.* at 174.

18. THE FIRST AMENDMENT, THE LEGACY OF GEORGE MASON 66 (T. Shumate ed. 1985).

19. R. RUTLAND, THE BIRTH OF THE BILL OF RIGHTS 1776–1791 202 (1971).

20. THE FIRST AMENDMENT, THE LEGACY OF GEORGE MASON 67 (T. Shumate ed. 1985).

21. 1 THE PAPERS OF GEORGE MASON 1725–1792, 1167n (R. Rutland ed. 1970).

22. THE FIRST AMENDMENT, THE LEGACY OF GEORGE MASON 67 (R. Rutland, ed. 1976).

23. *Id.* at 72.

24. 5 THE ROOTS OF THE BILL OF RIGHTS 1006 (B. Schwartz ed. 1980).

25. *Id.* at 1018.

26. *Id.*

27. *Id.* at 1020.

28. *Id.* at 1024.

29. *Id.* at 1025.

30. *Id.* at 1026.

31. *Id.* at 1027.

32. *Id.* at 1028.

33. *Id.*

34. *Id.*

35. 5 THE ROOTS OF THE BILL OF RIGHTS 1029 (B. Schwartz ed. 1980).

36.   *Id.* at 1029.
37.   *Id.* at 1033.
38.   *Id.* at 1031.
39.   Stated James Jackson:

> The gentleman [James Madison] endeavors to secure the liberty of the press; pray how is this in danger? There is no power given to Congress to regulate this subject as they can commerce, or peace, or war. Has any transaction taken place to make us suppose such an amendment necessary? An honorable gentleman, a member of this House, has been attacked in the public newspapers on account of sentiments delivered on this floor. Have Congress taken any notice of it? Have they ordered the writer before them, even for a breach of privilege, although the constitution provides that a member shall not be questioned in any place for any speech or debate in the House? No, these things are offered to the public view, and held up to the inspection of the world. These are principles which will always prevail. I am not afraid, nor are other members I believe, [that] our conduct should meet the severest scrutiny. Where, then, is the necessity of taking measures to secure what neither is nor can be in danger?

1 THE BILL OF RIGHTS: A DOCUMENTARY HISTORY 1034–35 (B. Schwartz ed. 1971).

40.   Anderson, *The Origins of the Press Clause*, 30 UCLA L. REV. 478 (1983); 5 THE ROOTS OF THE BILL OF RIGHTS 1050 (B. Schwartz ed. 1980).
41.   Anderson, *The Origins of the Press Clause*, 30 UCLA L. REV. 478 (1983).
42.   Bernard Schwartz submits: "It is fair to say that the Committee version made no substantial alteration in the original Madison draft. The Committee did, however, make certain stylistic changes which brought the amendments closer to the final Bill of Rights version. The most important of these are: the direct use of the term 'freedom of speech, and of the press.'" 5 THE ROOTS OF THE BILL OF RIGHTS 1050 (B. Schwartz ed. 1980).
43.   Anderson, *The Origins of the Press Clause*, 30 UCLA L. REV. 481 (1983).
44.   *Id.* at 478–79.
45.   5 THE ROOTS OF THE BILL OF RIGHTS 1096 (B. Schwartz ed. 1980).
46.   Anderson, *The Origins of the Press Clause*, 30 UCLA L. REV. 480 (1983).
47.   5 THE ROOTS OF THE BILL OF RIGHTS 1145–46 (B. Schwartz ed. 1980).
48.   Anderson, *The Origins of the Press Clause*, 30 UCLA L. REV. 480 (1983).
49.   Bogen, *The Origins of Freedom of Speech and Press*, 42 MD. L. REV. 429, 438 (1983).
50.   Anderson, *The Origins of the Press Clause*, 30 UCLA L. REV. 481 (1983). "[T]he change made the construction parallel to that of the religion clause as adopted by the House, which also began with the words 'Congress shall make no law.'" *Id.*

51. *Id.* at 481–82.

52. *Id.* at 482.

53. U.S. Const. amend. I (1791). *See* McConnell, *Political and Religious Disestablishment*, 1986 B.Y.U. L. Rev. 405 (1986), where Michael McConnell identifies a confluence in constitutional values underpinning the religion and speech clauses.

54. 4 Annals of Congress 934 (1794).

55. The pertinent part of the Act, Sections 2 and 3, provide:

> Sec. 2. . . . That if any person shall write, print, utter or publish, or shall cause or procure to be written, printed, uttered or published, or shall knowingly and willingly assist or aid in writing, printing, uttering or publishing any false, scandalous and malicious writing or writings against the government of the United States, or either house of the Congress of the United States, or the President of the United States, with intent to defame said government, or either house of the said Congress, or the said President, or to bring them or either of them, into contempt or disrepute; or to excite against them, or either or any of them, the hatred of the good people of the United States, or to stir up sedition within the United States . . . shall be punished by fine not exceeding two thousand dollars, and by imprisonment not exceeding two years.
>
> Sec. 4. . . . That if any person shall be [tried] under this act, for the writing or publishing any libel aforesaid, it shall be lawful for the defendant, upon the trial of the cause, to give evidence in his defense, the truth of the matter contained in the publication charged as a libel. And the jury who shall try the cause, shall have a right to determine the law and the fact, under the direction of the court, as in other cases.

Quoted in J. Smith, Freedom's Fetters: The Alien and Sedition Laws and American Civil Liberties 441–42 (1956).

56. In a May 13, 1789, letter to Thomas Jefferson, James Madison remarked: "Perhaps it is a universal truth that the loss of liberty at home is to be charged to provisions against dangers real or pretended from abroad." *Quoted in* D. Malone, Jefferson and the Ordeal of Liberty 379 (1962).

57. Thomas Jefferson perceived the true purpose of the Act to be "suppression of the Whig presses." *See* D. Malone, Jefferson and the Ordeal of Liberty 386 (1962); *see also* Gibson, *The Supreme Court and Freedom of Expression from 1791 to 1917*, 55 Fordham L. Rev. 263, 273–76 (1986).

58. "Madison's Report on the Virginia Resolutions," House of Delegates Session of 1799–1800, 4 The Debates in the Several State Conventions on the Adoption of the Federal Constitution, as Recommended by the General Convention at Philadelphia in 1787, Together with the Journal of the Federal Convention 561 (J. Elliott ed. 1937).

59. *Id.* at 569.

60. *Id.*

61. *Id.* at 569–70.

62. *Id.* at 570.

63. *Id.* at 571.

64. James Madison in his Virginia Resolutions, House of Delegates Session of 1799–1800, 4 THE DEBATES IN THE SEVERAL STATE CONVENTIONS ON THE ADOPTION OF THE FEDERAL CONSTITUTION, AS RECOMMENDED BY THE GENERAL CONVENTION AT PHILADELPHIA IN 1787, TOGETHER WITH THE JOURNAL OF THE FEDERAL CONSTITUTION 561 (J. Elliott ed. 1937).

65. *See* Gibson, *The Supreme Court and Freedom of Expression from 1791 to 1917,* 55 FORDHAM L. REV. 263, 271, 275 (1986).

66. *Id.* at 263, 275.

67. For a detailed treatment of the First Amendment's history during the period from roughly 1798 to 1931 and for critical analysis of the Court's failure to form any developed theory of First Amendment jurisprudence during this period, *see* Rabban, *The First Amendment in Its Forgotten Years,* 90 YALE L. J. 513 (1981); *See also* Hunter, *Problems in Search of Principles: The First Amendment in the Supreme Court from 1791–1930,* 35 EMORY L. J. 59 (1986); Gibson, *The Supreme Court and Freedom of Expression from 1791 to 1917,* 55 FORDHAM L. REV. 263 (1986).

68. *Gitlow v. New York,* 268 U.S. 652, 666 (1925).

69. *Respublica v. Oswald,* 1 U.S. (1 Dall.) 319 (1788).

70. *Patterson v. Colorado,* 205 U.S. 454, 464 (1907). Wrote Justice Harlan in dissent: "I go further and hold that the privileges of free speech and a free press, belonging to every citizen of the United States, constitute essential parts of every man's liberty, and are protected against violation by that clause of the Fourteenth Amendment forbidding a state to deprive any person of his liberty without due process of law."

71. *Ex Parte Jackson,* 96 U.S. 727, 733 (1878).

72. *See* Rabban, *The First Amendment in Its Forgotten Years,* 90 YALE L. J. 516, 526 (1981).

73. *Robertson v. Baldwin,* 165 U.S. 275, 281 (1897).

74. *Davis v. Massachusetts,* 167 U.S. 43 (1897), *rev'd, Hague v. CIO,* 307 U.S. 496 (1939).

75. *See* Gibson, *The Supreme Court and Freedom of Expression from 1791 to 1917,* 55 FORDHAM L. REV. 263, 271 (1986).

76. *Id.* at 263, 271 n.34.

77. *See* Hunter, *Problems in Search of Principles: The First Amendment in the Supreme Court from 1791–1930,* 35 EMORY L. J. 59, 89 (1986).

78. *See* Gibson, *The Supreme Court and Freedom of Expression from 1791 to 1917,* 55 FORDHAM L. REV. 263, 271, 281–85, 206–84, 288–325, 350–58 (1986).

79. *See* Hunter, *Problems in Search of Principles: The First Amendment in the Supreme Court from 1791–1930*, 35 EMORY L. J. 59, 90 (1986).

80. *Patterson v. Colorado*, 205 U.S. 454, 462 (1907).

81. *Turner v. Williams*, 194 U.S. 279 (1904).

82. *See generally* Rabban, *The First Amendment in Its Forgotten Years*, 90 YALE L. J. 514, 578–79 (1981). FREEDOM OF SPEECH (1920) by Zechariah Chafee, Jr., was perhaps the single most influential piece of scholarship of the time.

83. *Schenck v. United States*, 249 U.S. 47 (1919).

84. *Frohwerk v. United States*, 249 U.S. 204 (1919).

85. *Debs v. United States*, 249 U.S. 211 (1919).

86. *See* Hunter, *Problems in Search of Principles: The First Amendment in the Supreme Court from 1791–1930*, 35 EMORY L. J. 59, 101–10 (1986).

87. *See* Rabban, *The First Amendment in Its Forgotten Years*, 90 YALE L. J. 514, 585 (1981).

88. *See Abrams v. United States*, 250 U.S. 616, 627 (1919) (Holmes, J., dissenting).

89. *Schaefer v. United States*, 251 U.S. 466, 495 (1920).

90. *Whitney v. California*, 274 U.S. 357, 376 (1927).

91. *See* Hunter, *Problems in Search of Principles: The First Amendment in the Supreme Court from 1791–1930*, 35 EMORY L. J. 59, 125–26 (1986); *Stromberg v. California*, 283 U.S. 359 (1930).

PART II

CHOOSING A FIRST AMENDMENT STANDARD

What kind of First Amendment would best serve our needs as we approach the 21st century may be an open question. But the old-fashioned First Amendment that we have is the Court's only guideline; and one hard and fast principle which it announces is that Government shall keep its hands off the press. That principle has served us through days of calm and eras of strife and I would abide by it until a new First Amendment is adopted.*

---

*CBS v. Democratic Nat'l Comm., 412 U.S. 94, 160–61 (1973) (Douglas, J., concurring).

9

MODERN THEORIES OF FIRST AMENDMENT CONSTRUCTION

In the modern era, how one accommodates the conflicting forces of stability and change determines how one stands on the issue of constitutional construction. Because the body of scholarship on how best to construe the First Amendment is so rich and diverse, to treat each separate, competing perspective in detail would consume far more space than has been allotted for this book. Furthermore, such an exercise would be of dubious value. Instead, presented here are three of the most prominent modern perspectives on First Amendment construction: what may be termed the Literalist, the Narrow Intentionalist, and the Relativist Perspectives. The principal criticisms proffered against each perspective are also presented. Finally, a new perspective is offered, one designed to avoid the ills of the three principal theories and to preserve the core values of the First Amendment in the new media age.

THE LITERALIST PERSPECTIVE

The Literalist Perspective, popularly termed the "absolutist" view, is perhaps most often associated with Justice Hugo L. Black.[1] Justice Black believed the First Amendment "to mean what it says."[2] In other words, to Black, the amendment has a plain meaning: "no law means no law."[3] The strict Literalist focuses on the text of the amendment without regard to extrinsic evidence of intent and defines the language according to definitions believed current at the time of the amendment's ratification, 1789 to 1791. The perspective is designed to keep the law's meaning permanent and thereby predictable. The power to change the law is to be reserved to the people. In this way judicial discretion is to be held in check, subservient to the limited definitional compass of the Constitution's language.

Critics of the Literalist Perspective have variously argued that the approach is exceedingly naive, for it presumes the existence of a single definition for First Amendment terms such as "abridging," "speech," and "press," which are inherently multidefinitional.[4] Some believe these words to have been chosen with the intent that they be given the widest possible interpretive latitude.[5] Some have argued that the Literalist is limited to an anachronistic definition of the press that would include only the print medium known in 1789 but not the broadcast and cable "press" of this century or would include only political expression but not artistic or symbolic forms of expression.[6] The Literalist's definitional approach is said to be incapable of principled development, for it provides no clear guidance "whether [for example] singing, flag-waving, flag-burning, picketing, and criminal conspiracy are within the protected ambit of the first amendment's 'freedom of speech.' "[7] Lawrence Solum explains that the plain language of the First Amendment "refers only to Congress"; however, it would be odd indeed if the amendment did not also reach "executive and judicial action."[8] He also argues that no one could seriously maintain that the Constitution would invalidate "a law forbidding incitement to mutiny on a naval vessel or falsely shouting 'fire' in a crowded theater," and yet, quite literally, these pronouncements are "speech."[9]

Others find fault in the failure of the Literalists to examine extrinsic evidence to elucidate the specific intent of those who framed or ratified the First Amendment. For example, Richard Kay believes the constitutional text "meaningless marks on paper . . . until we posit an intelligence which selected and arranged them."[10] Henry Monaghan comments that the "textual language embodies one or more purposes, and the text may be understood and usefully applied only if its purposes are understood."[11] Essentially, without discerning a purpose for the amendment's terms, the jurist cannot know how to apply the definition posited by the Literalist to varying situations in a principled manner.

THE NARROW INTENTIONALIST PERSPECTIVE

Unlike the advocates of Literalism, the advocates of the Narrow Intentionalist Perspective "look behind the text to the original understanding."[12] In the words of Justice Sutherland, proper constitutional construction is accomplished when one "ascertain[s] and give[s] effect to the intent of the framers and the people who adopted" the Constitution.[13] "All that counts," states Robert Bork, "is how the words in the Constitution have been understood at the time [of the founding]. The original understanding is thus manifested in the words used and in secondary materials, such as debates at the conventions, public discussion, newspaper articles, dictionaries in use at the time, and the like."[14] Narrow Intentionalists regard the supremacy clause[15] as fixing the Constitution with its intended meaning in a comparatively static state.[16] The Justices are to fulfill the intended meaning of the Constitution and are duty bound by the supremacy clause to avoid infusing the law of the land with their own personal prejudices and predilections.[17] Changes in interpretation are reserved to the people who, through a supermajority, may effect such changes as they think fit through constitutional amendments. To permit judicial construction to bring about change would undermine public faith in the Constitution and produce instability in government, or perhaps, over time, would transform our limited federal republic into a new form of government entirely, an autocracy of executive magistrates.

A key criticism raised against Narrow Intentionalism is that it is difficult to discover who *the* Framers or ratifiers were and what their intentions were.[18] Which spokesmen embody the Framers' intent? Are the state ratification debates or the Congressional floor debates dispositive? Which secondary materials reveal the Framers' intent? How are conflicting intentions to be reconciled? Richard Kay answers these criticisms by explaining that "the relevant intentions are those of the human beings whose assent was necessary to give the Constitution the force of law."[19] Moreover, he argues that although a specific intention may not be known to exist, a general intention is always ascertainable. He further posits that the judicial object need not be to determine *specifically* what the Framers contemplated but rather what result would more properly comport with their intended meaning.[20]

Another criticism is that there exists no "collective mind" of the Framers but only a series of competing justifications for each constitutional provision.[21] Some argue that no evidence exists to suggest that the Framers wanted future generations to be bound by their intentions.[22]

Other critics of Narrow Intentionalism argue that it is not enough to merely invoke the Framers' intentions as a justification for deciding constitutional questions; those who would abide by the Framers' intentions must explain why, substantively, those intentions should be decisive. Writes Ronald Dworkin:

The historicist might say that the historical statements of the framers must be decisive because the Constitution is law and the content of law is settled by the publicly declared intentions of its authors. That begs the question too crudely. *His task* is to show *why* the Constitution as law should be understood to be what the framers concertedly thought it was, and he cannot simply assume that it should be. He might say that the declarations of the framers are decisive because they intended them to be. That is silly for two reasons: we have no evidence of this meta-intention, and even if we did, enforcing it would beg the question once again.[23]

The argument most often raised against Narrow Intentionalism concerns its supposed inability to keep pace with the ever-changing conditions of modernity. Those who oppose the Narrow Intentionalist doctrine often find that it is too wooden, requiring adherence to a constitutional understanding largely defined by the pre-industrial Newtonian views of the eighteenth century. Such views, contend the doctrine's detractors, are out of touch with fundamental, widely accepted modern values. In short, the Framers' views are said to be irrelevant in our time; such views are said to be obsolete in light of social and technological change. The Constitution of 1787 is said to be a dead letter; writes Erwin Chemerinsky:

> The Constitution should protect values that are fundamental now, not those that were important 200 years ago. In 1787, slavery was acceptable, women were disenfranchised, notions of free speech and due process were limited. Without the possibility of evolution, the Constitution would be confined to anachronistic beliefs. If the Constitution does not evolve, it will contain values that are universally rejected by society. A document that sanctions slavery and counts a slave as only three-fifths of a person for purposes of representation would be repugnant in modern society.[24]

Robert Bork believes the underlying objective of such argumentation to be the advancement of the proposition that "courts should be free to write into the Constitution freedoms from democratic control that the Framers omitted."[25] Bork finds great danger in this, for he views it as a process of substituting autocracy for democracy in areas where the Constitution provides for democratic governance.[26]

Those who find fault with Narrow Intentionalism typically favor an evolving constitutional understanding. They prefer incorporating into the Constitution contemporary values that countenance the exercise of government power to counteract the abuses of private power. Private power, they believe, if left unchecked, will be misallocated or will do injustice to innocent minorities. According to John Hart Ely, such malfunctioning in the market is to be counteracted by government power.[27] Those who support Narrow Intentionalism find the conclusion of market failure to be predicated not on some objective standard but on the simple fact that the person in a position to decide dislikes the result reached by the free play of market forces.[28]

THE RELATIVIST PERSPECTIVE

Advocates of the Relativist Perspective regard the Constitution's language "as a vessel that can be filled with new meanings through interpretation."[29] They consider adjudication to be "the social process by which judges give meaning to our public values."[30] Relativists submit that the Constitution, if it were to function according to eighteenth-century principles, would protect inequalities in wealth and political power that they believe are unfair. They advocate the use of governmental power to restrain private power, believing the concept of individualism to be outmoded and dangerous. Writes Owen Fiss:

> In truth, the individual participation axiom is rooted in a world that no longer exists. It is rooted in a horizontal world, in which people related to one another on individual terms and on terms of approximate equality. It is rooted in a world that viewed the law of contracts as The Law. . . . Our world, however, is a vertical one; the market has been replaced by the hierarchy, the individual entrepreneur by the bureau. In this social setting, what is needed to protect the individual is the establishment of power centers equal in strength and equal in resources to the dominant social actors; what is needed is countervailing power.[31]

The role of courts in this system is to guard against legislative and market failures—government or private action that perpetuates or condones certain differences in wealth, differences in access to economic goods, or differences in political clout (all said to be undesirable).[32]

Relativists argue that it is the essential role of the court to prevent "victimization of a discrete and insular minority."[33] They want a pervasive economic and social equality. Natural inequalities in ability are to be arrested by the state with enforced equality of results. Explains Kenneth Karst:

> The principle of equal citizenship does not call for the dismantling of the structures of capitalism, such as they remain in the era of the "welfare-corporate state." On the other hand, the principle does call for judicial intervention when economic inequalities make it impossible for a person to have "a fully human existence" and the political branches of government turn a blind eye.[34]

Relativists argue that modern liberal political values, such as equality,[35] enhancement of minority rights,[36] or redistribution of political or economic power,[37] are public interest objectives of *constitutional* dimension that must serve as unifying principles of decision.

Some Relativists believe that the Bill of Rights should be read to state "affirmative rights . . . to education, shelter, subsistence, health care and the like, or to the money these things cost."[38] Frank Michelman finds these "affirmative rights" in the "spacious locutions of . . . section one of the fourteenth amendment."[39] Following the affirmative rights theory, courts need not wait for legislative action "to define a state toward which we should want to move." Rather, the courts can assume the role of the legislature and can order the use of government resources to ensure fulfillment of a "constitutional" objective.[40] The court need not avoid action merely because society "is not fully and maturely just" or because its "material circumstances, or political and social maturation, have not yet reached a point admitting full implementation of the principles."[41] Instead, the court may compel the legislative or the executive branches to act. The historical separation of powers doctrine serves as no impediment to judicial attainment of the constitutional objective under this Relativist view of judicial power.

[T]his notion [of separation of powers] by itself fails to distinguish our welfare rights case clearly from cases involving school desegregation and finance, and legislative reapportionment. In such cases courts have been willing to try remedial devices designed to harness to the court's announced principle the competence and accountability of nonjudicial public officials—most typically, a judicial mandate to legislative, executive or administrative officers to prepare, submit, and carry out a corrective plan. Indeed the prognosis for one or another of these approaches would seem good, assuming a modicum of willingness to comply on the part of these nonjudicial officers.[42]

In the Relativists' view, procedure is a means to a substantive end, not an end in itself. Fusing new political principles with the Constitution to attain substantive ends is deemed far more important than avoiding establishing a precedent for the unlimited exercise of powers by the judiciary. Rather, the court is to become the nation's moral conscience and to create new welfare rights at propitious moments. Writes Frank Michelman:

[A]s judges go about their business of selectively translating constitutional and statutory offerings into welfare rights—as they play their role in the authorship of positive entitlements—they should conscientiously try to clarify in their own minds some systematic moral theory which justifies and accounts for these decisions, should not shrink from incorporating such thought in their public explanations of what they do, and should be prepared at an appropriate state in the emergence of a welfare right to declare that such a right exists.[43]

Mark Tushnet believes that adherence to precedent is a confining exercise that can be dispensed with readily. Tushnet has written that in deciding a case, the proper procedure should be "to make an explicitly political judgment," to ask "which result is, in the circumstances now existing, likely to advance the cause of socialism."[44] Once that political result has been identified, the next step is to "write an opinion in some currently favored version of Grand Theory."[45]

Some Relativists have not altogether abandoned an historical view. Calling their vision "modern republicanism," certain Relativists allude to select aspects of the formative constitutional tradition that lend support for their contemporary views and values. The "republican revival," as it has been termed, is inspired in part by the recognition that "republican theories of politics have a tenacious hold on political actors and observers, inside and outside the judiciary."[46]

Cass Sunstein has identified four "modern republican" principles for decision. The first principle denies the existence of prepolitical (or fundamental) rights and defines "private interests" as "relevant inputs into politics" and as "the object of critical scrutiny" by government.[47] The second principle calls for an elimination "of sharp disparities in political participation or influence among individuals or social groups."[48] Sunstein explains that "economic equality may, but need not, accompany political equality."[49] The third principle calls for deciding normative disputes with substantively "right" answers.[50] The fourth principle defines citizenship in largely public terms whereby civic virtue is inculcated into the law through political participation and whereby private interests are subordinated to conceptions of the "public good."[51]

The primary use of modern republicanism in the Relativist lexicon is to justify the exercise of essentially legislative powers by the judiciary. Modern republicanism interprets the historical roots of left-wing political values as bases for government redistribution of political or economic power. Writes Sunstein: "In the republican view, for example, the distribution of wealth is a matter for political disposition; there is no hostility to redistributive measures."[52] Proponents also rely on the theory to define "private interests" as necessarily distinct from and often in opposition to the "public interest," which they view as *superior* to private interests.[53] In fact, all interests, whether private or public, are to be understood as being public and therefore regulatable by the state. "Republicans see the private sphere as the product of public decisions, and deny the existence of natural or prepolitical entitlements. . . . On the republican point of view, the existence of realms of private autonomy must be justified in public terms," Sunstein writes.[54]

The advocates of modern republicanism welcome government regulation of the political process to "reduce the effects of wealth" and of the media "to furnish access" to certain groups.[55] Sunstein explains:

> [R]epublican ideas offer reasons to reject recent attacks on the fairness doctrine in the broadcast and print media. Such ideas suggest that efforts to promote access to sources of public deliberation should be treated quite hospitably; and that the exclusive use of the economic market to regulate such access is undesirable. It is for this reason that on the republican view a principal current threat to a well-functioning system of free expression lies, not in government regulation, but in government "inaction" that allows the political process to be excessively influenced by disparities in private wealth and private access.[56]

Through adoption of modern republicanism, courts that are inclined to favor a Relativist Perspective may argue that judicial remedies involving redistribution of wealth, political power, or rights of access are mandated by and are in accord with certain aspects of the formative republican tradition.

The attack on the Relativist Perspective comes from many fronts. The Relativist's preference for expanding the role of the judiciary to include policymaking functions is said to be an assumption of power antithetical to the maintenance of a free state. Doug Bandow writes:

> [T]he judiciary was vested with the role of defining, not redefining, constitutional liberties. Judges take an oath "to support this Constitution," not to enforce the one they wish the Founders had written. The reason for this is obvious: the purpose of a written Constitution, argued Supreme Court Justice Hugo Black, was "to make certain that men in power would be governed by law, not the arbitrary fiat of the man or men in power," even if they be high-minded judges.[57]

The Relativist approach is said to subvert the amendment process of Article V by denying the people and their representatives an opportunity to vote on the reallocation of powers within the government and between the government and the people.[58] A court guided by the Relativist Perspective is said to usurp these democratic powers and replace them with a judicial authority superior to any legislative power. From its role as least dangerous branch, the judiciary through liberal construction becomes the most dangerous branch, one that is not bound to uphold the law but is in fact *the source* of all law.

Most significantly, the accumulation of executive and legislative authority in the judiciary is said to replace an ideology in favor of limited government with one in favor of "an ever-expanding federal establishment." The consequence is said to be a replacement of "the limited government/individual freedom framework established by the nation's Founders" with "an ideology of egalitarian social justice," which forces us to view traditionally private affairs as public and regulatable by the state and which mandates that free will continue to be free only if it is deemed in fulfillment of the grand egalitarian designs of the executive magistrates.[59] Summarizes Bandow:

> Where judges treat the nation's fundamental law as an archaic and irrelevant parchment, they destroy the basis for the secure protection of any right. The government becomes one of men, not laws, where those who control the judiciary control our freedom, economic and civil.[60]

The threat envisioned is one of power without balance—judges reordering consensual private relationships and diluting or transferring rights to liberty and property to serve their favored view of an elusive public interest. In the process, the judges violate the rights of certain private individuals (the disfavored) in order to enhance the rights of others (the favored). The public becomes beholden to legal standards of morality not brought about by legislative action or the supermajoritarian process of constitutional amendment but by the decisions of a single judge or group of judges whose own conceptions of right and wrong are, by virtue of position, the law of the land. This "lawmaking" is outside the scope of judicial review, contends Raoul Berger[61]:

> [A]ll power must be drawn from the Constitution. Activist theorizing . . . is a very recent phenomenon, seeking to justify judicial exercise of ungranted power by moral theories that have no constitutional roots in order to undergird judicial governance that supports activist aspirations.[62]

In short, Relativism, unbounded by a need to follow any settled doctrinal concepts creates an unpredictable, rights-violative, and freedom-violative power center in the judiciary that cannot long co-exist with any regime but an authoritarian one.

AN APPRAISAL OF THE THREE PRINCIPAL PERSPECTIVES

Our Constitution is a framework for government by the majority that protects the liberties of the minority. It creates a delicate balance between public and private spheres that cannot be upset by the judiciary without sacrificing individual rights or replacing majority rule with autocracy. In construing our basic charter, the court must try to preserve this delicate balance. The three principal perspectives on constitutional construction presented earlier in this chapter all lend themselves to abuses of power or unprincipled results, some more than others.

The *Literalist Perspective* would require us to adopt a definitional understanding of the First Amendment's terms. However, the terms of the amendment cannot reasonably be limited to single definitions. Some of the amendment's terms, if understood literally, have meanings that are too narrow in definitional scope to provide adequate protection for speech and press liberty. Other First Amendment terms are ambiguous. The first word of the amendment, "Congress," if read literally, would deny only legislative power to "abridge" the freedom of speech or of the press. Such a narrow reading would condone judicial or executive deprivations of the liberty.

The phrase "no law," if understood literally, also begets certain results that cannot be justified by principle. It would require that society permit a speaker to say what he pleases, wherever, whenever, and in any manner he pleases. Such an interpretation would prohibit, for example, the arrest of an insubordinate soldier who, in the field of battle when silence was necessary, raised his voice in protest.

Few would question the right of a president to dismiss from command a general who defined a military mission for troops in a manner contrary to the Commander in Chief's express orders. Few would doubt that the police have a legitimate authority to remove a trespasser from one's living room, even if the trespasser has appeared there to express his views on pressing political issues. Few would question the power of government to remove a heckler from the gallery of the U.S. Senate, even if the heckler's protestations concerned questions then before the Senate. Few would doubt that a public school could rightfully expel a student who insists on bellowing obscenities at a teacher who is attempting to conduct a class lecture. However, each of these examples involves freedom of speech in its literal sense. At times, "no law" must not carry its literal meaning if the freedom and safety of others are to be protected adequately.

The word "abridging" in the First Amendment carries with it many definitions. If one construes the First Amendment to place primary emphasis on the phrase "no law," as Justice Black read it, then the term "abridging" becomes largely superfluous. However, if the amendment is read with a primary emphasis on the term "abridging" and that term is read as modifying the "no law" language, it is possible that some laws restricting speech and press could be construed as not constituting "abridgements." Indeed,

Federalist Judge Alexander Addison argued this point in his famous constitutional defense of the Sedition Act of 1798. Judge Addison explained that laws punishing seditious utterances were not regarded at common law as abridgements of speech or press and so could not properly be construed as violating the First Amendment.[63]

Likewise, the simple definite article "the" can be rendered all important by a Literalist reading of the First Amendment: "Congress shall make no law . . . abridging *the* freedom of speech, or of the press . . .," emphasizing a particular kind of freedom of speech and press, namely that recognized by the common law of 1791. By focusing on affording protection to only that understanding of "the" freedom extant in the common law of 1791, it is possible to limit the protective compass of the amendment to a mere proscription against prior restraints. Such a definition would permit subsequent punishments of all kinds, including those for seditious libel liberally tolerated under the law of Blackstone.

Any attempt to provide precise definitions for the terms "speech" and "press" is fraught with grave constitutional dangers. Communication often does not assume forms as immediately cognizable as the classic soap box "speech" or the newspaper "press" known at the founding. Limiting the definition of "speech" to verbal pronouncements and "press" to written works invites government to control many forms of expression that must be kept free from regulation if we are to enjoy the full benefits of the voluntary exchange of ideas and information. For example, "speech" in the idea marketplace may arise in the form of songs, silent marches, and the display of symbols such as armbands or painted placards. These forms are often powerful means by which the public becomes apprised of problems befalling the country, and yet they do not fit neatly into any single eighteenth-century definition of the term "speech." Likewise, broadcast, cable, and telephone transmissions now perform the same informational role for our society that the print medium did for Americans living in 1789; however, these media forms were not known to the Framers. In the future, videophone and holographic communication may also provide additional hybrid forms of information transmission. Were one to create a limited definition for the term "press," it is quite conceivable that the Constitution would be incapable of withstanding the test of time. Such anachronistic understandings would fail to fully incorporate new media forms under the amendment's protective shield.

Fundamentally, the Literalist Perspective provides us with no guidance concerning what *substantive purpose* the amendment serves (what it is for or what it is against) or how it has functioned to protect speech and press liberty in our history. Without knowing *why* the amendment is necessary we cannot know *which* definition best fits the constitutional crisis confronting us at any moment. This lack of principle precludes the Literalist Perspective from ensuring adequate protection for the speech and press liberty.

Unlike the Literalist Perspective, the *Narrow Intentionalist Perspective* contains many appealing aspects. It provides us with a reason for the First Amendment by informing us of what purposes certain of its Framers intended for it. It requires jurists to develop and appreciate much of the history that led to the amendment's inclusion in the Constitution. However, if one adopts too narrow a view of that intellectual history, one may end up condoning precisely the kind of governmental invasion into private communication that the amendment was designed to prevent. For example, from Leonard Levy's book, *Emergence of a Free Press,* it is possible on Narrow Intentionalist grounds to find historical support for the proposition that the amendment protects only political speech or only that speech which does not impugn the integrity of public officials or private persons. It is possible on Narrow Intentionalist grounds to argue for a limited First Amendment scope, leaving unprotected such communicative *actions* as streetside protests and the placement of newsstands or placards on public sidewalks. Without a purposive view of the amendment and its role in the entire constitutional scheme, it is quite possible to argue from the original understanding that the amendment should serve only limited ends. In the process, one will condone precisely that expansion in regulation which is inconsistent with the maintenance of a limited federal republic and with the overall design of the Constitution.[64]

The strength of Narrow Intentionalism lies in its assurance to the public that the Constitution does provide defined limits to government power. It permits speech and press to exist in an environment of fixed barriers against government. Its downfall is its narrow interpretive sense, its failure to provide for a means to incorporate nonpolitical forms of expression within the protective "speech" and "press" compass.

Unlike the Narrow Intentionalist Perspective, the *Relativist Perspective* contains many unappealing aspects. It transforms the meaning of the Bill of Rights from a denial of government power to an affirmative grant of power coupled with new constitutional requirements that mandate use of that power. Moreover, this dramatic reversal in the constitutional scheme, this investiture of expansive, new governmental authority, is not accompanied by any power limitations to stem the dangers created by such a power shift. Nor do the Relativists offer means to limit or eliminate the dangers of abuse of power inherent in the transfer. Rather, they merely presume the illogical: that a grant of total power over private liberties will be exercised consonant with those liberties (and in a manner consistent with their own desires).

The Relativist Perspective rests on the unproven and counterintuitive assumption that government, if granted unlimited power to reorder fundamental constitutional relationships between the public and private sectors, will exercise that power only to enhance individual rights when in fact the vesting of such power has always been the prelude to the deprivation of civil rights. The Relativist Perspective offers no limitation, let alone a clear or principled one, on the judicial exercise of power. The private sphere is to be entirely subsumed by and rendered subservient to the public sphere. Private acts, presumed public and thus regulatable, are permitted only so long as they serve the public interest. That interest is not for the individual to decide, but is placed squarely in the province of executive magistrates, who ensure that freedom is never free enough to threaten or contravene their own political views of the public good.

In the area of the First Amendment, the Relativist view is a justification for government to structure the idea marketplace by mandating a certain preferred mix of ideas. Private selection is believed to be burdened by problems of market failure: domination by the few who own communication properties at the expense of the many who do not. Government is to set the scales aright. The irony is that the government, the greatest lawful monopoly ever created, is to make the subjective decisions. Government is the great sanitizer and equalizer in the Relativist's world of equality. It determines what views are "underrepresented" and what speakers deserve government-mandated access to the private media.

The Relativists fail to recognize that the exercise of government control over editorial selection is the very antithesis of freedom. Such control robs existing speakers of their own freedoms of speech and press and establishes not merely a "Robin Hood–like" redistribution of speech power from a few private hands to the many but a forced divestiture of private speech power to the state. When the state has the power to decide which views are "underrepresented" in the idea marketplace and which views deserve access to the media, it in fact has the power to create an official orthodoxy. There is nothing new about this system of coercion; it is censorship like that used by Henry VIII in the sixteenth century. In such a system, no man is free except the civil servant to whom government awards the authority to dictate who may speak and what may be said. The very essence of free speech and press is individual editorial selection. When this selection becomes subject either to state control or to the threat of it, freedom is at an end.

In their rush to embrace the power of government as a countervailing force against the private sector, the Relativists have ignored or minimized the consequences of censorship. They have failed to realize that when government can establish an orthodoxy, even speakers not directly regulated must adhere to the government's content standards. In short, any effort by government to favor particular content has a chilling effect on speech. It suppresses natural incentives for criticizing the government and for deviating from that orthodoxy. Over time, the government's efforts will promote and protect politically "safe," banal expression and discourage politically "unsafe," provocative expression.

Because none of the three essential perspectives of constitutional construction avoids major pitfalls that will permit the courts to violate speech and press liberties, an alternative is needed, one that benefits from the Narrow Intentionalists' respect for limitations on government power yet affords a principled, *substantive* basis for the analysis of modern speech and press problems. The *Preservationist Perspective* presented in the next chapter is submitted as that alternative.

ENDNOTES

1. *See* Cahn, *Justice Black and the First Amendment "Absolutes": A Public Interview,* 37 N.Y.U. L. REV. 549 (1962). *See also* Black, *The Bill of Rights,* 35 N.Y.U. L. REV. 865, 867 (1960) ("It is my belief that there are 'absolutes' in our Bill of Rights, and that they were put there on purpose by men who knew what words meant, and meant their prohibitions to be 'absolutes' "); H. BLACK, HANDBOOK ON THE CONSTRUCTION AND INTERPRETATION OF THE LAWS 20 (1911); T. M. COOLEY, A TREATISE ON THE CONSTITUTIONAL LIMITATIONS WHICH REST UPON THE LEGISLATIVE POWER OF THE STATES OF THE AMERICAN UNION 124 (Carrington's 8th ed. 1927); see also C. MILLER, THE SUPREME COURT AND THE USES OF HISTORY 153–55 (1969); Harris, *Bonding Word and Polity: The Logic of American Constitutionalism,* 76 AM. POL. SCI. REV. 34, 43–44 (1982); Schauer, *An Essay on Constitutional Language,* 29 UCLA L. REV. 797, 809–12 (1982); Holmes, *The Theory of Legal Interpretation,* 12 HARV. L. REV. 417, 419 (1898–1899).

2. Cahn, *Justice Black and the First Amendment "Absolutes": A Public Interview,* 37 N.Y.U. L. REV. 553 (1962).

3. *Quoted in* Solum, *The Freedom of Communicative Action: A Theory of the First Amendment Freedom of Speech,* 83 Nw. U. L. REV. 54, 58–59 (1989).

4. *See, e.g.*, L. LEVY, ORIGINAL INTENT AND THE FRAMERS' CONSTITUTION 336 (1988).

5. *Id.* at 349; *see also* E. CHEMERINSKY, INTERPRETING THE CONSTITUTION 36 (1987).

6. *See, e.g.*, E. CHEMERINSKY, INTERPRETING THE CONSTITUTION 53 (1987).

7. Brest, *The Misconceived Quest for the Original Understanding*, 60 B.U. L. REV. 204, 207 (1980).

8. Solum, *The Freedom of Communicative Action: A Theory of the First Amendment*, 83 Nw. U. L. REV. 54, 59 (1989). *But see* Denbeaux, *The First Word of the First Amendment*, 80 Nw. U. L. REV. 1156 (1986).

9. *Id.* at 59.

10. Kay, *Adherence to the Original Intentions in Constitutional Adjudication: Three Objections and Responses*, 82 Nw. U. L. REV. 226, 230 (1988).

11. Monaghan, *Our Perfect Constitution*, 56 N.Y.U. L. REV. 353, 375 (1981).

12. Perry, *The Authority of Text, Tradition, and Reason: A Theory of Constitutional Interpretation*, 58 S. CAL. L. REV. 551, 564 (1985).

13. *Home Building & Loan Ass'n v. Blaisdell*, 290 U.S. 398, 448 (1934) (Sutherland, J., dissenting); *see also* R. BERGER, GOVERNMENT BY JUDICIARY (1977); R. BERGER, DEATH PENALTIES 77–82 (1982); R. BORK, THE TEMPTING OF AMERICA 163 (1990).

    Bork states:

    > In short, all that a judge committed to original understanding requires is that the text, structure, and history of the Constitution provide him not with a conclusion but with a major premise. That major premise is a principle or stated value that the ratifiers wanted to protect against hostile legislation or executive action. The judge must then see whether that principle or value is threatened by the statute or action challenged in the case before him. The answer to that question provides his minor premise, and the conclusion follows.

    See also Grano, *Judicial Review and a Written Constitution in a Democratic Society*, 28 WAYNE L. REV. 1 (1981); Maltz, *Foreword: The Appeal of Originalism*, 1988 UTAH L. REV. 1; Maltz, *Some New Thoughts on an Old Problem—The Role of the Intent of the Framers in Constitutional Theory*, 63 B.U. L. REV. 811 (1983); Monaghan, *The Constitution Goes to Harvard*, 13 HARV. C.R.-C.L. L. REV. 117 (1978).

14. R. BORK, THE TEMPTING OF AMERICA 144 (1990).

15. U.S. CONST. art. VI.

16. U.S. CONST. art. V.

17. *See, e.g.*, STILL THE LAW OF THE LAND? (L. Roche ed. 1987).

18. *See* E. CHEMERINSKY, INTERPRETING THE CONSTITUTION 49 (1987) ("The initial indeterminacy problem stems from an inability to determine who the Framers were").

19. Kay, *Adherence to the Original Intentions in Constitutional Adjudication: Three Objections and Responses*, 82 Nw. U. L. Rev. 226, 235 n.46 (1988).

20. *Id.* at 242–59.

21. *See* L. Levy, Original Intent and the Framers' Constitution 323 (1988).

22. *See, e.g.*, Powell, *The Original Understanding of Original Intent*, 98 Harv. L. Rev. 885 (1985).

23. R. Dworkin, Law's Empire 363–64 (1986).

24. E. Chemerinsky, Interpreting the Constitution 54 (1987).

25. R. Bork, The Tempting of America 171 (1990).

26. Summarizes Bork:

> There is no satisfactory explanation of why the judge has the authority to impose his morality upon us. Various authors have attempted to explain that but the explanations amount to little more than the assertion that judges have admirable capacities that we and our elected representatives lack. The utter dubiety of that assertion aside, the professors merely state a preference for rule by talented and benevolent autocrats over the self-government of ordinary folk. Whatever one thinks of that preference, and it seems to me morally repugnant, it is not our system of government, and those who advocate it propose a quiet revolution, made by judges.

R. Bork, The Tempting of America 252 (1990).

27. J. Ely, Democracy and Distrust 103 (1980).

28. R. Bork, The Tempting of America 197 (1990).

29. E. Chemerinsky, Interpreting the Constitution 60 (1987).

30. Fiss, *The Supreme Court 1978 Term—Foreword: The Forms of Justice*, 93 Harv. L. Rev. 1, 2 (1979).

31. *Id.* at 44.

32. *Id.* at 6, 10. *See also* Michelman, *In Pursuit of Constitutional Welfare Rights: One View of Rawls' Theory of Justice*, 121 U. Pa. L. Rev. 962 (1973) ("Opinion abounds that our society is marked by evident and severe distributive injustice").

33. Fiss, *The Supreme Court 1978 Term—Foreword: The Forms of Justice*, 93 Harv. L. Rev. 1, 6 (1979).

34. Karst, *The Supreme Court 1976 Term—Foreword: Equal Citizenship under the Fourteenth Amendment*, 91 Harv. L. Rev. 1, 62 (1977).

35. *See, e.g.*, Karst, *Equality as a Central Principle in the First Amendment*, 43 U. Chi. L. Rev. 20 (1975).

36. *See, e.g.*, E. Chemerinsky, Interpreting the Constitution 27–36, 54 (1987).

37. Consider the concept of "modern republicanism" as developed by Sunstein in *Beyond the Republican Revival*, 97 Yale L. J. 1539, 1549, 1551, 1552

(1988) ("In the republican view, for example, the distribution of wealth is a matter of political disposition; there is no hostility to redistributive measures. . . . [T]he existence of realms of private autonomy must be justified in public terms"). *See also* Michelman, *The Supreme Court, 1968 Term—Foreword: On Protecting the Poor Through the Fourteenth Amendment,* 83 Harv. L. Rev. 7 (1969).

38. Michelman, *In Pursuit of Constitutional Welfare Rights: One View of Rawls' Theory of Justice,* 121 U. Pa. L. Rev. 962 (1973).

39. *Id.* at 966.

40. *Id.* at 997.

41. *Id.*

42. *Id.* at 1006.

43. *Id.* at 1015.

44. Tushnet, *The Dilemmas of Liberal Constitutionalism,* 42 Ohio St. L. J. 424 (1981).

45. *Id.*

46. Sunstein, *Beyond the Republican Revival,* 97 Yale L. J. 1539, 1540 (1988).

47. *Id.* at 1540; *Id.* at 1546 ("[Lockean pluralism] . . . greatly overstates the real-world failings of deliberative government, and ignores the ways in which existing distributions and preferences are a product of law"). *See generally Symposium, Not Taken: Undercurrents of Republican Thinking in Modern Constitutional Theory,* 84 Nw. U.L. Rev. 1–219 (1990).

48. *Id.*

49. *Id.*

50. *Id.*

51. *Id.* at 1541–42, 1547.

52. *Id.* at 1549.

53. *Id.* at 1550 (". . . in their capacity as political actors, citizens and representatives are not supposed to ask only what is in their private interest, but also what will best serve the community in general—understood as a response to the best general theory of social welfare"). *See also* Michelman, *Law's Republic,* 97 Yale L. J. 1493, 1502 (1988) ("One possible way of making sense of this is to be conceiving of politics as a process in which private-regarding 'men' become public-regarding citizens and thus members of a people").

54. *Id.* at 1551. *See also* Michelman, *Law's Republic,* 97 Yale L. J. 1493, 1531 (1988).

Michelman explained:

Understandings of the social world that are contested and shaped in the daily encounters and transactions of civil society at large are of course conveyed to our representative arenas. They also, obviously, enter into determinations of policy that occur within nominally private settings but that can affect people's lives no less profoundly than government action. Those encounters and transactions are, then, to be counted among the sources and channels of republican self-government and jurisgenerative politics. They are areas of citizenship in the comparably broad sense in which citizenship encompasses not just formal participation in affairs of state but respected and self-respecting presence—distinct and audible voice—in public and social life at large.

55.   *Id.* at 1552.

56.   *Id.* at 1577–78.

57.   *See* Bandow, "The Conservative Judicial Agenda: A Critique" *in* Economic Liberties and the Judiciary 257, 259–60 (J. Dorn and H. Manne eds. 1987).

58.   R. Berger, Death Penalties 58 (1982).

59.   Bandow, "The Conservative Judicial Agenda: A Critique" *in* Economic Liberties and the Judiciary 257, 260 (J. Dorn and H. Manne eds. 1987).

60.   *Id.* at 263.

61.   R. Berger, Death Penalties 86–87 (1982).

62.   *Id.* at 193–94.

63.   *See* Addison, "Analysis of the Report of the Committee of the Virginia Assembly," Philadelphia, 1800, *in* 2 American Political Writing During the Founding Era 1760–1805 1055 (C. Hyneman and D. Lutz eds. 1983).

64.   *Compare, e.g.,* Bork, *Neutral Principles and Some First Amendment Problems,* 47 Ind. L. J. 1, 4 (1971) (wherein Bork first argued that only political speech was protected by the First Amendment) *with, e.g.,* R. Bork, The Tempting of America 333 (1990) (where Bork explains that on further reflection, he has abandoned the earlier position, for he now believes "the discovery and spread of what we regard as political truth is assisted by many forms of speech and writing that are not explicitly political").

10

A NEW FIRST AMENDMENT THEORY: THE PRESERVATIONIST PERSPECTIVE

To have pragmatic value, a theory of First Amendment construction must ensure stable protection of fundamental speech and press liberties, must be directed against the actual threat posed to those liberties, and must not upset the delicate balance of power among the branches of government and between the public and private sectors. From the First Amendment history set forth here, we have derived the values our ancestors understood to be a part of the speech and press liberties they revered. We have also established that government, not the private sector, has always posed the greatest threat to those values. With this knowledge in mind, we may form a theory of First Amendment construction.

In this chapter, a theory is propounded that protects the core free speech and press values, addresses the threat posed by government, preserves the essential power relationships created by the amendment at its founding, and requires judicial application of the amendment in a manner that will avoid a reduction in the protected private sphere.

THE CORE FREE SPEECH AND PRESS VALUES

From the time of Gordon and Trenchard's *Cato's Letters* until now, it is remarkable that great minds at different moments in history have recognized one or more of the same three values as beneficial by-products of the unencumbered communication of ideas. For more than 250 years these values have been found wherever the exchange of ideas has been unfettered, and they have been noticeably absent wherever government has tempered or suppressed speech and press liberty.

It is perhaps easiest to envision these fundamental values as functioning models, for they comprise several complex, self-regulating elements. As discussed in Chapter Three, the three models are (1) the Self-Government/ Checking-Value Model, (2) the Marketplace of Ideas/Search for Truth Model, and (3) the Personal Autonomy/Self-Fulfillment Model.

The Self-Government/Checking-Value Model was a central theme in *Cato's Letters* and has always been regarded as an aspect of freedom of speech vital to the proper functioning of democracy.[1] A fundamental part of the model is its acceptance of the sovereignty of the people. As Alexander Meiklejohn put it "[g]overnments . . . derive their just powers from the consent of the governed. If that consent be lacking, governments have no just powers."[2] Under the model, the people must have access to information necessary to make informed electoral choices and must be given the freedom necessary to express their views about their governors. This freedom enables the electorate to exercise a critical check on the actions of governors without fear of state retaliation. This freedom also enables the press to ferret out corruption and expose it, so that the public may condemn unfit governors or correct misguided policies.[3] In this way, public officials will know that they are subject to scrutiny and "will be much less likely to yield to the inevitable temptation presented to those with power to act in corrupt and arbitrary ways."[4]

On a number of occasions, the Court has embraced the Self-Government/ Checking-Value Model. The Court has determined that the First Amendment "was fashioned to [ensure] unfettered interchange of ideas for the bringing about of political and social changes desired by the people."[5] The Court has written:

> The maintenance of the opportunity for free political discussion to the end that government may be responsive to the will of the people and that changes may be obtained by lawful means, an opportunity essential to the security of the Republic, is a fundamental principle of our constitutional system.[6]

In the famous words of Justice Brennan in *New York Times Company v. Sullivan*, there exists a "profound national commitment to the principle that debate on public issues should be uninhibited, robust, and wide-open, and that it may well include vehement, caustic, and sometimes unpleasantly sharp attacks on government and public officials."[7] This commitment stems from the Self-Government/Checking-Value Model.

While the Self-Government Checking-Value Model focuses on the proper functioning of democracy, the Marketplace of Ideas/Search for Truth Model focuses on the discovery and dissemination of truth in all fields of inquiry, not merely political ones. The Marketplace of Ideas/Search for Truth Model defines a communications bazaar where ideas and information are exchanged freely and are contested through public inquiry and debate, and where truth, as a result of the contest, eventually prevails over falsehood. This model is the very antithesis of government censorship. It rests on a faith in free thinking and discussion. It presumes that although we may occasionally exercise our individual judgments wrongly, we will learn through trial and error to settle on reasonable theories and to come to reasonable conclusions because they will have greatest utility and value for us. The model calls for tolerance; it demands that those who believe they possess the "right" answers not impose their views on the rest of us through government fiat, but be content to argue their points in the communications bazaar, leaving each of us with the freedom to agree or disagree regardless of our reasons.

The Marketplace of Ideas/Search for Truth Model has extensive historical roots. John Milton in the mid-seventeenth century[8] and Thomas Gordon and John Trenchard in the early eighteenth century[9] were expositors of the model. In his Inaugural Address of March 4, 1801, Thomas Jefferson also advocated adherence to the model when he counseled his fellow Republicans: "If there be any among us who would wish to dissolve this Union or to change its republican form, let them stand undisturbed as monuments of the safety with which error of opinion may be tolerated where reason is left free to combat it."[10] In his 1859 classic *On Liberty,* John Stuart Mill perhaps best summarized the model when he wrote:

> [I]f any opinion is compelled to silence, that opinion may, for aught we can certainly know, be true. To deny this is to assume our own infallibility. . . . [T]hough the silenced opinion be an error, it may, and very commonly does, contain a portion of truth; and since the general or prevailing opinion on any subject is rarely or never the whole truth, it is only by the collision of adverse opinions that the remainder of the truth has any chance of being supplied. . . . [E]ven if the received opinion be not only true, but the whole truth; unless it is suffered to be, and actually is, vigorously and earnestly contested, it will, by most of those who receive it, be held in the manner of a prejudice, with little comprehension [of] or feeling [for] its rational grounds.[11]

In the Supreme Court, many Justices have written with eloquence about the value of the model. In his famous dissent in *Abrams v. United States,* Justice Holmes originated the "marketplace of ideas" metaphor with these immortal lines:

[W]hen men have realized that time has upset many fighting faiths, they may come to believe even more than they believe the very foundations of their own conduct that the ultimate good is better reached by free trade in ideas—that the best test of truth is the power of the thought to get itself accepted in the competition of the market and that truth is the only ground upon which their wishes safely can be carried out. That at any rate is the theory of our Constitution.[12]

In his dissent in *United States v. Schwimmer,* Justice Holmes emphasized the need for tolerance when he wrote: "[I]f there is any principle of the Constitution that more imperatively calls for attachment than any other, it is the principle of free thought—not free thought for those who agree with us but freedom for the thought we hate."[13] In his concurrence in *Whitney v. California,* Justice Brandeis in articulating a very broad compass for the protection of free thought and free expression emphasized that both freedoms were "means indispensable to the discovery and spread of political truth."[14]

The crux of the model is its premise that the best way to arrive at truth is through the exercise of free choice in an unfettered idea marketplace, not through a system of authoritative selection.[15] Whether in every case truth prevails over falsehood is not important. However, the argument *depends* on *that tendency.* It is not truth *per se* that is protected, because there are no absolute "truths." Rather, truth-seeking is protected, for it is the tendency of some things to be of more validity than others; it is debate that makes such tendencies apparent to us.

The Marketplace of Ideas/Search for Truth Model incorporates the view that authoritative selection cannot be countenanced because it supplants the contest of ideas, essential to truth-seeking, with propaganda. Authoritative selection requires adherence to a state dogma and violates the essential premise of the truth-seeking function by silencing voices that would otherwise be engaged in the process of discovery.[16] Explains Vincent Blasi:

[A]lthough an open marketplace of ideas might not lead to truth, any governmental intervention in the market is likely to exacerbate rather than ameliorate the preexisting distortions, thereby adding still another hindrance to the quest for truth. Furthermore, a policy of nonregulation at least leaves open the theoretical possibility that error can be corrected by persistent and persuasive appeals to the public consciousness, whereas a fully implemented policy of selective suppression permits some orthodoxies to be perpetuated in the face of the most irrefutable evidence of their falsity.[17]

The Personal Autonomy/Self-Fulfillment Model has always been appreciated by those who have lacked the freedom to express their sentiments.

It focuses on individuals and their cognitive side. It requires us to regard each person as an independent, free thinker possessing distinct views. "An autonomous agent [can]not accept the judgment of others as authoritatively deciding what the agent ought to believe or how the agent should act; the autonomous agent [is] required to have her own reasons for her beliefs and actions."[18] Advocates of the model reject the view that the public is a body of mindless viewers and listeners who uncritically accept the ideas presented to them. Rather, each of us is presumed to be a fully independent, thinking, rational being whose freedom of choice in decision making cannot be limited by authoritative controls without causing us to suffer an intolerable loss in liberty. C. Edwin Baker writes:

> A person's expressive behavior both directly defines or constitutes the person and is the person's major noncoercive, "direct" method for affecting the rest of the social world. From this view, the crucial reason to protect speech—as well as assemblies, associations, and practices dictated by religion or conscience, and, more generally, all value-based, self-expressive conduct—is that it has a direct role in controlling or influencing our destiny.[19]

The Personal Autonomy/Self-Fulfillment Model is based on the view that individuals "have an intellect—a rationality" that deserves protection even if the judgments made appear to others to be unsound. Writes Martin Redish:

> [I]f an individual wishes to buy a car because he believes it will make him look masculine, or to vote for a candidate because the candidate looks good with his tie loosened and his jacket slung over his shoulder, who are we to tell him that these are improper acts? We may prefer that he make his judgments (at least as to the candidate, if not the car) on more traditionally "rational" grounds, and hope that appeals made on such grounds will be heard. But in these areas society has left the ultimate right to decide to the individual, and this would not be much of a right if we prescribed how it was to be used.[20]

People must be free to cultivate their intellect as they see fit and must be able to consider all manner of information, not just political views, in order to satisfy their "personal needs and wants" and to develop the "power of reason," for "the development of the mind is an important goal in itself."[21] Writes Redish:

> An individual's "mental" processes cannot be limited to the receipt and digestion of cold, hard theories and facts, for there is also an emotional element that is uniquely human and that can be "developed" by . . . "non-rational" forms of communication.[22]

Under the model, the free flow of information is deemed necessary to stimulate "the development of reason and [to] provide an opportunity for the exercise of the powers of judgment and choice."[23] No content-based discrimination is permitted. Commercial speech and political speech each add to the ability of the individual to make informed judgments concerning "countless life-affecting decisions."[24] Likewise, the development of one's faculties is enhanced by art, plays, dance, and literature; these communication forms, too, fall within the scope of the model.[25]

Indeed, the model brings the great mass of information communicated in our society within the meaning of "speech," for it respects the by-products of thought, be they commercial information or works of art, literature, or politics. Lawrence Solum summarizes:

> Freedom of speech may allow the expression of powerful emotions and provide an outlet for the creative impulse in a variety of forms, including literature, drama, and the visual arts. Listeners and audiences may also be enriched by exposure to emotive or artistic expression. . . . Although some of the benefits of emotive or aesthetic expression might be realized by a solitary writer making an entry in a private diary, the self-realization value of free speech would surely be injured if the government were to forbid plays to be performed or pictures exhibited.[26]

Protection of the core values embodied in each of these three models of free speech and press is essential if the First Amendment is to protect that degree of freedom necessary for the maintenance of representative government, for the discovery and spread of truth, and for self-development. Each of the core values may be readily found in the absence of government regulation. However, arguments can be (and indeed have been) made that government intervention, if properly tailored, can promote one or more of the values without sacrificing the models' functional integrity.[27]

These arguments are made by those who fail to realize that the exercise of government power to change private editorial judgments is an act of oppression. Any effort by government to help one group have access to the mass media is an act of censorship against another group, any act by government to require the publication of certain information denies the publication of other information, and any act by government to determine which people may have the privilege to engage in speech through any particular medium is a determination that some other people may not have that same privilege. Any government intervention into the marketplace of ideas always reverberates throughout the entire media, stifling speech. As

Louis Jaffe understands, there is a great difference between private and public editorial license. The elimination of that distinction bodes ill for freedom:

> The proposition that the threat of government censorship is much less than that of private censorship cannot survive the lesson of the government's attempt to suppress publication of the Pentagon Papers. An argument of this sort can only be made by one who, not having lived under a system of governmental censorship, appears to have no idea what it really means. If one private person suppresses a fact, there are many others who may publish. Not so if the government forbids![28]

For these reasons, and for the many others developed throughout this volume, the government cannot be trusted with the power to effect changes in speech and press relationships, even when that power is said to be for a use that will enhance a particular value contained within a model. A precedent for the exercise of regulatory power (to effect a change in the composite message communicated to the public by the media) is a precedent favoring the substitution of government decision making for private decision making. This process, by its very nature, involves the suppression of some forms of communication in favor of others preferred by government. In the area of speech and press, a liberty for government translates into slavery for the press. Two hypothetical examples of authoritative selection exercised to promote certain values protected by a model will illustrate how, under the guise of enhancing speech, the government actually suppresses it.

Assume Congress enacted legislation that required regulatory agencies to promote a diverse mix of viewpoints in the private media through mandatory rights of access for those wanting to express views favored by Congress. The effects of such legislation would be immediate and profound. Owners of newspapers, radio stations, television stations, and cable systems would be obliged to engage in self-censorship, substituting the speech Congress preferred. By so doing, they would hope to avoid the wrath of government, legal expense, public outcry, and federal scrutiny. Hence, whether through direct compulsion by government or indirect coercion, the Personal Autonomy/Self-Fulfillment Model would be sacrificed. In addition, to minimize the risk of scrutiny by government regulators, the media would avoid criticism of government policy or policy-makers. Thus, the Self-Government/Checking-Value Model would also be impaired. Finally, the preferred views would likely become the predominant content of the media if government enforcement were particularly swift or consequential.

Therefore, the Marketplace of Ideas/Search for Truth Model would itself be sacrificed; innovations or discoveries that would have resulted from the free generation and exchange of ideas would be forfeited.

Or, consider a second example. Suppose the government subsidized the media presentation of certain kinds of information deemed in the "public interest." Assume that Congress provided the regulatory agencies with money to advertise. Assume the agencies could spend the money to promote public appreciation for their regulatory mandates. The primary results would be three-fold. While seeking to avoid offending the regulators, the media would tend to favor the government's advertising over comparably priced private advertising or even over their own programming. Furthermore, because the media would count on the government to pay cash on time and in full, its advertising would tend to be preferred. Last, because the government message would be an official pronouncement and because the media would not wish to invite federal inquiry, private messages opposing the public ones would tend not to be published or aired. One consequence of this government presence would be to reduce the amount of time or space available for publication of private matter, inducing a "crowding out" effect that would bid up the cost of remaining air time or advertising space. A second consequence would be that private ideas that would have ordinarily been presented would be supplanted by the government's message. Third, an official orthodoxy would be created as a result of the media's reluctance to present messages in opposition to the official ones. In short, effective self-censorship, induced by government, would impair the normal functioning of the models.

The normal functioning of the free speech and press models is possible only in the absence of government regulation. Consequently, to have meaning, the First Amendment must protect the private speech and press spheres from government.

THE FIRST AMENDMENT AS PROTECTOR RATHER THAN GUARANTOR

Considerable disagreement exists in academia over which free speech and press model should be viewed as embodying *the* central value of the First Amendment. Oliver Wendell Holmes believed that the Marketplace of Ideas/Search for Truth Model was central to the First Amendment.[29] Vincent Blasi has argued that the First Amendment's checking value is superior to the Personal Autonomy, Marketplace of Ideas, and Self-Government

Models of First Amendment construction.[30] Martin Redish disagrees with Holmes and Blasi; he submits, as Thomas Emerson did before him,[31] that the "constitutional guarantee of free speech ultimately serves only one true value . . . 'individual self-realization.' "[32] Alexander Meiklejohn believed the Self-Government Model was the only one protected by the First Amendment.[33] Although he no longer adheres to this thesis, Thomas Scanlon originally argued that the Personal Autonomy Model was *the* central value of the First Amendment.[34]

As expressed by these various scholars, the First Amendment *guarantees* the functional integrity of *one central* value either to the exclusion of or in preference to other values. The focus is result-oriented. The objective is to *create* and *sustain* a particular kind of free speech environment in service to the value espoused.

This result-oriented method is dangerous, for in arguing that the First Amendment *guarantees* a certain value, the various proponents of single-value construction either knowingly or unknowingly condone government regulation of the idea marketplace. A simple syllogism will illustrate the point. Major Premise: the First Amendment is designed to guarantee Value X; however, Value X is absent in the unregulated idea marketplace. Minor Premise: Government Speech Regulation Y will guarantee the existence of Value X. Conclusion: Government Speech Regulation Y must be imposed to ensure fulfillment of the First Amendment. In short, the result-oriented method of construing the First Amendment suggested by those who view the free speech and press models in a hierarchical manner condones rather than repudiates government regulation of communication. Viewing the First Amendment in this way invites the government to arm itself with powers to regulate speech and press when the very assumption of such powers (whether used to suppress speech generally or to enhance the speech rights of some at the expense of others) is antipathetic to the voluntary exchange of ideas.

If one considers the First Amendment to be a denial of government power, as James Madison did, it is entirely irrelevant whether free agents in the idea marketplace choose to engage in speech conducive to self-government, self-fulfillment, or truth-seeking. Indeed, Americans may decline to communicate, and this choice is provided the same degree of protection as the act of communicating. Decisions as to which free speech and press model is most valuable are left to each American. Differences are equally protected. There exists no lawful "preferred" mix of ideas, no required speech or disallowed speech. No free speech and press model is *mandated* by the First Amendment. Rather, each free model is descriptive of that government-free environment mandated by the First Amendment. Under this latter construct, when a free speech and press model fails to function properly, we do not focus on what form of government regulation may be imposed to alter the result. Rather, we focus on whether the malfunction is a result of government intervention or of private choice. If the former, the First Amendment is directly implicated. If the latter, no First Amendment issue arises.

A NEW APPROACH

If there is one lesson that the history of man's struggle for freedom of speech and press commands us to appreciate more than any other, it is that free speech and press are to reside in a protected private sphere. To ensure the unencumbered operation of the free speech and press models, the First Amendment must fulfill the essential role James Madison intended for it: it must serve as a static barrier against government regulation of communication. Moreover, to prevent this barrier from becoming porous, we must avoid limiting full First Amendment protection to the print media. Rather, we must understand "speech" and "press" to include not only the press of Madison's day but also the new media forms by which our people communicate ideas and information. In short, the approach advocated here is a *purposive* one, designed to protect the full intended scope of speech and press freedom regardless of the technological means selected to communicate or receive information.

This approach, termed the "Preservationist Perspective," is composed of two essential elements: (1) *Static Barriers* against government intervention and (2) *Adaptive Definitions* for the terms "speech" and "press."

The Static Barriers are designed to preserve the original protections of the private sphere that were made a part of the First Amendment in its formative years.[35] As Leonard Levy has explained, the amendment "was intended and understood to prohibit any congressional regulation of the press, whether by means of censorship, a licensing law, a tax, or a sedition act."[36] Any effort by government to invade the private speech and press sphere and to reorder existing relationships there will directly implicate the First Amendment and must be subjected to strict judicial scrutiny.

The Adaptive Definitions aspect of the Preservationist Perspective preserves the intended scope of the First Amendment's protective shield, despite the passage of time. This element is designed to prevent the amendment from becoming increasingly anachronistic, from being construed to condone precisely that intervention into a new medium that would clearly be unconstitutional were it to occur in an older print medium. The Adaptive Definitions aspect ensures that the protection afforded the print media and face-to-face communication will apply to all new media forms, guaranteeing that the Static Barriers remain virtually impenetrable, high, wide, and thick despite technological evolution. In this way, the compass of freedom from government will remain the same over time, and the essential antigovernment bias that is built into the amendment will retain its focus and potency.

The effect of the Preservationist Perspective is to rely on the private sphere as a self-correcting mechanism. Should the government attempt to violate the private sphere, it will be barred by a high constitutional barrier. Evidence of a violation would consist of proof of an adverse effect on the functioning of any free speech and press model. Under the Preservationist Perspective, government regulation of *who* may speak or *what* may be said would be strictly scrutinized and presumptively invalid.

ENDNOTES

1. *See generally* A. MEIKLEJOHN, POLITICAL FREEDOM: THE CONSTITUTIONAL POWERS OF THE PEOPLE 3 (1960); Bork, *Neutral Principles and Some First Amendment Problems*, 47 IND. L. J. 1, 21 (1971); BeVier, *The First Amendment and Political Speech: An Inquiry into the Substance and Limits of Principle*, 30 STAN. L. REV. 299 (1978); Brennan, *The Supreme Court and the Meiklejohn Interpretation of the First Amendment*, 79 HARV. L. REV. 1 (1965).

2. A. MEIKLEJOHN, POLITICAL FREEDOM: THE CONSTITUTIONAL POWERS OF THE PEOPLE 9 (1960).

3. *See generally* Blasi, *The Checking Value in First Amendment Theory*, 1977 AM. B. FOUND. RES. J. 523.

4. Greenawalt, *Free Speech Justifications*, 89 COLUM. L. REV. 119, 142 (1989).

5. *Roth v. United States*, 354 U.S. 476, 484 (1957).

6. *Stromberg v. California*, 283 U.S. 359, 369 (1931).

7. *New York Times Company v. Sullivan*, 367 U.S. 254, 270 (1964).

8. Milton, Areopagitica, *in* 4 THE WORKS OF JOHN MILTON 347 (F. Paterson ed. 1931).

9. 2 T. GORDON AND J. TRENCHARD, CATO'S LETTERS (L. Levy gen. ed.) 298–99 (Letter No. 100, *Discourse upon Libels*, Oct. 27, 1722) (1971 reprint).

10. Thomas Jefferson, First Inaugural Address, *reprinted in* JEFFERSON: WRITINGS 493 (M. Peterson ed. 1984).

11. J. MILL, ON LIBERTY 52 (S. Beer & O. Hardison, Jr., eds. 1947).

12. *Abrams v. United States*, 250 U.S. 616, 630 (1919) (Holmes, J., dissenting). *See also Whitney v. California*, 274 U.S. 357, 375 (1927) (Brandeis, J., concurring).

13. *United States v. Schwimmer*, 279 U.S. 644, 654–55 (1929) (Holmes, J., dissenting).

14. *See Whitney v. California*, 274 U.S. 357, 375–76 (1927) (Brandeis, J., concurring).

15. Solum, *Freedom of Communicative Action: A Theory of the First Amendment Freedom of Speech*, 83 Nw. U. L. Rev. 54, 68 (1989). *See also* M. Nimmer, Nimmer on Freedom of Speech § 1.02 (1984); F. Schauer, Free Speech: A Philosophical Enquiry 16 (1982); Baker, *Scope of the First Amendment Freedom of Speech*, 25 UCLA L. Rev. 964, 976–90 (1978); Ingber, *The Marketplace of Ideas: A Legitimizing Myth*, 1984 Duke L. J. 1.

16. Kent Greenawalt explains that "the truth-discovery justification combines a contained optimism that people have some ability over time to sort out true ideas from false ones with a realism that governments, which reflect presently concomitant assumptions and have narrow interests of their own to protect, will not exhibit requisite sensitivity if they get in the business of settling what is true." *See* Greenawalt, *Free Speech Justifications*, 89 Colum. L. Rev. 119, 131 (1989).

17. Blasi, *The Checking Value in First Amendment Theory*, 1977 Am. Bar Found. Res. J. 523, 550.

18. Solum, *Freedom of Communicative Action: A Theory of the First Amendment Freedom of Speech*, 83 Nw. U. L. Rev. 54, 77–78 (1989).

19. Baker, *Realizing Self-Realization: Corporate Political Expenditures and Redish's The Value of Free Speech*, 130 U. Pa. L. Rev. 646, 658–59 (1982).

20. Redish, *The Value of Free Speech*, 130 U. Pa. L. Rev. 591, 619 (1982).

21. *See, e.g.*, Redish, *The First Amendment in the Marketplace: Commercial Speech and the Values of Free Expression*, 39 Geo. Wash. L. Rev. 429 (1971); *see also* T. Emerson, The System of Freedom of Expression 6 (1970).

22. Redish, *The Value of Free Speech*, 130 U. Pa. L. Rev. 591, 628 (1982).

23. Solum, *Freedom of Communicative Action: A Theory of the First Amendment Freedom of Speech*, 83 Nw. U. L. Rev. 54, 80 (1989).

24. Redish, *The Value of Free Speech*, 130 U. Pa. L. Rev. 591, 630 (1982).

25. *Id.* at 627.

26. Solum, *Freedom of Communicative Action: A Theory of the First Amendment Freedom of Speech*, 83 Nw. U. L. Rev. 54, 80 (1989).

27. *See, e.g.*, Barron, *Access to the Press—A New First Amendment Right*, 80 Harv. L. Rev. 1641 (1967); Fiss, *Free Speech and Social Structure*, 71 Iowa L. Rev. 1405 (1986); Karst, *Equality as a Central Principle in the First Amendment*, 43 U. Chi. L. Rev. 20 (1975).

28.   Jaffe, *The Editorial Responsibility of the Broadcaster: Reflections on Fairness and Access*, 85 HARV. L. REV. 768, 786 (1972). *But see* Fiss, *Why the State?*, 100 HARV. L. REV. 781, 787 (1987) (where Fiss argues that the power of CBS to suppress speech is akin to the power of the FCC to suppress speech).

29.   *See, e.g., Abrams v. United States,* 250 U.S. 616 (1919).

30.   *See* Blasi, *The Checking Value in First Amendment Theory,* 1977 AM. B. FOUND. RES. J. 523, 544–67.

31.   *See, e.g.,* T. EMERSON, THE SYSTEM OF FREEDOM OF EXPRESSION 6 (1970).

32.   *See, e.g.,* Redish, *The Value of Free Speech,* 130 U. PA. L. REV. 591, 593 (1982).

33.   *See, e.g.,* A. MEIKLEJOHN, POLITICAL FREEDOM: THE CONSTITUTIONAL POWERS OF THE PEOPLE 9 (1960).

34.   Scanlon, *A Theory of Freedom of Expression,* 1 Phil. & Pub. Aff. 216 (1972). *But see* Scanlon, *Freedom of Expression and Categories of Expression,* 40 U. PITT. L. REV. 519 (1979).

35.   The Preservationist Perspective must exist in the world of the incorporation doctrine post-*Gitlow v. New York,* 268 U.S. 652 (1925), if it is to be useful to jurists and lawyers. Without evaluating the constitutional difficulties of that doctrine or its application in other contexts, I accept, for purposes of this analysis, the fact that the First Amendment has been made to apply to the states via the Fourteenth Amendment and believe, as James Madison did, that no state can truly be considered free without the protection for speech and press afforded by the First Amendment.

36.   L. LEVY, EMERGENCE OF A FREE PRESS 269–70 (1985).

PART III

PROTECTING THE CORE VALUES OF THE FIRST AMENDMENT IN THE NEW MEDIA AGE

If in the opinion of the People, the distribution or modification of the Constitutional powers be in any particular wrong, let it be corrected by an amendment in the way which the Constitution designates. But let there be no change by usurpation; for though this, in one instance, may be the instrument of good, it is the customary weapon by which free governments are destroyed.*

**George Washington, Farewell Address,* Sept. 19, 1796, *reprinted in* GEORGE WASHINGTON: A COLLECTION 521 (W. Allen ed. 1988).

11

THE ELECTRONIC PRESS AND THE INDUSTRY CAPTURE MOVEMENT

In the early twentieth century, the evolution of electronic technology paved the way for speech and press forms of great communicative reach and promise. The state of the law at that time was inadequate to meet the problems created by the new electronic media. As we have seen, the Supreme Court continued to rely on the Blackstonian definition of speech and press freedom well into the third decade of the twentieth century. The Court's general failure to form a developed theory of First Amendment protection for the traditional print media left the Court in no position to evaluate the free speech and press claims arising out of government efforts to suppress motion picture and radio industry activity.

In its 1915 decision, *Mutual Film Corp. v. Industrial Commission of Ohio*,[1] the Court first addressed free speech and press claims in the motion picture context. It considered whether a state law requiring prior approval from a board of censors before the exhibition of *any* film violated freedom of speech and press. Although the court briefs of both parties centered on free speech issues under the Ohio state constitution,[2] the Court, in construing that constitution, did not recognize censorship of motion pictures as involving either freedom of speech or of the press. Rather, relying on what it termed "common sense," the Court found that motion pictures do not constitute a "publication of ideas" and are not a "part of the press of the country," nor an "organ of public opinion."[3] In the minds of the Justices, a motion picture was akin to a carnival spectacle, not a work of literature.

This eighteenth-century mindset created an inhospitable legal environment for the unencumbered development of radio at the end of the nineteenth century. The government, especially the Department of the Navy and the U.S. Post Office, took an immediate interest in radio and endeavored to take control over the entire radio field. The interstate nature of radio made it an easy target for federal regulation. Congress would not be moved, however, until the 1920s, when private entrepreneurs suddenly used radio for mass communication and its propoganda potential caught the politicians' attention.

With the first general commercial use of radio for broadcasting, Congress discovered that whoever controlled radio possessed a means to persuade hundreds of thousands of people instantaneously. Congress admired and feared radio's great potential as the first national, spontaneous speech and press medium. They understood that the medium could be exploited to incumbents' political advantage if brought within the control of government. They believed the medium to be a source of great danger if left in the "uncontrolled hands" of individuals who, through the exercise of editorial discretion, could cause the medium to oppose the machinations and electoral desires of certain incumbents.

From 1922 until 1925, through a series of four national radio conferences, select representatives from the government's departments, members of Congress including the principal authors of the Radio Act of 1927, and radio industry leaders effected a tradeoff, a classic press-state symbiosis, which culminated in the most comprehensive system of press licensing America has ever known. The regulatory regime instituted then persists to this day and has recurred on the local level in regulation of the cable industry.

THE HISTORY OF RADIO AND OF EARLY GOVERNMENT EFFORTS TO CONTROL IT

In 1895, Guglielmo Marconi, an Italian physicist, was one of the first to demonstrate successfully that a message could be communicated by radio.[4] In 1896, he was awarded the first commercial patent for a radiotelegraph system.[5] The world's governments quickly became interested in the possibilities of radio. In 1903, representatives from Austria, France, Germany, Great Britain, Hungary, Italy, Russia, Spain, and the United States attended the First International Radio Telegraphic Conference in Berlin.[6] The conference reconvened in 1906 with 19 new nations' representatives in attendance.[7] Nations of the world began to use radio for military communication.

By 1904, twenty-four U.S. Navy ships were equipped with radiotelegraph systems and ten others were being similarly outfitted. A total of 200 shoreline radio stations were planned. Six such stations were already operated by the U.S. Army and one by the Weather Bureau. The U.S. Navy had erected twenty radio stations on the nation's shorelines, and about seven private companies had operational shoreline stations.[8]

That same year, at the direction of President Theodore Roosevelt, an Inter-Departmental Board was created to study the "entire question of wireless telegraphy" and to issue a report for the edification of the President. The Board consisted of two rear admirals and one lieutenant commander in the U.S. Navy, one brigadier general in the U.S. Army, and one person appointed to represent the interests of the Department of Agriculture. No representatives of private corporations operating wireless telegraphic stations were on the Board. In its report, the Board complained that private operators had interfered with some U.S. Navy ship-to-ship and ship-to-shore communications. To prevent this interference in the future, the Board recommended that the entire wireless telegraphy industry be placed "under full Government supervision." The Board's objective, however, was not simply to end interference. "Aside from the necessity of providing rules for the practical operation of such stations," wrote the Board, "it seems desirable that there should be some *wholesome supervision* of them to prevent *the exploitation* of speculative schemes based on public misconception of the art" [emphasis added]. The Board argued that government regulation of the new medium would prevent "control of wireless telegraphy by monopolies or trusts"—this despite an absence of evidence that the new art had fallen into a single, controlling private hand.[9] The President approved the Board's recommendations and had his secretary, William Loeb, Jr., order Secretary of the Navy Paul Morton to carry out these recommendations.[10]

In 1906, Reginald A. Fessenden, a Canadian who had worked with Thomas Edison, helped the General Electric Company produce the first continuous radio-wave transmission of the human voice, proving that the new art would not be confined to merely aiding ships at sea. Transmitting from General Electric's laboratories in Brant Rock, Massachusetts, Fessenden sent Christmas greetings to the U.S. Navy's ship operators. These greetings heightened the Navy's interest in removing the medium from private hands.[11]

Inspired by the fascinating new medium, amateur radio buffs began popping up everywhere. The materials necessary for creating a small amateur radio receiver or transmitter were almost universally available. Boy Scouts, country youth, college students, and the curious everywhere formed wireless clubs and, later, radio clubs to exploit the new technology. "Boys—and men—were constantly filing down nickels to make coherers, or winding wires around objects—broken baseball bats or, later on, Quaker Oats boxes," wrote Erik Barnouw. "In attics, barns, garages, woodsheds, apparatus took shape."[12]

Between 1907 and 1912, unregulated amateur radio use began to flourish in America, much to the consternation of the Navy. The Navy disapproved of the general dissemination of radio science, fearing that it would engender intolerable levels of interference and would endanger sea navigation. Increasingly, amateurs enjoyed trying to talk with Navy wireless operators. Knowledge of tuning was not well-developed at this early stage, and amateurs roamed the meter band in search of a responsive signal.[13]

The Navy never sought legislation establishing civil penalties for interference. Instead, it relied on the existence of sporadic interference to press its claim for full federal regulation over the entire radio field. The Navy insisted that the only solution was to declare the airwaves government property and the science of broadcasting exclusively within the government's domain. In Senate testimony concerning the Wireless Telegraphy Act of 1910, the Navy's spokesman described the situation thus:

> Calls of distress from vessels in peril on the sea go unheeded or are drowned out in the etheric bedlam produced by numerous stations all trying to communicate at once. . . . It is not putting the case too strongly to state that the situation is intolerable, and it is continually growing worse.[14]

Charles Nagel, Secretary of Commerce and Labor, echoed the Navy's sentiments in a 1911 report. He argued that the "ether is common property" and that private, unregulated use was fraught with peril, for "with the cheapest apparatus unrestrained trivial messages can create Babel."[15] He described private development of the art of telegraphy as wasteful duplication of government efforts and argued that further private development would bring either "wasteful" competition or monopoly.[16]

The Wireless Telegraphy Act of 1910[17] did not specifically address the Navy's concerns nor did it nationalize the private radio telegraphy industry in accordance with the suggestions of the Secretary of Labor and Commerce. Instead, it was designed to improve maritime safety in ship-to-shore and ship-to-ship communications by requiring all vessels that had more than 50 people aboard and that traveled between ports that were more than 200 miles apart to be equipped with efficient radio equipment. The Secretary of Commerce and Labor was vested with authority to enforce the Act.[18]

In 1912, Congress again considered the radio interference problem. It enacted the Post-Titanic Radio Communications Act,[19] which prohibited the use of any apparatus for radio communication unless the operator first obtained a license from the Secretary of Commerce and Labor. The Act required applicants to designate a specific wavelength on which they proposed to operate. The wavelength could not be between 600 and 1,600 meters. Ships were limited to wavelengths of 300 meters and 600 meters. The Act also prohibited private or commercial shore stations from using their transmitters during the first fifteen minutes of each hour, to prevent interference with naval vessels that reserved this time to transmit their signals and radiograms. Amateur operators were limited to a transmitting wavelength of up to 200 meters. The Act afforded the Secretary of Commerce and Labor the power to change the meter-band limitations and to revoke licenses for "good cause," although the Secretary was left powerless to deny any applicant a license.

A bit late in entering the political contest for control of radio, the Postmaster General drafted a report in 1913 in which he, like the Secretary of the Navy and the Secretary of Commerce and Labor, advocated that radio be brought under government control. Not surprisingly, the Postmaster General argued that the proper repository of regulatory power over the new medium was the Postal Service. He submitted that his powers would be derived from the Constitution under Article I, Section 8 ("Congress shall have Power. . . . To establish Post Office and post Roads"). After arguing that the "founders of this nation" would have wanted the Postal Service to own all means of communication, the Postmaster general noted that "[t]he United States alone of the leading nations has left to private enterprise the ownership and operation of the telegraph and telephone facilities" and concluded by advocating that "Congress declare a Government monopoly over all telegraph, telephone, and radio communication and such other means for the transmission of intelligence as may hereafter develop."[20]

With the United States' entry into World War I in 1917, private radio use was effectively suspended and replaced by Navy operations. By Executive Order, the President required 6,089 licensed amateur radio operators who were engaged in transmitting or receiving to discontinue their operations.[21] The Navy purchased almost all private coastal stations.[22] Following the war, the Navy argued strenuously before Congress that the government monopoly it enjoyed during the war should continue during peacetime, because radio, said Commander S. C. Hooper, is a natural monopoly; either the government must exercise that monopoly by owning the stations or it must place the ownership of these stations in the hands of some one commercial concern and let the government keep out of it.[23]

Secretary of the Navy Josephus Daniels expressed his "profound conviction" that radio "must be a monopoly" and believed it "up to the Congress to say whether it is a monopoly for the government or a monopoly for a company."[24]

However, at this moment, before the advent of mass communication by radio, Congress could not be persuaded to arrest the private development of the art. Instead, the peacetime regulation of radio communication was returned to the Secretary of Commerce.[25] The Secretary continued to issue licenses for private radio telegraphy, and the feared monopoly ownership of radio never materialized.

By 1920, it became apparent that radio was particularly well suited, not only for point-to-point communication, but also for mass communication. The switch in direction generated keen interest on the part of those in power who, in a very short time, established a comprehensive federal licensing scheme for the governance of the broadcast press. In 1920, commercial broadcasting to mass audiences commenced in earnest. This new use of radio technology was entirely unanticipated by the authors of the Radio Act of 1912.

From the very start, the Department of Commerce was predisposed to exercise control over the *content* of broadcasting. The Department first licensed broadcasting stations on two frequencies. Licenses for one frequency were expressly limited to stations "broadcasting news, concerts, lectures, and such matter."[26] Licenses for the other were limited to stations "broadcasting crop reports and weather forecasts."[27] In August 1922, the Department created a third class of stations that were termed "Class B" stations. These were awarded power levels between 500 and 1,000 watts; non-Class B stations were restricted to a maximum of 500 watts. The Department required the higher power Class B stations to use "[m]echanically operated musical instruments . . . only in an emergency and during intermission periods in regular program[s]." The Department also required these stations to maintain programming "satisfactory to the public" under threat of license revocation.[28]

MASS COMMUNICATION BY RADIO

Frank Conrad, a Westinghouse engineer in Pittsburgh, Pennsylvania, is one of those given credit for having first used radio to broadcast mass entertainment.[29] An amateur radio buff with considerable talent, Conrad constructed a transmitting unit in his garage and intermittently broadcast phonograph records. These transmissions caught the attention of other local amateurs and of one department store interested in capitalizing on the sale of radio receiving sets. The Joseph Horne department store published the following advertisement in the *Pittsburgh Sun* newspaper:

AIR CONCERT "PICKED UP" BY RADIO HERE

Victrola music, played into the air over a wireless telephone, was "picked up" by listeners on the wireless receiving station which was recently installed here for patrons interested in wireless experiments. The concert was heard Thursday night about 10 o'clock, and continued 20 minutes. Two orchestra numbers, a soprano solo—which rang particularly high and clear through the air—and a juvenile "talking piece" constituted the program.

The music was from a Victrola pulled up close to the transmitter of a wireless telephone in the home of Frank Conrad, Penn and Peebles avenues, Wilkinsburg. Mr. Conrad is a wireless enthusiast and "puts on" the wireless concerts periodically for the entertainment of the many people in this district who have wireless sets.

Amateur Wireless Sets, made by the maker of the Set which is in operation in our store, are on sale here $10.00 up.[30]

Harry P. Davis, Vice President of Westinghouse, saw this advertisement and realized that Westinghouse could make money if it had Conrad set up shop with the company. Thereafter, Westinghouse constructed a broadcasting facility for mass entertainment and capitalized on Conrad's work; it obtained a permit from the Secretary of Commerce to operate on 360 meters with the call letters KDKA on October 27, 1919.[31] The station became fully operational in November 1920. KDKA's opening broadcast was a popular success; for the first time, Americans heard presidential election returns by the radio wave.[32]

In 1921, a few more stations were presenting mass entertainment on the radio. In 1922, more than 500 commercial broadcasting stations were licensed by Secretary of Commerce Herbert Hoover. These began airing mass entertainment to audiences across the country. In the same year, technological innovations in transmitters and receivers greatly improved the quality of radio communication and enabled "a much greater number of transmitting stations . . . [to] be operated in . . . close proximity" than was possible in 1921.[33] Erik Barnouw describes the prolific growth in the industry:

So widespread was the feeling that broadcasting was a key to influence and power, that the rush was joined by many different interests. They included, not surprisingly, telephone and telegraph companies and the makers and sellers of electrical equipment. But educational institutions also took a prominent role. Scores of universities had long been active in radio experimentation and felt especially ready for this moment. By January 1923, broadcasting licenses had been obtained by 72 universities, colleges and schools, while many others prepared to follow. Newspapers were only very slightly less numerous; in the same period 69 newspapers became broadcasting licensees, along with 29 department stores, 12 religious organizations, several city governments, and a sprinkling of automobile dealers, theaters and banks.[34]

Licenses for broadcasting were available free of charge on application to the Secretary.

THE ZERO-PRICED SYSTEM

As the economist Thomas Hazlett has explained, this zero-priced system quickly produced an excess demand for authority to broadcast, causing Hoover to withhold licenses on grounds that interference would result.[35] When a Long Island licensee, Intercity Radio Company, sought a license renewal, Hoover denied it on grounds that no area frequency existed that would permit interference-free operation. In *Hoover v. Intercity Radio Co.*, the U.S. Court of Appeals for the District of Columbia held that by this action Hoover exceeded his statutory authority. The court determined that the Secretary lacked power under the Radio Act of 1912 to refuse a license to an applicant.[36]

Despite this holding, from 1923 until 1926, Secretary Hoover continued to limit the number of licenses that the Department issued by restricting the number of available frequencies, locations, and wavelength assignments, and by withholding action on a number of license applications.[37] The government's extreme limitation on the spectrum available for private use and on the issuance of licenses artificially limited broadcast opportunities while the concept of "free" licenses induced an artificially high demand among those who, under a market pricing structure, would have been eliminated from competition by price.

The limitation on available wavelengths rendered it difficult for more than one station to operate in any given region without causing objectionable interference.[38] Nevertheless, any objectionable interference was handled through private agreements among parties. This cooperation is remarkable in light of the explosive growth of commercial broadcasting from 1920 to 1927. In 1925, the number of licensed commercial broadcasting stations increased to almost 600.[39] Between July 1926 and February 1927, almost 200 additional stations went on the air.[40]

THE ABSENCE OF INTERFERENCE DURING A PERIOD OF SELF-REGULATION

Each year from 1922 to 1925, the Secretary of Commerce held four national radio conferences in which industry leaders negotiated with representatives of the government to establish regulations for the new medium. From 1920 to 1926, government regulation consisted largely of controls on the assignment of wavelengths. Agreements by licensees were relied on to avoid interference problems. No pervasive system of federal regulation existed until 1927. In the absence of regulation, the development of broadcasting continued apace. Private parties negotiated agreements to minimize interference problems, and the government protected property rights arising out of these agreements.[41] In the reports of the Commissioner of Navigation during this period, the Department of Commerce repeatedly commented on the industry's ability to voluntarily agree on methods of operation that would not produce objectionable interference. In his 1924 report, the Commissioner explained:

> During the last session of Congress another unsuccessful effort was made to amend our radio laws. Several radio bills were introduced but none passed. Cooperation has enabled us to function under the existing law without serious hardship to anyone.[42]

In his address to the Fourth National Radio Conference in 1925, Secretary Hoover recognized that from 1920 to 1925 the radio industry had largely been governed by self-policing and had been successful in its efforts until then.

> We have great reason to be proud of the results of these conferences. . . . We have accomplished this [the development of radio] by a large measure of self-government in an art and industry of unheard of complexity, not only in its technical phases but in its relations both to the Government and to the public. Four years ago we were dealing with a scientific toy; to-day we are dealing with a vital force in American life. We are, I believe, bringing this lusty child out of its swaddling clothes without any infant diseases. We have not only developed, in the conferences, traffic systems by which a vastly increasing

number of messages are kept upon the air without destroying each other, but we have done much to establish the ethics of public service and the response of public confidence.[43]

In his 1925 report, the Commissioner of Navigation reiterated that although the Department of Commerce desired regulation, it could not deny that the industry was succeeding without regulation.

In the absence of specific law to cover the rapidly changing radio conditions[,] your annual conferences with those directly concerned with the development of radio . . . have made it possible to proceed in a somewhat orderly manner, although it seems essential that we have a better legal foundation which will permit regulations to keep pace with the progress of the science and to extend the present radio organization so as to carry on this work in an efficient manner.[44]

The fact that cooperation was feasible would not be remarkable except for the fact that the conventional wisdom, expressed most notably by Justice Frankfurter in *NBC v. United States*,[45] has convinced many that without regulation chaos reigned.

THE INDUSTRY-CAPTURE MOVEMENT

The minutes of the First National Radio Conference in 1922 reveal that even at this early date, industry leaders clamored for government limits on the number of licenses issued; they sought protection against entry by new licensees. For its part, the government desired control over the industry's structure and programming content. Certain members of Congress, joined by Hoover, agreed with broadcast industry leaders that the system of broadcasting in the United States would be brought within the federal government's control. The classic monopoly rent/content control *quid pro quo* soon developed: in exchange for regulatory controls on industry structure and programming content, industry leaders would be granted the restrictions on market entry that they wanted. These restrictions would ensure monopoly rents for licensees and would provide the government with assurance that the broadcast industry would not oppose regulatory controls.

THE NATIONAL RADIO CONFERENCES (1922–25) AND THE "PUBLIC INTEREST" THEORY OF GOVERNMENT CONTROL

On February 27 and 28, 1922, Hoover convened the First National Conference on Radio Telephony, which was attended by radio broadcasters, amateur radio buffs, and government officials. The conference was governed by a committee of representatives from various government departments that were concerned with the burgeoning new radio phenomenon. Dr. S. W. Stratton, Director of the Bureau of Standards at the Department of Commerce, was chairman of the committee. Other members included Major General George O. Squier, representing the War Department; Captain Samuel W. Bryant, representing the Navy; J. C. Edgerton, superintendent of Radio Service for the Post Office; W. A. Wheeler, representing the Bureau of Markets and Crop Estimates of the Department of Agriculture; Congressman Wallace H. White, Jr., from Maine (later a sponsor of the House version of the Radio Act of 1927); R. B. Howell, representing the Post Office; Dr. Alfred N. Goldsmith, Secretary of the Institute of Radio Engineers; Hiram Percy Maxim, President of the American Radio Relay League; L. A. Hazeltine from the Stevens Institute of Technology; D. B. Carson, Commissioner of Navigation of the Department of Commerce; C. M. Jansky, Jr., from the University of Minnesota; and Edwin H. Armstrong from Columbia University.

At the outset of the conference, Hoover announced a principle to which none present objected: that the field of radio communications was "one of the few instances that I know of in this country where the public—all of the people interested—are unanimously for an extension of regulatory powers on the part of the Government."[46] He bore witness to the phenomenal growth of this new medium, describing it as "astounding" and noting that "over 600,000 . . . persons" possessed wireless receiving sets in 1922, while just one year before there were but "50,000 sets nationwide."[47] "We are indeed today upon the threshold of a new means of widespread communication of intelligence," he said.[48]

Hoover described the electromagnetic spectrum as a public resource, insisting that there be a "public right over the ether roads" so that there would be "no regret that we have parted with a great national asset into uncontrolled hands."[49] This sentiment was shared by Congressman White who, in a colloquy with A. H. Griswold of the American Telephone and Telegraph Company, expressed his preference for asserting government ownership over the new medium and gaining control over the content of broadcasts.

> MR. WHITE: I take it, Mr. Griswold, that you recognize the right and probably the duty of the Government to exercise more or less plenary control of the wave lengths that a particular concern can use.

> MR. GRISWOLD: Not only the right, but the desirability.

MR. WHITE: I suppose you would also conceive that the situation might arise where the government could limit the range within which you might operate and also control the subject matter of the distributions. To illustrate what I have in mind: I suppose the general public has a greater interest in crop reports than in advertisement of a particular theater. That might be so—Do you agree that the Government should have that right of control over the subject matter, granting the priority as to subject matter, or do you question that?

MR. GRISWOLD: I really had not considered it, Mr. White. I think that the proposition will seek its own level by the demands of the public for the kind of stuff they really want.

MR. WHITE: At the present time there seems to be a great conflict in demands. I want to know whether the situation might not arise where it would be necessary for the Government to grant privileges of priority as to subject matter.

MR. GRISWOLD: That might be necessary. I could not state whether it might be desirable or even necessary, but it is certainly something to think about.[50]

W. A. Wheeler, from the Department of Agriculture's Bureau of Markets and Crop Estimates, also expressed his department's interest in government control over content to ensure that crop, market, and weather information held primacy in broadcasting.

MR. WHEELER: Is it not a peculiar field of radio that it is particularly useful in transmitting information of very timely, of news interest, rather than information that can be obtained through other channels, and if any type of information should be put down lower in the scale it should be music and such entertainment as could be furnished in other hours, and those things of news interest and crop, weather and market information should have first order of importance.

MR. E. P. EDWARDS: I should be prone to agree with you but from comments I have heard on broadcasting you can get ten different opinions from ten different people. Personally, I like jazz but I am told my tastes are low.[51]

In their examination of Frank E. Doremus of the *Detroit News,* licensee of WWJ, and a Mr. Sherley, counsel for the Association of Manufacturers of Electronic Supplies, Hoover and Congressman White let their interest in government control be known. Asked Hoover: "Suppose we get into the period where there is [an] insufficient number of wave lengths and you find a given town where the program is not as high grade as another town; would you advocate the Government taking any supervision over the programs? Had you given any thought to that?" White raised the point with Sherley:

> MR. WHITE: I was interested in the Secretary's question as to whether the Government might not find itself more or less a sponsor for the moral tone of the entertainments. To bring this out, assume that another paper in Detroit established a broadcasting service and on one of the nights when you were going to broadcast a sermon by one of your pastors, this newspaper thought it would broadcast reports of a prize fight. Should the Government undertake to distinguish between these two grades of service? Now that is more a matter of joke, but it may become a serious question as to what control, if any, the Government should exercise over these matters.

* * * *

> MR. WHITE: There are classes of service. Broadcasting is a class of service. Can you subdivide that class, for instance, can you say that crop reports shall have a priority over baseball reports?

> MR. SHERLEY: Yes.

> MR. WHITE: If you admit that, where are you going to draw the line? Shall you give a priority to baseball over horseracing? How are you going to establish broadcasting if you don't go pretty close to censorship?

> MR. SHERLEY: You might give priority to sermons as against sporting news without giving any class the right to pass upon the character of service of either class.

> MR. WHITE: That goes back to the question, would we give priority to a sermon over a prize fight?[52]

Just as White, Hoover, and Wheeler indicated a desire that government exercise "plenary" control over the medium and the message, L. R. Krumm, representing the Westinghouse Electric and Manufacturing Company, revealed the sentiment of industry leaders that government must act to limit the number of new entrants into the broadcast marketplace, which would ensure market leaders high profits for broadcasting. He did so by arguing that it is government's duty to police the quality of broadcasting content to protect the public and by arguing that without government limitations on market entry, low-quality operations would crop up everywhere and interfere with the high-quality operations his own company offered.

Mr. L. R. Krumm: . . . [I]t is perfectly possible to establish a so-called broadcasting station for about $500 or $1,000 initial investment [as opposed to $15,000 which was a conservative estimate for the establishment of a "high quality" station] and the entertainment outlay represents nothing but phonograph records and that sort of a station can interfere very disastrously with such a station as we are trying to operate [broadcasting original entertainment, grand operas from Chicago, etc.], and that I think is the prime question before this Committee.

* * * *

There is a limitation to the number of broadcasting stations that can operate successfully and if you are going to get the desired results there must be some regulation and possibly limitation of the number of these stations. We can stand pat on our stations—operating them to the best of our ability—we hope to continue them and possibly extend them, but we want to know what the future holds for us in that regard.[53]

When asked whether he would continue with his broadcasting program if the American Telephone and Telegraph Company entered his market, Krumm said that he would, explaining that a new entry from an industry leader, AT&T, would be acceptable to him; it was just the thought of competition from several entities not now in the market that troubled him. Krumm said:

I do not want to pledge myself, but I see no reason why they [AT&T] cannot operate their stations without interfering with ours. We are not troubled by that Company as badly as a whole lot of stations—as we are by stations that do not represent any time, thought, or money.[54]

When asked by Hoover how many stations would be appropriate nationwide "to give the country a complete service," Krumm stated: "I believe twelve good stations, certainly a maximum of fifteen, would supply most of the needs of this country."[55]

H. F. Breckel of the Precision Equipment Company of Cincinnati, Ohio, explained the smaller licensees' position on barriers to entry, enunciating a one city/one station rule:

With reference to the number of broadcasting stations which should be permitted to operate, we believe that they should be limited to a number sufficient to provide adequate entertainment and safeguard the interests of the general public who have invested in receiving equipment and further, [we] . . . feel that it would be inadvisable to allocate more than one broadcasting station to a city.[56]

A study of the minutes of the First National Radio Conference exposes an unsurprising unanimity by broadcast industry leaders in advocating federal regulations that would limit market entry and an equally unsurprising unanimity by government regulators in demanding content control in exchange for regulatory protection. By the time of the Fourth National Radio Conference, the agreement to exchange market protection for programming control had been sealed.

Paul B. Klugh, President of the National Association of Broadcasters, presented resolutions that accepted without reservation the proposition that the Secretary of Commerce should control broadcast content under a "public interest" standard (with a preference for existing stations). The 1925 resolution reads in part:

> *Resolved,* That it be the sense of the National Association of Broadcasters that in any congressional legislation or pending such legislation that the test of the broadcasting privilege be based upon the needs of the listening public served by the proposed station. The basis should be convenience and necessity, combined with fitness and ability to serve, and due consideration should be given to existing stations and the services which they have established; . . . [57]

The government representatives of the national radio conference, in turn, adopted a resolution granting licensed broadcasters the assurance that new legislation would limit the number of licenses to ensure market protection for existing licensees.

> The committee considered the question, Is it essential to limit the number of broadcasting stations in order to prevent further congestion? The committee was unanimous in their views that the number of broadcasting stations should be limited, as there was ample evidence already at hand to show that serious congestion was taking place due to the large number of stations not having sufficient frequency separation or repeating frequencies to prevent interference. The committee felt that this was so much in evidence that little time need be spent on the question. They concluded that discussion by adopting the following resolution:
>
> *Resolved,* That it is the sense of this conference that the bands of frequencies now assigned to broadcasting [are] overcrowded, causing serious interference. Therefore, the committee recommends, in the interest of public service, that no new stations be licensed until through *discontinuance* the number of stations is reduced and until it shall be in the interest of public service to add new stations. [emphasis added][58]

Despite Hoover's appeals to Congress each year from 1922 to 1925, to regulate broadcasting, Congress did not enact the kind of comprehensive legislation that he and industry leaders wanted until 1927.[59] In each of the conferences following the first, government leaders continued to state that content regulation was a paramount federal objective. In the Third National Radio Conference, Hoover remarked that "[i]t is not the ability to transmit but the *character* of what is transmitted that really counts" [emphasis added].[60] Hoover understood there to be a federal obligation "to see that . . . [radio] is devoted to *real* service and to develop the material that is transmitted into that which is *really* worthwhile" [emphasis added].[61]

As early as the First National Radio Conference in 1922, Secretary of Commerce Hoover had said that the "ether" was a "public" medium. By the Fourth National Radio Conference in 1925, he had developed a theory that the entire broadcasting industry was one necessarily imbued with a "public" character, that is, a nature that must be under government controls to ensure that it presented programming in the "public interest." At the Fourth National Radio Conference he said:

> The ether is a public medium, and its use must be for public benefit. The use of a radio channel is justified only if there is public benefit. The dominant element for consideration in the radio field is, and always will be, the great body of the listening public, millions in number, countrywide in distribution. There is no proper line of conflict between the broadcaster and the listener, nor would I attempt to array the one against the other. Their interests are mutual, for without the one the other could not exist.[62]

In Hoover's view, the broadcaster's freedom of speech had to be suppressed to ensure the propagation of a "preferred" message, one tailored by government for the benefit of the listening public. He assumed that programming in the "public interest" would not be profitable and so would not be presented.

The programming that the public desired to hear and that advertisers would support was not regarded by Hoover as synonymous with the programming that the public *should* hear. Rather, in Hoover's view, the government could, and indeed must, determine for the public what it should hear. In short, the public interest standard that Hoover wanted was in fact government control over broadcast content. Hoover believed that government would have to determine what programming was in the public interest, for, as the Commissioner of Navigation of the Department of Commerce admitted in his report of 1924, "the broadcast listener is an unknown quantity. . . . An accurate expression of its views is unobtainable."[63]

Hoover thought that radio was an industry destined for monopoly, and he feared that the industry would be dominated by a select few who would hold great power over public opinion, irrespective of their program offerings.[64] Despite this fear, Hoover nevertheless trusted the government, the single most pervasive monopoly in our society, with power to control the content and structure of broadcasting. Stated Hoover:

> We hear a great deal about the freedom of the air; but there are two parties to freedom of the air, and to freedom of speech, for that matter. There [are] the speechmaker and the listener. Certainly in radio I believe in freedom for the listener. He has much less option upon what he can reject, for the other fellow is occupying his receiving set. The listener's only option is to abandon his right to use his receiver. Freedom cannot mean a license to every person or corporation who wishes to broadcast his name or his wares, and thus monopolize the listener's set.[65]

Hoover's views were to form the theoretical basis for radio regulation. He, Congressman Wallace H. White, and Senator C. C. Dill pressed for and eventually attained enactment of comprehensive regulation of the electronic press, but not, however, before Hoover and certain industry leaders (who favored regulation) set in motion events that led inexorably to a predictable "breakdown" in the system of self-regulation. In his closing remarks at the Fourth National Radio Conference, Hoover predicted, on the basis of the sound understanding given him by allies in the House and Senate, that comprehensive federal regulation would soon come to pass.[66] From now on, the government would presume to know "the actual needs of the radio public," and its presumptions would form the basis of regulatory restraints on radio programming.

THE INDUCEMENT OF CHAOS

In the legislative history underlying the Radio Act of 1927, there is a startling pronouncement by Senator Key Pittman of Nevada. Breaking with those backing the new legislation, Senator Pittman charged that private forces lobbying for the bill had created an environment of broadcast interference to secure the monopoly protection afforded by the legislation. The proposition is difficult to prove, but few would deny that the industry certainly had a major economic incentive to participate in such a scheme. Pittman said it was curious that after six years of comparatively successful self-policing of radio interference, the industry now, during the debates on the bill, experienced widespread interference. He believed the new interference wars were a ploy by broadcasters to induce public support for legislation that would shield existing licensees from competition. Announced Pittman on the Senate floor February 18, 1927:

> Oh, yes; of course the radio broadcasters of this country want this bill passed. Does anyone doubt that? Do not Senators know that nearly every telephone company in the United States in every little town is getting someone to send a telegram saying, "Pass this bill"? What do the senders of those wires know about it? Why was it that just recently broadcasting concerns of the West all changed their wave lengths, sometimes a hundred degrees, to have them conflict, and the next day said, "If you do not pass this bill, you will have that same condition for another year"? Why have we not had that for a year? Why does it happen just now?
>
> Mr. President, I do not believe I am naturally suspicious, but when telegrams pour in from all over the United States to Senators from people who know nothing about this legislation, and cannot know anything about it, urging its passage, I know the stimulus comes from somewhere, and where should the stimulus come from for the passage of this bill?
>
> This bill is fair to only one institution. It is fair to the monopoly that will be created under it. The monopoly that may be created under it is practically free of control. There is nothing in the bill about charges, there is nothing in it about service, [and] there is nothing in it about discrimination, unless a complainant goes to another body created by another law for another purpose and there makes his protest.[67]

Senator Robert B. Howell of Nebraska voiced similar concerns about lobbying by broadcasters. Stated Howell on the Senate floor, February 18, 1927:

> As this bill now stands, it is what the great radio interests want. They are supporting it from every corner of the United States. They are telling their listeners, necessarily unacquainted with its details, that a filibuster is in progress against the measure, that it is in danger, and that if their listeners want the air cleared up, to wire their Senators immediately to pass the bill. Not stopping there, they are charging individual Senators, including myself, with attempting to kill the bill through filibuster, although, as previously pointed out, up to to-day I have occupied the Senate floor upon this subject, from the time the bill was introduced in 1925 until now, but 48 minutes. Why such misrepresentation? Merely a determination to leave no stone unturned to force through this bill as reported by the conferees, and thus preserve, if possible, their claimed vested rights.[68]

For years the conventional wisdom, set forth in *NBC v. United States,* has been that private market forces and efforts at self-policing from 1920 to 1926 failed and could not avert substantial interference that drowned out audible reception. Recently, in a pioneering work for the *Journal of Law and Economics*,[69] Thomas Hazlett presented evidence that adds credence to the view that the interference problems of 1926 were precipitated in principal part by government and by cooperative broadcast industry efforts. Hazlett's work supports the proposition that Hoover's licensing policies up to 1926 created definable property rights in the spectrum that were freely traded and substantially protected. It lends support to the position that government leaders feared that such rights could become vested, freeing licensees from government content controls.

Hazlett explains that from 1920 to 1926, "the pricing mechanism was the institutional tool that was used to allocate frequencies."[70] The private market system existed from the moment a license was awarded. "Trades of spectrum rights were commonplace," he writes. He finds "that such chaos as potentially could exist was explicitly remedied by federal establishment of property rights, followed by market trading to assign such rights to their highest valued employments."[71]

The licensing system itself inflated market demand, for license applications could be filed and licenses could be obtained at no cost. However, from 1920 until 1926, Hoover artificially kept demand in check by rationing operating times, frequencies, and locations, despite the holding in *Intercity Radio Co.* that denied him the authority to withhold licenses. Limitations on available wavelengths left some significant interference problems, but by and large private operators negotiated agreements among themselves to minimize the interference.[72] This system worked well until about July 1926.[73]

From November 1925 until April 1926, Hoover suddenly stopped issuing new licenses, contending that "it is a simple physical fact that we have no more channels."[74] In April 1926, in *United States v. Zenith Radio Corporation,* the U.S. District Court for the Northern District of Illinois determined that the Radio Act of 1912 did not authorize the Secretary of Commerce to deny the issuance of licenses or to require operation on a precise wavelength or under certain time constraints not specifically provided for in the Act. On June 4, 1926, Hoover solicited an opinion on the meaning of the case from Acting Attorney General William Donovan. Donovan confirmed the correctness of the Court's decision.[75] Hoover then abandoned all attempts at regulation, exacerbating the excess demand for free, yet valuable licenses. In the words of Senator C. C. Dill, Hoover "issued everybody a license who . . . made application, and that has brought the present chaos."[76]

Hoover's decision to grant more licenses created an environment conducive to interference.[77] A purported "breakdown of the law" ensued, leading President Calvin Coolidge to lament in December 1926:

> Due to the decisions of the courts, the authority of the department [of Commerce] under the law of 1912 has broken down; many more stations have been operating than can be accommodated within the limited number of wave-lengths available; further stations are in [the] course of construction; many stations have departed from the scheme of allocation set down by the department; and the whole service of this most important public function has drifted into such chaos as seems likely, if not remedied, to destroy its great value.[78]

By his decision to abandon any attempt at regulation, Hoover had provoked a crisis. He had already obtained the agreement of the broadcast industry's leaders to accept content controls, and, along with Congressman White, Senator Dill, and key members of both Houses, he was committed to providing the protection from new market entrants that the industry wanted. The "crisis" precipitated by radio industry and government action created the necessary impetus and justification for enacting comprehensive federal controls.

Although aware of the free-market alternative, neither Congress nor Hoover seriously considered a property rights approach. That approach would have placed the broadcast medium in "uncontrolled hands" and would have denied Hoover and his allies in Congress the authority that they wanted. Accordingly, they adopted the public interest justification for regulation first articulated by Hoover at the Fourth National Radio Conference.

THE REJECTED ALTERNATIVE:
A PROPERTY RIGHTS APPROACH

WGN, owned by The Tribune Company, had been broadcasting on frequency 990 KHz for a few years. In November 1926, the company filed suit in Circuit Court against Oak Leaves Broadcast Station, Inc., licensee of a new facility which broadcast in a manner that caused WGN to suffer objectionable levels of interference. The court held that the common law concept of "priority of time" created a "superiority in right" and ordered Oak Leaves to modify its operations to avoid interference.[79] The court noted that the unregulated media marketplace had developed its own rights definition for broadcasting.[80]

Fully aware of the court's common law solution (indeed the court's decision was reprinted in the *Congressional Record* for the year 1926 at page 216), Congress rejected it.

Again and again Representatives and Senators raised concerns not about interference (which was in fact a secondary matter for those debating the radio act) but about the pervasive, instantaneous, and influential nature of the new medium. Congress appears to have been fixated on the great promise of the medium, to have feared its use as a political weapon against incumbents, and to have wanted to prevent industry leaders from having the discretion to deny giving political candidates access to the airwaves. As a part of their campaign to pass the Radio Act of 1927, many in Congress contended, despite significant evidence to the contrary, that the medium would devolve into a private monopoly if not controlled by a state monopoly.

Once again, those in power had set the stage for a recurrence of the monopoly rent/content control *quid pro quo* established in the time of Henry VIII. The only major difference was in the sophistication of the dialogue. Unlike Henry VIII, the American politicians of the twentieth century had artfully covered their true intentions with a more digestible, public interest coating.

ENDNOTES

1. *Mutual Film Corp. v. Industrial Commission of Ohio,* 236 U.S. 230 (1915).
2. *See* Rabban, *The First Amendment in Its Forgotten Years,* 90 Yale L. J. 514, 532 n.74 (1981).
3. *Mutual Film Corp. v. Industrial Commission of Ohio,* 236 U.S. 230, 244 (1915).
4. Marconi was not alone. In the 1860s, Scottish physicist James Clark Maxwell "predicted the existence of radio waves." *See* Broadcasting/Cablecasting Yearbook 1988 at A–1. German physicist Heinrich Rudolph Hertz demonstrated that radio waves could be transmitted through space. *Id.* Many other scientific minds contributed to early knowledge about the fundamental aspects of wireless telegraphy. *See generally* S. Douglas, Inventing American Broadcasting: 1899–1922 (1987).
5. *See* L. White, The American Radio 11 (1971).
6. *Id.* at 7.
7. *Id.*
8. J. Robinson, Spectrum Management Policy in the United States, An Historical Account 6 (U.S. Federal Communications Commission, Office of Plans and Policy Working Paper Series, Apr. 1985); *[U.S.]*

Inter-Departmental Board [on] Wireless Telegraphy: Inter-Departmental Board Appointed by the President to Consider the Entire Question of Wireless Telegraphy in the Service of the National Government, Washington, D.C., 1904, in 1 DOCUMENTS IN AMERICAN TELECOMMUNICATIONS POLICY 7 (J. Kittross ed. 1977).

9.   *Id.* at 6–11.

10.   *Id.* at 3. In a letter of June 13, 1902, then Secretary of War William Howard Taft wrote the President a letter that revealed his concern that the Navy's advocacy of government control was an unnecessary and self-serving one:

> After reading the report of the Secretary of Agriculture I am by no means certain that the Navy Department ought to have control of all governmental stations for wireless telegraphy. It seems to me that it would be sufficient for the joint Naval and Army Board in time of peace to keep a record of all stations, both public and private, with power in the Navy Department to assume control of them in time of war. Provision as to control of private stations would probably need legislative action.

Id. at 18.

11.   E. BARNOUW, A TOWER IN BABEL 20 (1966).

12.   *Id.* at 28.

13.   Writes Barnouw:

> The relation of amateur to governmental authority was a topic of growing interest during the years 1907–1912, when [Everett L.] Bragdon [radio editor of the New York *Globe* in 1921] was experimenting in Maine. Ship traffic off the Maine coast was heavy, and included navy ships moving in and out of Portland. Every amateur "felt that the world was his to explore," and that he had the right to talk with anyone he could reach. Bragdon in Westbrook and two or three experimenters in Portland spent night after night "going up and down the dial" trying to talk to the steamship *Belfast* on her way east along the coast or the *North Star* out of Portland en route to New York. For a time there seemed no limit to the readiness of ship operators to converse. But so many official messages were blotted out that naval authorities became increasingly testy, and then indignant, about amateur interference.

Id. at 31.

14.   S. Rep. No. 659, 61st Cong., 2d Sess. 4 (1910); *see also* E. KRASNOW, L. LONGLEY, & H. TERRY, THE POLITICS OF BROADCAST REGULATION 10–16 (1982).

15.   *Selections from Reports of the Department of Commerce and Labor, 1911, in* 1 DOCUMENTS IN TELECOMMUNICATIONS POLICY 669 (J. Kittross ed. 1977).

16. Stated Secretary Nagel:

> [The] Government system is duplicated at some points and to a greater or less[er] degree of efficiency by commercial stations owned and operated by four or five corporations. . . . Waiving the matter of national defense, the dual system of Government and private shore stations means wastefulness to the people of the United States. This waste . . . must increase as competing companies extend their plants and duplicate among themselves apparatus, stations, and operators, or one company will in time absorb the others and establish a monopoly.

> *Id.* at 673.

17. Wireless Telegraphy Act of June 24, 1910, Pub. L. No. 61–262, 36 Stat. 629 (1910).

18. *Print and Electronic Media: The Case for First Amendment Parity,* Committee on Commerce, Science and Transportation, U.S. Senate, S. Print 98–50, 98th Cong., 1st Sess. 23–24 (May 3, 1983).

19. Radio Communications Act of Aug. 13, 1912, Pub. L. No. 62–264, 37 Stat. 302 (1912).

20. *Government Ownership of Electrical Means of Communication, in* 1 DOCUMENTS IN AMERICAN TELECOMMUNICATIONS POLICY 5–13 (J. Kittross ed. 1977).

21. *Selection from Reports of the Department of Commerce, 1917, in* 1 DOCUMENTS IN AMERICAN TELECOMMUNICATIONS POLICY 999 (J. Kittross ed. 1977).

22. *See* J. ROBINSON, SPECTRUM MANAGEMENT POLICY IN THE UNITED STATES, AN HISTORICAL ACCOUNT 28 (U.S. Federal Communications Commission, Office of Plans and Policy Working Paper Series, Apr. 1985).

23. *Quoted in* E. BARNOUW, A TOWER IN BABEL 53 (1966).

24. *Id.*

25. *Selection from Reports of the Department of Commerce, 1920, in* 1 DOCUMENTS IN TELECOMMUNICATIONS POLICY 952 (J. Kittross ed. 1977).

26. *See* J. Rosenbloom, *Appendix I, Authority of the Federal Communications Commission, in* FREEDOM AND RESPONSIBILITY IN BROADCASTING 100–1 (1961).

27. *Id.*

28. *Id.* at 101.

29. E. BARNOUW, A TOWER IN BABEL 67–69 (1966).

30. *Id.* at 68.

31. *Id.* at 68–69.

32. I. DE SOLA POOL, TECHNOLOGIES OF FREEDOM 112 (1983).

33. *Selection from Annual Report of the Commissioner of Navigation to the Secretary of Commerce for the Fiscal Year Ended June 30, 1922, in* 1

DOCUMENTS IN AMERICAN TELECOMMUNICATIONS POLICY 17 (J. Kittross ed. 1977).

34.   E. BARNOUW, A TOWER IN BABEL 4 (1966).

35.   *See* Hazlett, *The Rationality of U.S. Regulation of the Broadcast Spectrum*, 33 J. L. & ECON. 133, 139 (1990).

36.   *Hoover v. Intercity Radio Co.*, 286 F. 1003 (App. D.C. 1923).

37.   Hazlett, *The Rationality of U.S. Broadcast Regulation of the Broadcast Spectrum*, 33 J. L. & ECON. 133, 141 (1990).

38.   See *Print and Electronic Media: The Case for First Amendment Parity*, Committee on Commerce, Science and Transportation, U.S. Senate, S. Print 98-50, 98th Cong., 1st Sess. 25-28 (May 3, 1983), wherein it is noted:

> As late as 1919, the Radio Division of the Department of Commerce had allocated only two wavelengths for radio transmission. The 600 meterband was to be used for private broadcasting and the 485 meterband had been allocated for government broadcasting functions such as weather and crop reports. Thus, only one private broadcasting station could be accommodated in a given locale. . . .
>
> By 1921, the Commerce Department had allocated one more wavelength, [the] 400 meterband, for the transmission of private broadcasts, thus ostensibly accommodating two full-time radio stations per area.

39.   *See NBC v. United States*, 319 U.S. 190, 211 (1943).

40.   *See Id.* at 190, 212.

41.   In his testimony before the First National Conference on Radio Telephony in 1922, Max Loewenthal of the Pacific Radio Trade Association of San Francisco, California, explained:

> We on the Coast feel that we have given to the radio world an example of practical cooperation, having solved the broadcasting problem to the satisfaction of all interests. This we have done by deciding upon a broadcasting schedule based upon a division of hours rather than upon various wave lengths. All the stations operate on 360 meters and a printed schedule, which I am herewith leaving with you, is strictly adhered to by all of the stations.

Minutes of Open Meetings of Department of Commerce Conference on Radio Telephony, Feb. 27 and 28, 1922, at 54.

42.   *Selection from Annual Report of the Commissioner of Navigation to the Secretary of Commerce for the Fiscal Year Ended June 30, 1924, in* 1 DOCUMENTS IN AMERICAN TELECOMMUNICATIONS POLICY 20 (J. Kittross ed. 1977).

43.   *Proceedings of the Fourth National Radio Conference and Recommendations for Regulation of Radio,* Nov. 9-11, 1925.

44. *Selection from Annual Report of the Commissioner of Navigation to the Secretary of Commerce for the Fiscal Year Ended June 30, 1922, in* 1 DOCUMENTS IN AMERICAN TELECOMMUNICATIONS POLICY 18 (J. Kittross ed. 1977).

45. 319 U.S. 190 (1943).

46. *Minutes of Open Meetings of Department of Commerce Conference on Radio Telephony,* Feb. 27 and 28, 1922, at 1.

47. *Id.* at 2.

48. *Id.*

49. *Id.* at 4–5.

50. *Id.* at 11.

51. *Id.* at 25–26.

52. *Id.* at 92, 95–96. Later, in introducing his bill for comprehensive regulation of radio in the first session of the 69th Congress, before the House Committee on the Merchant Marine and Fisheries, Congressman White reiterated his view that content regulation was inevitable:

> Of course, it has always been my belief and is now, that ultimately someone will have to determine and fix priorities as to subject matter. In the bill of last year, which this committee reported out, the department was given not only authority to prescribe the nature of the service to be rendered, but to establish priorities as to subject matter. In the draft this year, I dropped that reference as to priorities, because of the fear which had been expressed by so many to me that [the priorities] did confer something akin to censorship. But my conviction is that sooner or later there will have to be some authority to establish priorities as to subject matter, to determine specifically whether church music will have a right of way, for instance, during the hours of Sunday when church services are held.

> *Hearings Before the Committee on the Merchant Marine and Fisheries,* House of Representatives, 69th Cong., 1st Sess. on H.R. 5589, Jan. 6, 7, 14, and 15, 1926, 39–40 (1926).

53. *Minutes of Open Meetings of Department of Commerce Conference on Radio Telephony,* Feb. 27 and 28, 1922, at 33–34.

54. *Id.* at 43.

55. *Id.* at 36.

56. *Id.* at 107a.

57. *Proceedings of the Fourth National Radio Conference and Recommendations for Regulation of Radio,* Nov. 9–11, 1925, at 10.

58. *Id.* at 22–23. *See also* Hazlett, *The Rationality of U.S. Regulation of the Broadcast Spectrum,* 33 J. L. & ECON. 133, 153 (1990). ("In November 1925 . . . the radio broadcast market was developing well, radio set sales

were brisk, programming was expanding, and interference from rival broadcasters was not an issue. What was at issue was the ability of the Secretary of Commerce to exclude new requests for spectrum space.")

59. Following the radio conference of 1922, Secretary of Commerce Herbert Hoover recommended to Congress that it enact legislation to afford him "broad powers of supervision, regulation and control." *See Selection from Annual Report of the Commissioner of Navigation to the Secretary of Commerce for the Fiscal Year Ended June 30, 1922, in* 1 DOCUMENTS IN AMERICAN TELECOMMUNICATIONS POLICY 18 (J. Kittross ed. 1977).

Reflecting upon the failure of Congress to adopt the legislation recommended by the Department in 1922, the Commissioner of Navigation of the Department of Commerce wrote: "The radio bill designed to give to the Secretary of Commerce the authority needed to better control radio communication, which was introduced in the last session of Congress, was passed by the House, but was not taken up for consideration by the Senate. The need for new legislation, such as recommended last year, has not diminished." *See Selection from Annual Report of the Commissioner of Navigation to the Secretary of Commerce for Fiscal Year Ended June 30, 1923, in* 1 DOCUMENTS IN AMERICAN TELECOMMUNICATIONS POLICY 18 (J. Kittross ed. 1977).

Reflecting upon the failure of Congress to adopt the legislation recommended to it by the Department of Commerce in 1923, the Commissioner of Navigation wrote: "During the last session of Congress another unsuccessful effort was made to amend our radio laws. Several radio bills were introduced but none passed." *See Selection from Annual Report of the Commissioner of Navigation to the Secretary of Commerce for the Fiscal Year Ended June 30, 1924, in* 1 DOCUMENTS IN AMERICAN TELECOMMUNICATIONS POLICY 20 (J. Kittross ed. 1977).

Sentiments similar to these were voiced by the Commissioner of Navigation in his reports for Fiscal Years 1925 and 1926. *See Selection from Annual Report of the Commissioner of Navigation to the Secretary of Commerce for the Fiscal Year Ended June 30, 1925, and Selection from Annual Report of the Commissioner of Navigation to the Secretary of Commerce for the Fiscal Year Ended June 30, 1926, in* 1 DOCUMENTS IN AMERICAN TELECOMMUNICATIONS POLICY 18, 20 (J. Kittross ed. 1977).

60. *Recommendations for Regulation of Radio,* adopted by the Third National Radio Conference, Herbert Hoover, Secretary of Commerce, Oct. 6–10, 1924, at 2.

61. *Id.* at 2–3.

62. *Proceedings of the Fourth National Radio Conference and Recommendations for Regulation of Radio,* Nov. 9–11, 1925, at 7.

63. *Selection from Annual Report of the Commissioner of Navigation to the
     Secretary of Commerce for the Fiscal Year Ended June 30, 1924, in* 1
     DOCUMENTS IN AMERICAN TELECOMMUNICATIONS POLICY 22 (J. Kittross
     ed. 1977).

64. *Hearings Before the Committee on Interstate Commerce,* U.S. Senate, 69th
     Congress, 1st Sess. on S. 1 and S. 1754 (Bills Reaffirming the Use of the
     Ether for Radiocommunication or Otherwise to be the Inalienable Posses-
     sion of the People of the United States and their Government, Providing
     for the Regulation of Radiocommunication, and for Other Purposes),
     Mar. 1 and 2, 1926, at 285. Speaking on behalf of Secretary Hoover and
     the Department of Commerce, Department of Commerce Solicitor Stephen
     B. Davis remarked:

> Of course, the purpose of [the proposed radio] commission is very
> evident, and it is a purpose that Secretary Hoover and the department
> are in entire sympathy with, and that is to bring about a situation where
> there is not a one-man control of radio. I agree, and Secretary Hoover
> agrees with everything that has been said before this committee along
> that line, that no one individual should be entrusted with the control of
> a situation as important as this is today and as important as it will be
> still more in the time to come.

65. *Proceedings of the Fourth National Radio Conference and Recommenda-
     tions for Regulation of Radio,* Nov. 9–11, 1925, at 7.

66. Hoover remarked:

> Much work has been done in past sessions of Congress looking to radio
> legislation. I cannot speak too highly of the constructive effort expended
> by Representative Wallace White and his committee associates in the study
> of radio needs and the preparation of measures to meet them; but until
> the present time I think we have all had some feeling of doubt as to the
> precise course which legislation should take, for changes have been so
> rapid and conditions so shifting that no one was ready to try to chart
> an exact course. I am glad that Congressman White and other members
> of the House and Senate committees are with us in this conference.
> I am certain that they have a hearty sympathy with, and understanding
> of, the actual needs of the radio public.

     Id. at 9.

67. 68 CONG. REC. 4111 (1927).

68. *Id.* at 4153.

69. Hazlett, *The Rationality of U.S. Regulation of the Broadcast Spectrum,* 33
     J. L. & ECON. 133, 145 (1990).

70. *Id.*
71. *Id.*
72. In his testimony before the U.S. Senate Committee on Interstate Commerce in January 1926, Department of Commerce Solicitor Davis spoke plainly to the point, admitting that private agreements among parties during the period from 1920 to 1926 had successfully averted interference problems.

> Senator Burton K. Wheeler of Montana asked: "What is done to control what goes out; what is broadcast?"
>
> Solicitor Davis responded: "Absolutely nothing, so far as the department [of Commerce] is concerned. We have no authority to do it, and there has never been anything in the way of censorship of program direction. The whole situation has been handled to a very considerable extent through annual conferences which the Secretary has called, and at which all of the different radio interests, including the radio public, have been represented. In those conferences the persons interested have to a considerable extent gotten together and made their own rules and regulations. And they have adopted certain resolutions which have been pretty well complied with, as to the use of radio stations, and as to what we now are doing."

Hearings Before the Committee on Interstate Commerce, U.S. Senate, 69th Cong., 1st Sess. on S. 1 and S. 1754, Jan. 8 and 9, 1926, at 24.

73. Hazlett, *The Rationality of U.S. Regulation of the Broadcast Spectrum,* 33 J. L. & ECON. 133, 147 (1990).
74. *See* J. Rosenbloom, *Appendix I, Authority of the Federal Communications Commission, in* FREEDOM AND RESPONSIBILITY IN BROADCASTING 109 (1961).
75. *Id.* at 112; *see also* 35 Ops. Atty. Gen. 126 (1926).
76. CONG. REC., 68 3031 (1927).
77. Rosenbloom, *Appendix I, Authority of the Federal Communications Commission, in* FREEDOM AND RESPONSIBILITY IN BROADCASTING 112 (1961).
78. *Id.* at 113.
79. *Tribune Co. v. Oak Leaves Broadcasting Station* (Cir. Ct., Cook County, Ill., 1926), *reprinted in* 68 CONG. REC. 216 (1927).
80. Explained Chancellor Francis S. Wilson:

> So far as broadcasting stations are concerned, there has almost grown up a custom which recognizes the rights of the various broadcasters, particularly in that certain broadcasters use certain hours of the day, while the other broadcasters remain silent during that particular period of time. Again, in this particular locality, a certain night is set aside as silent night, when all local broadcasters cease broadcasting in order that radio receivers may be able to tune in on outside distant stations.

Wavelengths have been bought and sold and broadcasting stations have changed hands for a consideration. (Broadcasting stations have contracted with each other so as to broadcast without conflicting and in this manner be able to present their different programs to the waiting public.) The public itself has become educated to the use of its receiving sets so as to be able to obtain certain particular items of news, speeches, or programs over its own particular sets.

The theory of the bill in this case is based upon the proposition that by usage of a particular wavelength for a considerable length of time and by reason of the expenditure of a considerable amount of money in developing its broadcasting stations and by usage of a particular wavelength educating the public to know that the particular wavelength is the wavelength of the complainant and by furnishing programs which have been attractive thereby [causing] a great number of people to listen in to their particular programs that the said complainant has created and carved out for itself a particular right or easement in and to the use of said wavelength which should be recognized in a court of equity and that outsiders should not be allowed thereafter, except for good cause shown, to deprive them of that right and to make use of a field which had been buil[t] up by the complainant at a considerable cost in money and a considerable time in pioneering.

Quoted in Hazlett, *The Rationality of U.S. Regulation of the Broadcast Spectrum,* 33 J. L. & Econ. 133, 150–51 (1990).

12

THE LEGISLATIVE HISTORY OF THE RADIO ACT OF 1927

In March 1926, the House Committee on the Merchant Marine and Fisheries began consideration of a bill for comprehensive federal regulation of radio. The bill was authored by Congressman Wallace H. White. Despite statements made by Department of Commerce Solicitor Stephen B. Davis, Jr. (also known as Judge Davis), that broadcast licenses were held by a diverse number of interests,[1] Congressman White railed against an alleged monopoly said to be arising in the manufacture of radio receiving sets and said to be on the verge of taking over the entire broadcasting industry.[2]

White deemed this concern a principal justification for regulation of programming content and industry structure.[3] In his testimony before the committee, Secretary Hoover joined White in demanding that the Congress not allow the "newborn system of communication to fall exclusively into the power of any individual, group, or combination."[4] Reiterating his theory supporting the regulation of radio, Hoover asked the committee to treat the businesses engaged in radio broadcasting as utilities that must not be conducted for private gain but must be forced to serve the "public interest."[5] In addition and in accordance with the *quid pro quo* established at the Fourth National Radio Conference, Hoover emphasized that "from the viewpoint of public service, we need fewer stations rather than more, and the present bill permits the correction of this."[6]

Department of Commerce Solicitor Davis confirmed that the purpose of the House bill was "to prevent any further increase" in the number of licensees.[7] When asked by Congressman Frank R. Reid whether such a purpose might not "tend to give a monopoly to those now in existence," Davis responded: "It will tend to give a substantial right to all the existing broadcasting stations. There can be no question whatever about that."[8] Congressman White said that a regulated monopoly would be far less egregious than an unregulated one in broadcasting, for "individual and corporate censorship" would be far worse than "government censorship."[9]

In May 1926, the Chairman of the Senate Committee on Interstate Commerce, Senator C. C. Dill, began work to secure Senate passage of a comprehensive bill for the regulation of radio. Dill recognized what he termed "the probable influence [the medium] will develop . . . in the social, political and economic life of the American people" and urged that "the use of the rights of way of every radio station . . . be retained under the control of the Government." He believed that "all power to regulate radio communication should be centered in one independent body, a radio commission, granting it full and complete authority over the entire subject of radio."[10]

After admitting that the Department of Commerce had not allotted all spectrum that could feasibly be allotted for broadcasting use,[11] Davis conceded to the committee that the goal of the Department had been to protect existing licensees against potential new market entrants. "There is only room for a certain number of stations in a given locality," Davis said. "We have never seen any reason for throwing out the people who are already in and putting in a newcomer, so we have protected the existing situation [as] far as possible."[12]

The House and Senate committees submitted their bills to both houses of Congress. In the Senate, Dill emphasized what has since become known as the spectrum scarcity rationale for regulation, pointing out that the number of available channels was limited under present scientific conditions. This, submitted Dill, was another principal reason why regulation was necessary.[13]

Repeatedly, senators expressed their concern that the medium was in danger of being controlled by a select few who could deny coverage to certain political topics and, most particularly, could deny members of the Senate an opportunity to present their campaign messages. Federal content controls could alleviate this problem, they argued. Each discussion of the right of access for candidates for federal office was carefully couched in public interest terms. The monopoly argument too was used to bolster the contention that the public would be denied what it should be permitted to hear. Senator Robert B. Howell of Nebraska opined:

I think it was the view of the committee that if any subject was to be presented to the public by any of the limited number of stations, the other side should have the right to use the same forum; and if such privilege were not to be granted, then there should be no such forum whatever. . . .

Mr. President, to perpetuate in the hands of a comparatively few interests the opportunity of reaching the public by radio and allowing them alone to determine what the public shall and shall not hear is a tremendously dangerous course for Congress to pursue. Only recently a public official called my attention to the fact that he was invited to utilize a radio station of one of the great broadcasting companies; that when he appeared to speak they insisted on censoring his remarks and blue-penciled certain portions criticizing "Pittsburgh plus." They said, "You cannot talk about that." Are we to consent to the building up of a great publicity vehicle and allow it to be controlled by a few men, and empower those few men to determine what the public shall hear? . . .

If any public question is to be discussed over the radio, if the affirmative is to be offered, the negative should be allowed upon request also, or neither the affirmative nor the negative should be presented.[14]

The senators recognized the persuasive potential of the medium and argued that regulation was essential to prevent America's youth from being subjected to mind control by media barons. Howell argued: "[T]he larger portion of the radio audience is the youth of the country. Give me control of the character of the matter that goes out over our broadcasting stations and I will mold the views of the next generation."[15]

In the House, Congressman White voiced the same concerns expressed by Dill and Howell. The available channels were all in use; unless the federal government imposed comprehensive regulation on the broadcast industry, there would soon be a "complete breakdown of broadcasting service in the United States."[16]

Congressman Ewin L. Davis, like Howell, objected to affording broadcasters freedom of editorial choice to deny air time to candidates whose views they opposed:

[Broadcast licensees] can permit one candidate to be heard through their broadcasting stations and refuse to grant the same privilege to his opponent. They can permit the proponents of a measure to be heard and can refuse to grant the opposition a hearing.[17]

Congressman Thomas Lindsay Blanton lamented that "one candidate might be able to pay $1,000 for one night's service over the radio, and another candidate might not be able to put up anything, and the radio could shut that man out and let the other in."[18] He asked insistently: "What are you going to do about this question? The night before election some fellow who might be favored by the Radio Corporation could get up in a Congressman's district and, with favored access to the radio, ruin any man running for Congress."[19] Congressman William R. Johnson predicted:

> If the strong arm of the law does not prevent monopoly ownership and make discrimination by such stations illegal, American thought and American politics will be largely at the mercy of those who operate these stations. For publicity is the most powerful weapon that can be wielded in a Republic, and when such a weapon is placed in the hands of one, or a single selfish group is permitted to either tacitly or otherwise acquire ownership and dominate those who dare to differ with them, it will be impossible to compete with them in reaching the ears of the American people.[20]

Unlike in the Senate, these views in the House met with significant opposition. Congressman Arthur M. Free refuted the notion that a monopoly on the production of receiving sets would affect the public's reception of radio or the number of firms that would engage in broadcasting. Besides, Free explained, there simply was no monopoly. The competing concerns included the Atwater-Kent Manufacturing Co.; A. H. Grebe & Co.; Splitdorf Manufacturing Co.; Stromberg-Carlson Manufacturing Co.; DeForest Radio Co.; Charles Freshman Co.; Crosley Radio Corporation; Andrea, Stewart-Warner; and Bosch Magneto.[21] Free explained that 350 companies manufactured radio sets and 1,600 made radio parts.[22] He said that although radio tubes originally sold for about $6, the price had steadily declined to about $2.50, and they could be bought for as little as $1.10 because of the presence of "general competition in every line [of production]."[23] Furthermore, a monopoly was unlikely to ever arise in the manufacture of receiving sets, for

> any boy can take, as my boy did, a bolt, a little wire, and a crystal, which costs him a few cents, and make a radio set, and he can listen in on any program anywhere in the United States. If he wants a little bit better set he can take a little bit more wire, a few more nuts and bolts, and get a tube, and he can make a tube set, paying $2.50 for the tube.[24]

Free also said that of the 536 broadcasting stations operating in the United States, only 12 were operated by the so-called "cross-licensed monopolies." Free believed there to be but "one monopoly in this thing . . . the individual listener" who with the turn of a dial could end receipt of a radio transmission: "The minute he turns off his set and refuses to listen, just that minute the radio is gone so far as the sellers of sets are concerned."[25] Free also found service in the public interest to be a by-product of natural market forces:

[Broadcast licensees] must put on good programs; they must maintain the public interest because the public is their asset. When they sell time to an advertiser, they have got to show that you and other people are listening, and if they cannot show that they cannot get money for broadcasting.[26]

The Radio Act of 1927 passed the House and Senate on February 18, 1927, after conferees, through a compromise, vested primary licensing authority in the Federal Radio Commission for a year (the power to be returned thereafter to the Secretary of Commerce with an appellate role reserved for the Commission).[27] Congress, however, three times renewed the authority of the Commission to act independent of the Secretary and the last time did so "until otherwise provided by law," which was until enactment of the Communications Act of 1934.[28]

With the support of Congress, the Federal Radio Commission interpreted the Radio Act of 1927 to permit it broad leeway in making content-based licensing determinations. The Commission kept Secretary Hoover's promise to existing broadcasters, grandfathering their rights to broadcast and "eliminating marginal competitors and all new entry."[29]

ENDNOTES

1. In his testimony before the Senate Committee on Interstate Commerce, Davis presented Department statistics establishing that no single owner controlled the broadcast industry as of January 1926. The evidence revealed that 536 licenses were outstanding and 250 applications were on file with the Department. He explained the following: stores dealing in radio supplies operated 124 broadcast stations; schools and colleges operated 94 broadcast stations; churches operated 43 broadcast stations; publishers of newspapers and magazines operated 35 broadcast stations; manufacturers of various kinds operated 30 broadcast stations; states, counties, and municipalities operated 15 broadcast stations; insurance companies and similar businesses operated 15 broadcast stations; hotels operated 12 broadcast stations; societies of various kinds operated 11 broadcast stations; and entities of various kinds operated the remaining 22 broadcast stations. This diffuse ownership was possible despite the imposition of restrictions by the Department of Commerce on the allocation of bandwidth for broadcasting. See *Hearings Before the Committee on Interstate Commerce*, U.S. Senate, 69th Cong., 1st Sess. on S. 1 and S. 1754 (Bills Reaffirming the Use of the Ether for Radiocommunication

or Otherwise to be the Inalienable Possession of the People of the United States and Their Government, Providing for the Regulation of Radiocommunication, and for Other Purposes), Jan. 8 and 9, 1926, at 20.

2. On January 15, 1923, the House Committee on the Merchant Marine and Fisheries issued a report expressing its concern that "certain companies and interests" were trying to establish "a monopoly in wireless communication through control of the manufacture and sale of radio instruments, through contractual arrangements giving exclusive privileges in the transmission and exchange of messages or through other means." The committee recommended that this matter be investigated and that "appropriate action [be] considered at an early date." In an apparent response to this recommendation, Congress adopted a resolution that called upon the Federal Trade Commission "to investigate and report to the House" concerning these matters so that the House might determine whether the antitrust laws were being violated.

   The FTC reported to the House on December 1, 1923. The report was said to demonstrate "that patents were being used to obtain a monopoly of radio apparatus, and that there were many factors tending to lessen competition in the field of radio." On January 25, 1924, responding to pressures from Congress, the FTC filed a complaint against the General Electric Company, the American Telephone and Telegraph Company, Western Electric Company, Westinghouse Electric and Manufacturing Company, International Radio Telegraph Company, United Fruit Company, Wireless Specialty Apparatus Company, and Radio Corporation of America. The complaint alleged that these companies had engaged in "unfair methods of competition" and that they had tried to create "monopolies in the 'manufacture, purchase, and sale, in interstate commerce, of radio devices and apparatus, and other electrical devices and apparatus, and in domestic and transoceanic radio communication and broadcasting.' " After compiling a voluminous amount of testimony in the case, the FTC chose not to prosecute and dismissed its complaint on December 19, 1928. *See* Lovett, *The Antitrust Provisions of the Radio Act*, 2 J. RADIO L. 5–6 (1932).

   Increasingly, those who argued that the industry was falling prey to the monopolists relied on this report and echoed Hoover, who insisted that the radio industry be subject to some sort of public utility regulation. *See also* E. BARNOUW, A TOWER IN BABEL 60 (1966).

3. *Regulation of Radio Communications*, H.R. REP. No. 464, 49th Cong., 1st Sess., Mar. 5, 1926, at 4.

4. *Id.*

5. *Id.*

6. *Hearings Before the Committee on the Merchant Marine and Fisheries*, House of Representatives, 69th Cong., 1st Sess. on H.R. 5589, Jan. 6, 7, 14, and 15, 1926, at 10.

7. *Id.* at 38.
8. *Id.* at 38.
9. *Regulation of Radio Communications*, H.R. REP. NO. 464, 49th Cong., 1st Sess., Mar. 5, 1926, at 16. Congressman Ewin L. Davis shared these concerns, stating that he was "even more opposed to private censorship" than to government censorship. 67 CONG. REC. 5484 (1926). The historical evidence quite clearly demonstrates that the leading congressional advocates of comprehensive federal regulation (Congressman Davis and Senator White) and Hoover understood that the new legislation would create a lawful monopoly (through restrictions on the licensing of any new stations) in exchange for the censorial powers granted to the state. A December 5, 1924, letter from Hoover to White (inserted in the *Congressional Record* by Davis) in part reads: "There is growing up a demand for the limitation of the number of stations in a given area, and that such a limitation would be based on the service needs of the community, just as public utilities are generally limited by the rule of public convenience and necessity. . . . [T]his enters a dangerous field of recognizing monopoly and implied censorship." J. Rosenbloom, *Appendix I, Authority of the Federal Communications Commission, in* FREEDOM AND RESPONSIBILITY IN BROADCASTING 107-8 (1961).
10. REGULATION OF RADIO TRANSMISSION, S. REP. NO. 772, 69th Cong., 1st Sess., May 6, 1926, at 1-3.
11. *Hearings Before the Committee on Interstate Commerce*, U.S. Senate, 69th Cong., 1st Sess. on S. 1 and S. 1754, Jan. 8 and 9, 1926, at 30, 34:

> SENATOR [ROBERT B.] HOWELL: And . . . this field [of radio broadcasting] could be very much broadened if the Department of Commerce saw fit to broaden the field?
>
> MR. DAVIS: That is correct.

12. *Hearings Before the Committee on Interstate Commerce*, U.S. Senate, 69th Cong., 1st Sess. on S. 1 and S. 1754, Jan. 8 and 9, 1926, at 88.
13. 67 CONG REC. 12335 (1926).
14. *Id.* at 12503-04.
15. *Id.* at 12504.
16. *Id.* at 5479.
17. *Id.* at 5483.
18. *Id.*
19. *Id.* at 5489.
20. *Id.* at 5558.
21. Congressman Frank Crowther concurred with these views of Congressman Free, explaining:

Now, Mr. Chairman, overnight almost, an invention may upset this whole condition of control that exists now. There has been a great deal of attention and a good deal of discussion about the monopolistic tendency that may develop under this legislation. I want to say that so far as the manufacture of the products is concerned, I do not think there is anything in the United States that is as free from danger of monopolistic control as radio apparatus, parts, and complete sets.

The fact of the matter is, gentlemen, in one of the most expensive instruments made to-day, costing from $200 to $300, there is not a thing used in the construction of that instrument that cannot be constructed by the average bright, intelligent American young man from 15 to 18 years of age. He can make everything that is in that set. He can buy the materials, he can buy individual parts, and he can construct a set for probably $50 to $75 that commercially sells as high as $300. You may think the latter price is high, but they have combined furniture with radio building and customers are now largely buying furniture in the shape of fancy cabinets, consoles, and so on, which appeal to the artistic ideals of our American women.

Id. at 5562.

22.   *Id.* at 5490.

23.   *Id.*

24.   *Id.* at 5490–91. Joel Rosenbloom has astutely observed that monopoly claims "lent urgency to the demand that Congress act before rights which the courts might construe as vested and immune to governmental action could be established." *See* J. Rosenbloom, *Appendix I, Authority of the Federal Communications Commission, in* Freedom and Responsibility in Broadcasting 106 (1961).

25.   67 Cong. Rec. at 5491 (1926).

26.   *Id.*

27.   J. Rosenbloom, *Appendix I, Authority of the Federal Communications Commission, in* Freedom and Responsibility in Broadcasting 113 (1961).

28.   *Id.* at 141.

29.   Hazlett, *The Rationality of U.S. Regulation of the Broadcast Spectrum,* 33 J. L. & Econ. 133, 154 (1990); *see also* 1 F.R.C. Ann. Rep. 11 (1927).

13

THE FEDERAL
RADIO COMMISSION

The Radio Act of 1927 created a comprehensive licensing scheme to control not only what frequencies would be available for public use but also who would be permitted to use them and, to a degree, what content would be permitted over-the-air. The system was similar to the licensing regime established by the Crown and Parliament in the sixteenth and seventeenth centuries. It coupled a police power to enforce its judgments with a promise of monopoly protection, thereby taunting and tempting the press into broadcasting in a manner favored by the government.

The Act created a five-member commission of licensors, the Federal Radio Commission, which was to implement its provisions and the will of Congress. The Act empowered the FRC to classify radio stations; prescribe service limitations; assign wavelengths; determine class locations and power levels; regulate stations carrying network programming; require that programming logs be maintained by licensees; and grant, renew, and deny licenses.[1] One pervasive, virtually limitless standard was to govern the FRC's exercise of discretion: the "public interest, convenience or necessity."[2] The FRC was given broad power to revoke licenses if licensees violated its regulations, made false representations to the FRC, or did not abide by the technical standards of the station license.[3]

The Act specified that if a candidate for public office were granted access to a broadcasting facility, the licensee must afford other candidates for the same office a reasonable opportunity to broadcast.[4] Through the license renewal process, the FRC controlled the content of all broadcasting. It was "the prerogative of the FRC" to examine programming content:

> The character of the programs furnished is an essential factor in the determination of [the] public interest but a most difficult test to apply, for to classify on this basis is to verge on censorship. . . . But in spite of the troublesomeness, these very features may be the controlling consideration in Commission decisions.[5]

The system was premised on a utility regulation model. Under the FRC's regulatory regime, broadcasters were deemed "public trustees" who were "privileged" to use a scarce public resource. So characterized, broadcasters were obliged to abide by model standards of conduct established by the FRC to ensure programming that was responsive to community problems, needs, and interests.[6] The FRC summarized its theory this way:

> [Despite the fact that] the conscience and judgment of a station's management are necessarily personal, . . . the station itself must be operated as if owned by the public. . . . It is as if people of a community should own a station and turn it over to the best man in sight with this injunction: "Manage this station in our interest. . . ." The standing of every station is determined by that conception.[7]

In practice, most licensees found it prudent to abide by the FRC's programming preferences to avoid either a loss of license or a costly renewal challenge. From the beginning, broadcasters took these threats seriously. They knew they had no property right in the spectrum and were entirely beholden to the government for their authority to operate.

Early in its history, the Federal Radio Commission made clear that it intended to use its license revocation powers to punish broadcasters whose view of public interest programming significantly deviated from its own. Such deviations violated the original *quid pro quo.* The D.C. Circuit Court, in cases such as *Great Lakes Broadcasting Co.*[8] and *Chicago Federation of Labor,*[9] not only condoned the FRC's content-based determinations but also engaged in content scrutiny of its own in assessing the merits of the FRC's action.

The Radio Act did contain an anticensorship provision that read, in part:

> Nothing in this Act shall be understood or construed to give the licensing authority the power of censorship over the radio communications or signals transmitted by any radio station, and no regulation or condition shall be promulgated or fixed by the licensing authority which shall interfere with the right of free speech by means of radio communication.[10]

On the face of it, this provision would seem to bar the FRC from controlling content. But because of the courts' adherence to Blackstone's conception of freedom of the press, what would now pass for censorship was then merely viewed as a permissible "subsequent punishment." In *KFKB Broadcasting Association, Inc. v. FRC,*[11] the Circuit Court of Appeals for the District of Columbia, as in so many other cases, found that because the FRC had not attempted "to subject any part of appellant's broadcasting matter to scrutiny prior to its release" a license revocation based on *content* was entirely permissible.[12] Thus the anticensorship provision was deemed inapplicable.

In 1927, the FRC expounded at length on the plenary nature of its authority over programming:

> [We are] . . . unable to see that the guaranty of freedom of speech has anything to do with entertainment programs as such. Since there are only a limited number of channels and since an excessive number of stations desire to broadcast over these channels, the commission believes it is entitled to consider the program service rendered by the various applicants, to compare them, and to favor those which render the best service. If one station is broadcasting commercial phonograph records in a large city where original programs are available and another station is broadcasting original programs, for which it is making a great financial outlay, the commission believes that the second station should be favored and that the question of freedom of speech is not involved.[13]

Three notorious cases from the time reveal the FRC's preoccupation with broadcast content. The cases, although atypical factually, are representative of the extent to which the FRC considered regulation of content well within its jurisdiction. In practice, the FRC had institutionalized a bureaucratic cadre of roving speech police whose aim it was to rein in all broadcasters whose programs were not in accordance with the FRC's own conception of programming in the public interest.

THE CASE OF DR. BOB SHULER

The Reverend Doctor Bob Shuler was an irascible man who also happened to be a broadcast licensee. Shuler referred to himself as "Fighting Bob," "a scrapper for God."[14] His Los Angeles station, KGEF, was authorized to operate twenty-three and one-quarter hours per week. The lively program Shuler broadcast was self-righteous and unorthodox, involving criticism of the government, of certain religions, and the low state of public morality.

No sinner passed without suffering Dr. Shuler's derision. Lucas Powe records that Dr. Shuler lambasted the mayor of Los Angeles for purportedly allowing a gangster to run the city and for altering the course of a boulevard to have it run by the gangster's property. He accused the chief of police of protecting mob figures, accused the police department of engaging in a coverup and murder, castigated the district attorney and the chief deputy for allegedly taking bribes, and argued that the bar association favored judges who would not invoke stiff penalties for vice.[15] He also voiced antisemitic and anti-Catholic views during his program.[16]

In 1931, as required, Dr. Shuler applied for a license renewal. Members of the public filed petitions to deny the application and a hearing was held. Although the presiding officer opted for renewal, on appeal to the full FRC, the commissioners reversed. The D.C. Circuit Court upheld the FRC on appeal. The court decision reveals the great power over content that the FRC could lawfully wield and the anemic state of the First Amendment in the area of broadcast regulation. The court expressly affirmed the FRC's scrutiny of content, finding such regulation not merely within the FRC's discretion but a "duty" necessarily exercised in the proper assessment of renewal applications. Wrote the court:

> However inspired Dr. Shuler may have been by what he regarded as patriotic zeal, however sincere in denouncing conditions he did not approve, it is manifest, we think, that it is not narrowing the ordinary conception of "public interest" in declaring his broadcasts—without facts to sustain or to justify them—not within that term, and, since that is the test the Commission is required to apply, we think it was its duty in considering the application for renewal to take notice of appellant's conduct in his previous use of the permit, and, in the circumstances, the refusal, we think, was neither arbitrary nor capricious.[17]

The FRC had based its determination not to renew Shuler's license almost entirely on adverse determinations concerning content. As the Circuit Court summarized, "Some of the things urging [the Commission] to this conclusion were that the station had been used to attack a religious organization . . . [and] that the broadcasts . . . were sensational rather than instructive."[18] Shuler argued that, among other things, the FRC's decision violated his First Amendment rights. The court summarily rejected the notion that Shuler's freedom of speech was transgressed by the FRC's decision. Wrote Judge D. Lawrence Groner:

> [I]f it be admitted, as we think it must be, that, in the present condition of the science with its limited facilities, the regulatory provisions of the Radio

Act are a reasonable exercise by Congress of its powers, the exercise of these powers is no more restricted by the First Amendment than are the police powers of the States under the Fourteenth Amendment.[19]

THE CASE OF DR. J. R. BRINKLEY

Like Shuler, Dr. J. R. Brinkley was an unorthodox expositor of controversial subjects. Unlike Shuler, Brinkley concerned himself with the physical rather than the moral ailments of his listeners. He claimed to be a medical doctor and his quest was to turn a profit by touting the medicinal benefits of the various elixirs he concocted. Brinkley's station, KFKB, served a broad expanse from the Rockies to the Mississippi River.[20] Licensed to serve Milford, Kansas, his sizeable business was located in "one of eight states that would recognize his degree from Eclectic Medical University of Kansas City."[21] Station KFKB, the publicity arm of "Brinkley Hospital" and "Brinkley Pharmaceutical Association," served as a diagnostic center and mail order pharmacy.[22] In a program entitled the "Medical Question Box," Brinkley would read aloud letters sent to him by ailing listeners. He would diagnose their diseases and then prescribe an elixir from his store of drugs. The D.C. Circuit Court quoted from two such medical question box responses delivered by the doctor on KFKB:

> Here's one from Tillie. She says she had an operation, had some trouble 10 years ago. I think the operation was unnecessary, and it isn't very good sense to have an ovary removed with the expectation of motherhood resulting therefrom. My advice to you is to use Women's Tonic No. 50, 67, and 61. This combination will do for you what you desire if any combination will, after three months persistent use.
>
> * * * *
>
> Sunflower State, from Dresden Kans. Probably he has gall stones. No, I don't mean that, I mean kidney stones. My advice to you is to put him on Prescription No. 80 and 50 for men, also 64. I think that he will be a whole lot better. Also drink a lot of water.[23]

On April 1, 1930, a broadcast day said to be typical, Dr. Brinkley "prescribed for forty-four different patients and in all, save ten, he advised the procurement of from one to four of his own prescriptions."[24]

Few would doubt the medical impropriety of dispensing drugs without in-person diagnoses, but for the Federal Radio Commission the most important question concerned whether the *content* of Brinkley's broadcasts (rather than of his elixirs) was in the public interest. When KFKB applied for license renewal, the FRC determined, following a thorough assessment of the broadcasts, that renewal would not be in the public interest. The D.C. Circuit Court affirmed the FRC's decision, explaining that "because the number of available broadcasting frequencies is limited," the FRC has the authority to "consider the character and quality of the service to be rendered" and the "past conduct" of the licensee, for, as the court noted, quoting from Matthew VII:20, "by their fruits ye shall know them."[25]

The court cited approvingly the FRC's Second Annual Report of 1928, which had warned broadcasters against consuming "much of the valuable time allotted to them under their licenses in matters of a distinctly private nature which are not only uninteresting, but also distasteful to the listening public."[26] The court conceived the FRC's action not to be censorship, preferring a Blackstonian understanding of the term. The court found no prior restraint and deemed the subsequent penalty of laws appropriate even if it involved a judgment predicated solely on content. Wrote the court: "In considering the question whether the public interest, convenience, or necessity will be served by a renewal of appellant's license, the commission has merely exercised its undoubted right to take note of appellant's past conduct, which is not censorship."[27]

THE CASE OF NORMAN BAKER

Like Shuler and Brinkley, Norman Baker broadcast the unorthodox, and for that he paid. Baker was the licensee of station KTNT, Muscatine, Iowa. He regularly denounced a great number of people and institutions whose views or actions caused him discomfort. He also enjoyed submitting to the world his "cancer cure ideas." The commissioners found what Baker said and the way he said it intolerably offensive. In June 1931, his license came up for renewal. After examining Baker's broadcasts, the FRC issued its condemnation notice:

> This Commission holds no brief for the Medical Associations and other parties whom Mr. Baker does not like. Their alleged sins may be at times of public importance, to be called to the attention of the public over the air in the right way. But this record discloses that Mr. Baker does not do so in any high-minded way. It shows that he continually and erratically over the air rides a personal hobby, his cancer cure ideas and his likes and dislikes of certain persons and things. Surely his infliction of all this on the listeners is not the proper use

of a broadcasting license. Many of his utterances are vulgar, if not indeed indecent. Assuredly they are not uplifting or entertaining.

Though we may not censor, it is our duty to see that broadcasting licenses do not afford mere personal organs, and also to see that a standard of refinement fitting our day and generation is maintained.[28]

In the cases of Shuler, Brinkley, and Baker, we see that early in its regulatory life the Federal Radio Commission established precedent for the exertion of great influence over broadcast content. Although private suits could provide redress for fraud or libel perpetrated by licensees, the FRC took it upon itself to determine what content would be suitable for the public to hear. It was not enough for the FRC to regulate *who* would be permitted to have access to the airwaves. The FRC also found it necessary to determine *what* would be said.

THE PERVASIVENESS OF CONTENT CONTROLS

In determining which of two competing applicants would be permitted to improve its facilities, the Federal Radio Commission required the submission of evidence concerning "their past records of service, their program resources, etc." In assessing applications for renewal of license, the FRC required applicants to document the average amount of time devoted to entertainment, religious, educational, agricultural, and other programs, and to demonstrate how their programming served the "public interest, convenience or necessity."

In its General Docket No. 32, the FRC subjected 164 licensees to strict content review in response to public protests against these licensees' programming. In these proceedings, the FRC challenged the licensees to prove the public interest benefits of their service.[29]

In its 1929 *Great Lakes Broadcasting Co.* decision, the FRC again warned broadcasters that it deemed a certain mix of programming to be requisite to a finding of public interest benefit. Wrote the FRC:

The tastes, needs, and desires of all substantial groups among the listening public should be met, in some fair proportion, by a well-rounded program, in which entertainment, consisting of music of both classical and lighter grades, religion, education and instruction, important public events, discussions of public questions, weather, market reports, and news, and matters of interest to all members of the family find a place. . . . Insofar as a program consists of discussion of public questions, [the] public interest requires ample play for the free and fair competition of opposing views, and the Commission believes that the principle applies not only to addresses by political candidates but to all discussions of issues of importance to the public.[30]

This system of regulating content of the electronic press continued under the Federal Radio Commission's successor agency, the Federal Communications Commission. In creating the FCC, Congress reconfirmed its intention that broadcast licensees be held accountable for sustaining the government's conception of broadcasting in "the public interest."

ENDNOTES

1.   *See Print and Electronic Media: The Case for First Amendment Parity*, Committee on Commerce, Science, and Transportation, U.S. Senate, S. Print 98–50, 98th Cong., 1st Sess. 30 (May 3, 1983); §§ 4, 5, 44 Stat. 1162 (1927).
2.   § 9, 44 Stat. 1162 (1927).
3.   § 14, 44 Stat. 1162 (1927).
4.   § 18, 44 Stat. 1162 (1927).
5.   DAVIS, THE LAW OF RADIO COMMUNICATIONS 62 (1927).
6.   *FRC v. Nelson Brothers Bond & Mortgage Co.*, 289 U.S. 266 (1933).
7.   *See The Federal Radio Commission and the Public Service Responsibility of Broadcast Licensees*, 11 FED. COM. B. J. 5, 14 (1950).
8.   *Great Lakes Broadcasting Co. v. FRC*, 37 F.2d 993 (1930).
9.   *Chicago Federation of Labor v. FRC*, 41 F.2d 422 (1930).
10. *See* § 109, 47 U.S.C. (1927).
11. *KFKB Broadcasting Association, Inc. v. FRC*, 47 F.2d 670, 672 (1931).
12. *Id.*
13. *Quoted in* Caldwell, *Censorship of Radio Programs*, 1 J. RADIO L. 441, 467 (1931).
14. For an excellent and colorful account of Reverend Shuler's ordeal, *see* L. POWE, AMERICAN BROADCASTING AND THE FIRST AMENDMENT 13–21 (1987).
15. *Id.* at 14–15.
16. *Id.* at 15. In *Trinity Methodist Church, South v. FRC*, 62 F.2d 850, 852 (1932), the D.C. Circuit Court summarized Shuler's broadcasts thus:

> Appellant, not satisfied with attacking the judges of the courts in cases then pending before them, attacked the bar association for its activities in recommending judges, charging it with ulterior and sinister purposes. With no more justification, he charged particular judges with sundry immoral acts. He made defamatory statements against the board of health. He charged that . . . [a] temple in Los Angeles was a boot-legging and gambling joint. In none of these matters, when called on to explain or justify his statements, was he able to do more than declare that the

statements expressed his own sentiments. On one occasion he announced over the radio that he had certain damaging information against a prominent unnamed man which, unless a contribution (presumably to the church) of a hundred dollars was forthcoming, he would disclose. As a result, he received contributions from several persons. He freely spoke of "pimps" and prostitutes. He alluded slightingly to the Jews as a race, and made frequent and bitter attacks on the Roman Catholic religion and its relations to government.

Id. at 852.

17. *Id.* at 850, 852.
18. *Id.* at 850, 851.
19. *Id.* at 850, 852.
20. *KFKB Broadcasting Ass'n v. FRC,* 47 F.2d 670 (1931); L. POWE, AMERICAN BROADCASTING AND THE FIRST AMENDMENT 23 (1987).
21. L. POWE, AMERICAN BROADCASTING AND THE FIRST AMENDMENT 24 (1987).
22. *KFKB Broadcasting Ass'n v. FRC,* 47 F.2d 670, 671 (1931).
23. *Id.*
24. *Id.*
25. *Id.* at 670, 672.
26. *Id.*
27. *Id.*
28. *Quoted in* Caldwell, *Censorship of Radio Programs,* 1 J. RADIO L. 441, 473 (1931).
29. J. Rosenbloom, *Appendix I, Authority of the Federal Communications Commission, in* FREEDOM AND RESPONSIBILITY IN BROADCASTING 130-32 (1961).
30. *Quoted in* J. Rosenbloom, *Appendix I, Authority of the Federal Communications Commission, in* FREEDOM AND RESPONSIBILITY IN BROADCASTING 134-35 (1961).

14

THE FEDERAL
COMMUNICATIONS COMMISSION

The Congress enacted the Communications Act of 1934 to increase the membership of the Federal Radio Commission and to expand its powers. The newly created entity was named the Federal Communications Commission and had seven members (it now has five[1]). Congress gave the FCC jurisdiction over telephone and telegraph communications in addition to broadcasting.[2] Each member of the FCC was then and is now appointed by the President (an important factor that helps determine their political loyalties) subject to Senate confirmation. The President may appoint and the Senate may confirm a maximum of three commissioners from the same political party. The commissioners originally served staggered seven-year terms (they now serve fixed five-year terms[3]). The Act authorizes the President to select the FCC chairman, who, among other duties, presides over agency meetings and has authority to set the agency's administrative agenda.[4]

Despite its increased authority, the FCC has maintained essentially the same objectives as the Federal Radio Commission.[5] Between 1927 and 1934, the FRC developed an elaborate justification for content regulation. The FCC built its own system of controls atop this foundation, expanding federal power over both the content and structure of the broadcast press.

In practice, the commissioners danced on the head of a constitutional pin. In one direction, they bent over backwards to suggest that they had no power to censor. In the other direction, they stretched mightily to suggest that they had plenary authority to review a licensee's programming and determine whether it ought to be deemed "in the public interest." What the FCC and the courts agreed could not be done directly—specify in advance what kinds of programs would be aired—the FCC did indirectly (through the threat of subsequent punishments). Rather than simply ordering broadcasters to present specific kinds of programming, the FCC relied on administrative cajolery, after the fact, to keep licensees in line. The FCC deemed this regulation not to be censorship because it involved no prior restraint. The approach taken was akin to your informing a driver that he may freely use your car to drive in any manner he desires to any location he desires across the United States provided that at the end of his journey he will be subject to a detailed critique, which may result in the revocation of his license. The critique will include a determination of whether he avoided taking any right or left turns, did not stop except to relieve himself, observed all traffic signs, and arrived at a location somewhere in the mid-west, preferably Peoria, Illinois. In short, whether the restraints were imposed before the license was issued or after it was considered for renewal did not materially change the restraint on the licensee's liberty. As James Madison put it, "to be effectual" an exemption from punishment for matters published "must be an exemption, not only from the previous inspection of licensers, but from the subsequent penalty of laws."[6]

The FCC's elaborate system of administrative second-guessing became known by the pundits as regulation by "raised eyebrow."[7]

Increasingly, there arose at the FCC a philosophy of the "morality" of broadcast regulation. Broadcasters were not to air just any matter; they were, after all, "stewards" of the airwaves, public trustees, whose "privilege" to broadcast brought with it unique and heady responsibilities to ensure that programming content was for the public good. One of the first FCC commissioners, George Henry Payne (a former Bull Mooser for Theodore Roosevelt), expounded on the point, asserting the need to use federal power to keep licensees broadcasting "the right kind" of programming. In 1937, in a speech before the National Conference on Educational Broadcasting, Payne stated:

> First, we must establish in practice what has been accepted in theory and law— that the radio waves are the inalienable property of the public. Program standards must be established corresponding to technical standards. The broadcaster should be required at regular intervals to account for his stewardship, and if he has not met the standards set, the frequency he enjoys should be thrown into the public domain and made available to those who can and will meet the program standards, for program standards are more important than technical standards.[8]

Payne was joined by Commission Chairman Eugene O. Sykes, who observed in a less direct fashion:

> That act [the Radio Act of 1927] puts upon the individual licensee of a broadcast station the private initiative to see that those programs that he broadcasts are in the public interest. . . . Then that act makes those individual licensees responsible to the licensing authority to see that their operations are in the public interest.[9]

The FCC maintained the *quid pro quo* that operated under the Radio Act. In exchange for granting the FCC certain concessions on programming and for ensuring compliance with the FCC's technical rules, broadcasters could expect that their licenses would be renewed and that they would be insulated from market competition during their license terms. The FRC's system of second-guessing broadcast editorial judgments was strengthened under the FCC. The FCC's *McGlashan* decision confirms the point.[10]

THE CASE OF BEN S. MCGLASHAN ET AL.

In October 1935, the FCC was considering five applications for renewal submitted by: Ben S. McGlashan, licensee of KGFJ; Warner Brothers Broadcasting Corporation, licensee of KFWB; Beverly Hills Broadcasting Corporation, licensee of KMPC; Radio Broadcasters, Inc., licensee of KRKD; and Cannon System, Ltd., licensee of KIEV. In addition, three applicants (Warner Brothers Broadcasting Corporation; Radio Broadcasters, Inc.; and Cannon System, Ltd.) had applications to improve their facilities pending before the FCC. The FCC withheld action on the improvement applications pending its resolution of a content matter that caused the commissioners to question whether these stations' licenses ought to be renewed.

Each station had the misfortune of having broadcast a single program that the FCC found offensive. The peculiar program, created by the Alhambra Electronic Institute (later known as the California Electronic Institute), lauded the benefits of a mysterious device called the "Electron-o-meter." An entrepreneur named Fred Bezuzi and a California chiropractor named Stephen T. Mayes marketed the device, which they termed "good news for all those who are sick or in ill health." The Electron-o-meter was said to be "a machine that shows you definitely the cause of your illness, the condition of your internal organs, the severity of the ailment, and how to correct the faulty condition." Bezuzi and Mayes had station announcers at each facility broadcast an advertisement that read in part:

You have heard about this new marvel instrument called the electronometer installed at the Alhambra Electronic Institute at 1811 West Main Street in Alhambra. It is an instrument that is causing a sensation before us in Southern California, for this reason, it shows you visually the underlying and basic cause of your ailment. Many of you have spent many dollars trying to regain your health and today you are at a loss to know what is causing your ailment. You say to yourself, "If I knew what was causing my sickness, I certainly would regain health." All right you would, and here is your opportunity, that is for ten people; we are authorized to make appointments for ten people at this time for this examination. Now this examination usually costs $10.00, but for these ten people it is going to be given to them for just $1.00 and that is the total cost without any obligation.[11]

The FCC assessed the case under Section 309(a) of the Communications Act of 1934, which the FCC understood to be "an exact restatement of Section 11 of the Radio Act of 1927." The standard for Section 11 was set forth in *KFKB Broadcasting Association Inc.* by the D.C. Circuit Court. Under this precedent, the FCC found it necessary to "consider the character and quality of the service to be rendered" and to focus on "the past conduct of the applicant."[12] The FCC determined that "the broadcast of the programs of the Electronic Institute [were] . . . inimical to public welfare and therefore not in the public interest, convenience, and necessity." Finding that each of the licensees in question had discontinued the broadcasts and had expressed an intention not to air the program again, the FCC renewed the licenses, making it clear that programs of this nature would not be tolerated.[13] The *McGlashan* case and others like it reveal that the FCC's content control policies under the Communications Act were, at a minimum, just as pervasive as the FRC's. As we shall see, the FCC had, in fact, substantially increased its authority over broadcast content and over the structure of the broadcast industry generally.

THE SUPREME COURT ENDORSES FCC CONTROLS

As early as 1940, the Supreme Court became convinced that the business of broadcasting, unlike that of newspaper publishing, must be subject to federal regulation. The Court either was unaware of or was unwilling to accept the fact that the exercise of plenary authority over broadcasting was a choice among several and not an unavoidable result. The Court does not seem to have understood that a property rights alternative was available but had been rejected out of hand by Congress.

In *FCC v. Sanders Bros. Radio Station*,[14] the Supreme Court described FCC regulatory control over the medium as a "necessity." It found that "unless Congress had exercised its power over interstate commerce to bring about allocation of available frequencies and to regulate the employment of transmission equipment the result would have been an impairment of the effective use of these facilities by anyone."[15] The Court did not appreciate that the purported "breakdown in the law" had been the product, at least in part, of conscious efforts by those in power, along with industry leaders, to create an environment hospitable for new regulation.

It became accepted that, without pervasive federal regulation, there would arise a cacophonous collision of voices on the air waves, drowning out all intelligible sounds in etheric bedlam. The least restrictive alternative, federal protection for private broadcast property rights, was not considered by the Supreme Court.

In 1943, the Court decided a case that was to set to rest until quite recently any serious question concerning the "necessity" of comprehensive federal control over radio. The decision also settled the constitutionality of the FCC's authority to regulate the structure of the broadcast industry and the content of broadcast programming.

THE CASE OF THE NATIONAL BROADCASTING CO.

In *NBC v. United States*,[16] the Supreme Court, in considering the First Amendment validity of the FCC's so-called "chain broadcasting" rules, justified at length the government's regulatory regime over broadcast industry structure and broadcast programming. In recounting the history of federal intervention, Justice Felix Frankfurter described the government's takeover as ineluctable because of the physical and economic scarcity of the usable spectrum and because of interference wrought by radio communication. Justice Frankfurter explained that these problems required that some who desired to broadcast be precluded from doing so. In Frankfurter's mind, this condition of scarcity justified federal regulation. In *NBC v. United States*, Frankfurter made the FCC's theory of regulation constitutional law. He wrote:

> The plight into which radio fell prior to 1927 was attributable to certain basic facts about radio as a means of communication—its facilities are limited; they are not available to all who may wish to use them; the spectrum is not large

enough to accommodate everybody. There is a fixed natural limitation upon the number of stations that can operate without interfering with one another. Regulation was therefore as vital to its development as traffic control was to the development of the automobile.[17]

For Frankfurter, the FCC's unproven assumption, that the economic and physical scarcity in radio had no equals in other media, served as a pivotal First Amendment distinguishing principle: "Unlike other modes of expression, radio inherently is not available to all," he wrote. "That is its unique characteristic, and that is why, unlike other modes of expression, it is subject to government regulation."[18]

This "scarcity rationale" persists as the constitutional predicate for almost all FCC broadcast regulations.[19] However, at no time has the FCC or the Court ever explained precisely why economic or physical scarcity is relevant to First Amendment analysis or why it should cause us to reduce the protection afforded the broadcast press but not to the print press. The print medium relies on products such as paper, ink, presses, and delivery trucks, which are not universally available, and yet the Court forbids regulation of the print media.[20]

In his *NBC* decision, Frankfurter appeared entirely unaware that the demand excesses that plagued radio would not have occurred if channels were allocated through a pricing system like other scarce goods—including paper, ink, presses, and delivery trucks for newspaper publishing facilities. Instead, he viewed demand excesses as an *inherent* and *unique* characteristic of radio rather than a by-product of a regulatory regime that permitted applications for broadcast licenses to be filed free of charge.

Frankfurter did not regard broadcasting as somehow not "the press" within the meaning of the First Amendment. Rather, his sole basis for reducing the level of First Amendment protection for broadcasters rested on the fickle concept of scarcity and the alleged inevitability of objectionable interference without federal regulation.

The Court submitted that without regulation no broadcast voice could be intelligibly received on radio sets: this, despite proof of the success of industry self-regulation from 1922 to 1926. Although the Court could have restricted FCC authority to technical regulation, it chose to condone the FCC's regulations over technical *and* programming matters. In his most famous passage in the *NBC* decision, Frankfurter found regulation of mere technical matters inadequate:

The Act itself establishes that the Commission's powers are not limited to the engineering and technical aspects of regulation of radio communication. Yet we are asked to regard the Commission as a kind of traffic officer, policing the wave lengths to prevent stations from interfering with each other. But the Act does not restrict the Commission merely to supervision of the traffic. It puts upon the Commission the burden of determining the composition of that traffic. The facilities of radio are not large enough to accommodate all who wish to use them. Methods must be devised for choosing from among the many who apply. And since Congress itself could not do this, it committed the task to the Commission.[21]

The Court also affirmed what has become a central principle of the FCC, namely that, unlike printers, the rights of broadcasters are not to be construed as paramount. Rather, the controlling consideration was to ensure that "the interest of the listening public in 'the larger and more effective use of radio' " would govern in every case.[22] In short, Herbert Hoover's view of the public interest had been vindicated by the Court; it had now become *constitutionally legitimate* for the government to determine *what* the public would hear and see through the broadcast press and *who* would be permitted to broadcast in the first place.[23]

Having broadly justified the FCC's authority, Frankfurter gave the FCC the assurance it needed to embark on a grandiose regulatory course that until quite recently has grown as prolifically as weeds in an unkempt garden.[24]

ENDNOTES

1. In 1982, Congress reduced the FCC's membership from seven members to five. Pub. L. No. 99–334, 100 Stat. 513 (1982).
2. *See* T. CARTER, M. FRANKLIN, & J. WRIGHT, THE FIRST AMENDMENT AND THE FIFTH ESTATE 32 (1986).
3. *See* Act of June 6, 1986, Pub. L. No. 99–334, 100 Stat. 513 (1986).
4. *See* §§ 4, 5, 47 U.S.C. (1988); T. CARTER, M. FRANKLIN, & J. WRIGHT, THE FIRST AMENDMENT AND THE FIFTH ESTATE 32 (1986).
5. *FCC v. Pottsville Broadcasting Co.,* 309 U.S. 134, 137 (1940).
6. *Madison's Report on the Virginia Resolutions, quoted in* IV THE DEBATES IN THE SEVERAL STATE CONVENTIONS ON THE ADOPTION OF THE FEDERAL CONSTITUTION 570 (J. Elliot ed. 1888).
7. *See, e.g.,* E. BARNOUW, THE GOLDEN WEB 28–36 (1968). In the following extended passage, Erik Barnouw reveals the standard method used by the FCC to ensure that content broadcast met its conception of "preferred" programming fare.

While the ultimate weapon was non-renewal of a license, the FCC had at its disposal a device for exerting influence that had evolved under the FRC. When used, it usually aroused rage.

In the early 1930's the air bristled with lotteries. In answer to complaints, the commission said it had no right to forbid lotteries; that would be censorship. But a few days later it made an additional statement:

> There exists a doubt that such broadcasts are in the public interest. Complaints from a substantial number of listeners against any broadcasting station presenting such programs will result in the station's application for renewal of license being set for a hearing.

The threat of hearings—and perhaps parades of hostile witnesses—was eloquent. Radio lotteries began to melt away. They were later outlawed by the Communications Act.

In 1934 the technique was used again. With repeal of prohibition, liquor advertising appeared on many stations. Protests followed: should radio be urging the young to drink whiskey? Again the commission said it could not forbid such advertising; that would be censorship. Again it followed with another statement. It reminded broadcasters that the radio audience included children. Therefore—

> The commission will designate for hearing the renewal applications of all stations unmindful of the foregoing, and they will be required to make a showing that their continued operation will serve the public interest, convenience and necessity.

Id. at 32–33.

8.   *See* Zaragoza, Bodorff, & Emord, *The Public Interest Concept Transformed: The Trusteeship Model Gives Way to a Marketplace Approach, in* THE BROADCAST INDUSTRY LOOKS AT PUBLIC INTEREST AND THE BUSINESS OF BROADCASTING 43 n.13 (J. Powell & W. Gair eds. 1988).

9.   *Quoted in* Rosenbloom, *Appendix I, Authority of the Federal Communications Commission, in* FREEDOM AND RESPONSIBILITY IN BROADCASTING 151–52 (1961).

10.   *McGlashan et al.*, 2 F.C.C. 145 (1935).

11.   *Id.* at 145, 149–50.

12.   *Id.* at 145, 149.

13.   *Id.* at 145, 157.

14.   309 U.S. 470 (1940).

15.   *FCC v. Sanders Bros. Radio Station*, 309 U.S. 470, 474 (1940).

16.   *NBC v. United States*, 319 U.S. 190 (1943).

17.   *Id.* at 213.

18. *Id.* at 190, 226.
19. In addition to the scarcity rationale, the FCC relies on what has become known as the "impact rationale" to justify regulation of certain kinds of broadcast programming deemed "violent," "indecent," or "obscene." The impact rationale focuses on the pervasive presence and influential nature of the broadcast medium and suggests that this justifies regulation as a constitutional matter. *See FCC v. Pacifica Foundation,* 438 U.S. 726 (1978); *Sable Communications of California, Inc. v. FCC,* 109 S. Ct. 2829 (1989); *Enforcement of Prohibitions Against Broadcast Indecency in 18 USC § 1464,* 67 R.R. 2d 1714 (1990). The rationale has been soundly refuted elsewhere and will not be subject to further discussion here. *See* M. SPITZER, SEVEN DIRTY WORDS AND SIX OTHER STORIES 67–118 (1986).
20. Judge Bork observed in *Telecommunications Research & Action Center v. FCC,* 801 F.2d 501 (D.C. Cir. 1986), *cert. denied,* 107 S.Ct. 3196 (1987):

> All economic goods are scarce, not least the newsprint, ink, delivery trucks, computers, and other resources that go into the production and dissemination of print journalism. . . . Since scarcity is a universal fact, it can hardly explain regulation in one context and not another. The attempt to use a universal fact as a distinguishing principle necessarily leads to analytical confusion.

Id. at 508.
21. *NBC v. United States,* 319 U.S. 190, 215–16 (1943).
22. *Id.* at 190, 216.
23. In a closing passage, not much quoted or relied on by the FCC or the courts since 1943, Frankfurter did write that "Congress did not authorize the Commission to choose among applicants upon the basis of their political, economic, or social views, or upon any other capricious basis. If it did . . . the issue before us would be wholly different." *NBC v. United States,* 319 U.S. 190, 226 (1943).
24. In 1941, the FCC began licensing television stations. Consequently, they too were affected by the new and comprehensive regulatory regime. The content regulations applicable to radio generally were also applied to television. Licensing of new television stations ended in 1948 when, concerned about tropospheric interference, the FCC decided not to license any more television stations. In 1952, the FCC lifted the freeze in its *Sixth Report and Order on Television Allocations. See, e.g.,* THE FIRST AMENDMENT AND THE FIFTH ESTATE 46 (Carter, Franklin, & Wright eds. 1986).

15

THE MODERN EXPANSION OF FCC CONTENT CONTROLS

Bolstered by a Supreme Court victory affording it a constitutional basis for expanded content-based regulation, the FCC added to its system of regulation the new "unofficial" requirements set forth in its famed "Blue Book," officially entitled *Public Service Responsibility of Broadcast Licensees*.[1] The Blue Book, released to the public in 1946, was the product of the determined efforts of FCC Chairman Paul Porter, who believed that the FCC should, in considering license renewals, compare a licensee's promises to the FCC with its actual performance during a license term.[2] Promise versus performance became the accepted criterion for evaluating license renewals and continued to be used until 1984.

In the Blue Book, the FCC's policy and plans staff recommended that broadcasters sponsor what was termed "balanced programming fare." These programming recommendations or guidelines became an unofficial requirement for broadcasters. To hedge their bets in favor of renewal, licensees had to follow the guidelines. Explains Ben C. Fisher:

> The Commission proposed a quantitative evaluation of a station's overall performance. A half-dozen categories of programming were established. . . . So long as stations maintained a fair balance between the various categories, their renewals were automatic.[3]

The FCC's policy and plans staff identified a number of preferred programming categories to assist licensees in making editorial judgments.

The staff construed "responsive programming" to be that which is locally produced and live, relying on local talent, and that which covers issues of public importance. Consistent with these criteria, the Blue Book emphasized the need for local, non–network programming carried on a sustaining (that is, noncommercial) basis, local live programming, and public issues programming. Consistent with its historical inclination to regard advertising-supported programming as being of less public interest value than non-commercial programming, the staff recommended hourly limitations on the frequency of advertising.[4]

In 1949, the FCC added another requirement atop its Blue Book "recommendations." It ordered licensees to broadcast controversial issues of public importance and to air contrasting views on those issues (what has become known as the "Fairness Doctrine").[5]

THE 1959 AMENDMENTS TO SECTION 315
OF THE COMMUNICATIONS ACT

Following the introduction of television to America in 1941 and the expansion in the number of stations nationwide after the FCC adopted its television allocation plan in 1952, Congress and the FCC began to devote increasing attention to regulating this new broadcast medium.

In 1959, Congress amended Section 315 of the Communications Act. That section generally requires licensees who permit a candidate for public office to appear in broadcasts to afford a reasonable opportunity for all other candidates for the same office to make an appearance.[6] The amendment was triggered by actions that the FCC had taken in response to complaints filed concerning television coverage during the Chicago mayoral elections of 1959.

In that year, a third-party candidate, Lar Daly, asked a local CBS affiliate to give him equal time in response to the station's series of brief news reports that featured the Republican and Democratic candidates for mayor. The reports included one that pictured Mayor Richard J. Daley and his Republican opponent filing their campaign papers; another that showed the Republican answering a reporter's question about why he was running for office; a third that pictured Mayor Daley participating in the March of Dimes campaign; and a fourth that showed Daley greeting a foreign dignitary at the airport.[7]

Lar Daly argued to the FCC that these limited appearances triggered the right of access provision of the Act and insisted that he be given equal time. The FCC agreed and required the CBS affiliate to alter its programming schedule to permit Daly's appearance.[8]

Congress expressed its displeasure with the FCC's action by amending the Communications Act to exclude the following from the right of access requirement: *bona fide* newscasts, news interviews, news documentaries, and on-the-spot coverage of news events.[9] In a segment of the amended section that would later vex interpreters of legislative intent (during the Fairness Doctrine debates), Senator William Proxmire added the following language:

> Nothing in the foregoing sentence shall be construed as relieving broadcasters, in connection with the presentation of newscasts, news interviews, news documentaries, and on-the-spot coverage of news events, from the obligation imposed upon them under this Act to operate in the public interest and to afford reasonable opportunity for the discussion of conflicting views on issues of public importance.[10]

Proxmire stated that this section "merely expresses the philosophy that the media of radio and television are in the public domain, and that they must render, under the law, public service, and that wherever it is practical and possible the situation must bring to light all sides of a controversy in the public interest."[11] As a consequence, although broadcast licensees were generally relieved of the obligation of affording equal opportunities to opposing candidates whenever other candidates appeared in news broadcasts, the licensees were put on notice by Congress that the FCC was not relieving them of its requirement that they present what the FCC thought was balanced programming on controversial issues of public importance.

NEWTON MINOW'S RAISED EYEBROW

Following the imposition of Blue Book content guidelines and the renewal criterion of promise versus performance, the next major jolt for broadcasters in the content area came shortly after Newton N. Minow became chairman of the FCC at the behest of President John F. Kennedy. In a 1961 address to the National Association of Broadcasters, Minow shocked the audience with his stark vision of television programming. What has become known in broadcast circles as "*the* speech" had the unintended effect of revealing to a mature broadcast industry in one instant that the *quid pro quo* agreed to in the 1920s was perhaps too great a sacrifice of a most precious liberty.

Standing before the broadcast industry conventioneers was a man who regarded their handiwork as substandard. Minow's opinion was not merely a passing editorial; it was the judgment of one who commanded a mighty regulatory body and who had behind his words an accumulation of precedent that made it possible for him to wield regulatory muscle to effect the changes he wanted. Therefore, the audience listened intently and with trepidation when Minow said:

> When television is bad, nothing is worse. I invite you to sit down in front of your television set when your station goes on the air and stay there without a book, magazine, newspaper, profit and loss sheet or rating book to distract you—and keep your eyes glued to that set until the station signs off. I can assure you that you will observe a vast wasteland. You will see a procession of game shows, violence, audience participation shows, formula comedies about totally unbelievable families, blood and thunder, mayhem, violence, sadism, murder, western badmen, western good men, private eyes, gangsters, more violence, and cartoons. And endlessly, commercials—many screaming, cajoling, and offending. And most of all, boredom. Sure, you will see a few things you will enjoy. But they will be very, very few. And if you think I exaggerate, try it. . . .
>
> Gentlemen, your trust accounting with your beneficiaries is overdue. Never have so few owed so much to so many. . . .
>
> I understand that many people feel that in the past licenses were often renewed *pro forma*. I say to you now: renewal will not be *pro forma* in the future. There is nothing permanent or sacred about a broadcast license.[12]

No doubt, many an Adam's apple remained lodged high in the throats of the assembled. At once, free editorial choice truly seemed at an end. It was as if each broadcast executive present were looking up the barrel of a cocked gun under orders to satisfy this one man's view of what the rest of us *should* find worth listening to and watching. This speech can be regarded as the first sign of a breakup in industry-wide faith in the monopoly rent/content control *quid pro quo*.

One year later, in 1962, Minow made good on his promise to rein in press freedom. The FCC published its *En Banc Programming Inquiry Report and Statement of Policy*.[13] This report supplanted the Blue Book's general encouragement with a series of direct content requirements. It defined as a licensee's obligation the necessity of engaging in a "diligent, positive and continuing effort . . . to discover and fulfill the tastes, needs and desires of [its] service area."[14]

Despite the presence of market incentives for licensees to provide programming their audiences wanted, the FCC nevertheless continued pressuring licensees to abide by its own conception of what the public should listen to and watch. Fourteen elements were identified as essential to overall programming in the public interest. Programs of the kind listed were henceforth expected of broadcasters if they wished to minimize the probability of losing their licenses at renewal time. Licensees were expected to broadcast programs that would provide

(1) opportunity for local self-expression; (2) development and use of local talent; (3) programs for children; (4) religious programs; (5) educational programs; (6) public affairs programs; (7) editorialization by licensees; (8) political broadcasts; (9) agricultural programs; (10) news programs; (11) weather and market reports; (12) sports programs; (13) service programs for minority groups; and (14) entertainment programs.[15]

In 1968, the FCC added yet another content regulation, a corollary to the Fairness Doctrine: the "personal attack doctrine," which required licensees to afford free air time for a response by individuals whose honesty, character, integrity, or like personal qualities had been impugned during the broadcast of a controversial issue of public importance.[16]

EXPANSION OF THE CONTENT REGULATORY LABYRINTH

In the 1960s and early 1970s, the FCC created a plethora of additional content-focused requirements that stood as obstacles to the free exercise of editorial discretion. The FCC imposed an "ascertainment" requirement on applicants for new licenses and renewals (that is, they were forced to conduct sophisticated statistical surveys of their communities in an effort to identify data indicative of programming needs and they were expected to ensure that their programming was responsive to these identified needs).[17] Licensees were (since 1934 and the codification of Section 303(j) of the Communications Act) already required to keep detailed logs of their programming,[18] documenting how their programming was responsive to community problems and needs. They were also (and still are) required to keep detailed records of all requests for air time from candidates for elective office, of the station's disposition of such requests, and of any charge made for air time given a candidate.[19]

This information had been considered, since the early days of radio regulation, the principal proof of a licensee's community responsiveness during a renewal contest.[20] Licensees were expected to regularly present programs covering local issues and to originate at least some programs locally.[21]

FCC "primers" were issued, periodically updating licensees on the acceptable way to conduct ascertainment surveys.[22] News and public affairs programming guidelines were issued, requiring licensees to provide a minimum percentage of programming devoted to the FCC's favored areas.[23] Quantitative guidelines were established for promise versus performance renewal reviews. These guidelines required licensees to explain decreases of 15 percent or more in three nonentertainment categories of programming or of 20 percent or more in overall nonentertainment programming, from the amounts presented in the applicant's last renewal application.[24] Regulations were promulgated limiting the amount of advertising that a licensee could broadcast.[25] Affiliates of networks were (and still are), with but few exceptions, prohibited from broadcasting more than three hours of network programming during prime time, purportedly to aid the growth of a market in local and independent programming, a circumstance that has not occurred in accordance with FCC predictions.[26] Regulations were also promulgated requiring broadcasters to present children's programming—to air such programs over the course of more than two days a week, to reduce the number of commercials during children's programs, and to clearly segregate commercial matter from children's programs.[27]

These and other content-focused regulations formed a complex matrix of regulatory restraints that grew up amid the general growth of the federal government. The restrictions tempered the willingness of licensees to engage in controversy, coerced them into offering certain kinds of bureaucratically "preferred" programming, and caused them to become tools for the use of incumbent politicians and special interest groups who desired to influence the nature of public debate.

By the mid-1970s to the end of the decade, the FCC began to take its first steps away from the regulatory course followed since its creation.[28] These steps were part of a movement that would culminate with the major deregulatory initiatives undertaken in the 1980s during the Reagan administration. In the 1970s through deregulatory initiatives euphemistically termed "re-regulation," the FCC modified or eliminated several long-standing technical regulations, including those concerning mandatory periodic meter readings, transmitter inspections, station identification announcements, certain advance FCC notification requirements, and technical logging requirements. For example, the FCC replaced its requirement that technical operators work at each broadcast station with a provision for automated transmission, monitoring, and control.[29] Perhaps most significantly, in 1978 the FCC asked its Broadcast Bureau Office of Plans and Policy and its General Counsel to review the existing scope of radio regulation and supply the full Commission with a set of options for potential reduction or elimination of regulations which no longer fit the current economic marketplace of radio in the major markets, whose cost could no longer be justified against the social benefits they provide, and whose elimination would be consistent with the FCC's overall public interest obligations.[30]

These initiatives signaled the start of a movement that would gain greatest momentum in the 1980s, when the commissioners appointed by President Ronald Reagan made deregulation the centerpiece of the FCC's agenda.

ENDNOTES

1. FCC, PUBLIC SERVICE RESPONSIBILITY OF BROADCAST LICENSEES (1946); *see also Eugene J. Roth (Mission Broadcasting Co.)*, 12 F.C.C. 102 (1947); *Howard W. Davis*, 12 F.C.C. 91 (1947); *Community Broadcasting Co.*, 12 F.C.C. 85 (1947).

2. *See* E. BARNOUW, THE GOLDEN WEB 228 (1968).

3. Fisher, *Program Control and the Federal Communications Commission: A Limited Role*, 14 VILL. L. REV. 602, 607 (1969).

4. *See* FCC, PUBLIC SERVICE RESPONSIBILITY OF BROADCAST LICENSEES 18 (1946).

5. *Report on Editorializing by Broadcast Licensees*, 13 F.C.C. 1246 (1949); the Report overruled the FCC's 1940 decision in *Mayflower Broadcasting Corp.*, 8 F.C.C. 333, 340 (1940), that prohibited all commercial broadcasters from editorializing.

6. § 315(a), 47 U.S.C. (1988).

7. *See Columbia Broadcasting System, Inc. (Lar Daly)*, 26 F.C.C. 715 (1959); T. CARTER, M. FRANKLIN, & J. WRIGHT, THE FIRST AMENDMENT AND THE FIFTH ESTATE 187 (1986).

8. *See Columbia Broadcasting System, Inc. (Lar Daly)*, 26 F.C.C. 715 (1959).

9. *See* § 315(a) (1–4), 47 U.S.C. (1959).

10. *See* § 315(a), 47 U.S.C. (1959).

11. 105 CONG. REC. 14,457 (1959).

12. *Quoted in* E. BARNOUW, THE IMAGE EMPIRE 197 (1970).

13. 44 F.C.C. 2303 (1962).

14. *Id.* at 2312.

15. 44 F.C.C. 2314; *see also* Comment, 56 U. CIN. L. REV. 999, 1022 (1988).

16. *See* § 73.1930, 47 C.F.R. (1989).

17. *See In re Primer on Ascertainment of Community Problems by Broadcast Applicants*, 27 F.C.C.2d 650 (1971); § 73.4020, 47 C.F.R. (1981).

18. *See In re Primer on Ascertainment of Community Problems by Broadcast Applicants*, 27 F.C.C.2d 650, 655 (1971).

19. *See, e.g.,* § 73.1940(d), 47 C.F.R. (1988), which reads in part:

> Every licensee shall keep and permit public inspection of a complete record (political file) of all requests for broadcast time made by or on behalf of candidates for public office, together with an appropriate notation showing the disposition made by the licensee of such requests, and the charges made, if any, if the request was granted. When free time is provided for use by or on behalf of such candidates, a record of the free time provided shall be placed in the political file. All records required by this paragraph shall be placed in the political file as soon as possible and shall be retained for a period of two years.

20. *See Commission Policy on Programming,* 20 R.R. 1901, 1915–16 (1960); *see, e.g., Johnston Broadcasting Co. v. FCC,* 175 F.2d 351, 358–59 (D.C. Cir. 1949).

21. *See, e.g.,* § 73.1120(b) (2), 47 C.F.R. (1980).

22. *See, e.g., Primer on Ascertainment of Community Problems by Broadcast Applicants,* 27 F.C.C.2d 650 (1973).

23. *See, e.g., Television Program Form,* 5 F.C.C.2d 175 (1966); *Renewal of Broadcast Licenses,* 44 F.C.C.2d 405 (1973); *Ascertainment of Community Problems by Broadcast Applicants,* 57 F.C.C.2d 418 (1976); *Revision of FCC Form 303,* 54 F.C.C.2d 418 (1976); § 0.281(l) (8), 47 C.F.R. (1981); § 0.281(l) (8) (i), 47 C.F.R. (1981).

24. *Matter of Revision of FCC Form 302, Application for Renewal of Broadcast Station Licenses,* 59 F.C.C.2d 750 (1976).

25. *See* § 73.4010, 47 C.F.R. (1982).

26. *See National Association of Independent Television Producers & Distributors v. FCC,* 516 F.2d 526 (2d Cir. 1975); *see* § 73.658, 47 C.F.R. (1988). The FCC created an exception to the rule whereby a licensee "may show one half-hour of network news if it is shown immediately adjacent to at least one full hour of local news or public affairs," an exception responsible for the standardization of the one hour of local news/one half-hour of network news national format. *See* Spitzer, *The Constitutionality of Licensing Broadcasters,* 64 N.Y.U. L. REV. 990, 1005–6 (1989).

27. *See Children's TV Report and Policy Statement,* 50 F.C.C.2d 1 (1974); *Children's TV Programming and Advertising Practices,* 96 F.C.C.2d 634 (1984); *National Ass'n for Better Broadcasting v. FCC,* 830 F.2d 270 (D.C. Cir. 1987).

28. For example, in its 1974 Fairness Report, the FCC "affirmed the need for the Fairness Doctrine and said strict adherence to it was the single most important requirement of operation in the public interest and an absolute necessity for the granting of a renewal license." FCC, 40th ANNUAL REPORT/FISCAL YEAR 1974 16 (1974).

29. *See* FCC, 38th ANNUAL REPORT/FISCAL YEAR 1972 51 (1972); FCC, 40th ANNUAL REPORT/FISCAL YEAR 1974 33–34 (1974); FCC, 43rd ANNUAL REPORT/FISCAL YEAR 1977 63–64 (1977).
30. FCC, MAJOR MATTERS BEFORE THE COMMISSION 25 (1978).

16

BROADCAST PRESS LICENSING: GOVERNMENTAL DETERMINATIONS OF WHO MAY SPEAK AND WHAT MAY BE SAID

In 1965, the FCC issued a statement formally recognizing and, to a degree, honing the inexact criteria that it had historically used to assess competing applicants for new facilities. The FCC's *Policy Statement on Comparative Broadcast Hearings*[1] identified two principal objectives that it sought to accomplish through comparative broadcast hearings. The first, considered "of primary significance," was the attainment of "a maximum diffusion of control [over] . . . media of mass communication." The second factor, considered of lesser, but still substantial, importance, was the attainment of "best practicable service to the public."[2]

Since the very origins of the FCC, the agency's regulators have vowed their commitment to an unending quest for ever more diversity of views—in the words of the Supreme Court "the widest possible dissemination of information from diverse and antagonistic sources."[3] To attain this end, the FCC has elected to assign demerits to any applicant whose principals have ownership interests[4] in the media of mass communication. The gravity of such demerits hinges on the percentage of ownership interests in other media held and the proximity of media in question to the community to be served.[5] Underlying this criterion are two unproven assumptions: (1) that there exists a close nexus between diversity in *ownership* of mass media and diversity in *viewpoints* propagated by mass media and (2) that a sufficient level of diversity will not occur in the marketplace without government intervention. Also underlying this criterion is the view that it is proper for the government to take affirmative steps to ensure diversity in ownership of the mass media in order to attain a bureaucratically preferred diversity of viewpoints.

The criterion of "best practicable service to the public" or "integration" has been designed, in part, to attain "localism" or "community responsiveness" by licensees. Integration is subdivided into two components—one quantitative, the other qualitative—for which the FCC asigns credit. Quantitative integration concerns the extent to which owners who are in voting control of the applicant will work in full-time positions of management at the station. For example, a corporation that has two 50 percent voting stockholders and proposes to have just one work in a management position at the station would receive only 50 percent integration credit. Qualitative integration concerns the extent to which owners who are in voting control of the applicant and will assume management-level positions at the station are residents of the community to be served, have civic participation in that community, are minorities, are female, and have broadcast experience. An applicant that receives no quantitative credit is ineligible to receive qualitative credit. Qualitative credit is said to "enhance" quantitative credit and is assigned by degrees—very slight, slight, moderate, or substantial.

The FCC formerly required new applicants to prove that they would provide an "adequate [program] service" by supplying statistical data setting forth the problems, needs, and interests of the community of license (a formal process known as "ascertainment") and submitting plans to "meet the needs and interests of the public in [the] . . . area" with nonentertainment programming.[6]

Underlying these various criteria was the FCC's unproven assumption that local owners would be better attuned to area concerns and more capable of addressing an area's problems, needs, and interests than nonlocal owners. Also underlying these criteria was the view that, in any event, it was proper for government to attempt through regulation to influence the message communicated to the public.

"Spectral efficiency"[7] is a third factor considered whenever there are substantial differences in the areas and populations that are proposed to be served by competing applicants. This element typically involves an assessment of the areas and numbers of people to be served and the extent to which applicants propose to serve underserved populations. Significant disparities in service to underserved populations can result in significant preferences for the applicant with the greatest coverage advantage.

In the early 1970s, the FCC added minority race and ethnicity to its qualitative considerations, presuming that nonwhites would tend to select programming inherently different from that selected by whites. At first, the FCC adopted the position that it could award a preference to a minority applicant only if that applicant would prove that his or her race would beget a programming difference.[8] Later, in 1973, the FCC was required by the D.C. Circuit Court's *TV 9, Inc. v. FCC* decision to *assume* that minority ownership would result in program diversity.[9] In 1978, the FCC added female gender to its comparative preference policies, presuming that women would tend to select programming inherently different from that selected by men.[10] In *Metro Broadcasting, Inc. v. FCC* (a five to four decision), the Supreme Court upheld the minority preference against a challenge that was based on the equal protection component of the Fifth Amendment. The Court held that "the FCC's conclusion that there is an empirical nexus between minority ownership and broadcasting diversity is a product of its expertise, and we accord its judgment deference."[11] In dissent, Justice Sandra Day O'Connor observed that "social scientists may debate how peoples' thoughts and behavior reflect their background, but the Constitution provides that the Government may not allocate benefits and burdens among individuals based on the assumption that race or ethnicity determines how they act or think."[12] The Court was not presented with a First Amendment challenge to the viewpoint diversity premise underlying the preferences. However, in her dissent (which was joined by Chief Justice William Rehnquist, Justice Antonin Scalia, and Justice Anthony Kennedy), Justice O'Connor warned:

> The FCC's extension of the asserted interest in diversity of views in this case presents, at the very least, an unsettled First Amendment issue. The FCC has concluded that the American broadcasting public receives the incorrect mix of ideas and claims to have adopted the challenged policies to supplement programming content with a particular set of views. Although we have approved limited measures designed to increase information and views generally, the Court has never upheld a broadcasting measure designed to amplify a distinct set of views or the views of a particular class of speakers. Indeed, the Court has suggested that the First Amendment prohibits allocating licenses to further such ends.[13]

A PLETHORA OF SHAM APPLICATIONS

Throughout the 1980s the FCC's peculiar complex of quantitative and qualitative integration factors created an environment conducive to fraud and abuse. Time and again, applicants purportedly controlled by minorities or women were in fact controlled by shadow figures of male gender and white race who were often owners of existing broadcast properties. These *actual* controllers remained concealed from the FCC unless, through good fortune in cross-examination by counsel for competing applicants, their presence became known.[14] Often, the controllers appeared as purported nonvoting stockholders or limited partners who, under the FCC's attribution-of-ownership policies, were not evaluated under the integration or diversification criteria (unless substantial proof was presented to demonstrate that they were indeed active principals).[15] These purportedly passive individuals often possessed the vast majority of equity in the corporations or partnerships concerned, and they exercised *de facto* control.[16] In 1989, then FCC Chairman Dennis Patrick commenced a rule-making proceeding (which has since been terminated) that revealed the Commissions' discontent with the comparative hearing process and its willingness to consider random selection to decide new facilities cases.[17]

In the 1988 *Religious Broadcasting Network* case, as in so many others like it before and since, the FCC's Review Board expressed disgust at the tremendous number of sham application filings that were appearing at the FCC.[18] Wrote Board Member Norman Blumenthal:

> Because of this recent outbreak of sham broadcast applications, *bona fide* applicants and the Commission's [Administrative Law Judges] have been compelled to examine much more closely the alleged ownership structures and, more specifically, the purported "integration" designs of numerous competing applicants to determine whether their proposals reflect the [actual] composition of the particular applicant or whether that applicant is, in reality, an utterly artificial construct devised exclusively for the purpose of deceitfully exploiting the Commission's comparative system. . . . Unless sham applicants are stoutly rebuffed, the very fabric of the Commission's licensing process will be irreparably rent, and our broadcast license rolls reduced to a shabby sodality of frauds, mountebanks, and sundry speculators of the very lowest echelon.[19]

Indicative of how unsuccessful the FCC has been in its administrative selection of broadcast licensees are certain statistics compiled by the FCC's Office of Plans and Policy in the early 1980s. The peculiar mix of policy preferences imposed by the FCC has resulted in only Pyrrhic victories for the agency. More often than not, the party that is awarded the construction permit, after considerable government resources are spent in hearings, either sells the FCC's construction permit at no profit or assigns the license to operate to another party (which may bear no resemblance to the original applicant in its owners' race, gender, residence, or broadcast experience). This assignment of license has often been made at a considerable profit directly following station construction.[20]

RENEWAL REVIEW

When a license is up for renewal, anyone may file an application for the communications frequency that is used by an existing licensee. An FCC Administrative Law Judge conducts a hearing to resolve the contest.

The inquiry focuses on the existing licensee's past programming performance and the challenger's proposed performance. These proceedings are quite lengthy and expensive, sometimes lasting several years and costing millions of dollars.[21] Their purpose, according to the FCC, is to provide "broadcasters . . . [an] incentive to put forward their best programming efforts at serving the needs and interests of their communities."[22]

In the early days, the FCC extensively scrutinized a licensee's quantity of "news, public affairs, and other informational programs" in evaluating past performance. FCC administrative law judges would also compare the licensee's programming performance with the licensee's promises contained in its last renewal application.[23] The agency no longer looks at quantity *per se* but still considers generally whether programming has been responsive to community problems, needs, and interests.[24] As the FCC explained in its *Pillar of Fire* decision:

> While overtly eschewing quantitative program standards, [the Commission still has in place] delegation of authority rules [which have] instructed the staff to filter broadcast station applications to detect whether an applicant proposed certain levels of prosocial programming. . . . For commercial FM stations . . . the thresholds were 5% total local programming, 5% informational (news plus public affairs) programming, and 10% total non-entertainment programming.[25]

A licensee in a comparative renewal proceeding must prove a nexus between issues of local import and the licensee's programming choices. The judge, with unavoidable subjectivity, determines whether the programming has been responsive. Proof to the judge's satisfaction results in a determination that the licensee is deserving of a "renewal expectancy," a weighted presumption in favor of renewal.[26] In the past, to acquire a renewal expectancy, a licensee had to establish that his programming was not merely minimally acceptable but rather substantially responsive to community problems, needs, and interests and that its pledges of performance to the FCC equaled its actual performance. As the D.C. Circuit Court stated in *Office of Communication of the United Church of Christ v. FCC*, "on a renewal application the 'campaign pledges' of applicants must be open to comparison with 'performance in office.' "[27] If a licensee kept its promises

and demonstrated community responsiveness, that licensee would be preferred over competitors.[28]

The D.C. Circuit has recently required the FCC to judge a licensee's
performance against a "meritorious" service standard rather than a "substantially responsive" standard.[29] Neither standard significantly limits the
discretion of FCC administrative law judges in assessing a licensee's performance.[30] The process remains highly subjective.

THE CASE OF SIMON GELLER

In recent years, before the FCC abolished its promise-versus-performance
renewal criteria and its ascertainment requirement, the topsy-turvy case
of Simon Geller illustrated the odd nature of the FCC's content-focused
regime. The case is illustrative of the interplay of factors present in the
comparative renewal context as the FCC strives to have its licensees adhere
to its conception of programming in the public interest.

Simon Geller owned a Class A FM station, WCVA, in Gloucester,
Massachusetts (which he ran single-handedly). On February 25, 1977, the
FCC issued a Memorandum Opinion and Order designating for comparative
hearing Geller's renewal application and a competing application filed by
Grandbanke Corporation.

Geller had filed his renewal application without the aid of legal counsel
in 1975. In the application, he failed to supply the kind of detailed responses
required to satisfy many FCC legal requirements. Working 85 hours a week
at his station and serving as the station's only employee, he did not have
the time to do a formal ascertainment survey, and he could not afford to
have one done professionally, with station revenues amounting to only $6,500
a year. So he refrained from submitting one. Instead, Geller submitted a
simple explanation for noncompliance: "such a survey would be meaningless since revenue is not available to employ qualified staff to produce
programs which would be evolved from a survey."[31]

Geller had also neglected to satisfy the FCC's nonentertainment programming guidelines. He completed the portion of the renewal application
concerning a composite week of programming for the 1972–75 license term
and reported that he had aired a total of 15 minutes of nonentertainment
programming, representing less than 1 percent of his programming overall.
Moreover, Geller did not indicate that any of this programming was responsive to area problems, needs, or interests, as the FCC required. Instead,
he argued that his classical music format was filling a unique niche

in the local market and that he knew that members of the community liked it.

In the section of his application concerning future programming, Geller refused to pledge to broadcast any precise amount of nonentertainment programs, preferring to devote the station's air time to broadcasting what he and his station's listeners liked most, classical music.

This did not sit well with the FCC, for it fell grossly below what the agency had long considered minimum levels of nonentertainment programming in the public interest. The Broadcast Bureau asked that special issues be tried at a hearing, including one concerning the adequacy of Geller's ascertainment efforts, another concerning whether his "non-entertainment programming . . . was reasonably responsive to community problems, needs, and interests," and another concerning "whether Geller is qualified to remain a licensee."[32] In addition to his troubles with the FCC, Geller had to face a competing applicant who had filed for his facility. Unlike Geller, this competitor could afford a lawyer and had substantial resources to fight.

At a hearing before Administrative Law Judge John H. Conlin, Geller faced two Washington communications attorneys who represented the competing applicant, Grandbanke Corporation, and an FCC attorney who represented the Broadcast Bureau.[33] The hearing was held on June 28–30, 1977, in Gloucester.

Under cross-examination, when asked about his failure to pledge more nonentertainment programming, Geller testified: "I [will] try to do much better . . . but I don't like to promise unless I am sure I can fulfill the promises. . . . I don't want to be caught in a lie."[34] Geller had received a letter from the Chief of the Broadcast Bureau's Renewal and Transfer Division informing him that his renewal application was deficient because of its failure to include an ascertainment survey. The only employee at his station, without a car and with a disabled leg, Geller simply could not conduct the "in-person" ascertainment interviews required, so he instead used the telephone. This method was not in accordance with the FCC's policy and rules. Geller had to work 105 to 110 hours a week to complete the survey and also maintain WCVA's regular on-air schedule. Geller educated himself about ascertainment from one of the FCC's ascertainment *Primers* and from the ascertainment survey Grandbanke had submitted to the FCC with its application. Geller amended his application to include the results of his survey. But he refused to promise that he would sponsor programming responsive to ascertained needs, explaining at the hearing that "I do not know what the revenue situation would be [at my station] and I have never made promises to the Commission that I did not feel I could fulfill."[35]

During the hearing some thirty-five local residents approached the Broadcast Bureau's counsel, Robert A. Zauner, and asked to testify. He arranged for them to do so. They were classical music lovers who came from all walks of life, including "teachers, restaurant owners, proprietors of art galleries, painters and craftsmen, an architect, an engineer, an airline employee, a student, [and] a volunteer worker."[36] They all lauded Geller's programming fare and his unique broadcasting manner.

On the merits, under the FCC's criteria, Geller's proposal was sorely lacking. He committed a major offense by not proposing nonentertainment programs to fulfill his ascertained community needs and by not broadcasting nonentertainment programs equal to the FCC's preferred quantities. Hence, he would not deserve the FCC's weighted preference in favor of renewal, its renewal expectancy. By pledging to devote 16.9 percent of its weekly programming to news, 5.9 percent to public affairs, and 5.9 percent to other nonentertainment programming, his competitor offered the FCC that content mix it had come to expect from licensees. Moreover, Grandbanke had performed its ascertainment survey properly and demonstrated how its programming would satisfy ascertained needs.

Nevertheless, Geller was a long-term local resident. Grandbanke proposed that one of its owners, holding a 66 percent equity interest, would move to Gloucester and work at the station, but that promise could not equal a history of local residence. Furthermore, Geller also had substantial broadcast experience, which Grandbanke lacked, and Geller did not have any other media interests, while one principal of Grandbanke, who had a 34 percent ownership interest in the applicant, owned WNCS (FM), a station licensed to Montpelier, Vermont. To its credit, Grandbanke's proposed technical plant would reach substantially more people than Geller served.

In examining Geller's past record, presiding Administrative Law Judge John H. Conlin did not fault Geller for his paucity of nonentertainment programming. Instead, deeming the case *sui generis,* he found Geller's promises in past renewal applications to in fact equal his performance, albeit not in a way the FCC would have preferred:

While news and more extensive and meaningful programs devoted to local needs and problems would have been desirable, "the pressures and demands of day-to-day operation," in this case, the lack of revenue and the concomitant lack of personnel, virtually compelled Geller to pursue a more modest course. His decision to confine his programming efforts almost entirely to recorded music was, in the circumstances of this case, a reasonable good-faith judgment.[37]

Conlin also found Geller's local residence and his record of broadcast experience unmatched by Grandbanke. The presiding officer faulted Grandbanke for its other media interest but did give the company a "small" advantage on coverage grounds. As to the two parties' proposed programming, despite the fact that Grandbanke's proposal satisfied the FCC's criteria and Geller's did not, Judge Conlin found Grandbanke's proposal and Geller's existing service to be about equal in public interest merit.

Recognizing that a failure to propose nonentertainment programming that specifically addressed community needs had caused the FCC to frequently deny applications for new facilities, the judge nevertheless professed that he had never seen a case where a license renewal had been denied on this ground. Therefore, in considering the special issue concerning ascertainment, Conlin found no basis to deny Geller's renewal and ample evidence of what he termed "mitigating factors" predicated on Geller's dire financial circumstances, "his physical condition and lack of an automobile."[38] The judge also accepted Geller's statements that he did provide adequately responsive programming in the form of classical music, albeit the music was entertainment programming, not the FCC's preferred variety. Assessing the record as a whole, Conlin granted Geller's application.

Grandbanke pressed its case all the way to the full Commission. Unlike Judge Conlin's decision which evinced sympathy for Geller's plight, the FCC sent a clear message to Geller and other small licensees: they must abide by the FCC's programming guidelines—regardless of their financial or physical burdens or risk losing their licenses. The FCC disagreed with the presiding judge: "Reviewing the record . . . we have concluded that Geller did not substantially comply with the Commission's ascertainment requirements."[39] In the FCC's view, Geller's failure to sponsor the agency's preferred programming mix violated the public interest:

> None of his programs . . . were presented in response to ascertained community needs and problems. . . . In our opinion, such a broadcast record is inadequate and reflects poorly on the likelihood of future service in the public interest.[40]

Classical music did not fit within the FCC's conception of programming in the public interest: "[We] . . . to whom Congress has assigned the responsibility for making judgments about what the public interest requires of broadcasts, [have] long held that a licensee must present *informational* programming to meet the needs of its community in addition to the entertainment programming it presents."[41]

Considering what it construed to be an "inadequate level of past performance," the FCC determined that Geller was not deserving of a renewal expectancy,[42] but only a "diminished preference" under the integration and diversification criteria. This preference was outweighed by Grandbanke's "substantial preference for its superior program proposal, and a slight preference for its more efficient use of the spectrum."[43] On reconsideration, the FCC affirmed its decision.[44]

Geller's saga did not end there, however. He appealed to the U.S. Court of Appeals for the District of Columbia. The court determined that the FCC had acted arbitrarily by failing to fully explain its decision to diminish Geller's diversification and integration advantages and by focusing primarily on Geller's past programming record.[45]

When he was back before the same Commission that had found his programming contrary to the public interest, Geller witnessed a little revolution. Suddenly, his diversification advantage took on weighty significance and overwhelmed Grandbanke's programming advantage. In a remarkable flip-flop, the FCC now awarded Geller his renewal.[46]

CURRENT RENEWAL STANDARDS

In the years since *Simon Geller,* the FCC has abolished its promise-versus-performance renewal criteria and its ascertainment requirement. Since the D.C. Circuit Court's *Central Florida Enterprises, Inc. v. FCC* decision, which imposed a meritorious programming standard,[47] the FCC's Review Board has devised what it terms "five discrete criteria" for determining whether a renewal applicant's past programming is meritorious and, so, deserving of a renewal expectancy. As always, almost all of the criteria concern programming either directly or indirectly. Only one criterion concerns compliance with the FCC's rules generally.

> Criterion 1. The licensee's efforts to ascertain the needs, problems and interests of its community;
>
> Criterion 2. The licensee's programmatic response to those ascertained needs;
>
> Criterion 3. The licensee's reputation in the community for serving the needs, problems and interests of the community;

Criterion 4. The licensee's record of compliance with the Communications Act and FCC rules and policies; and

Criterion 5. The presence or absence of any special effort at community outreach or toward providing a forum for local self-expression.[48]

From 1927 to the present, the FCC has maintained a significant influence over the content of the nation's electronic press through its power to award licenses to applicants proposing a particular ownership structure and through its power to review programming when licenses are up for renewal. As long as government remains in the business of licensing the electronic press, it seems certain that the it will, whether admittedly or not, continue to render judgments predicated on its view of what constitutes programming in the public interest.[49]

ENDNOTES

1. *Policy Statement on Comparative Broadcast Hearings,* 1 F.C.C.2d 393 (1965).
2. *Id.* at 394.
3. *Associated Press v. United States,* 326 U.S. 1, 20 (1945).
4. The FCC defines the term "interests" to include *inter alia* actual owner-ship interests of 5 percent or more as well as officer or director positions in media companies. *See Attribution of Ownership Interests,* 97 F.C.C.2d 997 (1984).
5. *Policy Statement on Comparative Broadcast Hearings,* 1 F.C.C.2d 393, 397 (1965).
6. *Id.*
7. *See, e.g., Ram Enterprises,* 57 F.C.C.2d 844, 853 (Rev. Bd. 1976).
8. *See Mid-Florida Television Corp.,* 33 F.C.C.2d 1, 17–18 (Rev. Bd.), *review denied,* 37 F.C.C.2d 559 (1972), *rev'd, TV 9, Inc. v. FCC,* 495 F.2d 929 (1973).
9. *TV 9, Inc. v. FCC,* 495 F.2d 929, 937–38 (D.C. Cir. 1973). In the elegant and poignant language of D.C. Circuit Judge Lawrence H. Silberman, "it seems passing strange that a policy purporting to promote diversity should itself rest on a racial generalization." *Shurberg Broadcasting of Hartford, Inc. v. FCC,* 876 F.2d 902, 921 (D.C. Cir. 1989), *rev'd Metro Broadcasting Inc. v. FCC,* (1990). 110 S. Ct. 2997.
10. *See Mid-Florida Television Corp.,* 69 F.C.C.2d 607, 652 (1978).
11. *See Metro Broadcasting, Inc. v. FCC,* 110 S. Ct. 2997, 3011 (1990).
12. *See Id.* at 3029.
13. *See Id.* at 3036.
14. *See, e.g.,* the surprising case of *Linda L. Crook,* 3 FCC Rcd. 1867 (Rev. Bd. 1988), where before the FCC's Review Board an applicant previously

said to be a sole proprietor black female and local resident was suspected of engaging in acts of misrepresentation and of serving as a "front" for a previously undisclosed non-minority owner.

15. *See, e.g., Attribution of Ownership,* 97 F.C.C.2d 997 (1984), *on reconsideration,* 58 R.R.2d 604 (1985), *clarified,* 1 FCC Rcd. 802 (1986). *See also, e.g., Susan S. Mulkey,* 4 FCC Rcd. 5520 (1989).

16. *See, e.g., KIST Corp.,* 99 F.C.C.2d 173 (Rev. Bd. 1984); *N.E.O. Broadcasting Co.,* 103 F.C.C.2d 1031 (Rev. Bd. 1986); *Jarad Broadcasting Co., Inc.,* 1 FCC Rcd. 181 (Rev. Bd. 1986); *Pacific Television Ltd.,* 2 FCC Rcd. 1101 (Rev. Bd. 1987); *Tulsa Broadcasting Group,* 2 FCC Rcd. 6124 (Rev. Bd. 1987); *Magdalene Gunden Partnership,* 2 FCC Rcd. 5513 (Rev. Bd. 1987); *Metroplex Communications, Inc.,* 4 FCC Rcd. 8149 (Rev. Bd. 1989); *Poughkeepsie Broadcasting Limited,* 5 FCC Rcd. 3374 (Rev. Bd. 1990).

17. *See In the Matter of Amendment of the Commission's Rules to Allow the Selection from Among Competing Applicants for New AM, FM, and Television Stations by Random Selection (Lottery),* 4 FCC Rcd. 2256 (1989). The FCC has terminated this proceeding. *See Amendment of the Commission's Rules to Allow the Selection from Among Competing Applicants for New AM, FM, and Television Stations by Random Selection (Lottery), Order* 67 R.R.2d 1514 (1990).

18. *Religious Broadcasting Network,* 3 FCC Rcd. 4085 (Rev. Bd. 1988).

19. *Id.* at 4085, 4088.

20. In 1990, the FCC tried to enact measures to reduce the number of sham applications filed. It started a rule-making that proposed institution of, among other things, procedural measures to reduce the average time taken for processing applications through comparative hearings and to eliminate the policy basis for exempting limited partners and nonvoting stockholders from having "attributable" ownership interests for purposes of the FCC's integration and diversification analyses. *See Notice of Proposed Rule Making,* Gen. Docket 90–264, FCC 90–194, released June 26, 1990. Regarding competing applications for new facilities, the FCC started a rule-making to limit settlement payments. *See Notice of Proposed Rule Making,* MM Docket No. 90–263, FCC 90–193, released June 26, 1990.

The FCC changed its rules to limit settlement payments for the withdrawal of pleadings called "petitions to deny" which are filed against applications. Settlement payments were to be limited to the "legitimate and prudent expenses" of the petitioner in an effort to dissuade filings by insincere petitioners who might seek to extort money from applicants. *See Abuses of the Broadcast Licensing and Allotment Processes,* 67 R.R.2d 1526 (1990).

For license renewals, the FCC has elected to limit settlement payments to competing renewal applicants to "legitimate and prudent expenses" payable only after a presiding judge has issued an initial decision in order to discourage the filing of fraudulent applications by those seeking profit from the FCC's processes rather than an opportunity to broadcast. *See Broadcast Renewal Applicants (Abuses in the Comparative Renewal Process)*, 67 R.R. 2d 1514 (1990).

21. *See* Dyk, *Full First Amendment Freedom for Broadcasters: The Industry as Eliza on the Ice and Congress as the Friendly Overseer*, 5 YALE J. ON REG. 299, 308 at n.51 (1988):

Even if a broadcaster were certain of ultimate success, it would often be reluctant to take actions that would increase the risk of challenge because the defense of a comparative proceeding may run into millions of dollars [citing *Communications Daily*, Oct. 20, 1987, at 4; D. Patrick, Remarks before the Nat'l Ass'n of Broadcasters 8-9 (Apr. 12, 1988)].

22. *See Second Further Notice of Inquiry and Notice of Proposed Rule Making*, 3 FCC Rcd. 5179, 5185 (1988).

23. *See* Dyk, *Full First Amendment Protection for Broadcasters: The Industry as Eliza on the Ice and Congress as the Friendly Overseer*, 5 YALE J. ON REG. 299, 305 (1988); *Central Florida Enterprises*, 683 F.2d 503-10 (1982).

24. *See* Dyk, *Full First Amendment Freedom for Broadcasters: The Industry as Eliza on the Ice and Congress as the Friendly Overseer*, 5 YALE J. ON REG. 299, 306 (1988); *see also Columbus Broadcasting Coalition v. FCC*, 505 F.2d 320, 326 (D.C. Cir. 1974) ("A renewal applicant must literally 'run on his record' in demonstrating that past programming performance has been responsive to the needs of his broadcast area"); *Alianza Federal de Mercedes v. FCC*, 539 F.2d 732, 735 (D.C. Cir. 1976); *see also Commercial Television Licensing (Separate Statement of Commissioner Rivera)*, 56 R.R.2d 1066 (1984).

25. *Pillar of Fire*, 57 R.R.2d 601, 607 (1984).

26. *See, e.g., Victor Broadcasting Inc. v. FCC*, 722 F.2d 756 (D.C. Cir. 1983).

27. *Office of Communication of the United Church of Christ v. FCC*, 359 F.2d 994, 1005 (D.C. Cir. 1966).

28. *See, e.g., Policy Statement Concerning Comparative Hearings Involving Regular Renewal Applicants*, 22 F.C.C.2d 424 (1970).

29. *See Central Florida Enterprises v. FCC*, 683 F.2d 503, 506 (D.C. Cir. 1982).

30. *See Second Further Notice of Inquiry and Notice of Proposed Rule Making*, 3 FCC Rcd. 5179, 5191-92 (1988).

31. *Simon Geller*, 65 F.C.C.2d 161, 162 (1977).

32. *Id.* at 161, 164.

33. *Simon Geller*, 90 F.C.C.2d 284 (1978).

34. *Id.* at 284, 291.

35. *Id.* at 284, 295.

36. *Id.* at 284, 287–88.
37. *Id.* at 284, 298–99.
38. *Id.* at 303.
39. *Simon Geller,* 90 F.C.C.2d 250, 260–61 (1982).
40. *Id.* at 250, 265.
41. *Id.* at 250, 266.
42. *Id.* at 250, 271.
43. *Id.* at 250, 276–77.
44. *Simon Geller,* 91 F.C.C.2d 1253 (1982).
45. *Committee for Community Access v. FCC,* 737 F.2d 74 (D.C. Cir. 1984).
46. *Simon Geller,* 102 F.C.C.2d 1443, 1453 (1985).
47. *Central Florida Enterprises, Inc. v. FCC,* 683 F.2d 503 (D.C. Cir. 1982).
48. *Seattle Public Schools,* 4 FCC Rcd. 625, 637 (Rev. Bd. 1989).
49. *See, e.g., In the Matter of Enforcement of Prohibitions Against Broadcast Indecency in 18 U.S.C. § 1464 Report of the Commission,* 67 R.R. 2d 1714 (1990) (wherein the FCC announces that it will prohibit the broadcast of programming it regards as "indecent" on a 24-hour per day basis by reviewing licensee programming, upon receipt of a complaint, and coming to the inherently subjective determination of whether that programming "describes, in terms patently offensive as measured by contemporary community standards for the broadcast medium, sexual or excretory activities or organs").

17

STRUCTURAL REGULATION AND THE NEVER-ENDING QUEST FOR DIVERSITY

In addition to the regulations that determine *what* may be said, a considerable number of regulations determine *who* may speak over the broadcast medium. These regulations come in various forms: some prevent broadcasters from owning more than one station in a particular area, others prevent broadcasters from owning more than a certain number of stations nationwide, and others prevent broadcasters from owning certain nonbroadcast media in a particular area. Still others, in the past, have required nonbroadcast cable operators to set aside a specific number of their channels for public access use or to carry local broadcast signals.[1] These regulations, which do not impose direct constraints on content, are said to be "structural" and to affect the freedoms of speech and press only *incidentally* or tangentially. Many view these regulations as less onerous infringements upon speech and press liberty than direct content-based regulations.[2] However, these regulations often prevent certain individuals (those with media interests) from exercising speech rights in specific locales across the United States. They are also as susceptible to political abuse as content-based regulations.

The *constitutional* basis for structural regulations is the Supreme Court's decision in *Associated Press v. United States*.[3] The government has consistently relied on this decision for authority, and will almost certainly continue to rely on it to justify further structural regulations on the broadcast and nonbroadcast media. The latter category includes cable and telephone companies engaged in interactive audio, video, and data services.

Structural controls, purportedly designed to promote economic and viewpoint diversity in local markets, have sometimes served as tools for attaining partisan political objectives[4] and have often been used to prohibit speech, to limit access to certain kinds of speech, or to restrict private editorial discretion.

BROADCAST STRUCTURAL REGULATIONS

Enmeshed in the legislative history of the Radio Act of 1927 and adhered to by both the Federal Radio Commission and the Federal Communications Commission is a central tenet that has rarely been questioned outside the FCC and the courts. That tenet is a presumption that if government does not structure the broadcast marketplace, there will ineluctably arise a single, omnipotent private voice, which will command the people's attention and will dominate their thinking.[5] Government is said to have a legitimate right to prevent this by restricting ownership of stations.

As a result of structural regulations, there is a constant tension in the law between the First Amendment's prohibition on government action and the *Associated Press v. United States* decision's so-called "diversity" principle, which has been construed to require constant governmental intervention into the media marketplace. William E. Lee has noted:

> Any attempt to use government power to achieve a limited objective and simultaneously keep that power under control . . . "is a risky enterprise." Thus, government intervention in the market must be restrained or it may actually inhibit the public interest in a vigorous press. This is the central problem in applying the antitrust laws to the press, and it is a problem that the Court has not sufficiently addressed.[6]

Purported fears of ownership concentration have enabled regulators to justify sundry barriers to market entry in broadcasting since 1927. Without any conclusive proof of anticompetitive practices in the broadcasting field, the FCC continues to impose these barriers and to limit "broadcasters' rights to free speech in markets across the country."[7]

Indeed, from the outset the FCC viewed its authority as not limited to denying licenses to antitrust law violators.[8] Rather, it has sought to ensure an ever-increasing diversity of ownership regardless of the actual state of concentration in the marketplace.[9] The FCC's goal is not to attain mere economic diversity but to use economic diversity as a lever to attain a governmentally predetermined diversity of viewpoints.[10] The FCC has persisted in this quest despite the absence of proof that economic diversity does indeed beget viewpoint diversity and despite the presence of evidence that economies of scale in the broadcasting industry actually promote program diversity by ensuring that there is enough money for it.[11]

THE REPORT ON CHAIN BROADCASTING

On May 2, 1941, the FCC issued its *Report on Chain Broadcasting*,[12] purportedly in an effort to encourage diversity of ownership. In the report, the FCC enacted eight separate regulations designed to limit the power of the nation's broadcasting networks.[13] The regulations prohibited the licensing of entities having exclusive programming arrangements with a network,[14] limited term of network affiliation contracts to two years,[15] prohibited network contracts that did not allow a licensee discretion to reject network programming,[16] prohibited a broadcast license for a network that owned a station serving the same area as the proposed station,[17] and prevented networks from contracting with their affiliates to set uniform rates for network and nonnetwork advertising time.[18]

BARRIERS TO MARKET ENTRY

The "Chain Broadcasting" rules were merely the first major structural rules to circumscribe the speech and press rights of broadcasters. From 1940 to 1977, the FCC added further rules that prohibited the following: a licensee from possessing an ownership interest in a second station in the same area;[19] a licensee from possessing three stations within 100 miles of each other if any two stations' service contours overlapped;[20] a licensee from having joint business relationships with a competing same market broadcaster;[21] a licensee from owning more than a maximum number of stations providing the same service;[22] and a licensee from having certain same area broadcast/cable system, national network/cable, newspaper/broadcast,[23] and telephone/cable system cross-ownership relationships.[24]

The rules have imposed restraints on the exercise of speech by existing broadcast station owners without proof of either specific antitrust violations or of a diminution in programming diversity. They have created one class (nonmedia owners) who have been given rights to speak in preference to another class (media owners). Moreover, the rules have limited the freedom of existing licensees by placing geographic limitations on their right to speak.

ASSOCIATED PRESS V. UNITED STATES AND
THE DIVERSITY PRINCIPLE

The First Amendment does not embody antimonopoly principles. Indeed, at the time of the ratification of the amendment, no one cared that there were only eight daily newspapers in America, seventy weeklies, ten semi-weeklies, and three tri-weeklies.[25] The press was to be free from government controls nonetheless. The history of the First Amendment provides no basis for concluding that it was designed to provide government the power to *guarantee* a media environment most conducive to fulfillment of one or more of the core speech and press values. The core values served by the First Amendment were to be fostered in the absence of government. Nevertheless, in *Associated Press v. United States,* the Supreme Court fundamentally changed the constitutional relationship between the state and the press. *Associated Press* stood for the proposition that the government has a duty to intervene to ensure that the diversity value will be served in the manner it deems appropriate.

In that case, the Court considered whether the Sherman Anti-Trust Act could be applied to the Associated Press (AP), a newswire service.[26] The government had alleged that AP violated the Sherman Act by entering into a "combination and conspiracy in restraint of trade and commerce in news among the states" and by attempting "to monopolize a part of that trade."[27]

AP's appeal to the Supreme Court proceeded from a District Court's grant of a government motion for summary decision.[28] The District Court found that AP's newswire subscribers contracted to become members of an AP association. That association was governed by by-laws that included certain anticompetitive provisions.[29] Among them were provisions requiring each member newspaper to publish the service's news and to furnish AP with all news within a member's "district," an area to be defined by AP's board of directors. The news furnished by AP and discovered by its association members was not to be made available to nonmember competitors before publication.[30] The District Court found the AP by-laws to contain "provisions designed to stifle competition in the newspaper publishing field."[31] According to the District Court's findings, out of 1,803 English-language newspapers in the United States, 1,179 were contractually bound "not to supply either AP or their own 'spontaneous' news to any non-member of AP."[32]

The Supreme Court affirmed the District Court's judgment in favor of granting the government's motion for summary decision. The Court found it unnecessary for the government to prove the presence of an actual restraint of trade, noting that under the law, "combinations are no less unlawful because they have not as yet resulted in restraint."[33] Turning to the First Amendment considerations at stake, the court stated that "it would be strange indeed . . . if the grave concern for freedom of speech which prompted adoption of the First Amendment should be read as a command that the government was without power to protect the freedom."[34]

This apparently simple premise produced a revolutionary change in the law. The government was not to be deprived of all power over the press; rather, the government was to have the power to regulate the industry's structure in order to promote a particular level of ideological commerce in the idea marketplace.

This mighty power to shape the media was vested in a part of the government under the political control of the executive branch, the Department of Justice. The antitrust laws, which are enforceable by the DOJ, could now be applied to the press so that the core value of diversity might be served. "The First Amendment, far from providing an argument against application of the Sherman Act, here provides powerful reasons to the contrary," wrote the Court.[35] The Sherman Act was but a tool for use by government in fulfilling the First Amendment's diversity principle. The "amendment rests on the assumption that the widest possible dissemination of information from diverse and antagonistic sources is essential to the welfare of the public, that a free press is a condition of a free society," wrote the Court.[36]

The great sweep of the Court's reasoning invited the government to determine what level of diversity constituted a competitive level and to apply the antitrust laws to punish or constrain stations not supplying the kind of information that would produce what the government deemed competitive. Despite the fact that such government policing of the information marketplace would be under the ultimate control of political powers who could, without much difficulty, abuse their authority and interfere with private editorial judgments, the Court determined that affirmative government regulation of the structure of the press was mandated by the First Amendment. Moreover, the Court for the first time found *private* censorship to be the equivalent of *government* censorship and ruled that the state could regulate private censorship. The court reasoned that the "freedom of the press from governmental interference under the First Amendment does not sanction repression of that freedom by private interests."[37] In footnote 18 to the decision, the Court tried to separate the concepts of repression of content from repression of others' economic opportunity to publish AP news or the news of its members.[38] However, the Court did not explain how government regulation of the media's structure could avoid falling prey to those in power who might favor limiting the freedom of the press to attain partisan objectives.

This danger did not escape the attention of the dissenters in *Associated Press*.[39] Justice Owen B. Roberts understood that affording government a role in structuring the mass media would enable the state to unduly restrict freedom of speech and the press even if the direct suppression of content was not at stake:

> It is not protecting a freedom, but confining it, to prescribe where and how and under what conditions one must impart the literary product of his thought and research. This is fettering the press, not striking off its chains.[40]

Justice Frank Murphy understood that for the first time the Sherman Act was being "used as a vehicle for affirmative intervention by the Government in the realm of dissemination of information."[41] He believed that the Court failed to recognize the unique mission of the entity being regulated; that entity was not in the business of "manufacturing automobiles, aluminum or gasoline" but was in the business of "collecting and distributing news and information."[42] In Murphy's view any "governmental action directly aimed at the methods or conditions of such collection or distribution is an interference with the press, however differing in degree it may be from governmental restraints on written or spoken utterances themselves."[43] He thought the majority had ignored the inherent dangers of abuse of political power that teach us "to hesitate before creating a precedent in which might lurk even the slightest justification for . . . interference by the Government in these matters."[44]

The *Associated Press* diversity principle has led to many regulations. It underlies the FCC's regulations of ownership.[45] It underlies the U.S. District Court for the District of Columbia's Consent Decree that governs the extent to which the Bell operating companies may enter the electronic publishing, video programming, information services, and cable industries.[46] The principle also underlies congressional and court considerations about the propriety of imposing on cable systems ownership restrictions, requirements for local broadcast signal carriage, and requirements for public access.[47]

THE DANGERS OF GOVERNMENT ENFORCEMENT
OF THE DIVERSITY PRINCIPLE

"Although a chilling effect on the press may result from antitrust actions instigated by a President who is hostile toward the press," writes William E. Lee, "the Court has consistently ignored this possibility."[48] The *Associated Press* principle poses a direct threat to freedom of speech because it relies on that entity (the government) which has historically suppressed freedom of speech and press to remedy anticompetitive effects in the media marketplace. Unavoidably, affording the government authority to structure the media allows people with political power to punish those whose views they dislike and to reward those whose views they like.

Government enforcement of the antitrust laws has been characterized as "arbitrary" because the degree of enforcement depends to a large extent on the regulatory agenda of each administration.[49] Enforcement of the antitrust laws is often a political determination, because many of the initial decisions that must be made before a suit is brought are subjective and invite political manipulation. For example, the government decides how to define the market for analysis under the antitrust laws (will it be all newspapers? newspapers in a specific locale? all television stations? all television stations in a certain locale? newspapers, television, radio, and cable?). The outcome of any antitrust case depends on how one defines the relevant market. Thus how government discretion is exercised is important. The government bases its decisions about whom to prosecute on its own policy considerations. The determination is necessarily fraught with dangers of selective enforcement to punish political enemies or to reward political favorites competing with the defendant. Finally, the enforcement taken by the government may result in agreements between it and the defendant, such as the AT&T Consent Decree, which can enable the courts to wield considerable control over the defendant's operations long into the future.

Events from the Nixon administration illustrate the extent to which antitrust enforcement can be used for political ends. In his *American Broadcasting and the First Amendment,* Lucas Powe documents the efforts of the Nixon administration to use the antitrust laws to silence political opposition voiced through the nation's (then) three major networks.[50] President Nixon's Chief of Staff, H. R. ("Bob") Haldeman, asked that White House aide Jeb Magruder draft a "talking" paper "on specific problems we've had in shot-gunning the media and anti-Administration spokesmen on unfair coverage."[51] In response, Magruder produced a memo entitled "The Shotgun versus the Rifle."[52] Among the proposals Magruder offered was one to use the Department of Justice's Antitrust Division to investigate the media. Magruder wrote: "Even the possible threat of anti-trust action I think would be effective in changing their views."[53]

In December 1974, the administration brought suit against the three television networks, alleging violations of Sections 1 and 2 of the Sherman Act (that is, combinations in restraint of trade, monopolization, and attempts to monopolize prime time television programming).[54] The networks believed that the suit was a product of Nixon's alleged grudge against the media. The support for this charge, the networks alleged, could be found in White House tapes that purportedly documented "planned retribution against the Washington Post."[55] The congressional investigation of Watergate disclosed that on September 15, 1972, Nixon, Haldeman, and John Dean had in fact discussed a possible renewal challenge to the *Washington Post*'s Miami, Florida, television station. The discussion revealed considerable animus:

> PRESIDENT: The main thing is the *Post* is going to have damnable, damnable problems out of this one. They have a television station . . . and they're going to have to get it renewed.
> HALDEMAN: They've got a radio station, too.
> PRESIDENT: Does that come up, too? The point is, when does it come up?
> DEAN: I don't know. But the practice of non-licensees filing on top of licensees has certainly gotten more . . . active in . . . this area.
> PRESIDENT: And it's going to be Goddamn active here.
> DEAN: (Laughter) (Silence)
> PRESIDENT: Well, the game has to be played awfully rough.[56]

Before the end of 1972, the *Washington Post*'s Miami station did suffer a renewal challenge from a group of people including "two law partners of former Senator George Smathers, a close friend of Nixon's."[57]

The antitrust suit against the networks did not go very far. It became mired in an executive privilege legal thicket from which it could not be extricated. At the networks' request, discovery orders were issued requiring the government to produce "certain presidential documents which would allegedly show that the actions were" based on "improper" motives.[58] The government alleged that it need not produce the documents because they were "privileged." Other documents for which the government did not claim a privilege were simply not produced on time.[59] In response, the networks filed a motion to dismiss the government's suit and the court granted the motion, reserving to the government a right to refile later.[60]

Enforcement of the diversity principle is also prone to political abuse when Congress and the executive branch look to the FCC to enforce the multiple ownership rules. Recently, the FCC's selective policy of affording waivers to its newspaper-broadcast cross-ownership rule became embroiled in political controversy. An affiliate of Rupert Murdoch's News America Publishing, Inc., acquired television stations in Boston and New York, two cities where News America owned newspapers.[61] It obtained a temporary waiver of the rule from the FCC.[62] In the continuing appropriations legislation for fiscal year 1988, Congress "buried an obscure provision forbidding the Commission from extending any 'current grants' of temporary waivers."[63] The only two current grants in effect were News America's Boston and New York waivers.[64] Murdoch challenged this law on Fifth Amendment equal protection grounds in the U.S. Court of Appeals for the District of Columbia Circuit, alleging that it was "uniquely discriminatory." Among the pieces of evidence Murdoch marshaled were statements that were made by the amendment's sponsors that showed animus directed against News America.[65] Although the court seemed unimpressed with the evidence of ill-will, it did find that the "Hollings Amendment str[uck] at Murdoch with the precision of a laser beam," forbidding only his waiver request and no others. Accordingly, the court struck the provision as violative of the Fifth Amendment's equal protection clause.[66]

The executive branch has also relied on the diversity principle to express disdain for the press. In 1938, following the legislative defeat of his "court packing" plan, President Franklin D. Roosevelt began to turn on his critics.[67] In particular, with assistance of his FCC appointee, James Lawrence Fly, Roosevelt saw to it that an investigation was conducted of the newspaper industry to determine whether newspapers should possess ownership interests in radio stations.[68] The investigation was halted by the U.S. Court of Appeals for the District of Columbia Circuit which ruled that any general ban on newspaper entry into the broadcasting business would be an exercise of power beyond that delegated by Congress to the FCC.[69]

These few instances illustrate the extent to which political power can influence the use of structural regulations to force changes in the marketplace of ideas. Antitrust enforcement and the FCC's ownership rules can and have been used, like the FCC's content-based regulations, to restrict or suppress the ability of the press to exercise editorial discretion and to disseminate news and information freely. These dangers of abuse are too great to endure in a nation committed to free speech and press.

Nevertheless, the diversity principle will likely continue to be used to justify the FCC's broadcast ownership regulations, to justify government attempts to force carriage of broadcast signals on cable systems, whether operated by the telephone companies or not, and to require public access to a certain number of cable channels or to unused cable channels.

In the broadcast context, these regulations will continue to foreclose opportunities for existing broadcasters to speak and will continue to enhance the speech rights of non-media owners at the expense of media owners. In the cable context, these actions will force cable operators to associate with views they may oppose, to disseminate information against their will, to present programs of a quality they find unappealing, and to turn over a part of their forums to the government. In each of these actions there lurks a violation of the core values of the First Amendment. Each restricts the freedom of publishers and supplants it with government control.

Some have argued that merely carrying programs created by someone other than the cable operator does not involve an editorial function.[70] An analogous argument could be made that newspapers choosing to fill a substantial portion of their pages with newswire service reporting are also not engaged in editorial functions. However, decisions about which programs or articles to present and not present and about what channels or pages to reserve are editorial judgments that express the preferences of the medium owner. To the extent that government substitutes its choices for those of the owner or requires media to carry others' programming on a common carrier basis, government supplants private editorial freedom. This substitution entails speech suppression contrary to the purposes of the First Amendment.[71]

In the *Associated Press* case, the Court did not err by identifying diversity as a core value of the First Amendment. Indeed, that value inheres in the Marketplace of Ideas/Search for Truth aspect of the freedom. It erred by ascribing to government the role of deciding what amount and kind of diversity would be best. The First Amendment does not *require* any set amount of diversity in the marketplace. If everyone were to choose to remain silent, the First Amendment would not be violated, for the amendment's purpose is to deprive government of a power over the press and to leave to private citizens the decision of when to speak or not speak and what to say.

ENDNOTES

1. For surveys of the law in these areas from quite different First Amendment perspectives, *cf.* Emord, *The First Amendment Invalidity of FCC Ownership Regulations,* 38 CATH. U. L. REV. 401 (1989); with Nadel, *Editorial Freedom:*

Editors, Retailers, and Access to the Mass Media, 9 COMM/ENT 213 (1987); *See also* Mallamud, *Judicial Intrusion into Cable Television Regulation: The Misuse of O'Brien in Reviewing Compulsory Carriage Rules,* 34 VILL. L. REV. 467 (1989).

2. *See generally* Mallamud, *Judicial Intrusion into Cable Television Regulation: The Misuse of O'Brien in Reviewing Compulsory Carriage Rules,* 34 VILL. L. REV. 467 (1989).

3. 326 U.S. 1, 20 (1944).

4. *See, e.g.,* L. POWE, AMERICAN BROADCASTING AND THE FIRST AMENDMENT 72–74 (1987) (concerning President Franklin D. Roosevelt's efforts to persuade his appointed FCC chairman to " 'get the newspapers out of broadcasting' "); *Id.* at 83–84; 124–26 (concerning Nixon aide Jeb Magruder's memo entitled *The Shotgun versus the Rifle* in which he proposed to White House Chief of Staff H. R. Haldeman that the administration investigate whether "the possible threat of anti-trust action" could be relied on to punish the anti-Administration press); *see also* Note, *The Antitrust Implications of Network Television Programming,* 27 THE HASTINGS L. J. 1207 (1976) (concerning the Nixon administration's antitrust suit against the three major television networks in the 1970s. *See News America Publishing, Inc. v. FCC,* 844 F.2d 800, 803 (D.C. Cir. 1988) (documenting the discriminatory suspension of the Commission's newspaper-broadcast cross-ownership rule by members of Congress to prevent Rupert Murdoch's News America Publishing, Inc., from owning television stations in Boston and New York as well as owning daily newspapers in those two cities).

5. *See, e.g.,* Johnson, *Media Barons and the Public Interest,* ATLANTIC, June 1969, at 43–51.

6. Lee, *Antitrust Enforcement, Freedom of the Press, and the "Open Market": The Supreme Court on the Structure and Conduct of Mass Media,* 32 VAND. L. REV. 1249, 1338 (1979).

7. *See* Emord, *The First Amendment Invalidity of FCC Ownership Regulations,* 38 CATH. U. L. REV. 401, 405 (1989).

8. In FEDERAL COMMUNICATIONS COMMISSION, REPORT ON CHAIN BROADCASTING 83 (1941), the FCC explained:

    > While many of the network practices raise serious questions under the antitrust laws, our jurisdiction does not depend on a showing that they do in fact constitute a violation of the antitrust laws. It is not our function to apply the antitrust laws as such. It is our duty, however, to refuse licenses or renewals to any person who engages or proposes to engage in practices which will prevent either himself or other licensees or both from making the fullest use of radio facilities.

9. *See NBC v. United States,* 319 U.S. 190, 226 (1943); *FCC v. National Citizens Committee for Broadcasting,* 436 U.S. 775, 798–902 (1978).

10. *See Steele v. FCC*, 770 F.2d 1192, 1195 (D.C. Cir. 1985) ("Diversification seeks not only to avoid undue concentration of media outlets in the hands of a few individuals or entities, but also to promote diversity of programming and viewpoint.").

11. *See, e.g., Notice of Proposed Rulemaking, Amendment of Section 73.3555 of the Commission's Rules, The Broadcast Multiple Ownership Rules*, 2 FCC Rcd. 1138, 1140–41 (1987); OFFICE OF PLANS AND POLICY, FEDERAL COMMUNICATIONS COMMISSION, MEASUREMENT OF CONCENTRATION IN HOME VIDEO MARKETS iii, 10, 13, 55 (1982) (staff report).

12. FEDERAL COMMUNICATIONS COMMISSION, REPORT ON CHAIN BROADCASTING (1941), *aff'd, NBC v. United States*, 319 U.S. 190 (1943), amended by *Report, Statement of Policy, and Order*, 63 F.C.C.2d 674 (1977).

13. §§ 3.101–3.108, 47 C.F.R. (1941).

14. *See* § 3.103, 47 C.F.R. (1941).

15. *See Id.*

16. *See* § 3.105, 47 C.F.R. (1941).

17. *See* § 3.106, 47 C.F.R. (1941).

18. *See* § 3.108, 47 C.F.R. (1941).

19. *See* Emord, *The First Amendment Invalidity of FCC Ownership Regulations*, 38 CATH. U. L. REV. 401, 411–12 (1989).

20. *See Id.* at 401, 418–19.

21. *See Id.* at 401, 412–13.

22. *See Id.* at 401, 413–14.

23. *See Id.* at 401, 415–19.

24. *See In the Matter of Telephone Company-Cable Television Cross-Ownership Rules, Sections 63.54–63.58, Further Notice of Inquiry and Notice of Proposed Rulemaking*, 3 FCC Rcd. 5849 (1988).

25. *See Syracuse Peace Council*, 2 FCC Rcd. 5043, 5054 (1987).

26. *Associated Press v. United States*, 326 U.S. 1, 4 (1944); *see* Lee, *Antitrust Enforcement, Freedom of the Press, and the "Open Market": The Supreme Court on the Structure and Conduct of the Mass Media*, 32 VAND. L. REV. 1265–69 (1979).

27. *Associated Press v. United States*, 326 U.S. 1, 4 (1944).

28. *Id.*

29. *Id.* at 1, 11.

30. *Id.* at 1, 9.

31. *Id.* at 1, 11.

32. *Id.* at 1, 9 n.4.

33. *Id.* at 1, 12.

34. *Id.* at 1, 20.

35. *Id.*

36. *Id.*

37. *Id.* at 20 (1944).
38. *Id.*
39. *Id.* at 29 (Roberts, J., dissenting); *Id.* at 40 (Murphy, J., dissenting).
40. *Id.* at 48 (1944).
41. *Id.* at 51.
42. *Id.*
43. *Id.*
44. *Id.* at 52.
45. *See* Emord, *The First Amendment Invalidity of FCC Ownership Regulations,* 38 Cath. U. L. Rev. 401 (1989).
46. *See United States v. American Telephone & Telegraph Co.,* 552 F. Supp. 131 (D.D.C. 1982), *aff'd sub nom., Maryland v. United States,* 460 U.S. 1001 (1983); *see also* Note, *The Diversity Principle and the MFJ Information Services Restriction: Applying Time-Worn First Amendment Assumptions to New Technologies,* 38 Cath. U. L. Rev. 471 (1989); Winer, *Telephone Companies Have First Amendment Rights Too: The Constitutional Case for Entry into Cable,* 8 Cardozo Arts & Entertainment L. J. 257 (1990).
47. *See, e.g.,* Mallamud, *Judicial Intrusion into Cable Television Regulation: The Misuse of O'Brien in Reviewing Compulsory Carriage Rules,* 34 Vill. L. Rev. 467 (1989).
48. Lee, *Antitrust Enforcement, Freedom of the Press, and the "Open Market": The Supreme Court on the Structure and Conduct of Mass Media,* 32 Vand. L. Rev. 1249, 1275–76 (1979).
49. *See, e.g.,* D. Armentano, Antitrust Policy 1–9 (1986); *see also* DiLorenzo, *The Origins of Antitrust: An Interest-Group Perspective,* 5 Int'l Rev. of L. & Econ. 73–90 (1985); Tollison, *Public Choice and Antitrust,* 4 Cato J. 905–16 (1985).
50. *See* L. Powe, American Broadcasting and the First Amendment 121–41 (1987).
51. *Id.* at 124–25.
52. *Id.* at 124.
53. *Id.* at 125.
54. *See* Note, *The Antitrust Implications of Network Television Programming,* 27 Hastings L. J. 1207 (1976).
55. *Id.* at 1207, 1208 n.11.
56. Quoted in L. Powe, American Broadcasting and the First Amendment 131–32 (1987).
57. *See* L. Powe, American Broadcasting and the First Amendment 132 (1987). Powe explains that, in 1970, Nixon's friend Bebe Rebozo challenged the *Post*'s Miami station. That suit lasted seven and a half months and resulted in a settlement agreement for an undisclosed sum for legal fees. *Id.* at 131.
58. *See United States v. NBC, Inc.,* 65 F.R.D. 415 (1974).

59. *See Id.* at 415, 421.

60. *See Id.* at 415, 421–22.

61. *See* Emord, *The First Amendment Invalidity of Ownership Regulations,* 38 CATH. U. L. REV. 401, 417 n.87 (1989).

62. *See Metromedia Radio and Television, Inc.,* 102 F.C.C.2d 1334, 1353 (1985); *Twentieth Holdings Corp.,* 1 FCC Rcd. 1201 (1986).

63. H.R. REP. No. 498, 100th Cong., 1st Sess. 34 (1987).

64. *See* Emord, *The First Amendment Invalidity of FCC Ownership Regulations,* 38 CATH. U. L. REV. 401, 417 n.87 (1989).

65. *Id.*

66. *Id.* at 401, 417.

67. *See* L. POWE, AMERICAN BROADCASTING AND THE FIRST AMENDMENT 70 (1987).

68. *Id.* at 72.

69. *Id.* at 73.

70. *See, e.g.,* Nadel, *A Unified Theory of the First Amendment: Divorcing the Medium from the Message,* 11 FORDHAM URBAN L. J. 216–23 (1982); Mallamud, *Judicial Intrusion into Cable Television Regulation: The Misuse of O'Brien in Reviewing Compulsory Carriage Rules,* 34 VILL. L. REV. 467, 483 (1989).

71. *See, e.g., Buckley v. Valeo,* 424 U.S. 1, 48–49 (1976) (where the Supreme Court explained that "the concept that government may restrict the speech of some elements of our society in order to enhance the relative voice of others is wholly foreign to the First Amendment") *See also* Winer, *Telephone Companies Have First Amendment Rights Too: The Constitutional Case for Entry into Cable,* 8 CARDOZO ARTS & ENTERTAINMENT L. J. 257 (1990).

18

TOWARD A FREE
BROADCAST PRESS

Little changed in federal content and structural regulations until the election of Ronald Reagan to the presidency in 1980. Although previous administrations had taken some action toward deregulating the mass media, the 1980 election brought about an unprecedented deregulatory transformation at the Federal Communications Commission. For the first time in FCC history, a president appointed commissioners whose primary objective was to eliminate FCC regulations. Mark S. Fowler, President Reagan's first chosen FCC chairman, shared Reagan's free market philosophy. As Henry Geller later observed, "Like President Reagan, whom Fowler much admires, the former chairman has a clear and consistent philosophy: reliance on competition, the marketplace, and, as much as possible, deregulation."[1] In virtually every major FCC decision from 1981 to 1988, Fowler tried to roll back or eliminate the regulations that had accumulated since 1934.

Although efforts at deregulation had been made during earlier administrations, none had so pervasive an impact as the deregulatory efforts initiated by the two Reagan FCC Chairmen, Fowler and Dennis R. Patrick. In particular, Fowler spent the better part of seven years trying to tear apart central fibers in the regulatory tapestry, thereby making complete disassembly of the content and structural regulatory regime a possibility. In doing so, he repeatedly incurred the wrath of Congress, which viewed his efforts as a threat to its ability to gain access to the media and a threat to the control they had long exercised over the media. He also alarmed certain broadcasting industry leaders, as they realized that the erosion of FCC authority and increased competition would cost them monopoly rents.

The change in direction orchestrated by the Reagan FCC called into question the legitimacy of basic tenets of the regulatory regime, including the FCC's utility-based trusteeship model for regulation. As Matthew Spitzer has observed, the Patrick Commission "effectively attacked the reason for the Commission's existence" by abandoning the central underpinning for broadcast regulation, spectrum scarcity.[2] Despite the efforts of Fowler and Patrick, the decades old, utility-based "trusteeship model" of broadcast regulation remains very much a dominant force.[3]

When he assumed the chairmanship of the agency, Fowler introduced what he termed a "marketplace approach" to broadcast regulation. Early in his administration, Fowler made clear his intentions:

> Put simply, I believe that we are at the end of regulating broadcasting under the trusteeship model. Whether you call it "paternalism" or "nannyism," it is "Big Brother," and it must cease. I believe in a marketplace approach to broadcast regulation. . . . Under the coming marketplace approach, the Commission should, as far as possible, defer to a broadcaster's judgment about how best to compete for viewers and listeners, because this serves the public interest.[4]

THE DEREGULATION OF SELECT CONTENT CONTROLS

During the Reagan years, the FCC eliminated many regulations over what could be broadcast. It abolished its nonentertainment programming guidelines, its commercial guidelines, and its ascertainment requirement.[5] The FCC abolished its promise-versus-performance standard of renewal review[6] and its program log requirement (substituting for it a less-extensive issues/programs list requirement).[7]

The FCC eliminated or reduced the effect of a number of content-based or content-focused regulations. It abolished restrictions on broadcasting horse races and betting advertisements,[8] and it abolished its 1966 policy statement[9] limiting the broadcast of contests and promotions contrary to the public interest.[10] It eliminated regulations discouraging the broadcast of loud commercials;[11] the advertisement of alcoholic beverages; and the broadcast of astrological information, foreign language programs, repetitious records and tapes, sound effects in promotional announcements, and information that could encourage harassing or threatening telephone calls.[12] The FCC ended its policy against misleading concert promotion announcements, nonperformance of sales contracts, and false and deceptive advertising.[13] It also eliminated rules prohibiting fraudulent billing and network clipping (that is, airing advertisements that cut into part of network shows),[14] and its rule requiring broadcasters to originate certain programming within their communities.[15]

THE DEATH OF THE FAIRNESS DOCTRINE AND THE FCC'S DISAVOWAL OF THE "SCARCITY RATIONALE"

By far the most extraordinary action against content control was the FCC's 1987 decision to abolish the Fairness Doctrine set forth in *Syracuse Peace Council*.[16] The Fairness Doctrine imposed a two-fold editorial duty on broadcast licensees. Under threat of fines or license renewal challenges,[17] broadcasters were required to provide coverage to "controversial issues of public importance" and to afford "a reasonable opportunity" for the airing of contrasting views on those issues.[18] Although the Fairness Doctrine was eliminated, its corollaries remain in force.[19]

In *Syracuse Peace Council*,[20] the FCC repudiated the spectrum scarcity rationale that had served as the constitutional underpinning for all broadcast regulation. The FCC wrote:

> The evil of government intervention into the editorial process of the press (whether print or electronic) and the right of individuals to receive political viewpoints unfettered by government interference are not changed because the electromagnetic spectrum (or any other resource necessary to convey expression) is scarce or because the government (in conjunction with the marketplace) allocates that scarce resource. . . .
>
> [I]n analyzing the appropriate First Amendment standard to be applied to the electronic press, the concept of scarcity—be it spectrum or numerical—is irrelevant. . . .
>
> Consequently, we believe that an evaluation of First Amendment standards should not focus on the *physical differences* between the electronic press and the printed press, but on the *functional similarities* between these two media and upon the underlying values and goals of the First Amendment. We believe that the function of the electronic press in a free society is identical to that of the printed press and that, therefore, the constitutional analysis of government control of content should be no different.[21]

Because the constitutionality of virtually every content and structural regulation is premised on spectrum scarcity, the FCC's repudiation of this rationale "is destined to have a profound impact."[22]

Although in its *Syracuse Peace Council* decision the FCC disavowed any interest in ending its public trusteeship model for broadcast regulation (contending that it "may still impose certain conditions on licensees in furtherance of . . . [the] public interest"[23]) it is clear that without spectrum scarcity, there can be little left of the notion that a broadcaster must abide by a pre-ordained federal conception of what constitutes broadcasting in the public interest. As Henry Geller has astutely observed:

> The fairness doctrine flows directly from the public trustee notion, and to eliminate the fairness doctrine one must also eliminate the notion that broadcasters should act as public trustees. Moreover, the public trustee notion must be erased before a broadcast journalist can be guaranteed the same First Amendment rights as a newspaper journalist.[24]

Although the Congress or the FCC may seize upon some other doctrine to regulate broadcasting, the current legal basis for broadcast regulation is unquestionably in peril without further efforts by the Supreme Court to save it.[25]

Still the law of the land, the spectrum scarcity rationale has its constitutional foundation in *NBC v. United States*[26] and in *Red Lion Broadcasting Co. v. FCC*[27] In the aftermath of *Syracuse Peace Council,* the rationale now appears inexorably "in the course of ultimate extinction."[28]

THE ORIGINS OF THE SPECTRUM SCARCITY RATIONALE

Red Lion Broadcasting Co. v. FCC came twenty years after the Fairness Doctrine began to be enforced in 1949. In that decision, the Supreme Court reiterated Justice Frankfurter's conclusion in *NBC v. United States* that spectrum scarcity was a constitutional basis for distinguishing the broadcast medium from the print press and for affording the former less First Amendment protection.

Because in *Red Lion* the Fairness Doctrine was at issue, the decision of the Court put the law squarely in favor of federal control over broadcast content and premised this authority on a conception nowhere to be found in the First Amendment or print medium precedent.

In its 1949 report on *Editorializing by Broadcast Licensees,* the FCC announced that it was "[the] right of the public to be informed, rather than any right on the part of the Government, any broadcast licensee or any individual member of the public to broadcast his own particular views . . . which is the foundation stone of the American system of broadcasting."[29]

In particular, echoing the view articulated by Herbert Hoover at the Fourth National Radio Conference, the FCC determined that the right of the public to hear took precedence over the right of the broadcaster to speak:

> Licensee editorialization is but one aspect of freedom of expression by means of radio. Only insofar as it is exercised in conformity with the paramount right of the public to hear a reasonably balanced presentation of all responsible viewpoints on particular issues can such editorialization be considered to be consistent with . . . the public interest.[30]

In *Red Lion,* the Court wrapped the mantle of the First Amendment around this "foundation stone." It decided that the *degree* of First Amendment protection that would be afforded a message depended on the medium transmitting the message.[31] In the case of broadcasting, the Court decided that radio frequencies were a uniquely scarce resource in that demand for available frequencies far exceeded supply. This scarcity was said to justify abridgement of the First Amendment:

> Where there are substantially more individuals who want to broadcast than there are frequencies to allocate, it is idle to posit an unabridgeable First Amendment right to broadcast comparable to the right of every individual to speak, write or publish.[32]

The Court explained that:

> Because of the scarcity of radio frequencies, the Government is permitted to put restraints on licensees in favor of others whose views *should* be expressed on this unique medium. . . . *It is the right of the viewers and listeners, not the right of the broadcasters, which is paramount* [emphasis added].[33]

The Court's rationale included one significant caveat: "[if] experience" with broadcast technology post-1969 proved that "the net effect of [administration of the doctrine was to reduce] rather than [enhance] the volume and quality of coverage," there would be "time enough to reconsider the constitutional implications."[34]

In July 1984, the Supreme Court reemphasized that proof of technological changes could influence its constitutional considerations. In footnote 11 to *FCC v. League of Women Voters of Cal.,*[35] it stated:

> The prevailing rationale for broadcast regulation based on spectrum scarcity has come under increasing criticism in recent years. Critics, including the incumbent Chairman of the FCC [Mark Fowler], charge that with the advent of cable and satellite television technology, communities now have access to such a wide variety of stations that the scarcity doctrine is obsolete. . . . *We*

are not prepared, however, to reconsider our long-standing approach without some signal from Congress or the FCC that technological developments have advanced so far that some revision of broadcast regulation may be required [emphasis added].[36]

In 1987 in its *Syracuse Peace Council* decision, the FCC clearly gave the Court the signal it requested. In *Syracuse Peace Council,* the FCC stated:

We further believe, as the Supreme Court indicated in *FCC v. League of Women Voters of California,* that the dramatic transformation in the telecommunications marketplace provides a basis for the Court to reconsider its application of diminished First Amendment protection to the electronic media. Despite the physical differences between the electronic and print media, their roles in our society are identical, and we believe that the same First Amendment principles should be equally applicable to both.[37]

Two years before that decision, in its seminal 1985 Fairness Report, the FCC had comprehensively reexamined the doctrine in light of communications developments since 1949 and the experience of broadcasters under the doctrine. The FCC took seriously the First Amendment concerns of broadcasters and put their interests above those of the Congress in deciding what programming fare was responsive to the needs and interests of viewers and listeners.

The agency found that the administration of the doctrine had been both highly intrusive (into the editorial discretion of licensees) and quite costly.[38] It concluded:

We believe that the interest of the public in viewpoint diversity is fully served by the multiplicity of voices in the marketplace today and that the intrusion by government into the content of programming occasioned by the enforcement of the doctrine unnecessarily restricts the journalistic freedom of broadcasters. Furthermore, we find that the fairness doctrine, in operation, actually inhibits the presentation of controversial issues of public importance to the detriment of the public and in degradation of the editorial prerogatives of broadcast journalists.[39]

Virtually every broadcast journalist who participated in the 1985 proceeding on the efficacy of the Fairness Doctrine argued that because the second prong of the doctrine (which required balanced coverage), became operative only when controversial issues were broadcast, the doctrine discouraged broadcasters from airing controversial issues at all.[40] Broadcasters expressed fear that a Fairness Doctrine complaint could damage their renewal chances or force them to incur expensive legal fees in fending off the charges.[41] Moreover, broadcasters came to accept that the principal Fairness Doctrine complainants were well-financed special interest groups, which, regardless of the legal merit of their challenges, would file complaints knowing that the cost of defense alone could be enough to force the broadcasters to provide the groups with free air time.[42]

In hearings on the Fairness Doctrine, a former chief of the FCC's Mass Media Bureau, James McKinney, described in detail how FCC staffers were obliged to exercise their own editorial judgment in place of a licensee's in rendering a Fairness Doctrine decision:

> [I]t might be interesting for you to know the process that we go through here at the agency at the lower staff level before the Commissioners get [a case] for final decision. We . . . sit down with tape recordings [and] videotapes of . . . what has been broadcast on a specific station. We compare that to newspapers [and] other public statements that are made in the community, which may be 2000 miles away. . . . [W]hen it comes down to the final analysis, we take out stop watches and we start counting [the] seconds and minutes that are devoted to one issue compared to [the] seconds and minutes devoted to the other side of that issue. . . . [I]n the final analysis we start giving our judgment as [to] what words mean in the context of what was said on the air. What was the twist that was given that specific statement or that commercial advertisement? Was it really pro-nuclear power or was it pro some other associated issue?[43]

Mindful of its power limitations and uncertain whether the Fairness Doctrine was a creature of its own policies or mandated by statutory language, the FCC, despite finding that the doctrine abridged the First Amendment rights of broadcasters, deferred to Congress for further action.[44] While awaiting congressional action, the FCC continued to enforce the doctrine. It held that a licensee, Meredith Corporation, violated the doctrine when it denied the Syracuse Peace Council an opportunity to broadcast its opposition to three advertisements promoting the Nine Mile II nuclear power plant "as a sound investment for New York's future."

While the FCC considered Meredith's petition for reconsideration of the *Syracuse Peace Council* decision, Judge Robert Bork took a dramatic step, hinting at the D.C. Circuit Court's willingness to reconsider the validity of content regulation premised upon spectrum scarcity. In the 1986 decision *Telecommunications Research & Action Center v. FCC*,[45] Bork wrote that he regarded spectrum scarcity as an invalid basis for providing lessened First Amendment protection to the electronic media, believing broadcast frequencies to be no different from other economic goods in society, most notably paper for the print medium, and finding "scarcity" a "universal fact" that could not serve as a distinguishing principle.[46]

Significantly, Bork determined that the Fairness Doctrine was *not* codified by Section 315(a) of the Communications Act of 1934, but was a creature of FCC policy.[47] Thus, the FCC could abolish the doctrine against the will of Congress.

On reconsideration, the full FCC affirmed the Mass Media Bureau's decision that Meredith had violated the Fairness Doctrine. In the appellate review of the FCC's decision, the D.C. Circuit Court, viewing the 1985 Fairness Report in tandem with Judge Bork's *Telecommunications Research & Action Center* decision, determined that the FCC had acted arbitrarily by, on the one hand, deeming the Fairness Doctrine unconstitutional and, on the other, insisting on its enforcement. The court remanded the decision to the FCC, requiring it to address the constitutional issue.[48]

Considering the case on remand, the FCC determined that the Fairness Doctrine was unconstitutional and the D.C. Circuit Court thereafter affirmed the FCC's decision.[49] The Supreme Court refused to review the case, leaving the Circuit Court's decision standing.[50]

BENEATH THE PUBLIC INTEREST VENEER

The Fairness Doctrine can be viewed as the regulation that more than any other embodied the philosophical basis of the trusteeship model of broadcast regulation. It was, in fact, the most important content regulation of all, for its theoretical and constitutional foundations supported the FCC's authority to exercise a final editorial check over broadcast matters (an authority exercised more vigorously in the early days of radio regulation).

Moreover, the Fairness Doctrine was part of a number of regulatory and statutory rights that members of Congress had long used to attain political objectives and to gain access to broadcasting. Beneath the public interest veneer lay a partisan interest, one-half of the monopoly rent/content control *quid pro quo,* which now, by the FCC's own action in *Syracuse Peace Council,* was exposed and repudiated.

For more than fifty years the FCC had kowtowed to political pressure from Congress and had used the Fairness Doctrine and the political programming rules as part of the government's overall effort to require broadcast licensees to satisfy an often partisan conception of balanced journalism.[51] The Fairness Doctrine, its corollaries, the Personal Attack Rule,[52] and the political programming regulations set forth in Sections 312 and 315 of the Communications Act had become favorite tools of Congress and special interest groups in their struggle to prevent broadcasters from having free reign over programming. The elimination of the Fairness Doctrine called into question the same constitutional underpinnings relied on by Congress to support the mandatory access provisions of Sections 312 and 315. The FCC's action forced Congress to either resuscitate the Fairness Doctrine or come up with a new rationale for the Act's access provisions.

Section 312 gives the FCC power to "revoke any station license . . . for willful or repeated failure to allow reasonable access to or to permit purchase of reasonable amounts of time for the use of a broadcasting station by a legally qualified candidate for federal elective office on behalf of his candidacy."[53] Section 315 requires any licensee who permits one candidate to broadcast his message to provide "equal opportunities" for any other candidates for the same office to broadcast his messages.[54] The section also requires licensees to permit legally qualified candidates, during the forty-five days preceding a primary or the sixty days preceding a general election, to receive bargain rates on the air time that they have a statutory right to use. During this period, a licensee may not charge such candidates more than "the lowest unit charge of the station for the same class and amount of time for the same period."[55]

The Fairness Doctrine, the Personal Attack Rule, and the political programming rules were implemented through an elaborate FCC system for reviewing complaints brought by members of the public and candidates for federal office.

Under the Fairness Doctrine, when presented with a complaint, the FCC would determine whether broadcasters in the exercise of their editorial discretion had properly recognized an issue as controversial and had properly allowed appropriate groups a chance to oppose the view that had been presented. Through filing a Fairness Doctrine complaint, any partisan could create an immediate dilemma for the broadcast journalist, forcing him either to relent and air the complainant's views (no matter how noxious or contrary to the views held by the broadcaster) or to hire a lawyer and pay costly fees for a defense against the charges, waiting several months for the FCC to rule. An FCC investigation could result in a letter of admonishment, fines, or, conceivably, license revocation.

Similar to the Fairness Doctrine, Sections 312 and 315 require the FCC to ensure that members of Congress will be able to get on the airwaves anywhere in the country (to promote their candidacies) even if the station owners happen to oppose political programming in general or the politician in particular. By these and other content controls, Congress has built into the law a major disincentive for licensees to air controversial matters or to advocate, in a partisan way akin to the print press, the candidacy of any particular candidate.

THE POLITICS OF FAIRNESS

Although the FCC's decision to end the Fairness Doctrine did not eliminate content control, it did send a shock wave through Congress because it seemed to portend the decline of the entire content regulatory regime.

It should not be surprising that several members of Congress loudly condemned this bold and unorthodox move by the FCC. Many incumbents thought that the FCC, entrusted by Congress to keep the content controls in place, had shirked and betrayed the will of Congress.

Two months before the FCC's decision to end the Fairness Doctrine, President Reagan, himself a veteran sportscaster, vetoed a bill that would have codified the doctrine, stating that "policing of the editorial judgment of journalists" mandated by the doctrine was "antagonistic to the freedom of expression guaranteed by the First Amendment."[56]

In stark contrast to this reaction was that of Massachusetts Congressman Edward J. Markey, Chairman of the House Subcommittee on Telecommunications and Finance, which oversees the FCC. Markey had long demanded that the Reagan deregulators conform to the agenda preferred by Congress. Markey's reaction was typical of those members of Congress who did not appreciate the First Amendment victory at hand but instead lamented the loss of their power to control the press.

On the very day the FCC ended enforcement of the doctrine, Congressman Markey wrote:

> Over the past several months there have been consistent promises and commitments that the "Patrick Commission" would be less confrontational and more willing to work with the Congress than was the Fowler Commission. Well, the proof of the pudding is in the eating, and the rancid dish served up today is the same stale stuff that's been ladled out for the last six years.
>
> With its decision today, the Commission attempted to flout the will of Congress. The Commission's action was unconscionable, but it will be short-lived. I am certain that the Congress will reaffirm its overwhelming support for the Fairness Doctrine by recodifying the Doctrine again at the earliest possible opportunity. . . .
>
> The honeymoon between the Congress and the Patrick Commission is over.[57]

THE DEREGULATION OF SELECT STRUCTURAL CONTROLS AND THE CHANGE IN REGULATORY FOCUS

The Reagan Commission also eased certain barriers to market entry. It replaced its three-year prohibition on station sales with a one-year holding requirement, applicable only if the permit was awarded through the comparative hearing process.[58] The FCC ended its policies concerning broadcast business practices, deferring to local courts such matters as distortion of audience ratings and conflicts of interest of station employees.[59] It also stopped requiring that broadcasters disclose the arrangements by which sports announcers were hired and paid and ended its policy of discouraging the use of stations for pecuniary gain unrelated to station business.[60]

The FCC increased from seven to twelve (fourteen if minority owned or controlled) its limit on how many of the same service stations any one media entity could own.[61] It eliminated its regional concentration-of-control rules.[62] It lessened the geographic scope of its proscription on common or same market ownership.[63] It eliminated its term-of-network-affiliation rule,[64] and it relaxed its prohibition on the holding of employment in more than one same market mass medium.[65] In almost every case, it found data demonstrating ample competition in all markets to justify eliminating the policies.

Although the Reagan FCC removed many of the content and structural controls, it did not eliminate the fundamental licensing process. Applicants for new broadcast stations are still required to satisfy the FCC's policy preferences in favor of localism and diversification if more than one applicant wants a facility. Existing licensees are still confronted with the possibility that competitors may challenge their licenses at renewal time, causing the FCC to decide whether the licensee in question has engaged in meritorious service and deserves a renewal expectancy. Moreover, the Fairness Doctrine's corollaries and the political programming rules are still enforced, albeit without a constitutional basis. In short, the Reagan FCC did not replace the system of licensing with a property rights regime, despite its commitment to free market principles. Many content and structural controls remain in force.

The Bush administration has undertaken no significant effort to deregulate further, except for the FCC's two latest changes in policy to lessen the rigidity of its minimum distance separation requirements for certain FM stations and to improve the quality of AM radio. The FCC now permits certain Class A FM stations to increase their effective radiated power from 3 to 6 kilowatts even if they will violate the minimum distance separation required to another FM station that is also seeking improved facilities, provided both of the affected stations and the FCC agree to the change.[66] After years of argument that without extensive federal technical regulation the AM service would fall into chaos (as predicted in *NBC v. United States*), the FCC announced that it would encourage AM broadcasters to privately negotiate to reduce interference among their stations. Further, it would accept contingent applications by two AM licensees that were proposing modified operations designed to reduce interference between the stations. It would also lessen the rigidity of its "duopoly" rules that prohibit two AM stations operating in substantially the same area from having one owner.[67] The new rules would permit two AM stations to enter an agreement whereby one would reduce its power and area of service in exchange for payments from the other, which, in turn, would expand its service. This approach is the first movement in the direction of an unregulated broadcast service.

ENDNOTES

1. *See* Geller, *The FCC Under Mark Fowler: A Mixed Bag*, 10 COMM/ENT 521 (1988).
2. *See* Spitzer, *The Constitutionality of Licensing Broadcasters*, 64 N.Y.U. L. REV. 990, 991 (1989).
3. *See Metro Broadcasting, Inc. v. FCC*, 110 S. Ct. 2997, 3010 (1990).
4. Fowler, *The Public Interest*, 61 FLA. B. J. 213 (1982).
5. *See Deregulation of Radio*, 84 F.C.C.2d 968 (1981) *recon. granted in part*, 87 F.C.C.2d 797 (1981), *remanded in part, Office of Communication of the United Church of Christ v. FCC*, 707 F.2d 1413 (D.C. Cir. 1983); *modified in part*, 57 R.R.2d 93 (1984), *recon. denied*, 96 F.C.C.2d 930 (1984). *See also Deregulation of Commercial Television*, 98 F.C.C.2d 1076 (1984).
6. *Deregulation of Commercial Television*, 98 F.C.C.2d 1076 (1984).
7. *Id.*
8. *See Horse Racing Information*, 56 R.R.2d 976 (1984).
9. *See Policy Statement*, 2 F.C.C.2d 464 (1966).
10. *See Unnecessary Broadcast Regulation*, 57 R.R.2d 939 (1985).
11. *See Broadcast Stations (Loud Commercials)*, 56 R.R.2d 390 (1984).
12. *See Underbrush Broadcast Policies*, 54 R.R.2d 1043 (1983).
13. *See Unnecessary Broadcast Regulations*, 57 R.R.2d 913 (1985).
14. *See Elimination of Unnecessary Broadcast Regulation (Business Practices)*, 59 R.R.2d 1500 (1986).
15. *See Main Studio and Program Origination Rules*, 3 FCC Rcd. 3555.
16. *See Syracuse Peace Council*, 2 FCC Rcd. 5043.

17. *See, e.g., Committee for the Fair Broadcasting of Controversial Issues,* 25 F.C.C.2d 283, 292 (1970) (wherein the FCC stated that "strict adherence to the fairness doctrine"—including the affirmative obligation to provide coverage to controversial issues of public importance—was the "single most important requirement of operation in the public interest—[the] 'sine qua non' for grant of a renewal of license").

18. There are numerous corollaries of the Fairness Doctrine. Under one, the *Zapple* corollary, if a broadcast licensee sells time to the supporters of one political candidate to air an endorsement message, the licensee must also provide a reasonable opportunity for supporters of opposing candidates to air their endorsement messages. *See In re Letter to Nicholas Zapple,* 23 F.C.C.2d 707 (1970). *See also Fairness Report,* 48 F.C.C.2d 1, 33 (1974) (wherein the FCC subjects to the Fairness Doctrine's two-prong requirements such political matters as referendums, initiatives, recall propositions, bond proposals, and constitutional amendments). Under another, the *Cullman* corollary, if a licensee airs a paid advertisement that concerns one side of a controversial issue of public importance, it must either air a contrasting view itself or permit others to do so free of charge if no paid sponsor is available. *Cullman Broadcasting Co.,* 40 F.C.C. 576 (1963).

19. In a letter dated Sept. 22, 1987, from FCC Chairman Dennis R. Patrick to Congressman John D. Dingell, Chairman of the House Committee on Energy and Commerce, Patrick explained that "because the enforcement of the political editorial rules, the personal attack rules, the Zapple doctrine, or the application of the fairness doctrine to ballot issues were not before it in [*Syracuse Peace Council*], the Commission did not make any specific decision . . . regarding these issues." *See also Syracuse Peace Council,* 3 FCC Rcd. 2035, 2036 (1988): "We deny the [Freedom of Expression Foundation, Inc.] petition to the extent that it requests us to consider the continued validity of the personal attack and political editorial rules in this proceeding. . . . Those issues are beyond the scope of this proceeding."

20. *Syracuse Peace Council,* 2 FCC Rcd. 5043 (1987). The Commission first seriously questioned the constitutionality of the Fairness Doctrine in *In re Inquiry into Section 73.1910 of the Commission's Rules and Regulations Concerning the General Fairness Doctrine Obligations of Broadcast Licensees,* 102 F.C.C.2d 143 (1985), but did not abolish the doctrine at that time, deferring instead to the Courts and Congress.

21. *Syracuse Peace Council,* 2 FCC Rcd. 5043, 5055 (1987).

22. *See* Emord, *The First Amendment Invalidity of FCC Ownership Regulations,* 38 Cath. U. L. Rev. 401, 402 (1989).

23. *Syracuse Peace Council,* 2 FCC Rcd. 5043, 5055 (1987).

24. Geller, *Broadcasting and the Public Trustee Notion: A Failed Promise,* 10 Harv. J. L. & Pub. Pol'y 87 (1987).

25. *But see Metro Broadcasting, Inc. v. FCC*, 110 S. Ct. 2997, 3010 (1990) [where in dicta Justice Brennan endorses the spectrum scarcity rationale, calling into question the continuing validity of footnote 11 to *Federal Communications Commission v. League of Women Voters of Cal.*, 468 U.S. 364, 376–77n.11 (1984)]; consider Caristi, *The Concept of a Right of Access to the Media: A Workable Alternative*, 22 SUFFOLK U. L. REV. 103 (1988) [where Caristi argues that governmentally compelled rights of access to the broadcast press must be found constitutional and can be justified based on the *Marsh v. Alabama*, 326 U.S. 501 (1946), public function doctine]; *see also* Spitzer, *The Constitutionality of Licensing Broadcasters*, 64 N.Y.U. L. REV. 990 (1989) (where Spitzer argues that the Court may justify maintenance of the current broadcast regulatory regime on the basis of public forum law but submits that this would subvert the functional purpose of the First Amendment and would condone improper Congressional motives to structure the broadcast media marketplace.

26. *NBC v. United States*, 319 U.S. 190 (1943).

27. *Red Lion Broadcasting Co. v. FCC*, 395 U.S. 367 (1969).

28. In a June 16, 1858, speech in Springfield, Illinois, Abraham Lincoln described the pro- and anti-slavery forces thusly: "Either the opponents of slavery will arrest the further spread of it, and place it where the public mind can rest in the belief that it is in the course of ultimate extinction; or its advocates will push it forward, till it shall become alike lawful in all the States, old as well as new—North as well as South." THE LINCOLN-DOUGLAS DEBATES 14 (R. Johannsen ed. 1965). The spectrum scarcity rationale for broadcast regulation stands on similar footing.

29. *Report on Editorializing by Broadcast Journalists*, 13 F.C.C. 1246, 1249 (1949).

30. *Id.* at 1258; *see also* Zaragoza and Emord, *Electronic Media May Get Same Protection as Print Journalists*, Legal Times, Monday, Mar. 9, 1987, at 16.

31. *Red Lion Broadcasting Co. v. FCC*, 395 U.S. 367, 386 (1969): "Differences in the characteristics of news media justify differences in the First Amendment standards applied to them."

32. *Id.* at 388.

33. *Red Lion Broadcasting Co. v. FCC*, 395 U.S. 367, 390 (1969).

34. *Id.* at 388 (1969).

35. *FCC v. League of Women Voters of Cal.*, 468 U.S. 364 (1984).

36. *Id.* at 376–77 n.11 (1984).

37. *Syracuse Peace Council*, 2 FCC Rcd. 5043, 5058 (1987).

38. *See, e.g., Inquiry into Section 73.1910 of the Commission's Rules & Regulations Concerning Alternatives to the General Fairness Doctrine Obligations of Broadcast Licensees*, 102 F.C.C.2d 145, 164 (1985).

39. *See, e.g., Id.* at 145, 147.
40. *Id.* at 145, 147, 158–90.
41. *Id.* at 145, 167–68.
42. A survey of recently reported FCC cases reveals the extent to which the Fairness Doctrine can be manipulated by special interest groups to penalize broadcasters, regardless of the efficacy of the complaints involved. In *Ulster-American Heritage Foundation,* 96 F.C.C.2d 1246 (1984), a complainant unsuccessfully alleged that a television station's broadcast of "Ireland: A Television History" involved controversial issues of public importance in its segments concerning aid to the Irish Republic and Northern Ireland. The Commission disagreed. In *Joint Council of Allergy and Immunology,* 94 F.C.C.2d 734 (1983), a group's complaint alleged that coverage of the treatment of allergy sufferers constituted a controversial issue of public importance. The FCC disagreed.
43. *See Inquiry into Section 73.1910 of the Commission's Rules & Regulations Concerning Alternatives to the General Fairness Doctrine Obligations of Broadcast Licensees,* 102 F.C.C.2d 145, 191 at n.174 (1985).
44. *See Id.* at 145, 227.
45. *Telecommunications Research & Action Center v. FCC,* 801 F.2d 501 (D.C. Cir. 1986).
46. *Id.* at 501, 508. In 1975, Judge David Bazelon asked: "When we say there is a scarcity of frequencies, to what are we comparing this scarcity?" Bazelon, *FCC Regulation of the Telecommunications Press,* 1975 DUKE L. J. 213, 224.
47. *Telecommunications Research & Action Center v. FCC,* 801 F.2d 501, 509 (D.C. Cir. 1986).
48. *Meredith Corp. v. FCC,* 809 F.2d 863 (D.C. Cir. 1987).
49. *Syracuse Peace Council,* 2 FCC Rcd. 5043 (1987), *aff'd,* 867 F.2d 654 (D.C. Cir. 1989).
50. *Cert. den.,* 110 S.Ct. 717 (1990).
51. Evidence of the general use of the fairness doctrine and the licensing processes to award licenses to political friends, deny licenses to political enemies, and remove politically disfavored views from the airwaves can be found in L. POWE, AMERICAN BROADCASTING AND THE FIRST AMENDMENT 72, 127–28, 138–39, 113–15 (1987); Hazlett, *The Fairness Doctrine and the First Amendment,* THE PUBLIC INTEREST 103 (1989); Spitzer, *The Constitutionality of Licensing Broadcasters,* 64 N.Y.U. L. REV. 990 (1989); B. Schwartz, THE PROFESSOR AND THE COMMISSIONS (1959); Schwartz, *Comparative Television Licensing and the Chancellor's Foot,* 47 GEO. L. J. 665, 690–94 (1959).
52. *See* § 73.1920, 47 C.F.R. (1988) which provides in pertinent part: "When during the presentation of a controversial issue of public importance, an

attack is made upon the honesty, character, integrity, or like personal qualities of an identified person or group, the licensee shall, within a reasonable time and in no event later than one week after the attack" offer the person attacked a "reasonable opportunity to respond over the licensee's facilities."

53.   § 312(a)(7), 47 U.S.C. (1988).
54.   § 315(a), 47 U.S.C. (1988).
55.   § 315(b)(1), 47 U.S.C. (1988).
56.   *See Veto Message of the President,* 23 WEEKLY COMP. PRES. DOC. 715 (June 29, 1987).
57.   "Statement by Edward J. Markey, The Fairness Doctrine and the FCC," released by the congressman's office on Aug. 4, 1987, and on file with the author.
58.   *See Holding Period Rule,* 99 F.C.C.2d 971 (1985).
59.   *See Unnecessary Broadcast Regulations,* 57 R.R.2d 913 (1985), *aff'd, Telecommunications Research & Action Center v. FCC,* 800 F.2d 1181 (1986).
60.   *Id.*
61.   *See* Emord, *The First Amendment Invalidity of FCC Ownership Regulations,* 38 CATH. U. L. REV. 401, 425–27 (1989).
62.   *Id.* at 401, 427.
63.   *Id.* at 401, 427–29.
64.   *Id.* at 401, 429.
65.   *Id.* at 401, 429–30.
66.   *See Second Report and Order,* 4 FCC Rcd. 6375 (1989).
67.   *See Policies to Encourage Interference Reduction Between AM Broadcasting Stations,* 67 R.R. 2d 1612 (1910).

19

THE CABLE PRESS AND THE INDUSTRY CAPTURE MOVEMENT

Until recently, federal regulatory concern over the mass media appeared centered on broadcasting. The concern has now shifted with the rise of cable as a competitive source of news and entertainment programming and with the prospect that telephone companies will enter the interactive video and information services markets.[1] Cable television has had its own monopoly rent/content control *quid pro quo* operating on the local level for a decade. But now the federal government may be poised to implement its own *quid pro quo* through some kind of exchange with the cable industry.

Cable television is the first fully operational, national video alternative to broadcast television.[2] More than 53 million Americans subscribe.[3] Approximately 58 percent of America's 92.1 million television households now have access to cable from one or more of the 10,823 systems nationwide; of the cable households, more than 67 percent subscribe to 20 or more channels, with the average cable-system offering 30 to 53 channels.[4] More than 29 percent of America's television households have access to pay cable services.[5] Our society is becoming less and less dependent on spectrum for access to ideas and information. Consequently, new rationales for regulation will have to be invented if governments are to maintain their control over media content and structure.

The cable regulators have formulated two arguments for controlling the cable press. First, the states and localities invoke a police power rationale linked to states' authority to control the public streets and rights-of-way,

249

which are often traversed by cable wires. Second, they use a natural monopoly, or economic scarcity, rationale. The latter we have seen argued vociferously in support of media regulation during radio's formative years. Although no private broadcast monopoly ever arose in the broadcast marketplace, the regulators nevertheless assumed that it inevitably would. They preferred a state selected and controlled monopoly to private competition. With cable, the same assumptions and demands have been made.

Local government officials have united with cable industry leaders to exchange monopoly rent protection for rights of access and content controls. In thousands of cities and towns across America, licensing schemes like the FCC's system limit cable service in most cases to one firm and limit the cablecasters' press freedom through content controls and administrative cajolery. Significantly, in forty jurisdictions nationwide, cable systems directly compete with one another, one fact that undercuts the contention of regulators and incumbent cable franchisees that cable is a natural monopoly.

In exchange for their government-mandated monopolies, cable systems have ceded editorial discretion to local officials in order to satisfy the officials' appetites for self-promotion and favorable association with special interest groups. In almost every case, franchise agreements include a mandatory right of access for certain preferred local constituencies, as well as for the politicians themselves. Although typically labelled "nonexclusive," cable franchises are usually exclusive grants of authority to cablecast within a specified geographic area. Unlike the federal system of broadcast regulation, local cable regulation has been characterized by an extraordinary amount of corruption.

Throughout the 1980s, the FCC's role in regulating cable was quite limited and uncomfortable for the agency. Until recently, having not been told by Congress how best to deal with cable, the FCC largely responded to pressure from the broadcast industry. True to the historic *quid pro quo* with broadcasters (and not having a similar arrangement with cablecasters), the FCC repeatedly attempted to impose regulations on cable that were designed to fend off competitive challenges to local broadcasters. These regulatory efforts had limited success. The U.S. Court of Appeals for the District of Columbia Circuit has not tolerated the FCC's imposition of anticompetitive access requirements on cable. Without market protection from the FCC, the cable industry has had little incentive to cooperate with it and has been quite litigious, challenging almost every economically disadvantageous regulation the FCC has imposed. While existing cable franchisees have been quick to challenge FCC regulations, their record of challenging local municipal regulations has been less pronounced because a system of municipal licensing with its own *quid pro quo* keeps them in check.

As one would expect, the pervasive reach and persuasive potential of cable has not escaped the attention of Congress, whose members are maneuvering to wrest some control over cable from local authorities. The monopoly argument is foremost among their public reasons for promoting new federal controls. Although Judge J. Skelly Wright cautiously observed in *Quincy Cable TV, Inc. v. FCC,* "[t]he tendency toward monopoly, if present at all, may well be attributable [more] to governmental action—particularly the municipal franchising process—than to any 'natural' economic phenomenon,"[6] members of Congress (like Representative John Dingell, Chairman of the House Energy and Commerce Committee) increasingly argue that cable is "a deregulated monopoly" and have vowed to institute a "new regulatory regime."[7]

In response to pressures from Congress and broadcast licensees, the FCC commenced a series of public hearings at three locations across the country to hear public complaints about cable television's anticompetitive propensities but issued a report to Congress following these hearings which advocated competition in delivery of multichannel video services in line with the Bush administration's desires to the consternation of some in Congress.[8] The FCC also instituted two rule makings: one (a *Notice of Inquiry*) to examine the quality and competitiveness of cable, and another (a *Notice of Proposed Rule Making*) to redefine the FCC's "effective competition" standard, which exempts cable systems from local rate regulation.[9] These actions followed several unsuccessful attempts by the agency to introduce mandatory "must-carry" requirements that would have forced cable systems to dedicate some channels to carriage of local broadcasters' signals.[10] These actions respond to Congress's desire to gain greater control over the cable industry and respond to pressure from broadcasters who loudly complain that they have lost significant market share because of cable's phenomenal rise as a competing media outlet. It is a virtual certainty that the Congress will try to reregulate cable, perhaps in significant ways. If these regulations are to endure, some *quid pro quo* between Congress and the cable industry will probably be instituted at the federal level. Once again Henry VIII's proven technique for controlling the press may be used by the federal government to dominate yet another technology of mass communication.

THE UNSUCCESSFUL FCC CAMPAIGN TO PROTECT BROADCASTING FROM CABLE COMPETITION

The federal government's interest in cable was slow to develop. Throughout the 1950s, cable posed little threat to anyone. An unregulated medium limited to retransmitting broadcast signals and capable of providing fewer than twelve channels, cable was viewed favorably by broadcasters as a vehicle for carrying their signals into remote areas plagued by poor over-the-air reception.[11] As with radio before the advent of commercial broadcasting, those in power were at first unconcerned with cable, a medium having little independent influence and no apparently significant competitive potential.

In its 1958 *Frontier Broadcast Co.* decision and again in its 1959 *CATV and TV Repeater Services Inquiry,* the FCC denied that it had any regulatory power over the medium, deeming it neither broadcast nor common carrier in nature.[12] Soon, however, cable began to prove its great potential. Broadcasters came to view it as a competitive threat and politicians saw it as a potentially persuasive medium of mass communication. Cable thus became a candidate for comprehensive government regulation.

In the early 1960s, the cable environment underwent considerable change. Increasingly, cable systems began to use microwave facilities to import distant signals into their service areas. This development disturbed the broadcast community. Local broadcasters perceived that cable would soon develop this capability nationwide and would create a new source of competition. In response to the threat, the FCC reconsidered its decision not to regulate cable. Broadcasters encouraged the FCC to enact regulations that would retard the growth of the signal-importation industry: "Thirteen television stations complained to the FCC that 288 cable television operators in thirty-six states threatened their economic security."[13]

In its 1962 *Carter Mountain Transmission Corporation* decision,[14] the FCC responded to the broadcast industry's demands by requiring cable applicants for common carrier microwave facilities to establish that their proposed use of the facilities would not undermine local television service. This, in effect, required cable systems to carry local broadcast signals.[15] In 1965, the FCC made its *Carter Mountain* policy a formal rule, and in 1966 it imposed mandatory must-carry requirements on all cable operators, not just microwave-fed systems.[16] The must-carry rules forced cable operators to carry every broadcast signal that was local or had a loyal viewership in the service area.[17] In addition, the FCC's *Second Report and Order* required cable operators to avoid carrying distant signals that duplicated local broadcast programming.

In a move that sounded to the burgeoning signal-importation industry like a death knell, the FCC ruled that no distant signal could be imported into any of the top 100 television markets unless, in a hearing, the cable operator proved that importation of the signal "would be consistent with the public interest, and particularly the establishment and health and maintenance of [a] UHF television broadcast service." This effective ban on signal importation provided broadcasters with significant protection against competition from cable entrepreneurs and stymied the growth of cable for several years.[18]

The Supreme Court upheld the signal-importation ban in its *United States v. Southwestern Cable Co.* decision, deeming the regulation "reasonably ancillary" to "the regulation of television broadcasting."[19] The Court was not presented with a First Amendment challenge to the regulations; rather, the issue was the narrow one of whether the rules could fall within Section 152(a) of the Communications Act, affording the FCC broad powers to regulate "all interstate and foreign communication by wire or radio."

Encouraged by the *Southwestern Cable Co.* decision, in 1969 the FCC imposed Fairness Doctrine, equal time, and program origination requirements on all cable operators.[20] The FCC had come to recognize the great potential of cable: that cable could well increase "the number of local outlets for community self-expression without use of the broadcast spectrum."[21] By 1969, when videotape recorders had become relatively inexpensive and capable of high-quality production, it was understood that some cable operators would begin producing local programs.[22] This augmented the broadcasters' concern that their federally protected market shares could be eroded by enterprising cable competitors.

In 1970, the FCC enacted cross-ownership regulations, prohibiting a cable system from owning interests in telephone companies, TV networks, TV stations, and translator stations operating in the system's service area.[23] Also in that year, the FCC largely precluded pay cable systems from out-bidding broadcast television stations for the right to broadcast movies, television series, and sporting events.[24]

In its 1972 *United States v. Midwest Video Corp.*[25] decision, the Supreme Court expounded on its holding in *United States v. Southwestern Cable Co.* The Court upheld the FCC's authority to require, as it did in 1969, cablecasters to originate (locally produce) programming. The Court found that these regulations ensured "that in retransmission . . . viewers [were] . . . provided suitably diversified programming," and the Court stated that the regulations were "reasonably ancillary" to the FCC's broadcast jurisdiction within the meaning of the *Southwestern Cable Co.* decision.[26]

With renewed assurance, the FCC in 1972 issued a wide range of burdensome new structural and programming regulations applicable to cable. As modified in 1975, the rules removed a considerable amount of editorial discretion from cablecasters. These rules required each cable system to be equipped with a minimum twenty-channel capacity and two-way communication capability by certain dates; to provide public access to cable facilities at regulated charges; and to dedicate four cable channels to public, educational, local governmental, and leased access use. In addition, cable operators were required to make certain production equipment and facilities available to the public free of charge for their use in creating programming.[27]

In 1975, RCA put into orbit the nation's first domestic satellite. Other such satellites soon followed. Cable systems with earth station receiving dish antennas could now import signals from around the country and the world.[28] This prompted the arrival of the cable "superstations," which became increasingly regarded as mighty competitors to the broadcast networks. Within just a few years, cable systems began to transmit a plethora of programming options not offered by the three major networks. Moreover, cable television offered viewers better picture quality resulting largely from cable's inherent freedom from most forms of interference, which have always plagued spectrum-based modes of transmission.

COURT HOSTILITY TO FCC CABLE CONTENT CONTROLS

In 1977, in its *Home Box Office, Inc. v. FCC* decision, the D.C. Circuit Court struck down FCC rules that had largely prohibited pay cable systems from outbidding broadcast stations for movies, television series, and the right to cover sporting events.[29] The decision has had great influence with circuit courts across the country. Writing for the court, Judge J. Skelly Wright rejected the FCC's arguments that the spectrum scarcity rationale for broadcast regulation could be extended to support cable regulation. Wright found no scarcity of cable channels or interference that would cause the cable context to fall within the precedential breadth of broadcast law.[30] He also found unconvincing the government's argument that cable was a natural monopoly, explaining that even were it so,

> scarcity which is the result solely of economic conditions is apparently insufficient to justify even limited government intrusion into the First Amendment rights of the conventional press . . . and there is nothing in the record before us to suggest a constitutional distinction between cable television and newspapers on this point.[31]

However, in the absence of a clear explication by the Supreme Court of which First Amendment standard should be applied to the cable press, Wright analyzed the First Amendment question not under the strict scrutiny standard applicable when government directly regulates the content or structure of newspapers,[32] but under a less exacting standard. The standard came from a case involving not the press but rather draft card burning, *United States v. O'Brien*.[33] *O'Brien* concerned what the Supreme Court termed a "content-neutral" regulation (one not focused on regulating the specific message communicated) that created an "incidental" burden on speech (a burden that is the by-product of a regulation intended to control conduct). The *O'Brien* standard has four parts: a regulation is deemed constitutional if (1) it is "within the constitutional power of the Government," (2) it furthers "an important or substantial governmental interest," (3) the interest is "unrelated to the suppression of free expression," and (4) the "incidental restriction on alleged first amendment freedoms" is "no greater than . . . essential to the furtherance of [the state's] interest."[34]

The *Home Box Office* decision gave cable increasing confidence that it would be afforded greater First Amendment protection than the broadcast media. This decision could translate into greater market power for cable, by insulating it from costly federal regulations. However, the decision did not treat cable as equal with newspapers; thus, it left open the possibility of permitting more regulation of the cable than of the print press.

Despite the *Home Box Office* decision, the FCC hastened to prevent the cable industry from making significant inroads into broadcast markets. Unlike broadcast licensees, who since 1927 had enjoyed above market economic profits due to federal protection, cable operators bore the brunt of FCC policies designed to limit their competitiveness and paid the cost of the FCC's new editorial strictures. Without a *quid pro quo*, cable operators were unwilling to tolerate the burdens.

In its 1979 *FCC v. Midwest Video Corp.* decision, the Supreme Court first signaled its unwillingness to go along with the FCC's continuous expansion of cable regulation. The Court invalidated the FCC's 1972 and 1975 mandatory access regulations, holding them to be beyond the compass of the Communications Act. By wresting "a considerable degree of editorial control from the cable operator," the FCC had transformed cable into "a kind of common-carrier service," the Court ruled.[35] The Court found that this degree of control exceeded the intentions of Congress. However, unlike D.C. Circuit Judge Wright, the Court refused to address the First Amendment issues at stake and lamely noted at the end of the decision that it would "express no view on that question, save to acknowledge that it is not frivolous."[36] To this day, the Supreme Court has declined to articulate the precise First Amendment standard it will apply to cable. As a result, circuit courts across the country have imposed varying standards, which have produced conflicting results.

Nonetheless, the FCC is bound by the D.C. Circuit Court's holdings, which have severely limited the FCC's ability to erect barriers to competition. Perhaps the greatest defeat for the FCC in its effort to protect broadcasters from cable competition involves its ill-fated must-carry regulations.

THE D.C. CIRCUIT COURT'S REJECTION OF MUST-CARRY

Operative since 1966, the must-carry rules did not sit well with Judge Wright, who had already established himself as a pioneer advocate of extending First Amendment protection to the cable press in his *Home Box Office* decision. The must-carry rules required cable systems to carry local broadcast signals on some of their cable channels. On an appeal to the D.C. Circuit Court of an FCC refusal to eliminate the must-carry rules, Judge Wright in *Quincy Cable TV, Inc. v. FCC*[37] held that the rules violated the First Amendment. Announcing that it had now been "clearly established" that "cable operators engage in conduct protected by the First Amendment," Wright harkened back to his *Home Box Office* decision and applied the *United States v. O'Brien* standard to test the validity of the must-carry rules.

Significantly, Wright did not announce that the *O'Brien* standard was the *only* or the *most appropriate* analytical framework for assessing content regulations imposed on the new medium. Rather, in the absence of guidance from the Supreme Court, he deemed *O'Brien* adequate to the task, for even under the lower level of scrutiny afforded by *O'Brien* the must-carry rules were deemed violative of the First Amendment. Wrote Judge Wright: "Although our review leaves us with serious doubts about the appropriateness of invoking *O'Brien*'s interest-balancing formulation, we conclude that the rules so clearly fail under that standard that we need not resolve whether they warrant a more exacting level of First Amendment scrutiny."[38]

In further considering the propriety of the *O'Brien* standard, Wright made it clear that he regarded the must-carry rules as more than mere "incidental burdens on speech," as would justify application of *O'Brien*. Rather, he recognized that must-carry rules afforded one group (broadcasters) a right to restrict the speech rights of another, cablecasters, merely to bolster the economic position of the former at the expense of the speech liberty of the latter. Moreover, the rules constituted "coerced speech," requiring cable operators to present a message whether or not they agreed with it. The rules also limited the otherwise unfettered editorial discretion of cablecasters, and they interfered with the message communicated by cable to its viewers without any regard for the harm to these viewers.[39] Wright found "the conclusion that the must-carry rules burden First Amendment rights only incidentally . . . far from inevitable,"[40] holding the rules unconstitutional even under *O'Brien's* minimum threshold standard.

Wright rejected the notion that cable should be subjected to a lessened degree of First Amendment protection, one equivalent to that threshold afforded broadcasters. Following his reasoning in *Home Box Office,* he found the scarcity rationale inapplicable to cable. He also denied that cable's use of utility poles, streets, and public rights-of-way warranted a lessening in First Amendment protection. Wright analogized cable wires on public property to newspaper vending machines on public streets:

> The potential for disruption inherent in stringing coaxial cables above the city streets may well warrant some governmental regulation of the process of installing and maintaining the cable system. But hardly does it follow that such regulation could extend to controlling the nature of the programming that is conveyed over that system. No doubt a municipality has some power to control the placement of newspaper vending machines. But any effort to use that power as a basis for dictating what must be placed in such machines would surely be invalid.[41]

Moreover, as in *Home Box Office,* Wright could not be persuaded that any natural monopoly characteristics of cable could justify content regulations. In an extended analysis, he made clear his doubt that cable could actually be a monopoly, and he recognized that the First Amendment required protection of cable even if it were a monopoly because of its functional similarities with the print medium.[42]

The *Quincy Cable* decision came as a bitter defeat to the broadcast industry in its effort to create anticompetitive obstacles to the rapid advance of cable. Responding to the broadcasters' lamentations and to clear indications in the decision that a revised must-carry standard could possibly pass constitutional muster, the FCC spent two years trying to find a suitable alternative.

The revised rules finally adopted were in some ways comedic, for they did not eliminate any of the objectionable features of the old rules. Rather, they just tempered the old rules somewhat with a shorter duration and used a novel argument that was based on the previously unheard of need for an "input selector device." The new rules had a five-year duration—said by the FCC to be necessary to permit television viewers to become acclimated to the selector device, which was a simple mechanism known to electricians and consumers as an "A/B switch." Without the device, a typical television set hooked to cable will not receive signals over-the-air. Tuning to over-the-air channels not carried by cable without a selector device requires disconnecting the cable.

With the input selector device, the average cable viewer could turn off his cable reception with a switch. This, said the FCC, would create a "level playing field." According to the FCC, most people did not know how to use the switch. But, once convinced of its utility, they would install it and would learn to appreciate both broadcast and cable without being hoodwinked into becoming a cable-only customer.

To make sure this happened, the FCC required cable systems (but, conspicuously, not broadcast licensees) to educate the public about the A/B switch over five years. During that period, cable was to abide by a revised must-carry standard that based the number of select over-the-air channels a cable system had to carry on the number of cable channels the system offered.[43]

Like their predecessor, the revised must-carry rules got an unfriendly reception in the D.C. Circuit Court. In *Century Communications Corp. v. FCC*, Judge Patricia Wald refused to decide—in the absence of guidance from the Supreme Court—precisely what First Amendment standard ought to be applied to the revised must-carry rules. Instead, she deemed the new rules to fail even when tested under the lower *O'Brien* standard adopted in *Quincy Cable*. In particular, in assessing the governmental interest at stake, Wald found counterintuitive the FCC's assertion that the typical cable viewer was somnambulant and had to be goaded into using the A/B switch. Wrote Judge Wald:

> We simply cannot accept, without evidence to the contrary, the sluggish profile of the American consumer that the Commission's argument necessarily presupposes. In a culture in which even costly items like the video-cassette recorder, the cordless telephone, the compact disc-player and the home computer have spread like wildfire, it begs incredulity to simply assume that consumers are so unresponsive that within the span of five years they would not manage to purchase an inexpensive hardware-store switch upon learning that it could provide access to a considerable storehouse of new television stations and shows.[44]

This decision temporarily halted the FCC's efforts to enact must-carry regulations.

Nevertheless, the FCC has succeeded in applying to cable the numerous broadcast-type content restrictions that have not been eliminated in legal battles.[45] A cable operator must afford legally qualified federal candidates reasonable access to his origination channels (channels over which the operator exercises exclusive content control) and must provide access at the system's lowest unit charge.[46] The cable operator must also afford competing candidates reasonable opportunities to appear on its origination channels.[47] The operator must adhere to what is left of the Fairness Doctrine and also to the personal attack rule (by providing for any person whose character has been impugned a free opportunity to respond) on its local origination channels.[48]

Despite the FCC's failure in its anticompetitive efforts, cable has not been freed from significant constraints. Under the Cable Communications Policy Act of 1984, the bulk of authority over cable content and structure has been granted to the localities. Consequently, although the FCC has failed to prevent the cable industry from dominating the video marketplace, the localities have succeeded in exacting significant programming concessions in exchange for monopoly protection.

THE CABLE COMMUNICATIONS POLICY ACT OF 1984

In 1984, Congress placed its support behind comprehensive regulation of the cable industry by enacting the Cable Communications Policy Act of 1984.[49] The Act vested primary jurisdiction over cable in the states and localities. It specifically authorized local authorities to use a system of licensing, called franchising, to determine who would be permitted to erect and operate cable systems. Under the Act, no cable operator could provide service without a franchise.[50] Moreover, the local franchising authority was empowered to award "one or more franchises within its jurisdiction," a provision that has been interpreted by almost all localities to authorize the award of *de facto* exclusive franchises.[51]

The Act permits the franchising authority to require that cable systems reserve channels for "public, educational, or governmental use" and mandates that cable systems set aside certain channels for leased access by commercial concerns unaffiliated with the cable system.[52] Television licensees are barred from owning cable systems if the systems deliver programming within the primary service area of the television station, and the FCC is authorized to develop regulations to carry out the prohibition.[53] The Act permits the franchising authority to require a cable system to pay an annual franchise fee of up to 5 percent of the cable system's gross revenues, and it prohibits the FCC from regulating local fee collection.[54] The Act gives the FCC authority to regulate the rates charged by local franchising authorities for the provision of basic cable service in those markets where cable is not subject to "effective competition."[55]

The FCC has considered redefining its effective competition standard to permit greater regulation of cable rates. Under the standard existing at the time of this writing, the FCC has found there to be a lack of effective competition in cable markets not served by primary signals from at least three over-the-air television stations. Because almost no community in the United States receives fewer than three television signals, cable is virtually free of federal rate regulation. For the time being, cable remains largely in the regulatory province of the states and localities, and there, the imposition of content and structural controls has proceeded apace as a result of the monopoly rent/content control *quid pro quo.*

ENDNOTES

1. *See, e.g., In the Matter of Competition, Rate Deregulation, and the Commission's Policies Relating to the Provision of Cable Television Service,* 5 FCC Rcd. 362 (1989). *See also, In the Matter of Reexamination of the Effective Competition Standard for the Regulation of Cable Television Basic Service Rates,* 5 FCC Rcd. 259 (1990).

2. Formerly known as Community Antenna Television (CATV), in just fifty years, cable has become a major and, soon to be, predominant source of news, entertainment, and opinion in our society. In its early days, in the late 1940s and early 1950s, cable served principally as a retransmission system for local broadcast television. Cable provided broadcast signals to homes in remote areas where—because of terrain features—over-the-air reception was impaired or nonexistent. *See* G. Shapiro, P. Kurland, & J. Mercurio, "Cablespeech," The Case for First Amendment Protection 1 (1983); M. Hamburg, All About Cable, § 1.02, at 1–6 (1981). Today, cable has become directly competitive with over-the-air television, offering its own national programming and pay cable services in addition to the retransmission of over-the-air broadcast signals. *See* Brotman, "Cable Television," *in* Many Roads Home: The New Electronic Pathways 115–37 (National Association of Broadcasters, 1988).

3. *See* Broadcasting at 67, Aug. 20, 1990.

4. *Id.;* Broadcasting at 1, Feb. 5, 1990; Television and Cable Factbook C-384-C-385 (1990).

5. *See* BROADCASTING at 67, Aug. 20, 1990; JOINT NAB/CAB/CIRT Meeting Report, Sept. 25–27, 1988 (available from the National Association of Broadcasters' Research and Planning Dep't).

6. *Quincy Cable TV, Inc. v. FCC,* 768 F.2d 1434, 1450 (D.C. Cir. 1985).

7. *See Dingell: More Cable Regulation,* BROADCASTING at 22, Jan. 29, 1990.

8. *See FCC Hears Cable Complaints in Los Angeles,* BROADCASTING at 74, Feb. 19, 1990; *Report (In the Matter of Competition, Rate Regulation and the Commission's Policies Relating to the Provision of Cable Television Service),* MM Docket No. 89–600, FCC 90–276, released July 31, 1990 ("[T]his Commission steadfastly believes that robust competition will more efficiently provide both a better safeguard against undue rate increases or service failings and a greater diversity and choice than any web of rules and regulations . . .").

9. *See FCC to Review State of Cable TV,* BROADCASTING at 81, Dec. 18, 1989; *In the Matter of Competition, Rate Deregulation, and the Commission's Policies Relating to the Provision of Cable Television Service,* 5 FCC Rcd. 362 (1989).

10. *See Quincy Cable TV, Inc. v. FCC,* 768 F.2d 1434 (D.C. Cir. 1985); *Century Communications Corporation v. FCC,* 835 F.2d 292 (D.C. Cir. 1987).

11. *See* Fogarty and Spielholz, *FCC Cable Jurisdiction: From Zero to Plenary in Twenty-Five Years,* 37 FED. COM. L. J. 113, 114 (1985); G. SHAPIRO, P. KURLAND, & J. MERCURIO, "CABLESPEECH," THE CASE FOR FIRST AMENDMENT PROTECTION 1 (1983).

12. Fogarty and Spielholz, *FCC Cable Jurisdiction: From Zero to Plenary in Twenty-Five Years,* 37 FED. COM. L. J. 114–15 (1985); *Frontier Broadcasting Co. v. Collier,* 24 F.C.C. 251 (1958); *CATV and TV Repeater Services,* 26 F.C.C. 403 (1959).

13. *See* Brenner and Price, *The 1984 Cable Act: Prologue and Precedents,* 4 CARDOZO ARTS AND ENTERTAINMENT L. J. 19, 24 (1985); *see also* Judge J. Skelly Wright's majority opinion in *Quincy Cable TV, Inc. v. FCC,* 768 F.2d 1434, 1439 (1985) ("The Commission's objective was not merely to protect an established industry from the encroachment of an upstart young competitor, although that result was clearly the by-product of the regulatory posture that developed. Rather, the Commission took the position that without the power to regulate cable it could not discharge its statutory obligation to provide for the fair, efficient, and equitable distribution of service among 'the several States and Communities.' . . . If permitted to grow unfettered, the Commission feared, cable might well supplant ordinary broadcast television.")

14. *Carter Mountain Transmission Corp.,* 32 F.C.C. 459, 465 (1962).

15. *See* Shaffer, *Preferred Communications, Inc. v. Los Angeles: Broadening Cable's First Amendment Rights and Narrowing Cities' Franchising Powers,* 8 COMM/ENT L. J. 535, 539 (1986).

16.   *Id.; Microwave-Served CATV, First Report and Order,* 38 F.C.C. 683 (1965); *CATV, Second Report and Order,* 2 F.C.C.2d 725 (1966).

17.   Shaffer, *Preferred Communications, Inc. v. Los Angeles: Broadening Cable's First Amendment Rights and Narrowing Cities' Franchising Power,* 8 COMM/ENT L. J. 535, 539 (1986).

18.   *Second Report and Order,* 2 F.C.C.2d 725, 782 (1966); *see also* Brenner & Price, *The 1984 Cable Act: Prologue and Precedents,* 4 CARDOZO ARTS & ENTERTAINMENT L. J. 19, 26 (1985). ("The FCC's 1966 Second Report and Order extended these rules to non-microwave cable systems. Further, cable system importation of signals into the top 100 markets was made more difficult. The resulting scheme was extraordinarily burdensome and required a long and costly case-by-case analysis in determining which distant broadcast signals could be imported. Given the early outcome of hearings on these matters, it appeared that the FCC was freezing the growth of cable by inhibiting distant signal importation.")

19.   *United States v. Southwestern Cable Co.,* 329 U.S. 157, 178 (1968).

20.   *See Cable Television,* 20 F.C.C.2d 201, 218–19, 222–23 (1969).

21.   *Notice of Proposed Rulemaking and Notice of Inquiry in Docket No. 18397,* 15 F.C.C.2d 417, 421 (1968).

22.   G. SHAPIRO, P. KURLAND, & J. MERCURIO, "CABLESPEECH," THE CASE FOR FIRST AMENDMENT PROTECTION 2 (1983).

23.   Brenner & Price, *The 1984 Cable Act: Prologue and Precedents,* 4 CARDOZO ARTS & ENTERTAINMENT L. J. 19, 29 (1985).

24.   *Id.*

25.   *United States v. Midwest Video Corp.,* 406 U.S. 649 (1972).

26.   *Id.*

27.   *See Cable Television,* 36 F.C.C.2d 143 (1972); *Major Market Cable Television Systems,* 54 F.C.C.2d 207 (1975); *Cable TV Capacity and Access Requirements,* 59 F.C.C.2d 294 (1976).

28.   *See* Sibrary, *Cable Communications Policy Act of 1984 v. The First Amendment,* 7 COMM/ENT L. J. 381, 383 (1985).

29.   *See Home Box Office, Inc. v. FCC,* 567 F.2d 9 (D.C. Cir. 1977).

30.   *Id.* at 45.

31.   *Id.* at 9, 46.

32.   *See Miami Herald Publishing Co. v. Tornillo,* 418 U.S. 241, 247–56 (1974).

33.   *United States v. O'Brien,* 391 U.S. 367 (1968).

34.   *Id.* at 367, 377.

35.   *FCC v. Midwest Video Corp.,* 440 U.S. 689, 700 (1979).

36.   *Id.* at 689, 709 n.19.

37.   768 F.2d 1434 (D.C. Cir. 1985). Quincy Cable TV, Inc. was appealing a forfeiture imposed by the FCC for Quincy's violation of the rule.

38.   *Quincy Cable TV, Inc. v. FCC,* 768 F.2d 1434, 1448 (D.C. Cir. 1985).

39.   *Id.* at 1434, 1451–52.
40.   *Id.* at 1434, 1452.
41.   *Id.* at 1434, 1449.
42.   Explained Judge Wright:

> At the outset, the "economic scarcity" argument rests on the entirely unproven—and indeed doubtful—assumption that cable operators are in a position to exact monopolistic charges. . . . In any case, whatever the outcome of the debate over the monopolistic characteristics of cable, the Supreme Court has categorically rejected the suggestion that purely economic constraints on the number of voices available in a given community justify otherwise unwarranted intrusions into First Amendment rights[,] [citing to] *Miami Herald Publishing Co. v. Tornillo.* . . . While Miami Herald involved the conventional press, as this court has had prior occasion to observe, there is no meaningful "distinction between cable television and newspapers on this point." *Home Box Office, Inc. v. FCC.*

 Quincy Cable TV, Inc. v. FCC, 768 F.2d 1434, 1450 (D.C. Cir. 1985).
43.   *Century Communications Corp. v. FCC,* 835 F.2d 292, 296–97 (D.C. Cir. 1987).
44.   *Id.* at 292, 302.
45.   *See* Geller & Lampert, *Cable, Content Regulation, and the First Amendment,* 3 Cath. U. L. Rev. 603 (1983).
46.   *See* § 76.205, 47 C.F.R. (1988); § 315, 47 U.S.C. (1988).
47.   *See* § 76.205, 47 C.F.R. (1988); § 312, 47 U.S.C. (1988).
48.   *See* § 76.209, 47 C.F.R. (1988).
49.   § 521 et seq., 47 U.S.C. (1988).
50.   § 541(b)(1), 47 U.S.C. (1988).
51.   § 541(a)(1), 47 U.S.C. (1988).
52.   § 532, 47 U.S.C. (1988).
53.   § 533(a), (c), 47 U.S.C. (1988).
54.   § 542(a), (i), 47 U.S.C. (1988).
55.   § 543(a), 47 U.S.C. (1988).

20

THE FRANCHISING PROCESS

The press/state symbiosis in the cable industry has taken place on the local level through a system of licensing called "franchising." Typically, franchising results in the selection of one franchisee whose operation within a specified geographic area is afforded monopoly protection by the local authorities. Nationwide, the franchising process has been besmirched by scandal,[1] political cronyism and vote-selling,[2] illicit deals,[3] and extortion.[4]

In those areas where *de facto* exclusive franchises operate, local cable operators enjoy legally guaranteed monopoly rents in exchange for abiding by regulations on programming content and industry structure. These tradeoffs are a sordid political affair, often involving promises by competing applicants that cannot be kept, behind-the-scenes transfers of stock in cable companies to local political leaders, influence-peddling on a grand scale, lavish endowments to local charitable organizations or governments, favors for political constituencies preferred by those in power, and, in every case, added costs to consumers.[5] In a 1986 article for the University of Pennsylvania Law Review, Thomas Hazlett included numerous examples of corrupt practices that have epitomized this process in many local jurisdictions. Hazlett quotes Donald Sizemore, "a former consultant to the California State Senate's government operations subcommittee," who succinctly reported on the state of local franchising in that state:

> The lobbying process begins with the hiring of politically savvy and influential local consultants. These people are not chosen for their knowledge of cable

television or community needs. Rather, they are experts on the local officials and the political arena. These consultants trade upon the special relationships they have established with the local authorities in order to gain improved access and credibility for their employers.

The next stage in lobbying is to line up support for a company's proposal among influential community groups. Such support is gained by tailoring parts of the franchise proposal to benefit the goals of these groups. Thus, one company might dedicate a portion of its revenue to the maintenance of a deficit-ridden art museum. . . . .

Finally, there is the most controversial franchise-winning tactic of all—rent-a-citizen. Prominent local people are given stock in the subsidiary that will operate the franchise. These individuals are usually part of the local political scene and important to the continued political success of those who will grant the franchise.[6]

The franchising process lends itself quite readily to this kind of abuse. It also entails a sacrifice of the First Amendment, for the typical local authority expects significant content concessions in return for the franchise.

OBTAINING THE FRANCHISE

To operate a cable system, an individual or company must file a registration statement with the FCC[7] and obtain a franchise from the local government in that particular area.[8]

When establishing a franchising system, local authorities have often formed citizens' committees to advise them on franchising standards and, later, to help evaluate applicants' proposals. The authorities also obtain the aid of public-policy consultants to craft minimum legal requirements.[9] Invariably, in addition to setting franchise fees, determining rates, and requiring endowments to preferred local charities or governmental institutions, local franchising authorities establish cable channel access requirements. These requirements often include mandatory minimum numbers of cable channels that must be set aside on a common carrier basis for public, educational, or governmental (PEG) use. These requirements often include detailed descriptions of the kinds of PEG facilities, the minimum acceptable number and nature of PEG studios, and the extent of financing that must be made available to governmental units, citizen groups, and citizens for the production of their programs.[10]

Often, in the first phase of the franchising process, the local authority conducts public hearings, performs studies of its community, or requires prospective franchise applicants to perform "ascertainment surveys" to identify factual bases for program content regulations.[11] Public policy preferences, such as favoritism for minority, female, and local cable system owners and employees, are often factored into the criteria for selection.

Once the local franchising authority has adopted its programming and ownership guidelines, it then issues a public notice in local newspapers announcing its willingness to accept bids for the franchise. The bid solicitation is called a Request for Proposals.[12] The RFP or public notice alerts prospective bidders of the need to supply information about "background, financial qualifications, . . . system design, construction plan, rates, and services" to the local authority and also informs prospective bidders of the deadline by which proposals must be submitted.[13] The notice triggers an elaborate campaign by candidates for the franchise. The competition invariably degenerates into a political fight over whose proposed system promises the most PEG programming, the greatest system design, the most services, and the greatest number of economic concessions to the authorities. The established criteria for selection tend to form the minimum level for bidding. It is common for companies to promise significantly more concessions than are required or are economically feasible in order to curry favor with the authority.

The local authority next evaluates the bids in what is a highly politicized event. It often does so with the aid of consultants.[14] The background and character of each bidder is explored,[15] and public hearings are held to judge the various proposals.[16]

After hearings are held, the authority typically selects one bidder, creating a *de facto* monopoly franchise, and negotiates a franchise agreement with the bidder.[17] After the negotiations, the franchisee and the authority reveal the franchise's terms. The franchisee is then required to construct and operate in accordance with the agreement.[18]

Clint Bolick has noted in the case of a Denver, Colorado, franchise that a "massive regulatory scheme [was] imposed on the winner," including a 100-plus-page contract requiring the franchisee to do the following:

—pay 5 percent of its annual gross revenues as a franchise fee, plus an additional 2 percent for community programming;

—defray the city's expenses for the [Request for Proposals] . . . ($80,000);

—provide a $1 million construction bond and a $100,000 letter of credit;

—grant $1.5 million in loans and capital to small businesses and minority groups;

—wire the entire city according to a fixed construction schedule based on political rather than practical considerations;

—agree to pay a $1,000 penalty per day for franchise violations;

—submit to rate regulation;

—allow the city to veto programming changes;

—set aside all or part of 22 channels for programming access, and cede editorial control over them;

—build studios and other facilities for access to selected special-interest groups at a cost of $7.34 million; and

—provide an emergency override system that enables city officials to turn on subscribers' sets, adjust the volume, and broadcast "emergency" messages into their homes at any hour of the day or night.[19]

Provisions similar to these, albeit sometimes of lesser severity and scope, are a part of almost every cable franchise in America.

A cable franchise is not permanent. When the term ends, the local authority conducts a review of the franchisee's operations, paying particular attention to how the franchisee has operated and whether he has fulfilled the contract. Failure to satisfy the local authority can result in selection of a new franchisee. Fulfillment of promises nevertheless entails renegotiation of the franchise with the imposition of new requirements. In some instances, the system of local franchising has been challenged in the courts by those who have been denied a franchise by the municipality. These battles have called into question the First Amendment validity of the franchising process.

FRANCHISING AND THE COURTS

In *City of Los Angeles v. Preferred Communications, Inc.*,[20] the Supreme Court defaulted when first challenged to identify the proper First Amendment standard for assessing the constitutionality of a *de facto* exclusive franchise. Confronted with the propriety of the ninth circuit's refusal to grant a part of a motion to dismiss filed by the City of Los Angeles that concerned the First Amendment validity of the Los Angeles franchising process, the Court accepted as true the facts pled by the complainant but refused to settle on a First Amendment standard for evaluation.

On the basis of the factual record then before it, the Court recognized that First Amendment interests were "implicated" but refused to determine precisely what those interests were. In a vexing passage, the Court vacillated, on the one hand analogizing cable editorial functions to the kind exercised by the typical print journalist (suggesting that the *Miami Herald Publishing Co. v. Tornillo's* high level of protection might be appropriate), yet on the other hand analogizing cable to the broadcast press (suggesting that the *Red Lion Broadcasting Co. v. FCC's* low level of protection might be appropriate).[21]

Subsequently, by its refusal to review the *Chicago Cable Communications* case,[22] despite a light docket schedule in its fall 1990 term,[23] the Court demonstrated again a disinclination to resolve the ultimate First Amendment questions at stake. It is axiomatic that given the great import of these questions the Court will have to resolve them soon. However, it is not clear how it will do so.

Without guidance from the Supreme Court, the circuit courts have applied differing constitutional standards to assess the First Amendment validity of cable franchising and have, therefore, come to different conclusions. A survey of two of the more prominent circuit court cases reveals the extent of the diversity of opinion and the nature of the municipalities' primary arguments in favor of maintaining the monopoly rent/content control *quid pro quo*.

THE NINTH CIRCUIT COURT

The Ninth Circuit Court has adopted the most extensive degree of First Amendment protection for cable of all circuits in the nation. In *Preferred Communications, Inc. v. City of Los Angeles*,[24] the court assessed the First Amendment validity of a *de facto* exclusive franchise. Preferred Communications, Inc. (PCI), a cable company, sought to erect its cable system using public utility poles and conduits without participating in the city's franchising process. The city required cable companies to pay the typical high financial contributions and make access channel concessions. In particular, Los Angeles required potential bidders to pay, in addition to franchise fees, a $10,000 filing fee and a $500 good faith deposit. It also required bidders to agree to pay the city $60,000 for expenses incurred in the franchise process.[25] In addition to financial, character, and basic service requirements, the city expected bidders to pledge that they would provide two leased access channels and, at the cable company's expense, a number of mandatory access channels, including "two channels for use by the City and by other government entities, two channels for use by educational institutions, and two channels for use by the general public, along with staff and facilities to aid in programming."[26]

The city justified its licensing of the press and its limitations on the editorial discretion of cablecasters on essentially three grounds. The city alleged a "physical scarcity of space" on public utility structures akin to spectrum scarcity. It alleged that cable was a natural monopoly, and it alleged that it had a right to exercise plenary control over the medium because cable installation and maintenance would disrupt the public streets and rights-of-way.[27]

Writing for the court, Judge Joseph T. Sneed was not convinced by any of these arguments. None justified the franchising process limits on First Amendment rights. In the presence of an admission that the utility poles and conduits were capable of supporting more than one cable, Sneed could not accept the validity of the city's seemingly academic contention that in some undetermined respect the poles and conduits were physically limited.[28]

Sneed rejected the city's natural monopoly argument, citing to the *Miami Herald Publishing Co. v. Tornillo* newspaper standard. Echoing D.C. Circuit Court Judge Wright, Sneed explained that, even were cable a monopoly, the Supreme Court in *Miami Herald Publishing Co.* had rejected arguments based on difficulty of market entry as a basis for legitimizing a mandatory right of access to the press. He found the physical disruption to and burden on public rights-of-way also an insufficient basis for justifying the creation of a government-controlled monopoly.[29]

Sneed rejected the city's argument that cable installation and maintenance entailed significant disruption to public streets and rights-of-way, and that this disruption justified a lower First Amendment threshold of analysis. Rather, he found that such disruption justified only "some government regulation," provided it was "sharply focused" toward protecting public safety and was not an artifice for a wholesale restriction on access to the cable press.[30]

Sneed then adopted a new standard for evaluating the cable franchising system—relying heavily on precedent of the Supreme Court preceding its adoption of modern "public forum" law (namely, *Grayned v. City of Rockford*).[31] In *Grayned*, the high Court had determined that speech not "incompatible with the normal activity of a particular [public] place at a particular time" could not be restricted by the government without a compelling justification.[32] PCI's proposed cable installation was, of course, a compatible use and so could not be restricted on the basis of the city's arguments.

In conclusion, Sneed, like Judge Wright, analogized to the newspaper context, explaining that the city could not restrict the right to engage in speech over cable to one "highest bidder." He found this practice akin to allowing the government to restrict the grant of a permit for newspaper vending machines to the single paper regarded by the government as the "best" public servant, a circumstance unconstitutional under the *Miami Herald Publishing Co.* standard.

On remand to the U.S. District Court for the Central District of California Judge Consuelo Bland Marshall has expanded the application of the Ninth Circuit Court's holding in granting a motion for summary decision in favor of Preferred. The District Court found unconstitutional the city's requirements regarding "one area/one operator," "mandatory access/leased access," "character," "state of the art" equipment, and government consent before sale. It did so relying variously on the *O'Brien* intermediate scrutiny and the *Tornillo* strict scrutiny First Amendment standards.[33] Judge Marshall upheld a requirement that encouraged but did not require the cable franchisee to hire local residents; however, she strongly indicated that a mandatory requirement of this nature would be found unconstitutional.[34]

Like the Ninth and the D.C. Circuit Courts, the U.S. District Court for the Central District of California adheres to the view that the cable press is entitled to a more heightened degree of protection than is afforded the broadcast press.[35]

THE SEVENTH CIRCUIT COURT

In stark contrast to the decision of Judges Sneed and Marshall is that of Judge Richard Posner for the Seventh Circuit Court in *Omega Satellite Products v. City of Indianapolis*.[36]

Omega Satellite Products Company used a satellite master antenna television system (SMATV) to feed programs to an apartment complex. Because such systems do not use public streets or rights-of-way, they are not typically regulated by the franchising authority. However, in May 1981, Omega stumbled into the regulatory domain when it ran a cable through a public drainage culvert between two apartment complexes to avoid the expense of installing a second satellite dish. By using the public culvert, Omega had embarked on an illegal business venture: cablecasting without franchise authority. The city of Indianapolis sued Omega.

Before the Seventh Circuit, Omega contended that its simple, unobtrusive, and short-distance connection could not be prohibited by the city because of, among other things, the First Amendment. Omega did not convince the court, however, and was ordered to remove the cable from the ditch.

Judge Posner accepted without reservation the city's natural monopoly argument. He likewise accepted the city's argument about disruption to public property. And, indeed, he indicated his preference for treating cable more like broadcast television under the *Red Lion Broadcasting Co.* standard than like newspapers under the *Miami Herald Publishing Co.* standard.

Posner presumed that without regulation a monopoly would emerge from a competitive struggle and would exact monopoly rents from the public. Far better to permit a government-controlled monopoly from the start than to await the inevitable, reasoned Posner.[37]

Explaining that greater government intrusion in the affairs of the broadcast press was deemed permissible because of, in part, frequency interference, Posner found cable to involve an analogous kind of interference—"interference with other users of telephone poles and underground ducts."[38] Furthermore, he found greater regulation warranted for television (broadcast and cable alike) on the basis of the so-called "impact rationale" of *FCC v. Pacifica Foundation,*[39] whereby the pervasive presence and influential nature of a medium is said to justify regulation as a constitutional matter. Provided that the city did not use content-based criteria for selecting a franchisee, its *de facto* exclusive franchise would be deemed constitutional, according to Posner.[40]

The Eighth Circuit Court, like the Seventh, adheres to the view that the cable press is entitled only to the same First Amendment protection as the broadcast press.

The differences between the circuits are but part of a larger struggle over interpretation of the First Amendment. Boiled down to its essentials, this contest concerns whether the First Amendment constitutes a positive denial of government power to regulate access to and the content of the cable media or whether the First Amendment constitutes an affirmative grant of power to the states and localities to determine who will be afforded preferential access to the media and what messages may be communicated by the media. The ultimate resolution of this contest will determine whether the public sector or private sector will control the next century's principal communication pathways.

ENDNOTES

1. *See, e.g.,* Note, *The Collapse of Consensus: Effects of the Deregulation of Cable Television,* 81 Colum. L. Rev. 612, 614 n.20 (1981). ("The rewards of cable system ownership have caused abuses of the franchise bidding

process. There have been scandals in a number of cities as national cable companies 'rented a civic leader' by offering him a directorship of a local subsidiary set up to bid for a cable franchise. FORTUNE, July 2, 1979, at 64.")

2. *See, e.g., Central Telecommunications, Inc. v. TCI Cablevision,* 800 F.2d 711 (8th Cir. 1986); *Pacific West Cable Company v. City of Sacramento, California,* 672 F. Supp. 1322 (1987).

3. *See* Schildhause, *Should Cities Franchise Cable TV? Aren't We Forgetting Free Speech?,* Los Angeles Daily Journal, Thursday, Mar. 31, 1988.

4. *See* Lee, *Cable Franchising and the First Amendment,* 36 VAND. L. REV. 867, 869 (1988) (quoting Cablevision, Dec. 7, 1981, at 728, quoting Harold Farrow, counsel for petitioner in *Community Communications Co. v. City of Boulder,* 455 U.S. 40 (1982) that the "cities' franchising practices are more appropriately 'spelled e-x-t-o-r-t-i-o-n.' "); Hazlett, *Private Monopoly and the Public Interest: An Economic Analysis of the Cable Television Franchise,* 134 U. PENN. L. REV. 1335, 1357–61 (1986).

5. In a study conducted by the National Economic Research Associates, Inc., in 1984, typical costs associated with local government franchising requirements were said to result "in nearly a 30 percent increase in prices and a 12 percent decline in cable subscriptions." Shaw, *Costs of Cable Television Franchise Requirements* (National Economic Research Associates, Inc., 1984) at 3.

6. Hazlett, *Private Monopoly and the Public Interest: An Economic Analysis of the Cable Television Franchise,* 134 U. PENN. L. REV. 1335, 1360 (1986).

7. *See* § 76.12, 47 C.F.R. (1988).

8. For an overview of the franchising process, *see* C. FERRIS, F. LLOYD, & T. CASEY, CABLE TELEVISION LAW (1985); D. BRENNER, M. PRICE, & M. MYERSON, CABLE TELEVISION (1986); L. JOHNSON & M. BOTEIN, CABLE TELEVISION: THE PROCESS OF FRANCHISING (1973); W. S. BAER, M. BOTEIN, L. JOHNSON, C. FILNICK, M. PRICE, & R. YIN, CABLE TELEVISION: FRANCHISING CONSIDERATIONS (1974).

9. C. FERRIS, F. LLOYD, & T. CASEY, CABLE TELEVISION LAW § 13.17 (1985).

10. *Id.* at § 15 (1989).

11. *See, e.g.,* Lee, *Cable Franchising and the First Amendment,* 36 VAND. L. REV. 867, 871 (1983); Note, *Cable Television: The Constitutional Limitations of Local Government Control,* 15 SW. U. L. REV. 181, 185 (1984).

12. *See, e.g.,* Lee, *Cable Franchising and the First Amendment,* 36 VAND. L. REV. 867, 871 (1983).

13. *Id.*

14. *Id.*

15. *Id.*

16. Note, *Cable Television: The Constitutional Limitations of Local Government Control,* 15 SW. U. L. REV. 181, 185 (1984).

17. Note, *Cable Franchising and the First Amendment: Does the Franchising Process Contravene First Amendment Rights?*, 36 FED. COM. L. J. 317, 323 (1984).

18. *See* Lee, *Cable Franchising and the First Amendment,* 36 VAND. L. REV. 867, 872 (1983).

19. *See* Bolick, *Cable Television: An Unnatural Monopoly,* No. 34, CATO INST. POLICY ANALYSIS, Mar. 13, 1984.

20. 106 S.Ct. 2034 (1986).

21. Wrote Justice William Rehnquist:

> We do think that [cablecasting] . . . plainly implicate[s] First Amendment interests. . . . Thus, through original programming or by exercising editorial discretion over which stations or programs to include in its repertoire, respondent seeks to communicate messages on a wide variety of topics in a wide variety of formats. We recently noted that cable operators exercise "a significant amount of editorial discretion regarding what their programming will include." *FCC v. Midwest Video Corp.* Cable television partakes of some of the aspects of speech and the communication of ideas as do the traditional enterprises of newspaper and book publishers, public speakers, and pamphleteers. Respondent's proposed activities would seem to implicate First Amendment interests as do the activities of wireless broadcasters, which were found to fall within the ambit of the First Amendment in *Red Lion Broadcasting Co. v. FCC* . . . even though the free speech aspects of the wireless broadcasters' claim were found to be outweighed by the government interest in regulating by reason of the scarcity of available frequencies. . . .
>
> We do not think, however, that it is desirable to express any more detailed views on the proper resolution of the First Amendment question raised by the respondent's complaint and the City's response to it without a fuller development of the disputed issues in the case. We think that we may know more than we know now about how the constitutional issues should be resolved when we know more about the present uses of the public utility poles and rights-of-way and how respondent proposes to install and maintain its facilities on them.

City of Los Angeles v. Preferred Communications, Inc., 106 S.Ct. 2034, 2037–38 (1986).

22. *See Chicago Cable Communications v. Chicago Cable Commission,* 879 F.2d 1540 (7th Cir. 1989).

23. *See* 58 U.S.L.W. 1128 (1990).

24. *Preferred Communications, Inc. v. City of Los Angeles,* 754 F.2d 1396 (9th Cir. 1985).

25. *Id.* at 1396, 1400.

26. *Id.*

27. *Id.* at 1396.
28. *Id.* at 1396, 1404.
29. *Id.* at 1396.
30. *Id.* at 1396, 1406.
31. *Grayned v. City of Rockford,* 408 U.S. 104, 116 (1972).
32. *Preferred Communications, Inc. v. City of Los Angeles,* 754 F.2d 1396, 1408–9 (9th Cir. 1985).
33. *Preferred Communications, Inc. v. City of Los Angeles,* 3 Fed. Comm. Comm. R. Rep. (CCH) § 26, 272 (9th Cir. 1990).
34. *Id.*
35. *See, e.g., Quincy Cable TV, Inc. v. FCC,* 768 F.2d 1434 (D.C. Cir. 1985). Judge Eugene F. Lynch of the U.S. District Court for the Northern District of California granted a motion for summary decision filed by Century Federal, Inc., in its suit against the City of Palo Alto, California. The court held Palo Alto's *de facto* exclusive cable franchise and its mandatory access channel, universal service, and "state-of-the-art" technology requirements unconstitutional under the First Amendment. It decided that only "reasonable fees to help defray the administrative costs of necessary licensing may be permissible" under the First Amendment. *See Century Federal, Inc. v. City of Palo Alto,* 710 F. Supp. 1559 (1988).
36. *Omega Satellite Products v. City of Indianapolis,* 694 F.2d 119 (7th Cir. 1982).
37. Posner wrote:

> You can start with a competitive free-for-all—different cable television systems frantically building out their grids and signing up subscribers in an effort to bring down their average costs faster than their rivals—but eventually there will be only a single company, because until a company serves the whole market it will have an incentive to keep expanding in order to lower its average costs. In the interim there may be wasteful duplication of facilities. This duplication may lead not only to higher prices to cable television subscribers, at least in the short run, but also to higher costs to other users of the public ways, who must compete with the cable television companies for access to them. An alternative procedure is to pick the most efficient competitor at the outset, give him a monopoly, and extract from him in exchange a commitment to provide reasonable service at reasonable rates.

Omega Satellite Products v. City of Indianapolis, 694 F.2d 119, 126 (7th Cir. 1982).
38. *Id.* at 119, 126.
39. *FCC v. Pacifica Foundation,* 438 U.S. 726, 748–49 (1978).
40. *Omega Satellite Products v. City of Indianapolis,* 694 F.2d 119, 128 (7th Cir. 1982).

21

A REFUTATION OF ARGUMENTS FOR REGULATION

From the history of regulation set forth in this volume and from the law review literature favoring regulation, one can identify at least five principal arguments for not providing full First Amendment protection to the broadcast and cable press. These arguments hold the following:

1. That each mass medium should be assessed under its own peculiar First Amendment standard (the varying standards approach);
2. That the physical and economic scarcity said to be unique to the electronic media justify less than full First Amendment protection (the scarcity rationale);
3. That an economic and viewpoint monopoly will supplant viewpoint diversity if the content and structure of the broadcast and cable press are not regulated (the natural monopoly concept);
4. That the broadcast and cable press use public resources and should therefore be regulated according to the Supreme Court's First Amendment legal standard for speech on public property not traditionally open for speech purposes (the nonpublic forum approach); and
5. That the electronic press uses properties imbued with a "public character" for which private limitations on access are inappropriate, and that, without regulation, the marketplace of ideas will produce unacceptable inequalities, causing the views preferred by media owners to be the only ones presented (the public function approach).

Each of these arguments is derived from a demonstrably false premise. Each necessitates a redirection of the First Amendment from a prohibition on state suppression of speech to a prohibition on private speech, thereby limiting freedom in the manner described in this book's first chapter. Each authorizes government to select who may speak (and who may not freely speak) and what may be said (and what may not be said). A careful analysis of each argument reveals that each argument not only is void of factual support but also contravenes the core values protected by the amendment. Therefore, the arguments for government regulation of the broadcast and cable press must be rejected.

THE VARYING STANDARDS APPROACH

This approach was articulated by the Supreme Court in *Red Lion Broadcasting Co. v. FCC*. There, the Court announced the oft-quoted principle that "differences in the characteristics of news media justify differences in the First Amendment standards applied to them."[1] Justice Robert H. Jackson originated this principle in a case involving the First Amendment ramifications of communication by sound truck. He wrote:

> The moving picture screen, the radio, the newspaper, the handbill, the sound truck and the street corner orator have differing natures, values, abuses and dangers. Each, in my view, is a law unto itself, and all we are dealing with now is the sound truck.[2]

This argument assumes that the *same* message communicated by different technological modes should be accorded different levels of First Amendment protection because of the physical differences in the modes. The precise reason why a different technology should beget different First Amendment standards for the messages communicated has never been fully explained.

It might be argued that different modes of expression have differing impacts. However, upon close analysis, this focus appears to be an artifice for allowing government to engage in content discrimination.

Powerful language may leave an impression every bit as inspiring or traumatic as a visual recreation of the written word. The extraordinary diversity of the English language enables words in a classic work of literature to create as vivid, if not more vivid, an image as can be created by audio and video modes of communication.

The media, regardless of the mode of transmission, all use language (written or spoken) and images (still or moving) to captivate the viewer or listener; to evoke horror, outrage, shock, or consternation; to present information of immediate interest; to delve deeply into specific social, scientific, economic, political, or legal subjects in a serious and scholarly way; or to poke fun at the human condition. In each case, the message and the purpose for its transmission and receipt are the same regardless of the transmission mode chosen. The substantive commonalities between the various media forms militate against affording each evaluation under a different constitutional standard.

Additional arguments have been raised that the media differ because some forms intrude into the home while others do not. Broadcast and cable are said to invade directly through the television set, differing from literature, which must be obtained outside the home or by mail. In effect, the senses of the viewer are said to be involuntarily bombarded by audio and video transmissions. As Justice John Paul Stevens put it in *FCC v. Pacifica Foundation*:[3]

> The broadcast media have established a uniquely pervasive presence in the lives of all Americans. . . . Because the broadcast audience is constantly tuning in and out, prior warnings cannot completely protect the listener or viewer from unexpected program content. To say that one may avoid further offense by turning off the radio when he hears indecent language is like saying that the remedy for an assault is to run away after the first blow.

The fallacy in this argument is its presumption that the viewer or listener is a captive audience rather than a willing recipient of information. The set permits switching to other channels. Just as surely as one can tune in, one can tune out. Moreover, newspapers and magazines like *TV Guide* alert the TV viewer of television offerings and their nature. There are many channels and many information sources from which to choose. Furthermore, the fact that listening or viewing may cause one to hear or see something unpleasant is not an argument for suppression of speech; it is an argument for counterspeech. To be robust and diverse, the marketplace of ideas must be filled with information that some will find offensive or uninformative. The alternative, state censorship, grants the government authority to decide for us what will be deemed "offensive" and to impose that judgment on each of us—the willing and the unwilling alike—without permitting each viewer or listener to evaluate the material for himself. This suppression of speech not only stifles the right of speakers to present their messages, it also suppresses knowledge itself, for it is only by being subjected to speech, even speech we find offensive, that we will be able to understand precisely what it is that we do not like and why it is that we do not like it.

Moreover, the various media are becoming increasingly indistinguishable not only from a substantive but also from a technological standpoint. It has become more and more difficult to recognize any distinct differences between the print and nonprint modes of communication. The technologies have been merging into hybrid forms that do not lend themselves to *Red Lion Broadcasting Co.*'s superficial categorization approach. National newspapers and magazines, including *USA Today,* the *Wall Street Journal,* the *New York Times,* and *Time* all depend on satellite, telecommunications, and computer technologies to transmit and receive information from around the globe for their news stories.[4] Teletext (an electronic publishing service that permits viewers to receive pictographic and textual information from their viewing screens); videotext (a two-way communication service by telephone or cable for electronic mail, home-to-office data retrieval and transmission, home banking, etc.); home computers; and interactive cable technologies all permit data that historically appeared only in print to now occupy a video screen.[5]

Shortly after the turn of the twenty-first century, with the advent of fiber optic technology to the home, consumers will be able to retrieve national newspaper and magazine stories complete with pictures directly from teletext and electronic photography units that will be a part of or connected to a digital audio, video, and data retrieval and transmission unit. Newspapers will be "on line" and will be sampled through a viewing screen or retrieved in "hard copy" form through a teletext unit connected to the viewing screen. Newspaper and magazine pictures will also be accessible through electronic photography that will give viewers a hard copy of any image they want to pull from the viewing screen.[6]

The technology of television will carry the information of newspapers in print form as well as in combined print, live, and recorded audio and video formats. Viewers wanting more information on a story presented live may well be able to gain access to more detailed hard copy news reports that have been prepared to accompany live broadcasts or cablecasts. Newspapers, in turn, will rely increasingly on electronic modes of transmission both to retrieve and to transmit ideas and information.

In short, it has never been adequately explained why the mere (and now vanishing) technological differences in modes of disseminating ideas and information should produce differences in the First Amendment treatment accorded those ideas and that information. Furthermore, the superficial technological differences that have existed are fast disappearing as former "bright line" distinctions continue to be blurred by the fusing of print and electronic technologies. What remains are the profound commonalities that have always characterized the mass media, those substantive aspects of news, public affairs, and entertainment programming that reach people whether by book, motion picture, radio, or television.

THE SCARCITY RATIONALE: THE BROADCAST CONTEXT

Writ large in the law by the *NBC v. United States* and *Red Lion Broadcasting Co.* decisions, the scarcity rationale provides that government should be permitted to regulate the content and structure of the broadcast press because unlike the print press broadcasting suffers from "physical limitations" (the scarcity of the medium as a resource and the presence of an excess of demand for it) and "economic limitations" (the higher marginal cost associated with a less than universally available good).[7] In *FCC v. National Citizens Committee for Broadcasting,*[8] the Court summarized the essential physical scarcity argument when it wrote:

> Because of problems of interference between broadcast signals, a finite number of frequencies can be used productively; this number is far exceeded by the number of persons wishing to broadcast to the public. In light of this physical scarcity, Government allocation and regulation of broadcast frequencies are essential, as we have often recognized.[9]

In *Red Lion Broadcasting Co.*, the Court stated the essential economic scarcity argument when it wrote: "Only a tiny fraction of those with resources and intelligence can hope to communicate by radio."[10]

As an initial matter, no one has ever established in constitutional history preceding *NBC v. United States* a connection between scarcity and the First Amendment. In the history of print model constitutional jurisprudence, there is no analogue to the "scarcity rationale" that Justice Frankfurter made a distinguishing principle in the broadcast context. Despite newspaper shortages and the fact that presses have always been costly and have never been available to all who would like to (but who could not afford to) publish a newspaper, never has scarcity been deemed a constitutional reason for denying full First Amendment protection to the print press.

Indeed, in *Miami Herald Publishing Co. v. Tornillo,* the Court surveyed the history of newspaper concentration and of "one newspaper towns" but did not find this evidence a proper basis to impose a statutory right of reply for politicians castigated in print. Rather, the Court squarely backed the editorial discretion of the print journalist regardless of scarcity, finding "the choice of material to go into a newspaper, and the decisions made as to limitations on the size and content of the paper, and treatment of public issues and public officials—whether fair or unfair—[to] constitute the exercise of editorial control and judgment." These were understood to be private decisions deserving protection under the First Amendment.[11]

Even assuming the propriety of considering the presence of economic and physical scarcity in a medium as a basis for reducing the degree of First Amendment protection accorded that medium, the problem with the purported scarcity–based "distinction," militating against greater freedom for broadcasting than for printing is that, in fact, no such *distinction* exists. Rather than serving as a basis for differentiation between the two media forms, as we shall see, the spectrum scarcity rationale posits a double standard.

Because "all economic goods are scarce," it makes little sense to regard this universal fact as a distinguishing principle.[12] Like the electromagnetic spectrum, paper, presses, and ink are also scarce resources. In addition, scarcity is relative and varies constantly with technological innovation, resource availability, and demand. Therefore, if we predicate the degree of protection for a message on the relative scarcity of the medium, we may well find that messages communicated by newspapers (the costliest and the rarest medium today) would be subjected to the least First Amendment protection. Messages communicated by cable would get more protection than those communicated by the print medium. Messages communicated by broadcast stations would get the most protection. Tomorrow's changes in comparative scarcity would beget yet further changes in the degree of protection afforded the various media.

When universally applied, this "true" scarcity approach would produce numerous unprincipled and anomalous results. It would cause certain ribald matter to be fully protected when presented on a broadcast channel but would cause the same matter to be subject to regulation when presented on a cable channel.

Furthermore, there simply exists no true scarcity of outlets for mass communication. Means of mass communication that are comparable to broadcasting have always existed alongside radio and television, including books, magazines, newspapers, and motion pictures. Today, however, in addition to the thousands of radio and television stations, there are hundreds and thousands of nonspectrum-based substitutes such as cable, satellite master antenna television (SMATV) systems, video cassette recorders, and compact disc players. In the not-so-distant future, direct broadcast satellites will add yet another source of information. So-called "wireless" cable will create even more viewing options. Fiber optic networks will enable each home to receive a myriad of channels and each person to become a publisher who is capable of sending electronic transmissions anywhere in the country. These changes will increasingly render nonsensical the notion that scarcity of a media technology should serve as a distinguishing principle in First Amendment law.[13]

Some people have argued that because only one broadcast entity may transmit on a single frequency from a single location at a single time, this condition should justify a lessened degree of First Amendment protection for broadcasting. This construct erroneously presumes that only a government allocation rather than a market allocation scheme will suffice to solve the problem. It has also been rendered superfluous in light of the multiplicity of substitutable media forms that now exist.

The spectrum scarcity rationale is out of sync with the actual print and broadcast media marketplace (see Table 1). In 1934, there were 583 AM stations in the United States and no FM or television stations.[14] By contrast, in 1934, there were 1,929 daily newspapers in the United States.[15] An argument could have been made then that radio was more scarce than newspapers. In 1969, the year *Red Lion Broadcasting Co.* was decided, there were 577 VHF and 260 UHF television stations nationwide; there were 4,265 AM stations and 2,330 FM stations on the air. In addition, some 2,000 cable systems were operating, reaching approximately 2,800,000 people.[16] By contrast, in 1970, there were some 11,383 daily newspapers nationwide.[17] Despite the extraordinary growth in the number of broadcast and nonspectrum-based mass media outlets, an argument could still be made that the broadcast media were somewhat less bountiful than the print media.

TABLE 1
Comparison of Print, Broadcast,
and Cable Media in the United States.

Medium	1934	1969	1990
AM Stations	583	4,265	4,979
FM Stations	0	2,330	5,738
VHF TV Stations	0	577	674
UHF TV Stations	0	260	778
VHF LPTV	0	0	300
UHF LPTV	0	0	457
Cable Systems	0	2,000	10,823
Daily Newspapers	1,929	11,383[a]	10,457[b]

[a] Figure for 1970.
[b] Figure for 1989.

A decade later, in 1990, there were 674 VHF and 778 UHF television stations nationwide; there were 300 VHF low power television (LPTV) and 457 UHF LPTV stations; and there were 4,979 licensed AM stations and 5,738 licensed FM stations. In addition, some 10,823 cable systems were operating, reaching approximately 53,900,000 people.[18] In 1989, there were some 9,031 newspapers nationwide.[19] Given this environment, it is simply not the case that the broadcast media are more scarce than the print media. Indeed, the inverse is true and is exacerbated with each passing moment.

An examination of these figures reveals a consistent reduction in the number of newspapers and a consistent increase in the number of broadcast stations and cable systems. These changes suggest a basic shift in the media environment, rendering more acute the problem of lessened First Amendment protection for the broadcast and cable media. "In simple numerical terms, the electronic media have become the media of abundance and the print media have become increasingly scarce—reversing the essential premise of the broadcast scarcity rationale."[20]

Today, it is unquestionably true that there are far greater opportunities to enter the broadcast media than the print media. Moreover, the costs of entering the publishing business greatly exceed the costs of entering the broadcasting business.

In 1984, Michael O. Wirth conducted a comparative assessment of the broadcasting and newspaper markets for the National Association of Broadcasters and found the following:

Far less capital is required to start a new television station or radio station than to start a new daily newspaper. For example, starting a 250,000 circulation daily newspaper is estimated to be seven times more expensive than starting a Top 50 market television station. . . .

On average, entrepreneurs pay much less, per unit of average daily circulation purchased, for television and radio stations than they pay for daily newspapers. For example, the average 250,000 circulation daily newspaper sold for three times more per unit of daily circulation than the average Top 50 market television station. The costs of operating a daily newspaper are considerably higher than the costs of operating either a television or a radio station. For example, a typical 250,000 circulation newspaper costs five times more to operate than a typical Top 50 television station. . . .

Convincing consumers and advertisers to adopt a new media firm's product, when the new firm is in competition with one or more existing media firm [sic] of the same type, is a more difficult proposition for a daily newspaper than for either a television or a radio station.[21]

Wirth found the economic data to also hold true with smaller market stations, concluding that the cost of "starting a medium market television station . . . [was] almost one-fourth as expensive as starting a 65,000 circulation daily newspaper" and that the cost of "starting a small market television station . . . almost one-half as expensive as starting a 20,000 circulation daily newspaper."[22] Thus, scarcity as a basis for less constitutional protection for broadcasters makes little sense.

THE SCARCITY RATIONALE: THE CABLE CONTEXT

As with broadcasting, those who want cable regulated have argued that it is physically and economically scarce. Although no cacophonous collision of voices on the airwaves can be posited with cable, Judge Posner and others have argued that physical scarcity does plague cable because cable "involves another type of interference—interference with the users of telephone poles and underground ducts."[23] The City of Los Angeles, in the *Preferred Communications, Inc.* case has argued that the space on utility poles and in public streets and rights-of-way is limited and that this creates the requisite scarcity that justifies regulation. Posner has argued that cable, like broadcasting, is not available to all because it is a natural monopoly with formidable market entry costs.

The physical scarcity argument has only a modicum of factual support. Posner's analogy to broadcast interference is an erroneous one. Although the addition of cable lines to utility poles and public streets and rights-of-way may cause utilities some inconvenience in installing and maintaining their own lines, it assuredly will not prevent them from transmitting their messages or delivering power.

Furthermore, the inconvenience is small, for each cable line consumes but a *de minimis* part of utility pole and public street or right-of-way space. Of greater significance are natural physical obstructions such as large trees, shrubbery, and ice accumulations, as well as man-made obstacles such as traffic.

The lack of space argument is a weak one. For years, utilities and telephone companies have strung all manner of bulky cable lines on utility poles and under ground without concern that space on poles or public property would be so consumed as to leave little room for the installation of more utility lines. Moreover, for years utilities and telephone companies have not engendered even half as much concern by local governments as has surfaced in recent years surrounding the installation of cable lines for mass communication. Only with the advent of cable television has the need to preserve the unencumbered use of the streets and the availability of space on public utility poles become matters of grave import for local authorities.

The change is telling. The argument about lack of space appears to be disingenuous. There simply is no proof that adequate space is unavailable in fact rather than in theory. There is no logical reason or adequate explanation why minimal regulations, limited in duration and scope to protect the public from the disruption caused by the installation and maintenance of cable lines, are not fully adequate to protect public safety.

Cable poses no significant burden either from disruption during installation or from any shortage of space created by cable placement as would warrant anything but limited public safety regulation. As Sol Schildhause has explained, cable lines are far less disruptive than telephone and power lines. The cable itself is "small, light, and almost unnoticeable," composed of copper (and, increasingly, fiber) coaxial wires. The average size of a copper coaxial wire (the largest kind for cable use) is "the thickness of a man's thumb."[24] These cables are typically attached to utility poles or are buried a few inches under the ground in a neat crevice driven by a vibration plow.[25] The limited need to protect the public during periods of cable installation and repair does not justify denying the cable press full protection from government content and structure regulations.

THE NATURAL MONOPOLY CONCEPT

Another principal argument for affording cable less protection than the print media is the economic scarcity or natural monopoly argument. The costs of market entry and of maintaining mass communications services are said to be so great that without government regulation, cable markets will invariably fall into the hands of media giants, and these industry leaders will have no incentive to provide suitable service at reasonable rates. Furthermore, excess demand for a scarce good is said to plague cable in a manner akin to broadcasting. Much of the jurisprudential basis for this argument is borrowed from the economic scarcity argument for broadcast regulation. Like that argument, the cable economic scarcity argument is seriously flawed.

Initially, it is doubtful whether cable can be properly termed a "natural" monopoly, for the franchising system creates and sustains *de facto* exclusive monopoly franchises and insulates cable systems from direct intra-industry competition. Moreover, "market" definitions used to justify cable regulation do not include such alternative media services as broadcast television (including UHF, VHF, and LPTV stations); radio; wireless cable; satellite master antenna television systems (SMATV); multipoint distribution systems (MDS); and video cassette recorders. These all vie for the attention of the same consumers that subscribe to cable and provide consumers with the same kinds of news and entertainment services. In the near future, cable may well experience additional competition from sources such as direct broadcast satellites and fiber optic networks, the latter operated by the telephone companies.

Cable is now in direct competition with broadcast television and the home video cassette market for viewers. Moreover, with music programming, like MTV, cable has entered competition with the broader radio, compact disc, and video disc markets. In short, cable vies for the limited time of media consumers in a marketplace that abounds with options. Therefore, even when protected by local governments from cable competition, cable cannot be said to be void of significant competition.

Cable is a luxury item that has many low-cost substitutes. It differs from power and water utilities in that it provides a service that can be avoided without serious adverse effects. If cable sets its rates too high or diminishes its quality below that of over-the-air services, then media consumers can simply discontinue their cable subscriptions and still enjoy an ever-increasing plethora of video alternatives. The marketplace is so heavily saturated that cable is just another means to receive the same or similar sources of news, opinion, and entertainment.

In 1987, Peter Vestal of the National Association of Broadcasters' Research and Planning Department reported that the average media market from among those tracked by the A. C. Nielsen Company had "access to 36 cable channels . . . , 10 over-the-air television signals, 20.4 AM and 19.5 FM radio signals, 15.9 newspapers, 11.8 magazines each with subscription rate figures of at least 5 percent, and a VCR penetration rate of 48.7 percent."[26] From the largest to the smallest markets, there is simply no single predominant voice.[27] In a Policy Statement released February 28, 1989, in its "cross-interest policy" rule making, the FCC found remarkable the extraordinary proliferation of media sources in all markets. The Commission wrote:

> Whereas the top 25 markets average about 72 radio and television stations per market, even the smallest television markets average about 9 radio and television outlets per market. In addition, . . . analysis of Arbitron data by

288 PROTECTING THE CORE VALUES OF THE FIRST AMENDMENT

Metropolitan Statistical Area, the geographic market measure that may be more appropriate for radio reception, shows that while the top 25 radio markets average approximately 35 total AM and FM stations, even the smallest radio markets average approximately 10 commercial AM and FM stations. As these figures demonstrate, there are a significant number of commercial broadcast outlets throughout markets of all sizes. Further, if cable and VCRs are taken into account, listeners and viewers have even more sources of programs. Cable penetration actually increases as the size of television markets decreases, and VCR penetration appears to be relatively constant across market sizes.[28]

In this media-rich environment, it is difficult to contend seriously that cable can diminish public access to ideas and information. Furthermore, despite the general lack of local intra-industry competition for cable, it cannot be said that cable is less abundant than newspapers. Therefore, there exists no sufficiently persuasive reason why cable should not be afforded full First Amendment protection.

Indeed, cable is more abundant than newspapers are. Moreover, in at least forty jurisdictions nationwide where local laws do not forbid it, cable is in competition with cable.[29] Thomas Hazlett has provided detailed studies of the effects of duopolistic competition in the Orange, Dade, and Palm Beach counties of Florida and in the Sacramento, California, markets. He more generally notes the existence of duopolistic competition in, among others, Mobile and Huntsville, Alabama; Colorado Springs, Colorado; Shreveport and Baton Rouge, Louisiana; and Huntington, New York. Hazlett finds the trend toward "overbuilds" (head-to-head competition by cable firms) to be increasing in jurisdictions that allow competition.[30] He finds a significant reduction in rates (in some cases cutting basic subscriptions in half) for services in overbuilt areas. He finds in these same areas increases in the number of channels and the diversity of programs. Even in areas where "entry is possible, but unlikely to endure," Hazlett finds the threat of market entry "an important competitive constraint on incumbent behavior."[31]

An additional significant artificial anticompetitive obstacle exists in the form of federal law, FCC rules, and the *Modified Final Judgment* of the U.S. District Court of the District of Columbia.[32] These collectively prohibit cross-ownership of television station and cable systems if the cable system serves any part of the television station's primary service area.[33] They also prohibit the national networks from owning cable systems[34] and prohibit telephone companies from offering video and information services to people residing in their telephone service areas.[35] These anticompetitive obstacles effectively lock out of local cable markets certain logical sources for intra-industry competition; they afford cable an added barrier against competition atop the *de facto* exclusive franchise awarded by local authorities.

To the extent that it does exist, the intra-industry cable monopoly is a product not of natural market conditions but of the local franchising process and of federal law. There has yet to be posited a sufficient reason why cable ought not be subject to competition and ought not receive full First Amendment protection.

THE NONPUBLIC FORUM APPROACH

Identified by Matthew Spitzer as a dangerous rationale that the Supreme Court may adopt to support continued broadcast regulation,[36] the nonpublic forum approach has not been used by the Court to justify content and structural controls over either the broadcast or cable press. Nevertheless, this approach could be adopted as a substitute for the scarcity rationale. The nonpublic forum approach has its origins in the Supreme Court's treatment of certain knotty First Amendment problems that have arisen when private speakers have tried to exercise their speech rights on public property.

In its initial evaluation of speech on public property in *Davis v. Massachusetts*,[37] the Court defined government control over speech on public property as essentially proprietary in nature; that is, the government was said to have the same discretion to exclude some or all speech or speakers from its property as a private property owner. The government's greater power to "absolutely exclude" the public from public property was deemed to include a lesser power to abridge speech rights on that property as long as the government had a rational basis for its acts of suppression.[38]

The modern incarnation of *Davis* is *Lehman v. City of Shaker Heights*,[39] which is the law of the land. *Lehman* instituted a dichotomous standard for review of speech claims on public property. Under it, the Court examines particular property in light of its *traditional use* to determine if a public forum has been created. If the property is a public forum (if it has traditionally been made available by the government as a place for public expression), then any content-based regulation of speech on it will be subject to strict scrutiny, that is, the means chosen for regulation must be narrowly drawn to serve a compelling state interest to pass muster.[40] Content-neutral regulations such as those governing the time, place, and manner of speech are deemed constitutional only if they are "narrowly tailored to serve a significant governmental interest"[41] and if they leave open adequate "alternative channels for communication."[42]

If, however, the Court finds that the property in question has not been a traditional public forum, then it will almost invariably find the matter "not to rise to the dignity of a First Amendment violation."[43] Government suppression of speech entirely or as to specific content is then usually allowed, provided the government can show a mere rational basis for its regulations.

By avoiding an assessment of the core First Amendment values at stake and adhering to a traditional use basis, the Court ensures that government retains broad power to regulate speech on the property that it owns. The focus on mere traditional use of property leads the Court to avoid determining whether government has properly elected to close a forum at the outset—a treacherous move, for it gives the legislative and the executive branches final say-so over constitutional questions affecting fundamental individual rights. Instead of addressing whether property has *properly* been reserved to the government and is incompatible with the speech use proposed,[44] the Court almost invariably defers (without need for justification) to a legislative judgment that public property that is historically not open for speech purposes is, by virtue of that fact alone, properly a nonpublic forum. This failure of the Court to test the validity of the government's claim presents the crux of the problem when one contemplates, as Matthew Spitzer has, the application of nonpublic forum law to broadcasting.

Under a nonpublic forum theory, those who favor press regulation may assume that the broadcast spectrum has always been owned by the government and that it has never been held open for speech purposes like a public street or park. Since the inception of radio, government has assiduously regulated access to the airwaves.[45] Accepting this view, the Court would deem the airwaves a nonpublic forum and would countenance a level of constitutional protection for broadcast speech that is as low as the level afforded broadcast speech under the spectrum scarcity rationale.

The nonpublic forum approach should be rejected. None of the nonpublic forum cases is on point; the regulation of broadcast licensees and cable system operators is the regulation of the "press." Broadcasters and cablecasters have much in common with the traditional print press. The regulations in question do *not* preserve a *governmental use* of *public property;* they control the *press* as a medium of communication.

The mere fact that broadcast stations use what the government has deemed a public medium to communicate does not justify placing the entire industry into the government's province. Nor does it justify the government's use of its property to obstruct the free flow of ideas and information in our society. Application of nonpublic forum law to the media proceeds along a slippery slope. The mere fact that newspapers are distributed on the public streets and sidewalks does not, by virtue of that fact, give the government a legitimate claim of control over who may be in the printing business or what may be said in the newspapers.[46] Nor does the mere fact that cable communication travels in lines hung on public utility poles or run under public streets or through public rights-of-way give the government a legitimate claim to control who may be in the cable business or what may be said through the cable press. Likewise, government ownership of the airwaves is not a proper basis for government to claim control over the content and structure of the broadcast press.

Indeed, if the *Davis* syllogism were to apply, it would countenance a suppression of the press as great as, if not greater than, the Sedition Act of 1798. The government, the proprietor of the public communications pathways, could deny newspaper venders a right to distribute newspapers on the public streets or sidewalks; could prohibit cable systems from using the public utility poles, streets, and rights-of-way to reach subscribers' homes; and could withdraw the public airwaves from private broadcasting use entirely. The effect of government's possessing the power to severely restrict or preclude use of property deemed public for mass communication would clearly be discriminatory and burdensome within the meaning of cases like *Minneapolis Star & Tribune Co. v. Minnesota Commissioner of Revenue* (invalidating a tax that singled out the press for discriminatory treatment).[47] It would interfere with the "liberty of circulating," or disseminating, deemed an essential component of a free press (for "without the circulation, the publication would be of little value").[48] It would place an extraordinary censorial power within the "unbridled discretion" of government officials, an investiture of authority that has ever been the bane of tyrannical regimes and the enemy of the First Amendment.[49]

Traditional nonpublic forum cases do not concern the imposition of pervasive controls on an entire medium of communication. They concern discrete instances where people seek access to government property in order to speak. The issue in these cases is the permissible, temporary use of public property. The issue does not concern permanent government supervision and control over the press. Consequently, the nonpublic forum theory, which depends on the *Davis* proprietary approach, cannot apply to the press.

THE PUBLIC FUNCTION APPROACH

This approach has been advocated by a handful of scholars who ally themselves with the Relativist school of constitutional construction and has been strongly influenced by, and has itself influenced, the development of broadcast regulatory law. The public function approach lacks any developed Constitutional law foundation and is still very much a theoretical rather than an applied jurisprudential concept. Nevertheless, it is a theory worthy of refutation.

Under the public function approach, first stated by the Supreme Court in *Marsh v. Alabama*,[50] "the more an owner, for his advantage, opens up his property for use by the public in general, the more do his rights become circumscribed by the statutory and constitutional rights of those who use it."[51] The general public's use of private property, in other words, tends to transform it into public property: "Private property used to perform a traditional public function [will] be treated as government property."[52] Advocates of this approach (the access advocates) argue that the private press must be deemed imbued with a public character and thus be regulatable by the state. Jerome Barron writes:

> A right of access to the pages of a monopoly newspaper might be predicated on Justice Douglas's open-ended "public function" theory. . . . Such a theory would demand a rather rabid conception of "state action," but if parks in private hands cannot escape the stigma of abiding "public character," it would seem that a newspaper, which is the common journal of printed communication in a community, could not escape the constitutional restrictions which quasi-public status invites. If monopoly newspapers are indeed quasi-public, their refusal of space to particular viewpoints is state action abridging expression in violation of . . . the first amendment.[53]

For the access advocates, it is consistent with the First Amendment for government to take *affirmative steps* to create ideological balance in public debate. These steps consist of enforcing against media owners government-mandated rights of access for groups and individuals who hold minority views (or in the words of Dominic Caristi, "those views counter to the capitalistic goals of privately owned, for-profit media"[54]), but who cannot afford to own a press medium. The idea calls for a heavy-handed redistribution of editorial control from the private sector to the government and then from the government to certain preferred speakers. According to Caristi, "If free speech is necessary to promote robust discussion to enhance the process of self-governance, then government must take responsibility to provide channels for that opportunity."[55] Jerome Barron adds:

> The mass media's development of an antipathy to ideas requires legal intervention if novel and unpopular ideas are to be assured a forum—unorthodox points

of view which have no claim on broadcast time and newspaper space as a matter of right are in a poor position to compete with those aired as a matter of grace.[56]

The access advocates presume that private limitations on speech are as great as, if not more severe than, political suppression of speech. Writes Caristi: "When a select few individuals have the ability to restrict access, freedom of expression is endangered just as surely as if the restriction had been imposed by the government."[57]

Rather than understanding the First Amendment to be a *guardian* of the private sphere of communication, the access advocates interpret it to be a *guarantee* of a preferred mix of ideological viewpoints. Owen Fiss writes:

> The power of media to decide what it broadcasts must be regulated because . . . this power always has a double edge: It subtracts from public debate at the very moment that it adds to it. . . . To date we have ambivalently recognized the value of state regulation of this character on behalf of speech . . . [b]ut these regulatory measures are today embattled, and in any event, more, not less, is needed. . . . A commitment to rich public debate will allow, and sometimes even require, the state to act in these ways, however elemental and repressive [that] might at first seem. Autonomy will be sacrificed, and content regulation sometimes allowed, but only on the assumption that public debate might be enriched and our capacity for collective self-determination enhanced.[58]

In short, the access advocates have transformed the marketplace of ideas from a *laissez-faire* model to a state-control model. For them, if the marketplace of ideas can be viewed as the contents of a cauldron, it is not enough to await random stirring; government must burn an eternal flame beneath the cauldron, keeping it at the boiling point. Silence is not an option; the government implores: Let there be speech!

The access advocates' theory is predicated on the unproven assumptions that the media lack diversity of views, that government must compel diversity, and that government power to regulate the content of speech will be exercised beneficially, that is, consistent with, rather than suppressive of, freedom.

The notion that people with unorthodox ideas cannot gain access to the media is in error. To be sure, the exercise of editorial discretion causes some views to be preferred over others. This fact is a reflection of economic reality. Because resources are finite, not all of the infinite number of opinions and bits of information generated daily can possibly be published. However, no evidence exists that opinions useful to consumers are slighted. Moreover, there is no convincing evidence that the mass media act in concert to ignore those with unorthodox ideas. To the contrary, it is in the economic interest of the competing media to ferret out diverse opinions and information.

When the access advocates speak of minority views, they are almost always referring to views *they* believe to be inadequately represented in our society. The "views counter to the capitalistic goals of privately owned, for profit media" are what Caristi believes lack adequate attention. Of course, what constitutes an underrepresented minority view "deserving" of access to the media is inherently subjective and will vary from person to person. Just as the views of socialist Americans may be described as minority views by a socialist, so too may the views of the Ku Klux Klan, the American Nazi party, or the American communist party by their partisans.

That socialist, Ku Klux Klan, American Nazi, or communist party gatherings do not command coverage in the mass media is not indicative of a conspiracy by profit-seeking "media moguls" to suppress minority views. Rather, it is evidence of the public's preference for something else. The national media's failure to closely cover political fringe groups indicates that costly time and space must be devoted to subjects of general interest to ensure the viewership, listenership, or readership needed to economically support the media. Indeed, were the mass media required by bureaucratic fiat to present views and information unwanted by the public, the public would simply avoid the regulated mass media in favor of unregulated media more to their liking. Short of the totalitarian control exercised over the media in some countries, it would be impossible to prevent the public from exercising its freedom to flee from unwanted media offerings. The regulations sought by the access advocates would deprive people of free speech liberty and would cost the mass media the audience revenue needed for its survival.

Nevertheless, the access advocates prefer to have government, in the words of Jerome Barron, take "legal steps . . . to provide for the airing and publication of 'minority tastes or viewpoints.'" To take these steps requires that the government: (1) select particular views worthy of access, (2) select the particular media on which to impose mandatory rights of access, and (3) enforce a decree for a media owner to give up his property for use by another.

The first part entails discrimination against some views by political officials. The officials must decide what constitutes "minority tastes or viewpoints," a process that involves inherently subjective, arbitrary, and prejudicial selections. The second step entails the identification of appropriate media to regulate, a process fraught with dangers of discriminatory application of the law and of censorship. The third step entails direct censorship, which requires the regulatees to delete their scheduled or preferred program offerings to present the government's mandated message.

The access advocates' approach produces a temporary taking of property without just compensation, for it requires forum owners to forfeit their right to exclude others on that part of the forum usurped by government for access purposes. It forces media owners to publish information or views that they may not want to publish or may oppose. It also creates a chilling effect on speech by discouraging station owners and publishers from doing anything that might provoke the state to impose its censorial powers upon them. Without exception, the access advocates focus on neither the mechanics of enforced access nor its chilling effect. They presume that government regulation will only enhance diversity without causing the regulated entities to engage in self-censorship. They also presume that government control can be exercised benevolently when the history of state regulation of the press is characterized by the malevolent exercise of censorial powers. They seem ignorant of the fact that there can be no freedom where one political power determines the nature of national debate. They also seem to ignore that a government's power to suppress private speech will greatly discourage the media from ferreting out corruption and misguided policies.

Ironically, the access advocates appear to presume that those who agree with *their* ideological perspectives will be vested with power over speech and press. But, there can be no such guarantee in a democratic republic. Such powers will in fact be exercised by political operatives, of conservative or of liberal persuasion, according to the electoral preferences of the voting majority. These operatives may choose to deny rights of access to precisely those speakers whom the access advocates favor most and to grant those rights to others whom the access advocates regard as proponents of the "capitalistic goals of privately owned, for-profit media."

ENDNOTES

1. *Red Lion Broadcasting Co. v. FCC,* 395 U.S. 367, 386 (1969).
2. *Kovacs v. Cooper,* 336 U.S. 77, 97 (1949).
3. *See FCC v. Pacifica Foundation,* 438 U.S. 726 (1978).
4. *See* Emord, *The First Amendment Invalidity of FCC Ownership Regulations,* 38 CATH. U. L. REV. 401, 439 (1989).
5. *Id.*

6. For a general discussion of the aspects of new age television, see *COM/TECH Report Series*, TOMORROW'S TV, NAB Research & Planning Department, Jan. 1987.

7. Matthew Spitzer has further subdivided the scarcity rationale into five different parts: static technological scarcity, dynamic technological scarcity, excess demand scarcity, entry scarcity, and relative scarcity. *See* Spitzer, *The Constitutionality of Licensing Broadcasters*, 64 N.Y.U. L. REV. 990, 1013–18 (1989); M. SPITZER, SEVEN DIRTY WORDS AND SIX OTHER STORIES 9–18 (1986). Spitzer labels the essential interference problem (the fact that no two persons may broadcast on the same frequency at the same time without creating interference) "technological scarcity" and believes it to be but a truism characteristic of newspapers as well (i.e., no two individuals could write on the same piece of paper a message that would consume the same space without creating confusion). He regards the essential scarcity of resources used to broadcast and to print, "dynamic technological scarcity," as a distinction without a difference, explaining that all goods are scarce. He regards the excess demand problem, his "excess demand scarcity," a direct result of the governmental system of allocation that makes free or low-cost licenses available. He regards the ease of entry problem, "entry scarcity," to result from differences in the treatment of media by government rather than any inherent characteristics of the media.

8. *FCC v. National Citizens Committee for Broadcasting*, 436 U.S. 775 (1978).

9. *Id.* at 775, 799 (1978).

10. *Red Lion Broadcasting Co. v. FCC*, 395 U.S. 367, 388 (1969).

11. *Miami Herald Publishing Co. v. Tornillo*, 418 U.S. 241, 258 (1974).

12. *Telecommunications Research & Action Center v. FCC*, 801 F.2d 501, 508 (D.C. Cir. 1986).

13. The simple fact that the demand for broadcast channels is greater than the available channels has never been a consequence of the inherent nature of broadcast spectrum. Rather, the excess demand phenomenon has, since the 1920s, been a result of the absence of cost (or, currently, the low cost) for broadcast application filing. In other words, government allocation of resources necessarily has resulted in market dislocations, demand excesses, and inequitable channel allotments and allocations. Were a market pricing system present in broadcasting, price would eliminate demand excesses just as it does in the print medium and with all other unregulated consumer goods.

14. *See* Stern, Krasnow, & Senkowski, *The New Video Marketplace and the Search for a Coherent Regulatory Philosophy*, 32 CATH. U. L. REV. 563 (1983).

15. *See* U.S. BUREAU OF THE CENSUS, THE STATISTICAL HISTORY OF THE UNITED STATES SERIES R224–231, NEWSPAPERS-NUMBERS AND CIRCULATION OF DAILY AND SUNDAY NEWSPAPERS: 1920 TO 1970, at 809 (1976).

16. *See* TELEVISION AND CABLE FACTBOOK C–299, C–309, C–358 (1988).

17. *See* 1988 STATISTICAL ABSTRACTS OF THE UNITED STATES 528.

18.   *See* Broadcasting at 67 (Aug. 20, 1990).

19.   *See* 1990 Statistical Abstracts of the United States 555.

20.   *See* Emord, *The First Amendment Invalidity of FCC Ownership Regulations,* 38 Cath. U. L. Rev. 401, 440 (1989).

21.   M. Wirth, Economic Barriers to Entry: Daily Newspapers vs. Television Stations vs. Radio Stations: A Preliminary Analysis ii (National Association of Broadcasters, 1984).

22.   *Id.* at 10–11.

23.   *Omega Satellite Products v. City of Indianapolis,* 694 F.2d 119, 127 (7th Cir. 1982).

24.   *See* Sol Schildhause, *Can Local Franchising of Cable TV Be Trusted? (Not if You're Serious About the First Amendment and Are Leery of the Harm that Can Be Caused by the Sincere Who Would Do Good),* 6 Comm. Law. 1, 22 (Winter, 1988).

25.   *Id* at 1, 27.

26.   *Quoted in* Emord, *The First Amendment Invalidity of FCC Ownership Regulations,* 38 Cath. U. L. Rev. 401, 445–46 (1989); *see* P. Vestal, An Analysis of Media Outlets by Market, app. II (1987) (prepared for the Research and Planning Department, National Association of Broadcasters). The VCR penetration rate now exceeds 68% of all television households in America, *see* Broadcasting Yearbook A–3 (1990).

27.   *See generally* Emord, *The First Amendment Invalidity of FCC Ownership Regulations,* 38 Cath. U. L. Rev. 401, 444–48 (1989).

28.   *See Policy Statement,* FCC 88–344, released Feb. 28, 1989, at para. 23.

29.   *See* Hazlett, *Duopolistic Competition in Cable Television: Implications for Public Policy* 7 Yale J. on Reg. 65, 67 (1990).

30.   *Id.* at 92–96.

31.   *Id.* at 93, 100.

32.   *See United States of America v. Western Electric Company Inc.,* U.S. 714 F. Supp. 1 (1988).

33.   *See* § 76.501, 47 C.F.R. (1989).

34.   *See* § 76.501, 47 C.F.R. (1989); § 533, 47 U.S.C. (1989).

35.   *See* § 533, 47 U.S.C. (1989).

36.   Spitzer, *The Constitutionality of Licensing Broadcasters,* 64 N.Y.U. L. Rev. 990 (1989).

37.   167 U.S. 43 (1897), *rev'd Hague v. CIO,* 307 U.S. 496 (1939).

38.   *See* Werhan, *The Supreme Court's Public Forum Doctrine and the Return of Formalism,* 7 Cardozo L. Rev. 335, 346 (1986). ("The Davis opinion represents a fully realized view that, whatever the first amendment right of free expression may protect, it was no basis for a right of access to government property. The question concerned property ownership, not free expression.") *Davis v. Massachusetts,* 167 U.S. 43, 48 (1897).

39.   *Lehman v. City of Shaker Heights,* 418 U.S. 298 (1974).

40. *See, e.g., Consolidated Edison Co. v. Public Service Comm'n*, 447 U.S. 530, 540 (1980); *see generally* Lee, *Lonely Pamphleteers, Little People, and the Supreme Court: The Doctrine of Time, Place, and Manner Regulations of Expression*, 54 GEO. WASH. L. REV. 757 (1986).

41. In *Ward v. Rock Against Racism*, 109 S.Ct. 2746 (1989), the Court lessened the rigidity of its narrow tailoring component, permitting regulations not narrowly tailored to survive constitutional muster under the First Amendment provided they are reasonably related to the end in view.

42. *See, e.g., Clark v. Community for Creative Non-Violence*, 468 U.S. 288, 293 (1984); Lee, *Lonely Pamphleteers, Little People, and the Supreme Court: The Doctrine of Time, Place, and Manner Regulations of Expression*, 54 GEO. WASH. L. REV. 757 (1986).

43. *See Lehman v. City of Shaker Heights*, 418 U.S. 298, 304 (1974).

44. This preferred method was relied upon by the Supreme Court for one fleeting moment in *Grayned v. Rockford*, 408 U.S. 104, 116 (1972) (The Court defined a permissible content-neutral regulation of speech on public forums to be one wherein "the manner of expression" involved was found "basically incompatible with the normal activity of a particular place at a particular time").

45. For a full development of this theory, see Spitzer, *The Constitutionality of Licensing Broadcasters*, 64 N.Y.U. L. REV. 990, 1038–41 (1989).

46. *See, e.g., City of Lakewood v. Plain Dealer Pub. Co.*, 108 S.Ct. 2138 (1988).

47. *Minneapolis Star & Tribune Co. v. Minnesota Commissioner of Revenue*, 460 U.S. 575 (1983).

48. *See Ex Parte Jackson*, 96 U.S. 727 (1878); *Lovell v. City of Griffin, GA*, 303 U.S. 444, 452 (1938); *City of Lakewood v. Plain Dealer Pub. Co.*, 108 S.Ct. 2138, 2145 (1988) (explaining that "the circulation of newspapers" is a form of "expression or conduct commonly associated with expression").

49. *See, e.g., City of Lakewood v. Plain Dealer Pub. Co.*, 108 S.Ct. 2138, 2143 (1988) ("At the root of this long line of precedent is the time-tested knowledge that in the area of free expression a licensing statute placing unbridled discretion in the hands of a government official or agency constitutes a prior restraint and may result in censorship.").

50. *Marsh v. Alabama*, 326 U.S. 501 (1946).

51. *Id.*

52. Note, *Free Speech, Initiative and Property Rights in Conflict—Four Alternatives to the State Action Requirement in Washington—Alderwood Associates v. Washington Environmental Council, 96 WN.2d 230, 635 P.2d 108 (1981)*, 58 WASH. L. REV. 587, 612 (1983).

53. Barron, *Access to the Press—A New First Amendment Right*, 80 HARV. L. REV. 1641, 1669 (1967).

54. Caristi, *The Concept of a Right of Access to the Media: A Workable Alternative*, 22 SUFFOLK U. L. REV. 103, 108 (1988).

55. *Id.* at 103, 106.
56. Barron, *Access to the Press—A New First Amendment Right,* 80 HARV. L. REV. 1641 (1967).
57. Caristi, *The Concept of a Right of Access to the Media: A Workable Alternative,* 22 SUFFOLK U. L. REV. 103, 110 (1988).
58. Fiss, *Free Speech and Social Structure,* 71 IOWA L. REV. 1405, 1415 (1986).

22

IMPLEMENTATION OF THE PROPERTY RIGHTS ALTERNATIVE

To ensure adequate protection for the core values of the First Amendment, an entirely new system must replace the current broadcast and cable regulatory regime. For broadcasting, this means eliminating the licensing process and replacing it with a property rights approach. For cable, it means ending the franchising system and breaking down the barriers to the entry of telephone companies into the video and information services markets (and, conversely, breaking down barriers to the entry of cable systems into the telephone services market). What follows are recommended legislative alternatives to the current system. Given the necessity for brevity, the proposals advanced here are but broad outlines that must later be rendered more definitive.

BROADCASTING IN A FREE MEDIA MARKETPLACE

A free system of content-neutral, market allocation of broadcast property rights should replace the system of state ownership and control of the airwaves. This new system could take one of several forms and could be introduced in any number of ways but the form and the way that would ensure the least intrusion into the private communications sphere is by instituting a simple property title approach over a number of years.

Perhaps the most feasible, least disruptive way to attain this objective is through a multiyear transition from the current licensing system to the new property rights system. Title III of the Communications Act of 1934 and the jurisdiction of the Federal Communications Commission over broadcasting would be phased out of existence. A simple national title registry for public recordation of existing broadcast operating parameters would replace agency control. The Congress would phase out the need for advance government authorization of transfers of control and for assignments of licenses. It would also end the prohibition against private ownership of operating parameters, the need for mandatory licensing, the channel classification requirements, and the multiple ownership regulations.[1] In lieu of these provisions and processes, the new legislation would phase in a fee simple property rights system. The federal government's role would be limited to affording legal recognition to broadcast property rights defined by operating parameters and to providing protection for those parameters. In addition, the government would continue to ensure that broadcasters honored U.S. treaties with foreign countries.

Although revoking all existing licenses and starting anew would be satisfying from a theoretical standpoint, a draconian measure of this kind would unduly disrupt the broadcast marketplace and would violate the current rights of licensees, who have relied on the present system in good faith. Those who have invested hundreds of thousands of dollars in broadcast facilities and have operated these facilities under the costly and burdensome regulatory regime that now exists should not be forced to forfeit the value of their investments and the good will they have generated over the years. Consequently, starting anew by revoking existing licenses is not a viable or desirable option.

The far better approach would be to award licensees a fee simple property right in their existing operating parameters. In addition to receiving ownership in fee, licensees would be emancipated from all content and technical regulations on the condition that they not trespass on the recorded operating rights of other broadcasters.

The mandatory national title registry would be a computer storehouse to record the operating parameters owned in fee, to record proof of advance notification given to all broadcasters potentially affected by any proposed changes in station operating parameters, to reveal whether those holding rights to broadcast in fee have properly maintained the accuracy and completeness of their registration data, and to reflect instances of adjudicated trespass. To facilitate self-policing, the government could establish by statute a standard for ascertaining objectionable interference by requiring the use of certain kinds of receivers to detect interference.

Under such a system, station operating parameters, together with engineering evidence of actual field strength coverage contours, would have to be recorded in the registry. This information would define each broadcaster's property right and would have to conform precisely to technical requirements. Any fee holder wanting to change his operations, or any new market entrant wanting to institute a new broadcast service, would first be obliged to evaluate pertinent station data on file with the national title registry and to assess the danger posed to existing broadcasters. By statute and under threat of fines for noncompliance, each broadcaster proposing to change operations or to institute a new service would be required to provide advance notice to all current broadcasters potentially affected by the change. Affected parties would be free to negotiate mutually agreeable operating parameters in exchange for consideration. These agreements would have to be registered in the title registry.

The new operator could begin broadcasting only after notifying incumbent broadcasters of proposed operations, giving them a reasonable period of time set by statute to evaluate the proposal, and filing an appropriate registration form detailing the precise nature of the proposed operations with the national title registry.

The new federal statute governing this system would define and outlaw trespass. It would specify heavy fines (to be paid to the broadcaster adversely affected) for any trespass into an incumbent broadcaster's contour area and would permit the courts to enjoin the offending operation. Common law property "first in time, first in right" principles would govern. Proof of loss of audience reception within one's registered service area could be made *prima facie* grounds for seeking a mandatory injunction against an offending new broadcast use. Such injunctions would, wherever possible, merely stop the offending use, rather than shut down the new operations.

During the transition from the regulatory to a property rights approach, new applicants for FCC authority to construct facilities could be permitted to buy their right to operate in a national auction (following the FCC's "acceptability" review of an application for legal and technical compliance with the old rules). The highest bidder in such an auction would own the right to broadcast, as proposed, in fee.

Following the phaseout of licensing, new media entrants would be able to enter broadcasting in one of several ways. They could buy the operating rights of an existing station. They could conduct an engineering feasibility study and, after updating the national title registry and serving potentially affected broadcasters with notice, proceed to construct a new facility that would not interfere with existing operations. They could agree by contract to compensate existing broadcasters for mutually agreeable levels of interference or could pay a broadcaster to modify his operations to permit use of part of an existing broadcaster's service area. The system envisioned would cause the broadcasting business to be dominated by private transactions, void of any persistent governmental regulatory presence. As in the case of private property generally, enforcement actions would be pursued at the behest of private parties in courts of competent jurisdiction (in this case, the federal courts).

It would be the responsibility of broadcasters individually (as it is *de facto* today) to police their own coverage contours and check field monitoring equipment to detect objectionable interference (a trespass). This monitoring would be in their own economic self-interest and should therefore be expected to occur without regulation.

Disputes as to trespass could be resolved either through private negotiation or, barring agreement, in the federal court that has jurisdiction over the matter (much like the system of resolution employed by the Circuit Court of Cook County in *Tribune Co. v. Oak Leaves Broadcasting Station*[2]). An existing broadcaster who was found to have operated in accordance with recorded operating parameters would prevail under "first in time, first in right" common law principles over a newcomer who trespassed on the coverage contour area of the existing broadcaster. The incumbent could obtain an injunction against the offender's misuse of facilities and could, upon a final decision, be awarded damages set by statute.

Under this system, a successful broadcaster (one whose programming fare won favor with viewers and listeners) could have the flexibility to lease rights of access into the coverage contour area of less successful stations or to buy those stations' operating rights outright and increase the reach of his own station. Moreover, a broadcaster could experiment with new technologies, such as enhanced or high definition television or digital audio broadcasting, without need for government approval. Several commentators have recommended various other property rights alternatives to public control of broadcasting.[3]

CABLECASTING IN A FREE MEDIA MARKETPLACE

The process of liberating cable from the franchising system is a comparatively simple one. First Amendment interests of cable operators will be adequately protected by eliminating all federal, state, and local content regulations; by eliminating the franchising process; and by limiting the role of states and localities to protecting public safety during installation and repair of cable wires.

There is no genuine threat that space on utility poles or rights-of-way will become scarce anytime soon. However, in the unlikely event that space does become scarce, the same common law principle of priority in time, priority in right should govern. Then, those wanting to provide service by cable will either have to use a new cable delivery system or to buy access rights from existing cable systems.

In addition to elimination of federal, state, and local content regulations and the system of franchising, the courts (on First Amendment grounds) and the Congress (in order to foster competition) could eliminate the telephone company/cable cross-ownership ban and could eliminate the barriers to telephone company entry into the information and video services industry and to cable entry into telephone service contained in the Cable Communications Act of 1984, in the regulations of the FCC, and in the AT&T Consent Decree. Likewise, existing prohibitions against broadcast station and broadcast network ownership of cable systems ought to be eliminated. Broadcasters, cablecasters, and telephone companies should be free to use their technological expertise to create new hybrid communications forms. The elimination of existing barriers to competition can be expected to increase inter- and intra-industry service among broadcasters, cablecasters, and telephone companies, resulting in long-term benefits for the American consumer. The elimination of these barriers will permit the inevitable merging of broadcast and common carrier technologies, greatly enhancing opportunities for expression.

If the government continues to sustain the monopoly rent/content control *quid pro quo* and maintains barriers which prevent the proliferation of the new media, America's entry into tomorrow's communications age will likely lag behind that of certain more enterprising nations.

In a day when the speed of communications is vital to economic competitiveness, the maintenance of barriers to new communications technologies could well cause not only violations of precious liberties but also economic, social, and political repercussions that could place America at a disadvantage in the global economic marketplace.

If, on the other hand, the Supreme Court, Congress, the states, and the localities remove the content and structural regulations that now retard the development of the electronic media marketplace, the benefits of the latest communications technologies will come to fruition nationwide in the first decade of the twenty-first century. These technologies will hasten the arrival of the most prolific national and global communications age the world has ever known, an age replete with extraordinary social and economic benefits for our people.

ENDNOTES

1. *See* §§ 301, 303 (a–c), 304, 307(c), 308(b), 309, 310, 47 U.S.C.
2. *Tribune Co. v. Oak Leaves Broadcasting Station* (Cir. Ct. Cook County, Ill., 1926), *reprinted in* 68 Cong. Rec. 216 (1926).
3. *See, e.g.,* Coase, *The Federal Communications Commission,* 2 J. L. & Econ. 1–40 (1959) ; DeVany, Eckert, Meyers, O'Hara, & Scott, *A Property System Approach to the Electromagnetic Spectrum,* 21 Stan. L. Rev. 1499–1561 (1969); Webbink, *Frequency Spectrum Deregulation Alternatives,* FCC Office of Plans and Policy (Oct. 1980); M. Mueller, Property Rights in Radio Communication: The Key to the Reform of Telecommunications Regulation (No. 11, Cato Inst. Policy Analysis, June 3, 1982); Mueller, *Privitization of the Airwaves,* Reason Foundation Issue Paper, Apr. 4, 1988; Spitzer, *The Constitutionality of Licensing Broadcasters,* 64 N.Y.U. L. Rev. 990, 1068–69 (1989).

23

PRESERVING THE CORE VALUES OF THE FIRST AMENDMENT IN THE TWENTY-FIRST CENTURY

In the first decades of the twenty-first century, society will again witness the development of extraordinary technologies for the mass exchange of ideas and information. As before, the question will be: Will industry and government strike a deal that forfeits press freedom in exchange for market protection?

Fiber optic technology, developed in the 1960s, will likely bring about interactive voice, audio, video, and data communication early in the next century. Mass publication will soon be possible from the home and in the reach of almost every American. Because fiber optic cables are capable of transmitting hundreds of millions, and potentially billions, of bits of information per second (as opposed to copper cable wire that is capable of transmitting only 1.5 million bits of information per second),[1] the amount of data exchanged will multiply manifold. Exchanges will occur at high volume and at light speed.

Once fully implemented, a national, digital broadband series of fiber optic networks could enable people to send and receive the following from anywhere in the United States (and potentially the world): high-resolution, full-color graphics; live voice and color video transmissions; high-quality video/stereophonic transmissions; video telephone voices and images; teletext and videotext services; high-speed computer data transmissions; and high-definition television. Fiber optic lines will have unlimited channel capacity for television viewing, data retrieval, and transmission. This technology will enable people to conduct an enormous amount and variety of business from home. Shopping, banking, and medical diagnostic and professional counseling services will all be possible from the home.

The communications information and entertainment systems of tomorrow will likely include an integrated unit that will make it possible to watch a program on high-definition television, receive additional written information about the program through a teletext printer, record a program on another channel, and, for the first time, transmit any video image across fiber optic lines to homes or offices.

Indeed, for the first time, American television viewers will not merely be passive recipients of audio and video communication, they will become part of a great mass communications marketplace. They will be able to gain access to a potentially limitless amount of information from their viewing screens, voice channels, and data retrieval channels. Great computer bulletin board services will likely be created in response to consumer demand for more information on specific subjects. For the first time in history, each American household will become a miniature publishing center.

In time, given the global movement toward democracy, interactive voice, audio, video, and data exchanges will occur worldwide. The effects of such a market for goods, services, ideas, and information will be extraordinary. It will help break down barriers to free trade and market economies, will promote the transformation of totalitarian governments into democratic ones, and will cause certain local cultures to become more a part of the international cultural melange.

In addition to fiber optics, dozens of other technological innovations will end our dependency on the electromagnetic spectrum. Since 1975, more than two million households have installed satellite television receive-only (TRVO) earth stations to receive distant signals transmitted by satellite. As many as seventy-eight scrambled and sixty-nine clear video channels are transmitted from satellites to these stations. On the horizon, Direct Broadcast Satellites (DBS) will soon expand the television marketplace. DBS will use very high power to transmit television programming across the continental United States from a geostationary satellite to homes located within the geographic area (or "footprint") reached by the satellite. DBS holds out the potential of offering as many as 200 or more new channels (which will have High Definition Television compatibility). Reception will be possible from small, relatively inexpensive flat-plate antennas, that may be installed inside the home or office near a window.

Other, more traditional technologies may merge into hybrid forms that will offer still other services to the home. So-called "wireless cable" may add yet another source of competition to local cable and broadcast television markets. Capable of sustaining several channels through a one-way microwave transmission, wireless cable may bring new television programming to homes and apartment complexes. Low Power Television, relying on VHS and UHF frequencies operated at significantly reduced power levels, may also become a competitive force in local video markets.

Traditional television and radio may be transformed early in the next century through the technology of High Definition Television and Digital Audio Broadcasting. Television is currently restricted by a decades-old technological standard that limits picture quality. The National Television System Committee (NTSC) standard aspect ratio (the ratio of television picture width to height) is 4:3 with 525 scanning lines. Under the FCC's television allocation plan, only 6 MHz of spectrum are available per television channel. By contrast, advanced and high-definition television systems have an aspect ratio of between 14:9 and 16:9 with as many as 1,125 scanning lines. Various HDTV systems rely on 6 to 12 MHz. This difference enhances picture quality. HDTV is capable of producing as much as five times the picture elements (pixels) obtainable from standard television. As a consequence, HDTV can approximate on the home screen a picture quality equivalent to 35mm film.[2] HDTV systems now under development offer to provide television viewers movie theater picture quality accompanied by sound equivalent to that produced by compact discs.

Standard radio, like television, stands to benefit from technological innovations. Matthew Spitzer has observed that innovation permits us to "grow more spectrum"—an argument against the concept of technological scarcity.[3] One of the greatest proofs of Spitzer's theory may well be Digital Audio Broadcasting (DAB).[4]

Standard AM and FM radio are based on analog transmission schemes, that is, "the information they carry (such as the fluctuating tones of music or voice) causes a continuous range of variation in the frequency (FM) or amplitude (AM) of the carrier wave."[5] A European research and development consortium known as Eureka has developed a new digital radio transmission system that encodes "sound . . . as a series of binary (0/1, on/off) digits, with the sequence corresponding to a certain pitch, volume, etc."[6] European DAB is far superior to standard AM and FM because it uses a digital system that can overcome the "multi-path" interference plaguing traditional radio and can improve the quality of audible sound by masking inaudible sound. The result is compact disc sound quality in radio. The ingenius computer technology of DAB enables such systems to use far less power than conventional broadcasting stations to reach the same sized audience. AM and FM stations use high power to overcome problems of multipath interference. DAB uses digital technology to neutralize multi-path. Consequently, a DAB station operating on 2,500 watts of power can reach an audience equal to a typical FM station operating with 50,000 watts.[7]

Another advantage of DAB is that from one location it is possible to have three separate audio programs transmitted simultaneously using the same amount of spectrum currently relied on by an FM station to transmit just one audio program.[8] Thus, the technology has enabled us to "grow more spectrum." Furthermore, DAB can carry more information than just sound. It can transmit still pictures and data to properly designed receiving sets.

These and dozens of other technologies now on the horizon can be fully introduced into the American marketplace in the first few decades of the twenty-first century. Their introduction can enhance editorial freedom in our society to an extraordinary degree. The speed with which these technologies enter the marketplace and the degree of freedom that will be associated with them will depend largely on what constitutional standard is applied to protect the new press forms. At stake will be the freedom of speech and press for each American citizen. As always, the principal players will be industry leaders; key politicians in local, state, and national governments; and the courts.

Undoubtedly attempts will be made to subject these new technologies to the monopoly rent/content control *quid pro quo.* If we are to avoid the losses in freedom that would be associated with content and structural controls on the new media forms, it will be imperative for the courts to embrace the First Amendment print model standard and apply it to the new forms. Unless the Supreme Court rededicates itself to preserving the core values of the First Amendment and rejects the notion that each new technology should be subjected to a different standard of protection, speech and press in the next century will unnecessarily suffer regulatory restraints that will abridge freedom. Without a universal application of the print standard, the pattern of content and structural controls that has burdened the broadcast press since the 1920s will burden the new press forms.

By adopting the Preservationist Perspective introduced here, the Court can protect the core values of the First Amendment, permit the print model to transcend time and technology, and ensure that the blessings of a free press are enjoyed in their fullest latitude by the next generation.

ENDNOTES

1. *See* A HIGH-FIBER DIET FOR TELEVISION? Impact of Future Telephone, Fiber, and Regulatory Changes for Broadcasters 8, 11 (National Association of Broadcasters, 1988).
2. *See* HDTV: PLANNING FOR ACTION (National Association of Broadcasters, 1988).
3. *See* Spitzer, *The Constitutionality of Licensing Broadcasters,* 64 N.Y.U. L. REV. 990, 1015 (1989).
4. *See DAB: The Next Generation of Radio Broadcasting?* BROADCASTING 62 (June 4, 1990).
5. *See Bringing Radio Up to Date,* The Washington Post D3 (Sunday, June 3, 1990).
6. *See Id.*
7. *See Id.*
8. *See Id.*

INDEX

ABOUT THE AUTHOR

Jonathan W. Emord is a Senior Research Fellow at the Pacific Research Institute and a member of the First Amendment Task Force of the Center for Applied Jurisprudence. He is also an attorney who practices communications law in Washington, D.C. In 1985 and 1986, he served as an attorney in the FM Branch of the Federal Communications Commission's Mass Media Bureau.

PRESIDENT
William H. Mellor III, J.D.

SENIOR ECONOMIST
Terry L. Anderson, Ph.D.

BOARD OF ADVISORS
Charles W. Baird
California State University, Hayward

Yale Brozen
University of Chicago

James M. Buchanan
Nobel laureate in economics
George Mason University

Steven N. S. Cheung
University of Hong Kong

Robert W. Clower
University of South Carolina

Richard A. Epstein
University of Chicago

John Gray
Oxford University, England

Steve H. Hanke
Johns Hopkins University

Friedrich A. Hayek
Nobel laureate in economics
University of Freiburg, Germany

George W. Hilton
University of California, Los Angeles

Jonathan R. T. Hughes
Northwestern University

Michael C. Jensen
University of Rochester

Israel M. Kirzner
New York University

Gary D. Libecap
University of Arizona

Stephen C. Littlechild
University of Birmingham, England

Fred McChesney
Emory University

Michael McConnell
University of Chicago

Chiaki Nishiyama
Rikkyo University, Japan

Ellen F. Paul
Bowling Green State University

Jennifer Roback
George Mason University

Anna J. Schwarz
National Bureau of Economic Research

Julian L. Simon
University of Maryland

Edwin G. West
Carleton University, Canada

Leland B. Yeager
Auburn University

PACIFIC
RESEARCH
INSTITUTE
FOR PUBLIC POLICY

The Pacific Research Institute produces studies that explore long-term solutions to difficult issues of public policy. The Institute seeks to facilitate a more active and enlightened discourse on these issues and to broaden understanding of market processes, government policy, and the rule of law. Through the publication of scholarly books and the sponsorship of conferences, the Institute serves as an established resource for ideas in the continuing public policy debate.

Institute books have been adopted for courses at colleges, universities, and graduate schools nationwide. More than 175 distinguished scholars have worked with the Institute to analyze the premises and consequences of existing public policy and to formulate possible solutions to seemingly intractable problems. Prestigious journals and major media regularly review and comment upon Institute work. In addition, the Board of Advisors consists of internationally recognized scholars, including two Nobel laureates.

The Pacific Research Institute is an independent, tax exempt, 501(c)(3) organization and as such is supported solely by the sale of its books and by the contributions from a wide variety of foundations, corporations, and individuals. This diverse funding base and the Institute's refusal to accept government funds enable it to remain independent.

OTHER STUDIES IN PUBLIC POLICY BY THE PACIFIC RESEARCH INSTITUTE

URBAN TRANSIT
The Private Challenge to Public Transportation
Edited by Charles A. Lave
Foreword by John Meyer

POLITICS, PRICES, AND PETROLEUM
The Political Economy of Energy
By David Glasner
Foreword by Paul W. MacAvoy

RIGHTS AND REGULATION
Ethical, Political, and Economic Issues
Edited by Tibor M. Machan and M. Bruce Johnson
Foreword by Aaron Wildavsky

FUGITIVE INDUSTRY
The Economics and Politics of Deindustrialization
By Richard B. McKenzie
Foreword by Finis Welch

MONEY IN CRISIS
The Federal Reserve, the Economy, and Monetary Reform
Edited by Barry N. Siegel
Foreword by Leland B. Yeager

NATURAL RESOURCES
Bureaucratic Myths and Environmental Management
By Richard Stroup and John Baden
Foreword by William Niskanen

FIREARMS AND VIOLENCE
Issues of Public Policy
Edited by Don B. Kates, Jr.
Foreword by John Kaplan

WATER RIGHTS
Scarce Resource Allocation, Bureaucracy, and the Environment
Edited by Terry L. Anderson
Foreword by Jack Hirshleifer

LOCKING UP THE RANGE
Federal Land Controls and Grazing
By Gary D. Libecap
Foreword by Jonathan R.T. Hughes

THE PUBLIC SCHOOL MONOPOLY
A Critical Analysis of Education and the State in American Society
Edited by Robert B. Everhart
Foreword by Clarence J. Karier

RESOLVING THE HOUSING CRISIS
Government Policy, Demand, Decontrol, and the Public Interest
Edited with an Introduction by M. Bruce Johnson

OFFSHORE LANDS
Oil and Gas Leasing and Conservation on the Outer Continental Shelf
By Walter J. Mead, et al.
Foreword by Stephen L. McDonald

THE ENTERPRISE OF LAW
Justice Without the State
By Bruce L. Benson

For further information on the Pacific Research Institute's program and a catalog of publications, please contact:

PACIFIC RESEARCH INSTITUTE FOR PUBLIC POLICY
177 Post Street
San Francisco, CA 94108
(415) 989-0833